D1604434

# Intersectionality and Urban Education

## Identities, Policies, Spaces, and Power

A volume in
*Urban Education Studies*
Nicholas D. Hartlep, Thandeka K. Chapman, and Kenny Varner, *Series Editors*

# Intersectionality and Urban Education

## Identities, Policies, Spaces, and Power

*edited by*

## Carl A. Grant
*University of Wisconsin–Madison*

## Elisabeth Zwier
*Universidad Pedagógica Nacional Francisco Morazán*

INFORMATION AGE PUBLISHING, INC.
Charlotte, NC • www.infoagepub.com

LC
5115
.I57
2014

**Library of Congress Cataloging-in-Publication Data**

A CIP record for this book is available from the Library of Congress
http://www.loc.gov

ISBN:  978-1-62396-732-1 (Paperback)
       978-1-62396-733-8 (Hardcover)
       978-1-62396-734-5 (ebook)

Printed in the United States of America

# CONTENTS

## PART III
### THINKING INTERSECTIONALLY IN TEACHER EDUCATION AND HIGHER EDUCATION

## PART IV
### EDUCATIONAL POLICIES AND URBAN SPACES

# INTRODUCTION

**Carl A. Grant**
**Elisabeth Zwier**
*University of Wisconsin-Madison*

The first Global Civil Society Yearbook (2001) describes our global society as "...the sphere of ideas, values, institutions, organisations, networks, and individuals located between the family, the state, and the market and operating beyond the confines of national societies, polities, and economies" (Anheier, Glasius & Kaldor, 2001, p. 17). This definition points to the intersections of people and their different self-identified and/or ascribed characteristics within the spaces they take part in—urban, suburban, rural. The concept of a "global civil society" also suggests that ideas and values are equal because they are part of a global sphere. Moreover, the use of the term "global society" recognizes that these ideas and values are played out in institutions, organization and networks across the globe. What happens when these ideas and values intersect in institutions, organizations and networks is that people—and their worldviews—are treated differently based upon their self-identified or ascribed characteristics (race, gender, socioeconomic status, gender, sexual orientation and religion, to name a few). The goal of our book is to discuss how intersectionality theories operate within and across locations to produce shifting sites of privilege and oppression, helping illuminate what takes place in the global sphere, but plays out at the local level in urban settings.

*Intersectionality and Urban Education*, pages ix–xx
Copyright © 2014 by Information Age Publishing

In urban education, "urban" is a floating signifier that is imbued with meaning, positive or negative by its users. "Urban" can be used to refer to both the geographical context of a city and a sense of "less than," most often in relation to race and/or socioeconomic status (Watson, 2011). For Noblit and Pink (2007), "Urban . . . is a generalization as much about geography as it is about the idea that urban centers have problems: problems of too many people, too much poverty, too much crime and violence, and ultimately, too little hope" (p. xv). Recently, urban education scholars such as Anyon (2005), Pink and Noblit (2007), Blanchett, Klinger and Harry (2009), and Lipman (2013) have elucidated the social construction of oppression and privilege for urban students, teachers, schools, families, and communities using intersectionality theories. We echo Blanchett and colleagues' (2009) vision for urban education, in which the global sphere and the city are linked through an intersectional perspective:

> We dare say that the only way we will get an equitable education for all marginalized children and families affected by the intersection of race, culture, language, poverty, and disability is to identify them with oppressed children and families in urban settings and everywhere in the world. (p. 405)

Though the Yearbook's description of our global society is noteworthy in all that it addresses, what it does not fully articulate is that our twenty-first century global society and its cities, are multicultural. This means that people identify with or are ascribed identities on the basis of their socioeconomic status, race, ethnicity, religion and sexual orientation, etc. Therefore there is a need, perhaps greater than any other time in civilization, to accept and appreciate the diversity of people in world because of many socioeconomic, environmental, cultural opportunities and challenges we face. We believe this formidable task would be facilitated by using intersectionality theories, which show great promise in helping us to better understand the intertwining matrices of privilege and oppression that shape our experiences as individuals and members of societies. As markers of identity take upon increased significance both nationally and internationally, we think it wise to consider the intertwining of these markers in order to analyze urban educational issues holistically, work to improve student outcomes, and promote coalitional advocacy towards more just policies and practices.

## THE HEEDING

Social inclusion encompasses the idea that "a citizen has the right and ability to participate in the basic economic, political and social functioning of his or her society. It's more than economic enrichment, centered on access to basic public and private goods such as health care, formal employment, education, adequate housing, political and civil rights, and economic opportunity without discrimination" (Sabatini, 2012, p. 1). The concept of "social inclusion" is currently embraced and pursued throughout the world, albeit in some places more so than in others.

In the inaugural editorial of the journal *Social Inclusion*, Hedetoft (2013) contends that many societies view social inclusion as a value that is fundamental to their growth and development. In the United States, for example, social inclusion has longed served as part of a grand project. "We the people . . ." is the first line of the preamble to the US Constitution. Within the United States' education system social inclusion became a policy and practice mandate in 1975 with the passage of the Education for All Handicapped Children Act. This law (PL 94-142) states that in order for a state to receive federal funds for education it must develop and implement policies that guarantee a free and appropriate public education for all children, including those with disabilities. Incorporating students with physical and mental challenges in mainstream classrooms was a huge step toward the inclusion of students who had previously been marginalized. Other countries, such as the United Kingdom, also have social inclusion policies for physically and mental challenged students. In Latin America, for example, Sabatini (2012) contends that the index of social inclusion points to a number of differences and challenges. Citing Chile and Brazil as examples, Sabatini (2012) argues that Chile could be considered more inclusive than its other Latin American neighbors in the areas of political and civil rights, secondary school enrollment, the percent of the population living on more than $4 per day, access to adequate housing, and the percent of the population with formal jobs; the latter three taking into account race/ethnicity and gender. However, these advances pale in light of the fact that Chile's distribution of economic resources is among the most unequal of OECD member countries. Regarding Brazil, Sabatini (2012) reports on its impressive economic growth and indicates it spends more on social programs as a percent of its GDP than any other country (including the United States). Nevertheless, severe differences regarding access to education and formal jobs remain, with indicators skewed by race, gender, and poverty. Though social inclusion is a value pursued by many countries, its indicators give cause for both hope and for concern because of the unequal distribution patterns of various political and civil rights.

Social inclusion is now cast in a global frame. Discussions of social inclusion take place within official government spheres and everyday conversations about shared national and global identity, cultural recognition and respect among peoples, and ways to accept and appreciate differences within nation-states and among global partners. Silver (2010) enumerates this meaning of social inclusion when he states it involves "the provision of political and social rights to all individuals and groups in society, such as voting privileges, freedom of expression, opportunities for employment, adequate housing, health care, and education" (p. 87). According to the author, social inclusion is a "framework to accommodate social, cultural, or national 'differences' in plural or multicultural societies... more readily than one-dimensional redistributive frameworks insofar as it acknowledges and accommodates specific needs and rights of groups" (Silver, 2010, p.87).

Though the ideas of social inclusion and multiculturalism are widely accepted in many societies, they come under fire from proponents—who see these concepts as desirable but unfeasible—and opponents—who consider these ideas incompatible with an individualistic, market-driven world view. Paradoxically, the lived realities of ongoing exclusion are in part due to national and international political attention to concepts like "social inclusion" and "multiculturalism" which have circulated through government and civic policy statements and media coverage over the past several decades (Grant & Lei, 1991; Hedetoft, 2013). The more these concepts and values have been promoted by political and community leaders, the more difficult it becomes to deliver convincing, sustainable, and workable models to facilitate social and democratic acceptance of differences. In part, social inclusion and multiculturalism are difficult to deliver on because they generate high expectations across social and political sectors. Furthermore, these concepts face serious challenges from neoliberal discourses and actions in place (Lipman, 2011, 2013). By neoliberal discourses we mean policies and practices that demand that an individual be solely responsible for his or her personal well-being (Peters, 2001; Borwn 2003). In countries that implement neoliberal policies, the help or "safety net" that governments provide for the poor, low-income workers, and those in need of health services is greatly reduced or eliminated. According to Amble (2011), neoliberalism strives to teach people that individuals are only to be rewarded based on their personal effort; greatly reducing help or assistance from the government. With such "an ego-driven focus, the process of individualization engenders a climate where structural inequalities—racism, gender inequality, poverty—are converted into individual problems" (Smith, 2012, p. 1). In addition there is an increase in privatization and greater market control leading to a significant reduction of the core features of the social welfare state. Treanor (2012) states,

> Neoliberalism is a philosophy in which the existence and operation of a market are valued in themselves, separately from any previous relationship with the production of goods and services... and where the operation of a market or market-like structure is seen as an ethic in itself, capable of acting as a guide for all human action, and substituting for all previously existing ethical belief. (p. 1)

The significance of neoliberalism to social inclusion is that the latter argues for the inclusion every person, whereas neoliberalism advocates leaving individuals to fend for themselves. In a neoliberal world, education becomes a terrain of struggle for the "right to the city" of students and their families who are situated at intersections of exclusion (Lipman, 2013, p. 5).

Concepts like social inclusion have led to new kinds of contestation at the political and social level, new forms of nationalist and internationalist demagoguery, political discourses advocating cultural revanchism, along with English Language primacy, the construction of new walls against and blame of the "other," arguments for returning to "the way things used to be," and arguments that citizens are responsible for their own welfare at both national and local levels (Hedetoft, 2013). Such negative reactions toward inclusion and the up-swing of neoliberalism have tended to produce sentiments of powerlessness, frustration, and anomie among those who are *othered*—particularly urban residents—and have high hopes that social inclusion and multiculturalism will bring about change toward social justice (Grant & Lei, 2001; Grant & Portera, 2011; Hedetoftt, 2013; Silj, 2010).

In our global society social inclusion and multiculturalism are often challenged by proponents and opponents alike. Proponents argue that racial, ethnic, gendered, socioeconomic, religious, and gay and lesbian inequalities, as well as a deep resistance to positive change, turn the normative ideals of "inclusion" and "multiculturalism" into empty promises. The same governments that espouse these ideas fail to back relevant policies with the strategies and mechanisms that could ensure their success. For example, supporters argue that the normative ideal of "equal opportunity for all," a statement written and spoken by numerous governments, is a falsehood because empirical research shows inequalities continue and there is little official action to change the status quo. A 2005 report by the European Monitoring Centre on Racism and Xenophobia entitled *Majorities' Attitude Towards Minorities*, interviewed between 1,500 and 2,500 persons in each of the "old" 15 European Union (EU) Member States about majority population attitudes towards minorities. Several of their findings are useful to our discussion: One in four Europeans living in the 15 EU Member States indicate a resistance to a multicultural society; two in three people in the EU Member States believe that there are limits to a multicultural society; four in ten are opposed to civil rights for legal migrants, and one in five persons—an increasing minority—favor repatriation policies for legal migrants (European Monitoring Centre, 2005, p.12). The report also states that, "Overall, the level of resistance to multicultural society has remained the same in 2003 as it was in 1997—a minority of roughly one in four respondents in the EU 15 Member States displayed this attitude" (European Monitoring Centre, 2005, p. 13). Inclusion—acceptance and appreciation of a multicultural society—while located on the positive side of the rubric measuring attitudes for and against multiculturalism, is facing a stiff challenge.

Proponents of social inclusion argue that although a government may identify inclusion as fundamental to official policy and create structures to put it into practice, the efforts are purposefully weak in order to keep migrants and minorities on margins. Some proponents argue for taking direct action, such as civil disobedience, to pressure governments for inclusion for all. Proponents arguing from a "liberal" stance contend that inclusion fragments society and condemns liberal rights when defined as "group rights." Group rights include "the claims of religious groups to self-government in internal affairs and the demands for specific minority practices and legal exemptions from general rules for members of minority groups" (Barry, 2002, pp. 20–21).

Opponents argue that inclusion and multiculturalism can lead to ethnic Balkanization and can divide rather than unite people in the fight for social justice (Barry, 2002). Others contend inclusion and multiculturalism are utopian ideologies with simplistic and over-optimistic views of human nature (Njalsson, 2005). Still other critics argue that these ideas represent an attack on "traditional Christian values." Some opponents, such as Buchanan (2011), would go so far as to claim that social inclusion and multiculturalism are an assault on Anglo-American heritage and may mean the end of White America. Thus, "social inclusion, along with multiculturalism encounters powerful opposition—cohesiveness battling division, communities experiencing multiple forms of fragmentation, nuanced biases, narrow acceptance of diversity and individualism; and privileges for the few, often trump the needs of the many" (Hedetoft, 2013, p. 10). Social inclusion and multiculturalism also come under fire because many countries are facing stiff economic challenges, which result in some people with low education and income levels, such as the unemployed and manual workers, arguing that inclusion will increase immigration, spurring competition for an increasingly limited pool of jobs (European Monitoring Centre on Racism and Xenophobia, 2005). Thus, for some opponents, inclusion as an actionable concept has failed, though its value as an idea may remain. For other critics, inclusion and multiculturalism are antithetical to their world view.

The use of inclusive concepts may be fraught with difficulties, namely, the incompatibility between political rhetoric and the social and civic achievements of the *othered*, on the one hand, and a lack of appreciation and acceptance of concepts like social inclusion and multiculturalism by the general public, on the other. Nevertheless, it is difficult to identify models or ways of working (for e.g., conducting insightful research, writing policy, or making changes in teaching practice) that take into consideration the web of problems and issues facing people who live in urban, rural and suburban spaces and who experience exclusion for a host of intertwining identity-based factors. That said, intersectionality theories offer ways to examine cultural and social categories of inclusion and exclusion and the processes thorough which these interactions can produce systemic and individual inequalities (Hill Collins, 1998; Crenshaw, 1991; McCall, 2005; Winker & Degele, 2011).

## THE PROJECT

We perceive an ongoing lack of attention to intersectionality in education, despite growing interest in popular media and ongoing investment in intersectional-type work in the social sciences. Our collection invites urban educators and researchers to ask: How can our work benefit by incorporating intersectionality theories in research and in practice? What might we be able to better "see" using an intersectional lens? Though in many ways the literature on intersectionality and education echoes recommendations from studies of diversity over the years, we believe there is the potential for intersectionality to produce a serendipitous effect, revitalizing our theory and praxis around race, class, gender, and other identity axes in urban education. Building on the work of urban education scholars such as Anyon (2005), Pink and Noblit (2007), Blanchett, Klinger and Harry (2009), and Lipman (2013) , we see the need for an edited collection that would look across the different realms of urban education—theorizing identity markers in urban education, education in urban schools and communities, thinking intersectionally in teacher education & higher education, educational policies & urban spaces—seeking to better understand each topic using an intersectional lens. Such a collection might serve as a reference point for scholars and educators who are trying to address urban educational issues in light of identities and power. Secondly, we argue that education questions and/or problems beg to be conceptualized and analyzed through more than one identity axis. Policies and practices that do not take into account urban students' intertwining identity markers risk reproducing patterns of privilege and oppression, perpetuating stereotypes, and failing at the task we care most deeply about: supporting all students' learning across a holistic range of academic, personal, and justice-oriented outcomes.

This project was born out of a group of colleagues who joined together to present an *Intersectionality and Education* symposium at the 2011 National Association of Multicultural Education annual meeting. Based on the discussions generated, we decided to turn our presentations into an edited collection that would bring together scholars and practitioners that draw on intersectionality theories in their work. We hope to engage readers with a range of possibilities for applying intersectionality theories in their own educational settings; urban or otherwise.

## AN OVERVIEW

Crenshaw (2010) argues intersectionality is a project that is both academic and practical which seeks to "... illuminate and address discriminatory situations that would otherwise escape articulation" (n.p.). Though scholars have posited intersectional-type notions for over a century, Crenshaw's coining of the term "intersectionality" in 1989 led to a frenzy of empirical and theoretical work that still continues today. Within education, Grant and Sleeter first called for the use of race-, class-, and gender- analyses in 1986 in order to better understand schooling within a multicultural and inclusive context but intersectional work received limited scholarly attention until the current decade. Educational research that draws on intersectionality theories to better understand the inclusive and practices of multiculturalism is steadily growing and has been used to study social justice issues regarding policies and reforms (for e.g., Chapman & Antrop-Gonzalez, 2011; Ravnbol, 2009), teaching and learning (for e.g., Irizarry, 2007; Howard, 2008), relationships between families, communities, and schools (for e.g., Bhopal, 2004; Villenas, 2001), and teacher education (for e.g., DiAngelo & Sensoy, 2010; Heilman, 2010). Though in many ways the literature on intersectionality and education echoes recommendations from studies of diversity over the years, we believe there is the potential for intersectionality to produce a serendipitous effect, revitalizing our theory and praxis around race, class, gender, and other identity axes and fostering social inclusion.

The book explores the application of intersectionality theories in four main areas within urban education:

### Theorizing Identity Markers in Urban Education

These chapters introduce alternative ways of analyzing social relationships of inclusion and exclusion in urban settings with regard to difference and identities. Zwier and Grant review the literature on intersectionality and education, tracing its history and development over time and assessing the current state of the field. Baker encourages readers to shift away from a traditional social sciences focus on human-to-human interaction and power relations to examining how discourses of empiricism and vision shape our thinking. Christie proposes an amalgam of theories, combining spatial analysis with intersectional work to elucidate how social inequalities are produced and how they may be worked against, drawing on examples from South African students' journeys to and from school across urban, suburban, and rural spaces.

## Education in Urban Schools and Communities

This section highlights the relevance of intersectionality for teaching and learning in urban school and community settings. Boals, Macilla, and Castro explore how Latino students use the intersections of their multiple identity axes to navigate educational contexts. Noguera and Leslie inquire into the ways race, gender and class frame how black males are "seen" and configure the marginalization and risk they frequently experience in schools and society. Pacheco describes how Latina bilingual adolescents' identities shape and are shaped by their participation in out-of-school and online-settings. Chapman articulates how students of color in majority white schools articulate and assert their identities to defy common racial stereotypes.

## Thinking Intersectionally in Teacher Education and Higher Education

This group of chapters considers how college instructors and pre-service, and in-service teachers can use intersectionality to gain insight into the access to and experiences in higher education of their urban students, as well as their own experiences and instructional practices. Kraehe and Brown propose a combination of critical arts-based inquiry and intersectionality to help pre-service teachers develop critical socio-cultural knowledge. Hynds considers how the multiple identity markers of Indigenous Maori and non-Maori teachers in New Zealand influence their engagement in culturally responsive professional development. Kim uses quantitative methods to investigate how intersecting identities may affect Korean students' performances on the national standardized exam for college entrance. Bhopal describes how the experiences in higher education of a group of Asian women in the United Kingdom are shaped by their diverse identities.

## Educational Policies and Urban Spaces

These authors focus on educational policies for urban spaces from a variety of angles including critiques of existing policies, policy design and implementation, and policy as practice. Osler posits human rights education as both a right and a tool for enabling social justice in and through education. Allweiss describes how Chuj Mayan educators enact and make sense of national intercultural and bilingual education policies and practices. Agosto and Rolle look at the ways in which technology and obesity policies intersect in the experiences and identities of schoolchildren.

Our collection includes empirical research (qualitative and quantitative) and theoretical analyses. We offer readers a range of different uses for intersectionality theories, both theoretical and methodological. We have asked authors to be explicit about how their topic, theoretical framework, and/or methods draw on intersectionality theories. Chapters explore many of the salient discourses and topics under discussion in urban education today, suggesting ways in which intersectionality can be used to inform a wide range of areas within the field. We have asked contributors to consider the intersection of three or more identity markers as a sort of "minimum threshold." The contributions span intertwining identity axes such as race, ethnicity, gender, geography (rural, urban, suburban), immigration status, nationality, language, sexual orientation, religion, social class, and body (weight). Lastly, we invited both international and U.S. authors to contextualize intersectionality theories in multiple local and global settings. Our collection includes contributions from authors in South Africa, the United Kingdom, South Korea, New Zealand, and the United States.

Can educational policies and practices address the social justice issues faced in urban schools and communities today? We argue that doing intersectional research and implementing educational policies and practices guided by these frameworks can help improve the "fit." Particular attention needs to be paid to intersectionality as a lens for educational theory, policy, and practice. As urban educators we would be wise to consider the intertwining of these identity axes in order to better analyze educational issues and engage in teaching, learning, research, and policymaking that are better-tuned to the needs of diverse students, families, and communities.

## REFERENCES

Anheier, H., Glasius, M., & Kaldor, M. (Eds.). (2001). *Global civil society yearbook 2001*. Oxford, U.K.: Oxford University Press.

Anyon, J. (2005). *Radical possibilities: Public policy, urban education, and a new social movement*. New York: Taylor & Francis.

Barry, B. (2002). *Culture and equality: An egalitarian critique of multiculturalism* Cambridge, MA: Harvard University Press.

Bhopal, K. (2004). Gypsy travelers and education: Changing needs and changing perceptions. *British Journal of Educational Studies*, 52(1), 47–64.

Blanchett, W. J., Klinger, J. K., & Harry, B. (2009). The intersections of race, culture, language, and disability: Implications for urban education. *Urban Education*, 44, 389–404.

Buchanan, P. (2011). *Multiculturalism and the end of White America*. Retrieved May 25, 2013 from ww.wnd.com/2011/11/365357/.

Chapman, T. K., & Antrop-Gonzalez, R. (2011). A critical look at choice options as solutions to Milwaukee's Schooling Inequities. *Teachers College Record, 113*(4), 787–810.

Crenshaw, K. W. (1991). Mapping the margins: Intersectionality, identity politics, and violence against women of color. *Stanford Law Review, 43*(6), 1241–1299.

Crenshaw, K. W. (2010). *Intersection of race and gender.* University of Wisconsin-Madison, Sociology Department FemSem. Madison, WI. 23 Oct. 2010.

DiAngelo, R., & Sensoy, O. (2010). "OK, I get it! Now tell me how to do it!": Why we can't just tell you how to do critical multicultural education. *Multicultural Perspectives, 12*(2), 97–102.

Grant, C. A., & Sleeter, C. E. (1986). Race, class, and gender in education research. *Review of Educational Research, 56*(2), 195–211.

Grant, C. A. & Lei, J. (Eds.). (2001). *Global construction of multicultural education: theories and realities.* Mahwah, NJ: Lawrence Erlbaum.

Grant, C. A., & Portera, A. (Eds.). (2011). *Intercultural and multicultural education: Enhancing global interconnectedness.* New York: Routledge.

Hedetoft, U. R. (2013). Social inclusion: Inaugural editorial. *Social Inclusion, 1*(1), 1–2.

Heilman, E. E. (2010). Hoosiers, hicks, and hayseeds: The controversial place of marginalized ethnic whites in multicultural education. *Equity & Excellence in Education, 37*(1), 67–79.

Hill Collins, P. (1990) *Black feminist thought: Knowledge, consciousness and the politics of empowerment.* New York: Routledge.

Howard, T. C. (2008). Who really cares? The disenfranchisement of African American males in preK-12 schools: A critical race theory perspective. *Teachers College Record, 110*(5), 954–985.

Irizarry, J. G. (2007). Ethnic and urban intersections in the classroom: Latino students, hybrid identities and culturally responsive pedagogy. *Multicultural Perspectives, 9*(3), 21–28.

Lipman, P. (2011). *The new political economy of urban education: Neoliberalism, race, and the right to the city.* New York, NY: Routledge.

Lipman, P. (2013). *The new political economy of urban education: Neoliberalism, race, and the right to the city.* New York: Routledge.

McCall, L. (2005). The complexity of intersectionality. *Signs: Journal of Women in Culture and Society, 30*(3), 1771–1800.

Njalsson, G. K. A. (2005). *Multiculturalism.* Retrieved May 25, 2013 from http://wiki. owotw.net/wiki/index.php?title=Multicultural.

Noblit, G. W., & Pink, W. T. (2007). Introduction. In W. T. Pink, & G. W. Noblit (Eds.), *International handbook of urban education.* New York: Springer.

Peters, M. A. (2001). *Postructuralism, Marxism and neoliberalism: Between theory and Politics.* New York: Rowman and Littlefield.

Pink, W. T., & Noblit, G. W. (Eds.). (2007). *International handbook of urban education.* New York: Springer.

Ravnbol, C. I. (2009). *Intersectional discrimination against children: Discrimination against Romani children and anti-discrimination measures to address child trafficking.* UNICEF Innocenti Research Centre, Florence. Retrieved March 28, 2011 from http://www.unicef-irc.org/publications/pdf/iwp_2009_11.pdf

Sabatini, C. (2012). What is social inclusion, and how is it lacking in Latin America. CNN World. Global Public Square Blog, May 17, 2012. Retrieved June 1, 2013 from http://globalpublicsquare.blogs.cnn.com/2012/05/17/what-is-social-inclusion-and-how-is-it-lacking-in-latin-america/.

Silj, A. (Ed.). (2010). *European multiculturalism revisited.* London, UK: Zed Books.

Silver, H. (2010). Understanding social inclusion and its meaning for Australia. *Australian Journal of Social Issues, 45*(2), 183–211.

Smith, C. (2012). Neoliberalism and individualism: Ego leads to interpersonal violence? *The Society Pages: Sociology Lens,* December 4, 2012. Retrieved June 1, 2013 from http://thesocietypages.org/sociologylens/2012/12/04/neoliberalism-and-individualism-ego-leads-to-interpersonal-violence/

Treanor, P. (2012). The philosophy of neoliberalism. *Penny Wise,* April 4, 2012. Retrieved June 1, 2013 from http://econocat.wordpress.com/tag/paul-treanor/.

Villenas, S. (2001). Latina mothers and small-town racisms. *Anthropology & Education Quarterly, 32*(1), 3–28.

Watson, D. (2011). What do you mean when you say urban? *Rethinking Schools, 26*(1), n.p. Retrieved November 14, 2013 from http://www.rethinkingschools.org/restrict.asp?path+archive/26_01/26_01_watson.shtml.

Winker, G., & Degele, N. (2011). Intersectionality as multi-level analysis: Dealing with social inequality. *European Journal of Women's Studies, 18*(1), 51–66.

# PART I
## THEORIZING IDENTITY MARKERS
## IN URBAN EDUCATION

CHAPTER 1

# THINKING INTERSECTIONALLY IN EDUCATION

Elisabeth Zwier
Carl A. Grant
*University of Wisconsin-Madison*

Educational researchers first noted the need for intersectional theories
and intersectionally informed methodologies to address issues of oppression and inequality during the 1980s, but lacked a common language for
discussing these concerns (Grant & Sleeter, 1986; McCarthy & Apple, 1988;
Sleeter & Grant, 1988). Black feminist theorists (Hill Collins, 1990, 2000;
hooks, 1981), Critical Race Theorists (Crenshaw, 1989, 1991), and sociologists (Anthias & Yuval-Davis, 1983) can be credited with the development of
a range of intersectionality theories and notions that sought to understand
the workings of identity and oppression across a wide range of contexts.
Within the past decade, a growing number of education scholars draw on
intersectionality to analyze social justice issues in education such as individual experiences and counter-narratives of oppression (Connor, 2006;
Staunaes, 2003), groups experiencing intersectional oppression (Gillborn,
2010; Noguera, 2008; Villenas, 2001), and exclusionary policies (Cassidy &
Jackson, 2005; Chapman, Lamborn & Epps, 2010; Ravnbol, 2009).

*Intersectionality and Urban Education*, pages 3–27
Copyright © 2014 by Information Age Publishing
All rights of reproduction in any form reserved.

**3**

Since intersectionality theories do not originate in education, we begin by outlining a brief history of their development noting moments where educational theorists and researchers called for, proposed, and engaged in intersectional research. Next, we synthesize the current state of knowledge with respect to the use of intersectionality theories in education. We structure this discussion around two central questions: What has scholarship on intersectionality and education focused on and how has it been used to address social justice issues? How have authors drawn upon intersectionality theories? Grant and Sleeter (1986) caution, "A failure to consider the integration of race, social class and gender leads at times to an oversimplification or inaccurate understanding of what occurs in schools, and therefore to inappropriate or simplistic prescriptions for educational equity" (p. 197). This theoretical review of the literature heeds this call by inquiring into the scholarship on intersectionality theories and intersectionality and education to determine what these theories offer the field of education, and how they have sought to address social justice issues.

## BRIEF HISTORY OF INTERSECTIONALITY THEORIES WITH ATTENTION TO EDUCATION

Many histories of intersectionality theories situate their geneses with Critical Legal scholar Kimberle Crenshaw's coining of the term in her 1989 article *Demarginalizing the Intersection of Race and Sex: A Black Feminist Critique of Antidiscrimination Doctrine, Feminist Theory and Antiracist Politics*. While Crenshaw (1989, 1991) can be credited with naming and further theorizing the notion, other scholars suggest that this term was a nodal point for multiple ongoing feminist debates both before and after this time point (Lykke, 2010; Nash, 2008). Along with Davis (2008) we might ask, "If all these ideas were already 'in the air,' then, what was so special about intersectionality?" (p. 73). One argument is that intersectionality became a "buzzword" because it linked critical feminist theory and critical methodologies in novel ways, appealing to both generalist and specialist academic audiences (Davis, 2008). Others suggest it provided an "appropriate metaphor" for analyzing relationships of difference in previously unimaginable ways (Andersen, 2005, p. 444). Regardless of the source of its appeal, the coining of "intersectionality" as such marked a transition in the study of difference and categories of difference from single to multiple categories of difference, and then to intersecting categories (Hancock, 2007, p. 67).

Prior to intersectionality theories' arrival on the social science scene, scholars and social movements throughout the previous century had articulated similar notions, deploying them in research and in the political arena to address social justice issues. Sojourner Truth, with her *"Ain't I a Woman"* speech at the convention on women's rights in Akron, Ohio in 1851, arguably garners the honor of being the foremother of intersectionality theories. From her experiences and positionality as a Black female enslaved person, she argued for considering the raced and classed dimensions of gender in formulating the subjects of women's rights: "That man over there says that women need to be helped into carriages, and lifted over ditches and to have the best place everywhere. Nobody helps me any best place. And ain't I a woman?" (Cited in Brah & Phoenix, 2004, p. 77). Hints of intersectional thinking might also be identified in the writings of W.E.B. DuBois when he speaks of "the island within," suggesting an outsider perspective within his own position as a Black male due to class and educational differences. DuBois also articulates the need for joint efforts between feminist and Black social movements: "When, now, two of these movements—women and color—combine in one, the combination has deep meaning" (In Hancock, 2005, p. 77). DuBois' work acknowledges the interaction between individual agency and structural and political change (Hancock, 2005, p. 80). The origins of intersectional thinking can also be traced to conversations between feminist and socialist theorists in the late nineteenth and early twentieth centuries (Kocze, 2009). Marxist feminists' focus on gender and class challenged both the mainstream workers movement (predominantly comprised of men) and the bourgeois feminist movement to consider the relationships between these social markers (Lykke, 2010, p. 76). Intersectionality's birth out of identity politics taps into deep roots of strength, community, and intellectual development for oppressed groups (Crenshaw, 1991). Nevertheless, some scholars claim using one category as most salient for political explanation can be universalizing and result in static and enduring notions of categories (Hancock, 2007). Marginal members of these and other race-, class-, and gender-based social movements and theoretical traditions note how their experiences are "rendered invisible" through the discourses of single-category identity politics (Yuval-Davis, 2006, p. 195).

Black feminist scholars' and activists' conjoined focus on race, class, and gender begins with their critique of second-wave feminism, namely, that White women did not speak for all women (hooks, 1981). hooks (1981) argues against feminists' assumptions at the time that all Blacks were male and all Whites were women, indicating how this erases the existence of Black women. In 1977, the Combahee River Collective, a group of Black feminists issues a statement decrying the ways in which "interlocking oppressions" structured their lived experiences. They pronounce: "The most general statement of our politics at the present time would be that we are actively committed to struggling against racial, sexual, heterosexual, and class oppression, and see as our particular task the development of integrated analysis and practice based upon the fact that the major systems of oppression are interlocking. The synthesis of these oppressions creates the conditions of our lives" (Combahee River Collective, 1977, n.p.). Scholars from the United Kingdom seek to address similar issues and posit the notion of "triple oppression" of race, class, and gender (Anthias & Yuval-Davis, 1983). King (1988) elaborates on this iteration, proposing the concept of "multiple jeopardy" in attempt to capture multiple, simultaneous oppressions, the multiplicative relationships among them, and the multiple consciousness needed for resistance.

During this era, educational researchers were also wrestling theoretically and empirically with how to address race, class, and gender simultaneously. Scholars sought to understand how social inequalities are maintained through schools (Weis, 1988). Structuralists suggested students' race, class, and gender results in differential schooling through the hidden curriculum, whereas culturalists asserted minority students construct subcultures within schools, which then lead to inequalities, and post-structuralists analyzed race, class, and gender as processes of mediation and negotiation by embodied actors (McCarthy & Apple, 1988; Weis, 1988). In 1986, Grant and Sleeter engage in a seminal review of the literature within education in top education journals from the previous decade, finding only three articles that consider all three status groups and only one (Rumberger, 1983) that could be considered a fully integrated analysis. In subsequent writings the authors further develop their critique of the tendency within the field to subsume multiple forms of oppression under a Marxist analysis (Sleeter & Grant, 1988). They call for collective theory building around race, class, and gender by a group of diverse scholars that views categories as "... equally important and enduring forms of oppression that are interrelated but not reducible to one form" (Sleeter & Grant, 1988, p. 145). McCarthy and Apple (1988) argue for the use of an "interactive framework" that considers the intersection of the dynamics of race, class, and gender in schooling and attends to political, economic, and cultural spheres (p. 23). The authors contend, "We see social formation as an integrated though contested totality. Thus, though relations of race, gender, and class exist on autonomous and independent axes to capital, they intersect and are dependent upon each other for their reproduction and persistence" (McCarthy & Apple, 1988, p. 10). Nevertheless, these discussions of race-, class-, and gender-based oppression within education did not result their widespread use, in contrast with the intersectional theoretical developments taking place in the broader social sciences at the time.

In the ongoing scholarly discussion regarding the three categories, Crenshaw (1989) is credited with naming and elaborating the best-know iteration of intersectionality theory. The author posits a metaphor of intersections, like roads crossing one another, to argue that both identity politics and anti-discrimination policies miss the point in relation to the experiences women of color because they view race and gender separately (Crenshaw,

1989). Crenshaw (1991) asserts, "Either-or discourses marginalize women of color because their intersectional identities are both-and" (p. 1244). Moreover, Crenshaw (1991) suggests intersectionality could be useful for analyzing any type of marginalization. Throughout the subsequent decade, other scholars elaborate, contest, or reject Crenshaw's (1989) notion of "intersectionality." Black feminist theorist Patricia Hill Collins (1990, 2000) develops the concept of the matrix of domination, proposing intersectionality and interlocking as complementary concepts that operate through four interrelated domains of power: structural, disciplinary, hegemonic, and interpersonal. Hill Collins (2000) asserts, "Each domain serves a particular purpose. The structural domain organizes oppression, whereas the disciplinary domain manages it. The hegemonic domain justifies oppression, and the interpersonal domain influences everyday lived experience and the individual consciousness that ensues" (p. 276). Razack (1998) develops the idea of "interlocking systems" to understand how groups of people are produced so that neither exists without the other. Glenn (1999) puts forward a social constructionist framework for "integrated analysis" which clarifies how intersectionality processes operate. The author indicates "…race and gender share three key features as analytic concepts: They are relational concepts whose construction involves both representational and social structural processes, in which power is a constitutive element" (Glenn, 1999, p. 9). Latina and Chicana feminists' work (Anzaldua, 1987; Chela Sandoval, 2000) offers the notion of "border crossing" (Anzaldua, 1987) to capture the intersectional oppression experienced on the basis of race/ethnicity, gender, sexual orientation, language, and social class. This work by feminist scholars, activists, and social movements named and proposed concepts and frameworks for understanding and, in some iterations, working to transform intersectional oppression.

Intersectionality theories' articulation and development did not go unnoticed by stakeholders in the international policy sphere. Policymakers incorporate intersectionality in the United Nations (UN) Beijing Platform for Action, adopted by 95 countries at the Fourth World Conference on Women in September 1995. The framework calls for governments to ensure rights and freedoms of women and girls who "face multiple barriers" because of other identity-based factors (in Yuval-Davis, 2006, p. 196). Some scholars suggest this is the first instance where high-level policy organizations address intersectional or multiple discrimination (Makkonen, 2002, p. 45). The proposals emanating from the 2001 UN World Conference against Racism, Racial Discrimination, Xenophobia, and Related Intolerance contain numerous references to the concept of "multiple or aggravated forms of discrimination," another milestone in terms of considering identity categories intersectionally (Kocze, 2009; Makkonen, 2002, p. 48). However, Hankivsky and Cormier (2010) note that while the concept of intersectionality is referenced, no specific international policies have been developed to address intersectional inequalities. Policymakers within the European Union (EU) have been at the forefront of actually incorporating intersectionality into policymaking, with varying degrees of success (Kocze, 2009; Parken, 2010; Verloo, 2006). For instance, the 2007 European Year of Equal Opportunities for All makes intersectional thinking more visible and has led to the recognition of multiple differences and inequalities (Kocze, 2009). Furthermore, new EU policies are subject to equality impact assessments for all strands of inequality and multiple discrimination (Parken, 2010). However, Verloo (2006) suggests EU policymakers struggle with assuming similarity among inequalities, failing to incorporate structural approaches, and inadvertently fueling political competition among inequalities (p. 214).

Recent developments regarding intersectionality theories foreground the processual nature of oppression and privilege and attend to the social workings of power. Several scholars conceptualize intersectionality as dynamic process of "doing difference" (Staunaes, 2003; Lykke, 2010). Focusing on the individual or group level, these scholars examine how categories are made in interactions, in context, and in relation to "normative conceptions of in/appropriateness" (Staunaes, 2003, p. 104). Recent scholarship seeks to recognize "axes of difference" (Yuval-Davis, 2006) and how these processes interact with systems of domination in a "matrix of meaning-making" (Dhamoon, 2010) or through "transversal approaches" to encourage thinking across categories (Yuval-Davis, 2006). Nash (2008) claims intersectionality has become the new "gold standard" multidisciplinary approach for analyzing both identity and oppression. Given intersectionality theories' common goals of understanding inequalities and identifying potential for change in the status quo (Ferree, 2010), concepts should be chosen according to their critical capacity and remain open to change as theories continue to develop (Dhamoon, 2010).

## Levels or Domains of Power

Within the range of intersectionality theories, scholars attend to different levels or domains of power in their conceptualizations in keeping with whether micro- or macro-level phenomena or both are central to their concerns (Ferree, 2010). While significant overlaps exist among the foci, each iteration provides a slightly different lens for empirical research. Hancock (2007) claims, "Intersectionality is sympathetic and applicable to both the structural level of analysis, and individual-level phenomena via its domains of power thesis, which recognizes the various terrains on which politics plays out—structural and interpersonal" (p. 74). It is important to note that in intersectionality theories, these levels or domains are interactive rather than hierarchical (Yuval-Davis, 2006). Hill Collins (1990) posits four inter-related domains of power: structural (organization of social institutions), disciplinary (policies and bureaucracies that manage oppression), hege-monic (ideas and beliefs that rationalize oppression), and interpersonal (everyday interactions among individuals and groups). Crenshaw (1991) lays out three levels: structural, political, and representational intersection-ality (p. 1245). The structural level looks at individuals' experiences and positions within intersecting oppressions, the political level examines how policies marginalize intersectional groups, and the representational level explores how these individuals and groups are constructed within popular culture (Crenshaw, 1991). Both Hill Collins (1990) and Crenshaw's (1991) frameworks attend to micro- and macro-level phenomena, but empha-size the role of systems and policies in processes of differentiation. Glenn (1999) proposes, and Winker and Degele (2011) expand upon, a three-level conceptualization that includes symbolic representation (symbols, language, images), micro-interaction or identity constructions (norms and etiquette that orchestrate interaction in and across boundaries), and social structures (allocation of power and resources according power relations vis-à-vis identity categories). In contrast, "doing intersectionality" approaches (Staunaes, 2003; Lykke, 2010) call for an in-depth focus on the micro- or identity construction level categories as processes shaped by social norms and structures. Ferree's (2010) framework incorporates all of the previ-ous approaches into two types of analyses: locational intersectionality and relational intersectionality. According to Ferree (2010), locational inter-sectionality focuses on the identity categories and social positions where multiple forms of oppression co-occur, whereas relational intersectionality identifies processes (struggles, conflicts) that "interact to produce dynam-ic and complex patterns of inequality for everyone, not merely the most disadvantaged" through institutionalized practices and cultural discourses (p. 430). Ferree (2010) argues that the key difference among approaches is the degree to which institutional change is central to the analysis, given that all intersectional approaches are premised upon viewing privilege and oppression as inherently contradictory and multiple. When employed in tandem, locational and relational intersectional approaches "...balance attention to structures of inequality with a concern for agency and voice" (Ferree, 2010, p. 430).

## Definitions of Intersectionality Theories

Given the plurality of intersectional theories, no one definition can en-compass the diverse strands of scholarship that make up this arena. One point of consensus it that intersectionality is both a set of theories and their methodological and analytical applications to empirical research (Cassidy & Jackson, 2005; Hancock, 2007). A second substantive focus is explaining, critiquing, and in some cases, working to transform, the operations of power through institutional processes, interpersonal dynamics, or both (Ferree, 2010; Hawkesworth, 2006; Winker & Degele, 2011). Hill Collins and Anderson (1995) assert, "The very notion of intersections of race, class, gender as an area worthy of study emerged from the recognition of practitioners of each distinctive theoretical tradition that inequality could not be explained, let alone challenged, via race-only, class-only, or gender-only frameworks" (p. 492). A serious point of contention among theorists is whether the priority list of inequalities is infinite or finite (Choo & Ferree, 2010; Lykke, 2010; Verloo, 2006). Verloo (2006) asserts: "As of yet, no work has been done on whether all possible intersections might be relevant at all times, or when and where some of them might be more salient" (p. 214). These points of consensus and divergence highlight the diversity of approaches that make up intersectionality theories.

Depending on which domains of power they analyze, intersectional feminist theories may focus on "doing difference" or analyze processes within and across multiple social spheres. However, Yuval-Davis (2006) cautions against a strict division among levels because all of the levels are processes and each level has both material and symbolic production effects. Lykke's (2010) definition is representative of the "doing difference" focus: "Intersectional feminist theories focus on the ways in which gender/sex is "done" in intra-action with other socio-cultural classifications, and how societal power differentials and constructions of identity, based on gender, class, race, ethnicity, geopolitical position, nationality, sexuality, dis/ability, age, and so on mutually influence each other" (p. 208). Davis (2008) incorporates "doing difference" but situates it among multiple social spheres: "'Intersectionality' refers to the interaction between gender, race, and other categories of difference in individual lives, social practices, institutional arrangements, and cultural ideologies and the outcomes of these interactions in terms of power" (p. 68). Ferree (2010) clarifies the common foundational elements across all intersectional theories: "Despite differences in specifics, any perspective is today called intersectional if it takes multiple relations of inequality as the norm, sees them as processes that shape each other, and considers how they interactively define the identities and experiences—and thus analytic standpoints—of individuals and groups" (p. 428). Drawing on this scholarship, our working definition of intersectionality theories is as follows: Intersectionality theories and intersectionally-informed methodologies seek to explain, critique, and transform relationships of difference within and across one or more levels or social spheres, taking into account the workings of power through fluid, context-specific, co-constructed identity categories.

## Intersectionally Informed Methodologies and Methods

Intersectionality theorists have been subject to the criticism that they have failed to develop a coherent methodology (McCall, 2005; Nash, 2008). These critiques may be rooted in confusion over methodology—a disciplinary approach to research, and methods—the specific analytical tools researchers apply in the context of that approach. Crenshaw (2010) argues intersectionality cannot develop a methodology because methodologies are specific to disciplines. Methodological criticisms may also be grounded in a desire to more efficiently manage the complexity of intersectional research, which increases in proportion to the number of categories involved (Lykke, 2010). A frequently cited study of intersectionality theories and methods (McCall, 2005) divides research in the field into three approaches toward analytical categories: anticategorical, intercategorical, and intracategorical complexity. McCall (2005) describes anticategorical approaches as deconstructing identity categories and their accompanying normative assumptions, viewing those "simplifying social fictions" (p. 1783). Staunaes (2003) argues intersectional studies that understand subjects as determined by social systems obscure complexity and ambiguity at subject level. Intercategorical methods provisionally adopt existing categories to analyze changing relationships of inequality among multiple social groups (McCall, 2005). For instance, Matsuda's (1991) popular method of "asking the other question" takes the primary form of oppression in a situation and asks how this dimension interacts with other axes of power and exclusion that are less well articulated (p. 1189). Nevertheless, Choo and Ferree (2009) caution ". . . it is still easier to include multiply marginalized groups than to analyze relationships that affect them intersectionally" (p. 31). Lastly, intracategorical approaches focus on particular individuals or social groups at neglected points of intersection (McCall, 2005). For instance, Kumashiro's (2001) method of "troubling intersections" examines the intersections researchers find troubling or ignore and problematizes the ways they examine intersections (p. 2). However, intra-categorical approaches are subject to critiques of remaining on the experiential level of analysis and failing to distinguish between different levels (Yuval-Davis, 2006).

Collectively, intersectionally-informed methodologies and methods attune researchers to the operations of power through institutional processes and interpersonal dynamics, including those invisible to mainstream methods in the social sciences (Hawkesworth, 2006). Hancock (2007) claims intersectionality is a paradigm for conducting research, rather than a "content specialization" in populations with intersecting marginalized identities (p. 64). Crenshaw (2010) elaborates "...intersectionality applies to everyone—no one exists outside the matrix of power, but the implications of this matrix—when certain features are activated and relevant and when they are not—are contextual" (n.p.). While intersectionality theories do not claim to be a methodology, this paradigm for research informs methodologies and methods for research.

## INTERSECTIONALITY THEORIES IN EDUCATION

Though a few studies called for or incorporated intersectionality in the 1980s and 1990s (Grant & Sleeter, 1986; Grant & Sleeter, 1988; McCarthy & Apple, 1988; Sleeter & Grant, 1988), most of the empirical work informed by this theory has been published within the past decade. In this review of the literature, I draw upon studies that explicitly mention the term "intersectionality" or engage in intersectional-type work (Dhamoon, 2010), that incorporate three or more identity characteristics—a "minimum threshold" proposed by some scholars (Davis, 2008), and that topically focus on areas of direct relevance to K–12 education—policies and reforms; teaching and learning, relationships between schools, families, and communities; and teacher education. Several scholars argue all intersectionality research is social justice oriented because it is premised upon understanding the operations of power, critiquing or deconstructing these operations, and in some instantiations, seeking to disrupt and transform their workings (Dhamoon, 2010; Hawkesworth, 2006). This review will be structured around the following guiding questions: What has scholarship on intersectionality and education focused on and how has it been used to address social justice issues? How have authors drawn upon intersectionality theories? Educational research has been subject to criticisms of either ignoring intersections (Grant, Wieczorek & Gillette, 2000) or falling into the trap of "...speak[ing] in identity-constructed balkanizations, with little fluidity or intersectionality between those for whom race, class, sexuality, or gender has primacy" (Loutzenheiser & McIntosh, 2004, p. 155). This small, but steadily growing body of literature suggests otherwise.

### Policies and Reforms

*What has scholarship on intersectionality and education focused on and how has it been used to address social justice issues?* Educational researchers and policymakers are beginning to draw on intersectionality theories for formulating and analyzing policies and their role in reforms, in some cases (Au, 2009;

Bishwakarma, Hunt & Zajicek, 2007; Cassidy & Jackson, 2005; Chapman & Antrop-Gonzalez, 2011; Chapman, Lamborn & Epps, 2010; Kockze, 2009; McCall & Skrtic, 2010; Ravnbol; 2009). Kozce (2009) argues intersectionality can be used as a tool to formulate complex and responsive public policies. Other scholars employ this theoretical framework for critical analysis: "… [Policy] interpretation is not simply a neutral, technical undertaking, but rather a moral and political act with consequences for ethical practice and a just society" (McCall and Skrtic, 2010, p. 4). Intersectionality can also be used to critique the ways in which reforms perpetuate systems of oppression by underestimating the power of interacting identity axes (Au, 2009; Chapman et al., 2010; Chapman & Antrop-Gonzalez, 2011).

Several scholars suggest intersectionality theories can help design policies that better promote social justice and analyze their inclusionary or exclusionary effects once implemented (Bishwakarma, Hunt & Zajicek, 2007; Cassidy & Jackson, 2005; Kocze, 2009; McCall & Skrtic, 2010; Ravnbol, 2009). Bishwakarma, Hunt & Zajicek (2007) note intersectionality's limited use in formulating development policies and propose a model for intersectional analysis at each stage of the policy process. Other studies argue for integrating intersectionality into rights-based policymaking to protect Romani children from intersectional discrimination (Kocze, 2009; Ravnbol, 2009). Several scholars use intersectionality theories to frame and analyze the discriminatory effects of seemingly neutral policies (Cassidy & Jackson, 2005; McCall & Skrtic, 2010). One study examines the disproportionate representation of particular groups of already disadvantaged students in special education (McCall & Skrtic, 2010), while another traces the exclusion of students seen as "severe behavior problems" through anti-bullying practices and zero tolerance policies (Cassidy & Jackson, 2005).

Other scholars incorporate intersectionality into their critical analyses of social justice issues in school systems and the reforms that address or exacerbate these dilemmas (Au, 2009; Chapman et al., 2010; Chapman & Antrop-Gonzalez, 2011). Au (2009) explores the disproportionate negative impact of high-stakes testing on students of color and their schools. In the case of White and middle-class Black flight to suburban schools, school choice reforms purportedly targeting the racially diverse, low-income families that remain behind ignore the power of race and class on parental choice (Chapman & Antrop-Gonzalez, 2011). Chapman and colleagues (2010) argue reforms seeking to address the low achievement of many culturally and linguistically diverse students fail to consider how the inequitable distribution of resources and underlying racism and discrimination might affect these trends. These scholars call for school reformers to draw upon community assets and consider the social, historical and institutional contexts schools are situated in (Chapman et al., 2010).

*How have authors drawn upon intersectionality theories?* Intersectionality helps us look critically at policy and reform processes and is particularly useful for uncovering the adverse effects of purportedly neutral policies on students already experiencing intersectional discrimination (Au, 2009; Cassidy & Jackson, 2005; Chapman & Antrop-Gonzalez, 2011; McCall & Skrtic, 2010). Anti-discrimination policies which target separate identity axes (Kocze, 2009) and reforms that standardize identities (Au, 2009) can have unanticipated adverse effects on children experiencing intersectional discrimination. Inversely, intersectionality can help us trace the ways in which policies rhetorically address issues of oppression while actually benefitting those already privileged (Chapman et al., 2010; Chapman & Antrop-Gonzalez, 2011). Several studies use intersectionality as a theoretical lens and a tool to identify issues and formulate policies (Bishwakarma, Hunt & Zajicek, 2007; Kockze, 2009). Nevertheless, Ravnbol (2009) notes that educational policy studies are still transitioning from theory to practice in their engagement with intersectionality theories and points to the need for further research.

## Teaching and Learning

*What has scholarship on intersectionality and education focused on and how has it been used to address social justice issues?* Though educational research focused on the school and classroom level has long been interested in addressing role identities play in pedagogical relationships and the ways in which schooling itself structures identities (e.g., Grant & Sleeter, 1988), a body of recent scholarship suggests intersectionality theories may help us better understand questions around teaching and learning, identities, and student outcomes (Achinstein & Aguirre, 2008; Allard & Santoro, 2008; Briscoe, 2009; Bryan, 2009; Camarrota, 2007; Connor, 2006; Gallagher-Geurtsen, 2009; Howard, 2008; Irizarry, 2007; Kumashiro, 2001; Loutzenheiser & MacIntosh, 2004; Lugg, 2003; Noguera, 2008; Staunaes, 2003; Watkins & Aber, 2009; Zembylas, 2010). Grant and colleagues (2000) summarize the intersectional effects of this dilemma: "Often, however, we ignore these [intersectional] observations and just 'see' one or two or none of these social constructions and relationships and their influence on social justice issues such as inequality and stratification" (p. 12). Allard and Santoro (2008) suggest teachers need to know about differences and how these might intersect, but more importantly, "...become adept a working productively with differences..." (p. 212).

Intersectional studies of teaching and learning in K–12 school settings have been used to analyze and work to address an array of social justice topics and issues. We have organized our discussion of these articles by theme: teaching diverse students, curricular relevance, "doing difference," students' experiences and strategies for navigating their education, and the oppressive effects of schooling.

### Teaching Diverse Students

The scholarship on intersectionality and teaching diverse students (Achinstein & Aguirre, 2008; Allard & Santoro, 2008; Gallagher-Geurtsen, 2009; Irizarry, 2007; Kumashiro, 2001; Zembylas, 2010) centers teachers' wealth of culturally responsive, critical, asset-based beliefs, pedagogies, and experiences, but notes stereotypes and oppressive practices persist in many cases. Achinstein & Aguirre (2008) find that when new teachers of color experience sociocultural challenges by students of color, the majority draw on "emergent multicultural capital" to create teachable moments. These studies suggest teachers' multicultural capital might include critical self-reflection (Allard & Santoro, 2008), viewing students as global resources (Gallagher-Geurtsen, 2009), culturally responsive practices and constant efforts to become a "culturally connected" educator (Irizarry, 2007). Other scholars examine "harmful interactions" and "inaction" (Kumashiro, 2001) on the part of teachers and administrators that result in detrimental experiences for students. Kumashiro (2001) reports queer students of color experience verbal and physical violence, harassment, isolation, etc., which he proposes countering with anti-oppressive education. Zembylas (2010) studies how Turkish-speaking students are stereotypically racialized, ethnicized, classed by Greek-Cypriot teachers but finds individual instances of teachers working to counter these practices.

### Curricular Relevance

Two studies point to the ways in which curricula can either include or exclude students and their intersectional experiences (Bryan, 2009; Camarrota, 2007). Bryan (2009) shows how state-level discourses of intercultural education in Ireland are interpreted in one high school to diffuse conflict and maintain the status quo of nationalism and racism vis-à-vis recent immigrants. In another high school in Texas, United States, Camarrota (2007) describes how a year-long course on social justice, critical theory, and participatory action research engages Latino/a students previously in remedial tracks, promotes their sense of agency, and increases their chances of graduating.

### "Doing Difference"

Studies of intersectionality, teaching, and learning can also be used to highlight how students enact their identities in school (Connor, 2006; Staunaes, 2003). Such approaches to research can problematize how categories work and intersect in the lived experiences of students (Staunaes, 2003), producing exclusionary schooling experiences for many (Connor, 2006).

*Students' Experiences and Strategies*

Intersectional research can create spaces for students to voice their experiences through approaches such as counter storytelling (Howard, 2008), testimonies (Briscoe, 2009), and personal interviews (Grant & Sleeter, 1988; Noguera, 2008) or express their perceptions through surveys (Watkins & Aber, 2009). Briscoe's (2009) study of Mexican-American women's experience in their K–12 to PhD journey describes the wealth of strategies they deploy for navigating schooling. Howard (2008) and Noguera (2008) suggest African American males pursue academic success to counter stereotypes and experiences of racism. Another study reports middle school students' college and career dreams may be negatively impacted by a range of scholastic, community-based, economic, and personal factors over the course of their schooling experiences (Grant & Sleeter, 1988). Watkins and Aber (2009) find middle school students' perceptions of the school racial climate influence their achievement and sense of academic efficacy.

*Oppressive Effects of Schooling*

Several scholars draw on intersectionality theories and queer studies to research how school structures shape oppressive daily educational practices around gender and sexual orientation (Loutzenheiser & MacIntosh, 2004; Lugg, 2003). Loutzenheiser & MacIntosh (2004) suggest queer students are harmfully positioned as Other in educational research and schooling through curriculum and discourses; a focus Lugg (2003) shares and expands to encompass school policies.

*How have authors drawn upon intersectionality theories?* The body of scholarly work on intersectionality and teaching and learning incorporates intersectionality theoretically to expose the workings of identity and power (e.g., Staunaes, 2003; Zembylas, 2010) and transform teaching and learning (e.g., Camarrota, 2007; Irizarry, 2007). In the first focus, identities are viewed as a relational, micro-level (Connor, 2006) and/or macro-level processes (Briscoe, 2009) of meaning-making and negotiation (Achinstein & Aguirre, 2008), influenced by structures of power (Lugg, 2003), discourses (Bryan, 2009), and context (Zembylas, 2010). One approach to intersectional research is to study how social categories function as tools of inclusion/exclusion, positioning and hierarchy creation in daily interactions (Connor, 2006; Staunaes, 2003). Analytically, intersectionality theories highlight and interrupt normative assumptions (Kumashiro, 2001; Loutzenheiser & MacIntosh, 2004; Lugg, 2003) and focus on the tactics of power and participants' agentic strategies (Briscoe, 2009; Noguera, 2008). Drawing on intersectionality theories' critical possibilities also help scholars work to transform pedagogical relationships (Allard & Santoro, 2008; Irizarry, 2007), reframe the curriculum as a site of struggle against oppression (Camarrota, 2007; Kumashiro, 2001), and analyze where, how, and why social justice issues persist in schools (Howard, 2008; Grant & Sleeter, 1988; Noguera, 2008). These studies suggest intersectionality theories may help researchers and educators see through limitations of exclusively structural (determinism, lack of agency) or exclusively cultural (blame the victim) theses (Noguera, 2008, p. 24) and consider the interplay of student culture and social-structural inequality (Grant & Sleeter, 1988).

## Relationships between Schools, Families, and Communities

*What has scholarship on intersectionality and education focused on and how has it been used to address social justice issues?* Some studies of the relationships between schools, families, and communities forefront the diversity of experiences within minority status groups regarding valued channels for participation and whether they feel encouraged or discouraged from becoming involved (Bhopal, 2004; Howard & Reynolds, 2008; Levine-Rasky, 2009; West-Olatunji et al., 2010). Other scholars center the ways in which discourses frame students and their families as agents and assets or through deficit views (Gillborn, 2010; Villenas, 2001). However, the common thread throughout these studies is how elite groups maintain the status quo and exclude intersectionally marginalized individuals and groups materially (access, resources) and discursively.

Collectively, these studies incorporate intersectionality theories in attempts to address two sets of social justice issues: the pernicious effects of different concepts of schooling and participation on relationships among educational actors and the mechanisms of inclusion and exclusion. For instance, Villenas (2001) indicates that Latina mothers' views of a "good education" include moral and familial aspects that speak back to their deficit framing in public discourse in schools and in the community. Bhopal (2004) finds Gypsy Traveller parents whose children often experience similar patterns of underachievement, exclusion from enrollment, racism, and bullying, hold a wide range of views towards schooling from extremely negative (perceived exposure to immorality), to functional (access to basic literacy and numeracy), to future-focused (life skills acquisition). The author's intersectional analysis suggests consulting marginalized communities can help policymakers and school staff to be more responsive to within-group diversity (Bhopal, 2004). Another study suggests middle-class African American parents hold a similarly wide range of views regarding parent involvement in school, distinguishing between backstage and front stage involvement (Howard & Reynolds, 2008). Different concepts of education, schooling, and participation can lead to miscommunication or conflict between parents and communities and the schools in their mutual venture to support student learning. A second set of studies detail how particular mechanisms of parental and community inclusion and exclusion from schools operate (Gillborn, 2010; Levine-Rasky, 2009; West-Olatunji et al., 2010). Gillborn (2010) traces negative popular and political discourses about the White working class, elucidating a discourse of victimhood and a discourse of degeneracy. In another study, White middle-class parents reproduce their social class advantage in their relationships with school staff, thereby excluding low-income parents of color who value other forms of involvement (Levine-Rasky, 2009). In contrast, West-Olatunji and colleagues (2010) detail African American parents' strategies for successfully promoting their children's academic achievement. These authors uncover mechanisms that discriminate against individuals and groups situated at particular intersections or that actively work to foster their inclusion.

*How have authors drawn upon intersectionality theories?* These intersectional studies of the relationships among educational actors inside and outside schools integrate intersectional frameworks into their analyses to "give voice" to excluded individuals and groups (Bhopal, 2004; Villenas, 2001; West-Olatunji et al., 2010) and attend to complexity (Gillborn, 2010; Howard & Reynolds, 2008; Levine-Rasky, 2009). Bhopal (2004) suggests she uses intersectionality theories and interviews to center the perspectives of Gypsy Traveller parents regarding their children's schooling experiences. Through Villenas' (2001) approach of counter narratives, Latina women voice their vision of a "good education" for their children and speak back to "benevolent" and xenophobic racist discourses about themselves and their families. Lastly, intersectional analysis can highlight parents' coping mechanisms and resilience alongside risk factors for African American students' achievement (West-Olatunji et al., 2010). Intersectionality theories challenge scholars to recognize and attend to complexity (Choo & Ferree, 2010; Gillborn, 2010). Gillborn (2010) uses intersectionality to trace how specific discourses operate to privilege elite Whites and oppress working class Whites. For Howard & Reynolds (2008), intersectionality helps detail the complexity of the intersections between race and class in terms of parents' varying views of school involvement. An essential aspect of attending to complexity is a researcher's ability to use intersectionality theories flexibly because inequitable access to resources might be exacerbated by a set of intersections in one context and mitigated by it in another (Levine-Rasky, 2009, p. 341).

## Teacher Education

*What has scholarship on intersectionality and education focused on and how been used to address social justice issues?* Scholarship combining intersectionality theories and a topical focus on teacher education points to the need for increasing pre-service teachers' and teacher educators' intersectional awareness and suggests curricular and pedagogical approaches for doing so (Akom, 2009; Berry, 2009; DiAngelo & Sensoy, 2010; Ensign, 2009; Fernandez, 2009; Grant, Wieczorek & Gillette, 2000; Heilman, 2010). These studies seek to promote increased self-awareness for educators as socialized members of multiple intersecting groups, situated in a social and historical context (DiAngelo & Sensoy, 2010; Fernandez, 2009). Secondly, the authors hope to foster asset-based views of students and their families and communities through their curricular and pedagogical choices (Akom, 2009; Ensign, 2009).

The social justice foci of intersectional studies of teacher education include increasing teachers' sociocultural knowledge of self and others (DiAngelo & Sensoy, 2010; Ensign, 2009; Fernandez, 2009), understanding intersectionality (DiAngelo & Sensoy, 2010; Grant, Weiczorek & Gillette, 2000), awareness of students' assets (Akom, 2009), and skills for engaging in social justice education (Akom, 2009; Fernandez, 2009; Heilman, 2010). In order to promote these goals, the authors describe novel pedagogical and curricular approaches to foster teachers' engagement with intersectionality theories. Curricular approaches combine social justice education, critical theories, and intersectionality theories in iterations such as Critical Hip Hop Pedagogy (Akom, 2009), writing a new educational foundations textbook from an intersectional standpoint (Grant, Wieczorek & Gillette, 2000), and incorporating content on marginalized ethnic Whites (Heilman, 2010). Scholars suggest pedagogies to foster intersectional awareness include metaphors (DiAngelo & Sensoy, 2010; Fernandez, 2009), narratives or vignettes (Berry, 2009; Grant, Wieczorek & Gillette, 2000), and participatory action research in diverse communities (Akom, 2009; Fernandez, 2009). Nevertheless, Ensign (2009) cautions pre-service teachers' ability to interpret students' low achievement as a blame-game or include themselves in the issue will depend on whether programs incorporate a social justice focus in one or two courses or throughout the program. Heilman's (2010) work also points to the persistence of teachers' stereotypes, despite their critical coursework and attempts at teaching about intersectionality marginalized groups. Finally, one study encourages teacher educators to advocate with and on behalf of pre-service teachers of color in order to challenge their experiences of oppression in their teacher education coursework and practicum sites (Berry, 2009).

*How have authors drawn upon intersectionality theories?* Studies of teacher education that incorporate intersectionality theories support and challenge pre-service teachers in an ongoing process of learning to "read" stratified systems of oppression and privilege (Akom, 2009; Berry, 2009; DiAngelo & Sensoy, 2010; Ensign, 2009; Fernandez, 2009; Grant, Wieczorek & Gillette, 2000; Heilman, 2010) and engage in critical self-reflection (DiAngelo & Sensoy, 2010; Fernandez, 2009). Berry (2009) envisions increasing teacher educators' awareness of the multiplicity and intersectionality of the identities of students of color. Akom (2009) and Fernandez (2009) use intersectionality theories to help pre-service teaches and their students recognize and analyze systems of oppression and privilege, which DiAngelo and Sensoy (2010) argue should be contextualized and historicized. Fernandez (2009) wants teachers to be able to "analyze individuals in relation to one another, to interconnected communities, and to systems of power and privilege" (p. 1). Intersectionality theories might also be used to create new curricula, such as Grant and colleagues' (2000) textbook incorporating an integrated approach to intersectionality, or topical strands within existing courses, such as Heilman's (2010) addition of content on marginalized ethnic Whites. Lastly, studies of intersectionality and teacher education challenge teachers to engage in critical self-reflection (DiAngelo & Sensoy, 2010; Fernandez, 2009) and consider their own role in issues rather than blaming students and their families (Ensign, 2009). Through reflection, course activities, and course content, pre-service teachers can begin to engage in a process of learning to think and act in intersectionally-informed ways.

## Trends across Studies of Intersectionality and Education

When looking across studies of intersectionality theories and education, we might consider the identity categories they incorporate topically and analytically and identify what level of analysis the authors ground their work in. We selected the aforementioned studies for review because they consider three or more identity categories, which some scholars have argued is a minimum threshold for studies that use intersectionality theories (Leiprecht & Lutz, 2006 in Davis, 2008, p. 1), while others suggest such separations are analytically impossible (Lykke, 2010). Using the identity categories scholars mention or focus on their studies, we created a table (see Appendix 1) to analyze which categories they discussed and compare trends over time or by geographical region. This body of literature consistently focuses on the race, class, and gender "trinity," with very few exceptions. Educational researchers have also paid significant attention to language/dialect and geography (rural, urban, and suburban). Sexual orientation and citizenship or documentation status also appear as analytical categories in a number of studies. Scholars have paid considerably less attention to religion, (dis)ability, age, and caste, though a few studies consider one or more of these dimensions. Interestingly, there do not appear to be noticeable trends over time in terms of an increasing or decreasing focus on particular identity categories. One exception is that early studies in intersectionality and education included sexual orientation but this category has been relatively ignored in recent work. In terms of trends by geographical region, this body of literature primarily comes from North America (especially the United States) and European Union. There is one study from Australia (Allard & Santoro, 2008) and one from Southeast Asia (Bishwakarma et al., 2007). These trends could be possibly be attributed to the fact that intersectionality theories were developed and largely continue to be forwarded by North American and European theorists. Another plausible hypothesis is that intersectional-type theorizing in other regions may use different terminologies, not receive scholarly attention, or engage in different academic projects to address identities and oppression.

Scholars who have written about intersectionality and education ground their work in one or more analytical levels, stemming from their intellectual commitments to micro-level, macro-level, or crosscutting studies (Hancock, 2007; McCall, 2005; Winker & Degele, 2011; Yuval-Davis, 2006). Here we draw on Winker and Degele's (2011) analytical framework of identity constructions—interrelations of categories at the level of identity, symbolic representations—ideologies, norms of justification, values, symbols, legislation, and social structures—concrete relations of power expressed through the categories of class, gender, race, body and the accompanying –isms. Yuval-Davis (2006) argues each that each level of analysis has both material and symbolic production effects and cautions against constructing binary divides among levels because each level is a relational process. We selected examples of studies with a substantive focus on one level of analysis to argue that scholars tend to ground their work in one level. However, this list does not do justice to the fact that most incorporate two or three levels of analysis to varying degrees. Studies that center identity constructions analytically include Connor (2006), Loutzenheiser & MacIntosh (2004), and Staunaes (2003). Other scholars center symbolic representations such as discourses (Allard & Santoro, 2008; Gillborn, 2010) and policies (Cassidy & Jackson, 2005; Chapman & Antrop-Gonzalez, 2011). A final group of scholars focus their studies at the level of social structures (Achinstein & Aguirre, 2008; Bhopal, 2004; Howard, 2008; Zembylas, 2010). Cassidy and Jackson (2005) assert "... intersectionality as an analytic tool can be used to study, understand, and respond to the ways in which these factors do intersect and can expose different types of discrimination and disadvantage" (p. 438). Regardless of the analytical level(s) in which scholars ground their studies of intersectionality and education, the core phenomena of interest are identities and power.

**APPENDIX  Identity Axes in the Literature on Intersectionality and Education**

| Article | Race, Ethnicity | Gender | Social class | Sexual orientation | Citizenship, documentation status | Language, Dialect | Geography: rural, urban, suburban | Religion | (Dis) ability | Age | Caste |
|---|---|---|---|---|---|---|---|---|---|---|---|
| Grant & Sleeter (1988)* | X | X | X | | | | | | | | |
| Grant et al. (2000)* | X | X | X | | | | | | | | |
| Kumashiro (2001)* | | X | | X | | | | | | | |
| Lugg (2003)* | | X | | X | | | | | | | |
| Villenas (2001)* | X | X | X | | X | | | | | | |
| Staunaes (2003)** | X | X | X | X | X | | | | | X | |
| Bhopal (2004)** | X | | X | | | | X | | | | |
| Loutzenheiser & MacIntosh (2004)* | | X | | X | | | | | | | |
| Cassidy & Jackson (2005)* | X | | X | | | | X | | | | |
| Connor (2006)* | X | X | X | | | | X | | | | |
| Bishwakarma et al. (2007)**** | X | X | X | | | X | X | | | | X |
| Camarrota (2007)* | X | | X | | | X | X | | | | |
| Irizarry (2007)* | X | | | | | X | X | | | | |
| Achinstein & Aguirre (2008)* | X | X | | | X | X | X | | | | |
| Allard & Santoro (2008)*** | X | | | | X | X | X | | | | |
| Howard (2008)* | X | X | X | | | | X | | | | |
| Howard & Reynolds (2008)* | X | X | X | | | | X | | | | |
| Noguera (2008)* | X | X | X | | | | | | | | |
| Akom (2009)* | X | X | X | | | | | | X | | |
| Au (2009)* | X | | X | X | | | | | X | | |

*(continued)*

**APPENDIX   Identity Axes in the Literature on Intersectionality and Education (continued)**

| Article | Race, Ethnicity | Gender | Social class | Sexual orientation | Citizenship, documentation status | Language, Dialect | Geography: rural, urban, suburban | Religion | (Dis) ability | Age | Caste |
|---|---|---|---|---|---|---|---|---|---|---|---|
| Berry (2009)* | X | X | | | | X | | | | | |
| Briscoe (2009)* | X | X | X | | | X | | | | | |
| Bryan (2009)** | X | | | | X | | | X | | | |
| Ensign (2009)* | X | X | X | | | | | | | | |
| Fernandez (2009)* | X | X | X | | | X | | | | | |
| Gallagher-Geurtsen (2009)* | X | X | X | | X | | | | | | |
| Kocze (2009)** | X | X | X | | | | | | | | |
| Levine-Rasky (2009)* | X | | X | | | | X | | | | |
| Ravnbol (2009)** | X | X | X | | X | X | | | | | |
| Watkins & Aber (2009)* | X | X | X | | | | | | X | X | |
| Chapman et al. (2010)* | X | | X | | | | X | | | | |
| DiAngelo & Sensoy (2010)* | X | X | X | | | | X | | | | |
| Gillborn (2010)** | X | | X | | | X | X | | | | |
| Heilman (2010)* | X | X | X | | | X | X | | | | |
| McCall & Skrtic (2010)* | X | X | X | | | | | | X | X | |
| West-Olatunji et al. (2010)* | X | X | X | | X | | | X | | | |
| Zembylas (2010)*** | X | | X | | | X | | | | | |
| Chapman & Antrop-Gonzalez (2011)* | X | | X | | | | X | | | | |

*Region:* * = North America, ** = Europe, *** = Australia, **** = Southeast Asia.
*Note:* Table organized by publication date to examine trends in the field over time.

# REFERENCES

Achinstein, B., & Aguirre, J. (2008). Cultural match or culturally suspect: How new teachers of color negotiate sociocultural challenges in the classroom. *Teachers College Record, 110*(8), 1505–1540.

Akom, A. A. (2009). Critical hip hop pedagogy as a form of liberatory praxis. *Equity & Excellence in Education, 42*(1), 52–66.

Allard, A. C., & Santoro, N. (2008). Experienced teachers' perspectives on cultural and social class diversity: Which differences matter? *Equity & Excellence in Education, 41*(2), 200–214.

Andersen, M. L. (2005). Thinking about women: A quarter century's view. *Gender & Society, 19*(4), 437–455.

Anthias, F., & Yuval-Davis, N. (1983). Contextualizing feminism: Gender, ethnic, and class divisions. *Feminist Review, 15*, 62–75.

Anzaldua, G. (1987). *Borderlands: La Frontera = La Nueva Mestiza.* San Francisco, CA: Aunt Lute Books.

Au, W. W. (2009). High-stakes testing and discursive control: The triple bind for non-standard student identities. *Multicultural Perspectives, 11*(2), 65–71.

Berry, T. R. (2009). Women of color in a bilingual/dialectical dilemma. *International Journal of Qualitative Studies in Education, 22*(6), 745–753.

Bhopal, K. (2004). Gypsy travellers and education: Changing needs and changing perceptions. *British Journal of Educational Studies, 52*(1), 47–64.

Bishwakarma, R., Hunt, V. H., & Zajicek, A. (2007). Educating Dalit women: Beyond a one-dimensional policy formulation. *Himalaya, 27*(1–2), 27–39.

Brah, A., & Phoenix, A. (2004). Ain't I a woman?: Revisiting intersectionality. *Journal of International Women's Studies, 5*(3), 75–86.

Briscoe, F. M. (2009). "They make you invisible:" Negotiating power at the academic intersections of ethnicity, gender, and class. *Equity & Excellence in Education, 42*(2), 233–248.

Bryan, A. (2009). The intersectionality of nationalism and multiculturalism in the Irish curriculum: Teaching against racism? *Race Ethnicity and Education, 12*(3), 297–317.

Camarrota, J. (2007). A social justice approach to achievement: Guiding Latina/o students toward educational attainment with a challenging, socially relevant curriculum. *Equity & Excellence in Education, 40*, 87–96.

Cassidy, W., & Jackson, M. (2005). The need for equality in education. *McGill Journal of Education, 40*(3), 435–456.

Chapman, T. K., & Antrop-Gonzalez, R. (2011). A critical look at choice options as solutions to Milwaukee's schooling inequities. *Teachers College Record, 113*(4), 787–810.

Chapman, T. K., Lamborn, S. D., & Epps, E. (2010). Educational strategies for children of Milwaukee: A critical race theory analysis. *Multicultural Learning and Teaching, 5*(2), 4–27.

Choo, H. Y., & Ferree, M. M. (2010). Practicing intersectionality in sociological research. *Sociological Theory, 28*(2), 129–149.

Combahee River Collective. (1977). *The Combahee River Collective Statement.* Retrieved June 25, 2011 from http://www.circuitous.org/scraps/combahee.html

Connor, D. J. (2006). Michael's story: "I get into so much trouble just by walking": Narrative knowing and life at the intersections of learning disability, race, and class. *Equity & Excellence in Education, 39*, 154–165.

Crenshaw, K. W. (1989). Demarginalizing the intersection of race and sex: A Black feminist critique of antidiscrimination doctrine, feminist theory and antiracist politics. *University of Chicago Legal Forum,* 139–167.

Crenshaw, K. W. (1991). Mapping the margins: Intersectionality, identity politics, and violence against women of color. *Stanford Law Review, 43*(6), 1241–1299.

Crenshaw, K. W. (2010). *Intersection of race and gender.* University of Wisconsin-Madison, Sociology Department FemSem. Madison, WI. 23 Oct. 2010.

Davis, K. (2008). Intersectionality as a buzzword: A sociology of science perspective on what makes a feminist theory successful. *Feminist Theory, 9*(1), 67–85.

Dhamoon, R. K. (2010). Considerations on maintreaming intersectionality. *Political Research Quarterly, 20*(10), 1–14.

DiAngelo, R., & Sensoy, O. (2010). "OK, I get it! Now tell me how to do it!": Why we can't just tell you how to do critical multicultural education. *Multicultural Perspectives, 12*(2), 97–102.

Ensign, J. (2009). Multiculturalism in four teacher education programs: For replication or transformation. *Multicultural Perspectives, 11*(3), 169–173.

Ferree, M. M. (2010). Filling the glass: Gender perspectives on families. *Journal of Marriage and Family, 72*, 420–439.

Fernandez, A. E. (2009). Reconfiguring the borderlands of identity. *Journal of Praxis in Multicultural Education, 4*(1), 1–6.

Gallagher-Geurtsen, T. (2009). Inspiring hybridity: A call to engage with(in) global flows of the multicultural classroom. *Multicultural Perspectives, 11*(4), 200–203.

Gillborn, D. (2010). The White working class, racism, and respectability. *British Journal of Educational Studies, 58*(1), 3–25.

Glenn, E. N. (1999). The social construction and institutionalization of gender and race: An integrative framework. In M. M. Ferree, J. Lorber, & B. B. Hess (Eds.), *Revisioning gender.* Thousand Oaks, CA: Sage.

Grant, C. A., & Sleeter, C. E. (1986). Race, class, and gender in education research. *Review of Educational Research, 56*(2), 195–211.

Grant, C. A., & Sleeter, C. E. (1988). Race, class, gender and abandoned dreams. *Teachers College Record, 90*(1), 19–40.

Grant, C. A., Wieczorek, K., & Gillette, M. (2000). Text materials and the intersections of race, class, gender and power. *Race, Gender & Class, 7*(3), 11–34.

Hancock, A. M. (2005). W. E. B. DuBois: Intellectual forefather of intersectionality? *Souls, 7*(3), 74–84.

Hancock, A. M. (2007). Intersectionality as a normative and empirical paradigm. *Politics & Gender, 3*(2), 248–254.

Hankivsky, O., & Cormier, R. (2010). Intersectionality and public policy: Some lessons from existing models. *Political Research Quarterly, 64*(1), 217–229.

Hawkesworth, M. (2006). *Feminist inquiry: From political conviction to methodological innovation.* Piscataway, NJ: Rutgers University Press.

Heilman, E. E. (2010). Hoosiers, hicks, and hayseeds: The controversial place of marginalized ethnic Whites in multicultural education. *Equity & Excellence in Education, 37*(1), 67–79.

Hill Collins, P. (1990). *Black feminist thought: Knowledge, consciousness and the politics of empowerment.* New York: Routledge.

Hill Collins, P. (2000). *Black feminist thought: Knowledge, consciousness and the politics of empowerment, 10th anniversary edition.* New York: Routledge.

hooks, b. (1981). *Ain't I a Woman: Black women and feminism.* Boston: South End Press.

Howard, T. C. (2008). Who really cares? The Disenfranchisement of African American males in preK-12 schools: A critical race theory perspective. *Teachers College Record, 110*(5), 954–985.

Howard, T. C., & Reynolds, R. (2008, winter-spring). Examining parent involvement in reversing the underachievement of African American students in middle-class schools. *Educational Foundations,* 79–98.

Irizarry, J. G. (2007). Ethnic and urban intersections in the classroom: Latino students, hybrid identities and culturally responsive pedagogy. *Multicultural Perspectives, 9*(3), 21–28.

King, J. (1988). Multiple jeopardy, multiple consciousness: The context of a Black feminist ideology. *Signs, 14*(1), 42–72.

Kocze, A. (2009). *Missing intersectionality: Race/ethnicity, gender, and class in current research and policies on Romani women in Europe.* Budapest: Center for Policy Studies, Central European University.

Kumashiro K. K. (2001). Queer students of color and antiracist, antiheterosexist education. In K. K. Kumashiro (Ed.), *Troubling intersections of race and sexuality.* Lanham, MD: Rowman & Littlefield.

Levine-Rasky, C. (2009). Dynamics of parent involvement at a multicultural school. *British Journal of Sociology of Education, 30*(3), 331–344.

Loutzenheiser, L. W., & MacIntosh, L. B. (2004). Citizenships, sexualities, and education. *Theory into Practice, 43*(2), 151–158.

Lugg, C. A. (2003). Sissies, faggots, lezzies, and dykes. *Educational Administration Quarterly, 39*(1), 95–134.

Lykke, N. (2010). *Feminist studies: A guide to intersectional theory, methodology, and writing.* New York: Routledge.

Makkonen, L. L. M. (2002). *Multiple, compound, and intersectional discrimination: Bringing the experiences of the most marginalized to the fore.* Institute for Human Rights, Abo Akademi University, April, 2002.

Matsuda, M. J. (1991). Beside my sister, facing the enemy: Legal theory out of coalition. *Stanford Law Review, 43*(6), 1183–1192.

McCall, L. (2005). The complexity of intersectionality. *Signs: Journal of Women in Culture and Society,* 30(3), 1771–1800.

McCall, Z., & Skrtic, T. M. (2010). Intersectional needs politics. *Multiple Voices for Ethnically Diverse Exceptional Learners, 11*(2), 3–23.

McCarthy, C., & Apple, M. W. (1988). Race, class, and gender in American educational research: Toward a nonsynchronous parallelist position. In L. Weis (Ed.), *Class, race, and gender in American education.* Albany, NY: State University of New York Press.

Nash, J. C. (2008). Re-thinking intersectionality. *Feminist Review,* 89, 1–15.

Noguera, P. A. (2008). *The trouble with Black boys.* San Francisco, CA: Jossey-Bass.

Parken, A. (2010). A multi-strand approach to promoting equalities and human rights in policy making. *Policy & Politics, 38*(1), 79–99.

Ravnbol, C. I. (2009). *Intersectional discrimination against children: Discrimination against Romani children and anti-discrimination measures to address child trafficking.* UNICEF Innocenti Research Centre, Florence. Retrieved March 28, 2011 from http://www.unicef-irc.org/publications/pdf/iwp_2009_11.pdf

Razack, S. (1998). *Looking White people in the eye: Gender, race, and culture in courtrooms and classrooms.* Toronto, Canada: University of Toronto Press.

Sandoval, C. (2000). *Methodology of the oppressed.* Minneapolis, MN: University of Minnesota Press.

Sleeter, C. E., & Grant, C. A. (1988). A rationale for integrating race, gender, and social class. In L. Weis (Ed.), *Class, race, and gender in American education.* Albany, NY: State University of New York Press.

Staunaes, D. (2003). Where have all the subjects gone? *Nordic Journal of Feminist and Gender Research, 11*(2), 101–110.

Verloo, M. (2006). Multiple inequalities, intersectionality, and the European Union. *European Journal of Women's Studies, 13*(3), 211–228.

Villenas, S. (2001). Latina mothers and small-town racisms. *Anthropology & Education Quarterly, 32*(1), 3–28.

Watkins, N. D., & Aber, M. S. (2009). Exploring the relationships among race, gender, and middle school students' perceptions of school racial climate. *Equity & Excellence in Education, 42*(4), 395–411.

Weis, L. (Ed.). (1988). *Class, race and gender in American education.* Albany, N.Y.: State University of New York Press.

West-Olatunji, C., Sanders, T., Mehta, S., & Behar-Horenstein, L. (2010). Parenting practices among low-income parents/guardians of academically successful fifth grade African American children. *Multicultural Perspectives, 12*(3), 138–144.

Winker, G., & Degele, N. (2011). Intersectionality as multi-level analysis: Dealing with social inequality. *European Journal of Women's Studies, 18*(1), 51–66.

Yuval-Davis, N. (2006). Intersectionality and feminist politics. *European Journal of Women's Studies, 13*(3), 193–209.

Zembylas, M. (2010). Greek-Cypriot teachers' constructions of Turkish-speaking children's identities: Critical race theory and education in a conflict-ridden society. *Ethnic and Racial Studies, 33*(8), 1372–1391.

CHAPTER 2

# EMPIRICISM, PERCEPTION, VISION

## A Nomadology of Tactics in Social Scientific Thought

**Bernadette M. Baker**
*University of Wisconsin-Madison*

### INTRODUCTION

*History is always written from the sedentary point of view and in the name
of a unitary State apparatus, at least a possible one, even when the topic is nomads.
What is lacking is a Nomadology, the opposite of a history.*

—Deleuze and Guattari

I begin this chapter with two vignettes that are neither representative nor
exhaustive but which function as incitements to discourse around the question of intersectionality. They act as temporary signposts within a nomadology for what this chapter is going to unpack, which requires a step back
from invoking intersectionality automatically and from definitional, operational, and methodological issues to which intersectionality studies have
already spoken.

*Intersectionality and Urban Education*, pages 29–64
Copyright © 2014 by Information Age Publishing
All rights of reproduction in any form reserved.

The vignettes point toward an examination of one of the key discourses that has participated in systems of analysis that have both spawned the need for intersectionality studies in the first place and that also at times inhabit such studies through force of publishing requirements. That discourse is the discourse of empiricism and its allied investment in particular conceptions of reality, in relatively narrow strategies of perception, and especially, in (shifting) discourses of vision.[1]

## Vignette One

In *The Silent War: Imperialism and the Changing Perception of Race*, Frank Füredi examines "the evolution of the Western racial imagination and its relationship to international relations." Füredi argues that

> The greatest influence on racial thinking was the emergence of resistance to Western domination. Fears about the decline of the West were often expressed in a racial form and implicitly contested the idea of white superiority. Race, which was a positive ideal in the self image of the West, had become a source of anxiety by the end of the First World War; by the 1920s, the Anglo American foreign policy elites regarded racial thinking as having the potential to disrupt the world system; and by the end of the Second World War racism was so discredited that Western diplomats were forced to devote considerable resources to eliminating it from international affairs altogether. The changing dynamic between Western identity and racial thinking is most vividly expressed as a shift from racial confidence to racial fear. (1998, pp. 1–2)

Füredi's focus is the West as primarily Britain and the United States. His analysis of twentieth century shifts resonates at multiple levels and within multiple literatures. In Pan-Africanist analyses, postcolonial studies, and "Third World" feminisms, the intersection between national and international levels has been automatically expected and enacted, but less so elsewhere and especially less so when educational policy or curriculum are the focus within particular nation-states and racialized thinking becomes a moniker for internal, domestic, or apparently self-sealed cultures.

## Vignette Two

In *Comparative Theories of Nonduality: The Search for a Middle Way*, Milton Scarborough gives multiple examples of repetitive forms of dualistic thinking, where dualism is not reducible to just any kind of difference, but often acts to reduce multiple kinds of differences: "mere difference, opposition, polar opposition, and contradiction, however, still do not in the strictest sense constitute dualism. For both the West and Asia, dualism consists of a dichotomy, in which the paired concepts, terms, or things have a static substance or fixed essence.... Substance is an unchanging, underlying metaphysical reality in which the quality or attributes of a thing inhere. A fixed essence consists of changeless attributes, qualities or meanings that are essential to the nature or identity of the concept or thing" (2009, p. 6). Scarborough notes five different ways in which dualisms perform a particular kind of analytical restriction and reduction, including that they commonly mislead through prompting boundaries that are drawn too narrowly and precisely and they distort by numerical simplification. He elaborates the latter through examining the construct of gender:

> Are situations best understood in terms of two causes, classes, or features? Why not one, three, or ten? Consider sex, for example. It is usually described by a binary opposition that has become a full-blown dualism. Whether in theology ("male and female He created them") or biology, we have believed that there are two sexes, male and female. But why merely two? Is it because there are two kinds of chromosomes (XX and XY) involved in the genetic determination of sex? Yet the dualism of the sexes preceded our knowledge of chromosomes. And why choose the two-ness of the chromosomes in order to understand sex? More recently, other possibilities have been suggested.

Scarborough gives examples of "non-standard sexes" that even biologists have been forced to acknowledge in terms of their own conditions of proof and argues that if the notion of sexes proliferated to, say, twenty it would not accord seamlessly and effortlessly with an already well-established habit of thinking in terms of binary oppositions.

Both Füredi and Scarborough point to, without necessarily exploring, the inherent conditions of possibility for the complexities that they unpack and step to the side of. Both note the cultural constructedness of things, how language operates amid shifting classificatory regimes, the tie to strategies of perception, and the possibilities and limits this entails for onto-epistemological hierarchicization. But whether "cultures" asserts things as "empirically real" (e.g., "I can see it, you can see it, therefore it's real") or "metaphysical" (e.g., I can't see it, you can't see it, but we can infer that it operates," such as gravity, God, etc) or a "metaphysical reality" (e.g., "We all know that a concept has effects. It might not be able to be held in the hand like a glass, but a concept groups things together in useful ways that make sense of something we can hold in the hand") has come to matter for truth-, proof- and knowledge-production in the social sciences of what is now called the North. Moreover, even the classification system empirical, metaphysical, and metaphysical reality, however, bears the marks of its sites of production, ensuring a logocentrism that resecures what might otherwise be contested—or considered irrelevant—elsewhere.

The designation of what can count as real, and whether this is tied to be-lief in a substance that is both visible and agreed upon as proof of identical-ness has not been thoroughly unpacked in the vignettes above. Something is still not settled by shifting causality from nature to culture and something that established "the problem" to which both intersectionality and nondu-alist studies speak, different as their other starting assumptions may be, is still retained in their enactment within social science.

This chapter digs further and deeper into such something's. In particu-lar, it examines the role that various claims to empiricism—and especially post-empirical tactics—have played in the emergence of social scientific thought and in debates over discourses of vision, over claims made about what can and cannot be "seen," and over the claims to truth-, proof-, and knowledge-production that have ensued.

## PROBLEMS CONCERNING THE INTERROGATION
## OF EMPIRICISM IN SOCIAL SCIENTIFIC THOUGHT

Discourses of empiricism currently constitute a regime of truth in educa-tional research. The appeal to something called the empirical evidence which is meant to support narrative-formation is by now standard in a va-riety of locations that may have little else to do with each other, such as in contemporary federal educational policies in the United States, including evidence-based education (EBE) and as part of the common requirements transnationally for (post)graduate theses and dissertations to demonstrate analyses built from "data-sets." At the same time, teachers, parents, students, and full-time researchers note how contemporary methods, templates, in-terview techniques, populational checklists, and quantitative scales often cannot capture that which bears the most meaning for them in classroom interactions, childrearing, and other educational settings (Baker, 2012; Lather, 2007; Taubman, 2009).

The interplay between appeals to empiricism in some form and a sensibil-ity of a meaningful "something beyond" is an historical legacy in part of the formation of different social scientific logics, strategies of perception, and their relationship to philosophies, religions, and regionalisms. In occiden-talist educational philosophy, such interplay has generally and with good cause been understood as a function of post-Lockean, post-Humean, and post-Kantian debate, pointing toward a fairly common acceptance of a real-ist/idealist split. While such debates are indeed pivotal to both the instan-tiation of different versions of empiricism and allied counter-reactions, this chapter unpacks the baggage of the term empirical in occidentalist thought through a different yet related line of argument which concerns the vari-ety of now-abjected counter-moves that proliferated alongside empiricism's rise. Such counter-moves point both to the lack of settlement regarding the nature of what is and has been "seen" and valued in education and remind us in contemporary circumstance, especially where policies such as EBE and/or the quantitification of reality dominate, of the multitudinous possibilities for thought and for care within a social compact.

As a vantage point on such deeper and broader possibilities, then, the chapter provides a nomadology, examining the shifting tactics deployed to theorize what has been taken as abjected during empiricism's rise and reign in the so-called North. I am not referring here to empiricism as a monolith, but to the tightening of appeal to empiricism as a condition of proof amid a stricter subject/object spatialization post-Locke, where sensation became distantiated from reflection. I am also not discussing empiricism here as it relates in specific forms to northern trans-Atlantic movements, such as Comtean positivism or psychological behaviorism, although they intersect. I begin, rather, with the convoluted etymology of empiricism and the implications of this etymology for shifting discourses of vision in particular.

Discourses of vision and of visuality are reference to thresholds of noticeability that both include and exceed an ocular portal, and thus are not simplistically aligned with a blindness/seeingness binary reduced to a physiological conception of the human. An operational understanding of discourses of vision for the purposes of this analysis is thus concerned with what can be claimed as coming-to-notice (perception in this case) and crucially, as sciences are forged, with the formation of a consensus in regard to legitimate presence. Because of the diffusion and repetition of the simplistic appeal to "the empirical evidence" in the contemporary educational field—as if that shores everything up and makes things "scientific"—I am concerned here, too, with the stronger entrance of (beliefs about) the post-Lockean functioning of a sensorium into (beliefs about) knowledge-production and to the elevation of an ocular portal (and its destabilization) in particular.

These discursive confluences were part of the very formation of what was called Western and now Northern, part of the very fabrication of racialized, gendered, and able-ized "perceptions" of body-mind relations. While this chapter cannot elaborate the complexity of all such braidings, it is important to note at the outset that the very conditions of possibility for honing in on phenotype, faces, skin, general appearance, body parts, and functions and generating classificatory regimes and superiority effects on that basis were indebted to belief- and value-systems that elevated empiricism and especially the assumption of a visible-to-the-naked-eye objective reality embodied in the observed subject/object.

As such, the chapter illustrates three tactics, necessarily adumbrated, that have emerged post-empiricism (roughly, post-Locke) for mediating a presumed visible/invisible horizon, a horizon that becomes in part the hallmark of Northern social scientific analyses, yet a horizon continuously modified and contested. The concept of post-empiricism will be delineated below but it is important to note here that it exceeds the repetitive concern in occidentalist philosophy for Humean-Kantian debates and presumed realist/idealist binaries. It points instead to spatializations of discourse—how that which could come to notice could be spatialized onto different sides of a visible/invisible line and how changes or shifts in this coding could generate some new imaginal domains while restricting others.

Such changes or shifts generated unique responses to whatever was labeled as invisible, yet meaningful or significant, in the wake of various claims to truth-, proof-, and knowledge-production, and it is these never-settled legacies that the field of education still largely struggles with on the surface and that end up in the kind of sensibilities or "feelings" noted in the opening paragraph—that in already-reported cases, parents, teachers, researchers, etc, have noted that there is something important or meaningful beyond numerical data, beyond the coding of themes in interview transcripts, and beyond popular identity categories that one is often forced to claim or check.

Post-Lockean versions of empiricism rewrote the role of a sensorium in strategies of knowledge-production. The role of discourses of vision and visuality within such rearrangements are complex. Rather than reapproaching the tactics developed post-empiricism within contemporary disciplinary boundaries, which did not exist at all junctures considered here, the tactics utilized across a range of narrative-building projects are examined, giving the social sciences of the North a potentially longer and more convoluted heritage than the formation of professional associations at the turn of the twentieth century.

To this end, the analysis steps to the side of both existing sociological interrogations such as Boaventura de Sousa Santos' notions of the visible/invisible within the abyssal thinking of Western modernity and to the side of naturalized biomedical renditions of sight and seeing. In drawing from a wider range of sources, the tactics analyzed here have had to respond to the mark that the popularization of empiricism bequeathed and thus carry with them some aspects of what they have attempted to problematize. In addition, the propositions and assumptions within such tactics do not necessarily map neatly onto a clean, stable and omnipresent visible/invisible binary. They operated instead within contexts where such tactics for narrative-building were still trying to maintain or achieve legitimacy in regard to their imagined audiences and were doing so in the midst of changing conditions of truth-, proof-, and knowledge-production.

Given these complexities, then, the nomadology here draws its scaffolding, but not its content, from Deleuze and Guattari's *A Thousand Plateaus: Capitalism and Schizophrenia*. The tactics traversed below include *explanatory concepts, technicalizing instruments,* and *strategies of stabilization,* all of which have been developed and deployed to help theorize whatever was allocated as visible and invisible, and whatever was considered meaningful in emergent social sciences. Such tactics are not introduced here through a School of the Annales' assumption regarding a context/text division that marks traditional Statist and sedentary histories. Rather, they arise as Deleuze and Guattarian-inspired, treated deliberately and rhizomatically as unique plateaus, out of the center of which can suddenly arise further and new plateaus that in turn provide different planes of composition for social scientific thought: "A plateau is always in the middle, not at the beginning or the end. A rhizome is made of plateaus. . . . We call a 'plateau' any multiplicity connected to other multiplicities by superficial underground stems in such a way as to form or extend a rhizome" (Deleuze & Guattari, 1987, p. 22).

The three tactics are positioned here not as part of a linear and continuous historical narrative but *as tools for narrative-building* that have historically impacted the possibilities and limits for the formation of truth-statements, for what could count as a condition of proof, and for the allied knowledge-effects in social science research. *Explanatory concepts* are identified by their reach, by the power to draw together and explain the previously inexplicable without necessarily pointing to an exteriorized object visible to the naked eye. *Technicalizing instruments* act to render that which is taken as an active or shaping influence into visibility for public corroboration/consensus, such as transcripts, which operate as a point of return and appear to making moving forces (social, religious, biological, etc) legible to the attuned reader. *Strategies of stabilization* operate to settle a pluralized background and to crystallize a foreground against it, generating an impression of resolution of the differences preceding and surrounding. This has included forms of counting (*mathesis*—such as appeal to statistics) and styles of coding (*taxinomia*—such as identifying themes in ethnography or organizing timespaces historically).

There is something significant in recognizing and analyzing such tactics together and considering their relation to social scientific thinking. That "something significant" is their mutual relation to the theorization of (whatever was postulated as) "the invisible" from different angles and concerns, and the relationship of that coding and spatialization to evidence—a process and a relationship that has been and still is quite uneven and variegated. I suggest here that such efforts across several centuries have not necessarily been marginal practices within the formation of social scientific thinking but integral to it, becoming one of the vexed markers of geopolitical, disciplinary, and perceptual boundaries that have contributed to both the restriction *and* the proliferation of difference in certain forms.

Key to the formation of geopolitical, disciplinary, and perceptual boundaries that now inhabit the naming of the North is the consensual acceptance of some objects and not others as both scientific and real. I outline below, then, three different kinds of efforts to produce objects, to bring some "thing" to the threshold of noticeability, such that a consensus around presence could form and travel (or not), and such that debates around evidence and the nature of the "thing" could play out. Here, turning some "thing" that comes to notice into an object of study is one thing, into a *scientific* object another, and making it amenable to *tracking* another.

As an example of explanatory concepts, I examine the late 1700s and early 1800s northern trans-Atlantic fascination for extraordinary behavior, the turn to theorizing a conscious/unconscious border as an explanation for human behavior, and the successful attempt at making "mind" into a scientific object. As an example of technicalizing instruments, I re-visit the turn of the twentieth century fascination with spirit-return, the life/death border, and the unsuccessful attempt to make the ghost into a continuously studied *scientific* object via the use of transcripts. And as an example of strategies of stabilization, I unpack turn of the twenty-first century concerns over geopolitical borders (such as presumed within PISA, the Programme for International Student Assessment), mapping, and the making of the nation into an unstable (but trackable) scientific object. Together, these layers do not analyze a specific policy, school, curriculum, or classroom but rather complexify the methods we would bring to such analyses. The following sections ultimately suggest, then, some possibilities that have already been seeded for rethinking educational research, its classificatory regimes, and its preferred strategies for narrative-building.

Last, in doing so, it is important to note here that this chapter takes a step back to examine the conditions from which the plateaus and their tactics arose. It thus delves further into what was thought to be at stake in order for evidentiary, definitional, and explanatory projects to have purchase, that which enabled the debates, for example over the meanings of phenotype and over theories of external behavior, to have something on which to peg their hats. As such, it focuses on tactics in modern discourses of vision as an index of shifting incommensurabilities in value-systems, or that which Bruno Latour (2004) has characterized as a general shift from matters of fact to matters of concern. It offers, then, a counter-memory and a retrieval of differences that have sometimes been elided, and it makes less certain the appeal to categorical distinctions in contemporary educational research such as empirical/conceptual, quantitative/qualitative, and activist/removed.

## SHIFTS FROM MEDIEVAL TO MODERN DISCOURSES OF VISION: PLATEAU-FORMATION IN EMPIRICAL AND POST-EMPIRICAL TACTICS

> What is important is not whether the flows are "One or multiple"—we're past that point: there is a collective assemblage of enunciation, a machine assemblage of desire, one inside the other and both plugged into an immense outside that is a multiplicity in any case. (Deleuze & Guattari, 1987, p. 23)

What now falls under the label of discourses of vision has been plugged into an immense outside that is a multiplicity via nomadologies that have been both longer and shorter. In terms of the shorter, for several decades now, critiques of ocularcentrism in occidental thought have been well-formulated. The historicizing literature generally follows the Philosophy 101 arc—from ancient Greece to the nineteenth century West—pointing up shifting inscriptions of being, truth, light, vision, and knowing in different epistemes (Jay, 1994; Levin, 1997). In terms of the longer, the role of what are now called the senses in epistemology, and especially the eyes, has more recently been attributed to North Africa, particularly cosmologies circulating within ancient Egypt, subsequently modified by Aristotle, whose preservation and reinterpretation as text is then attributed to Islamic scholars and Celtic monks, and thereby reintroduced into medieval Latin Europe where Aristotelianism flourishes among the Scholastics (Bynum, 1999; Clark, 2007).

The difficulty of "looking backwards" as though a continuous line has been in place is, however, as Foucault (1970) noted in *The Order of Things* part of the problem—and expectation—of a modern episteme, where single origin is sought and continuous sequencing required, where the notion of continuity is protected and located in the generationalism and presumed volition of the conscious, human subject.

As Clark (2007, p. 9) has more recently pointed out ocularcentrism has been on the defensive for over a century: "mirroring, imaging, and anamorphosis were all part of the reconceptualizing of vision that was fundamental to the psychoanalytical theories of Jacques Lacan. Richard Rorty's influential assault on modern philosophy was built, likewise, on undermining its dependence on the mind as the 'mirror' of nature. Above all, perhaps, thanks to developments in art history, visual anthropology, and visual hermeneutics we now take for granted the constructed nature of vision and the extent to which visual perception and visual meaning are fused." This fusing, especially of optical theory with cognitive philosophy Clark attributes in part to the pivotal role of "the tenth- to eleventh-century Islamic scholar, Alhazen," who characterizes vision as transmission of image or picture through the optic nerve to the brain—a belief infused into medieval and early modern thought. A shift from attempts to make linear perspective equivalent to vision to the idea that vision itself was pictorial was facilitated by the idea of a point-by-point mapping onto the eye of rays of lights transmitted from objects along a "visual pyramid." Alhazen suggested that after leaving the object as a mosaic of visible color and light the custodial power of the optic nerve preserved the picture with perfect integral order to reach the forefront of the brain intact. Key here is the cosmological assumption that drives the process of attribution: "That the entire process was dictated by causal demands that made each form in the sequence a cause of its successor and an effect of its antecedent also helped to ensure that the picture of reality occurring in the brain was veridical" (Clark, 2007, p. 16). Perceptual certitude becomes assured because categories or species are taken as natural signs of their objects, making the external object, the species, and the mental representation of it ontologically continuous. The integrity and coherence of the image between object and brain was taken as a radical new line of thought in which it was postulated that if things external to us "are able to reproduce their essential qualities in our senses and minds, then the content of the mind is assuredly objective" (quoted in Clark, 2007, p. 16).

Even if, though, ocularcentrism is dubiously flattened out as a singular historical category and rendered backwards as that which links medieval and early modern sciences, the task is not the same for Alhazen, Galileo Galilei, or the seventeenth- and eighteenth-century Christian scholar, Sir Isaac Newton. Newtonian conceptions in particular shift the grounds upon which claims to objectivity are made.

What elaborates the radical new line of thought that linked vision to linear perspective and linear perspective to the pictorial was the emergence of observation and experiment in medicine especially. Here, the term empirical first appears in English-language documents and it captures Alhazen's sense of vision as though somehow objective and outside theory, principle, prejudice or affect. The term appears earliest in English in 1500s as a noun, *Empirik*, and refers to medical practitioners who attend to the body through trial and error. It draws initially from Latin, *empiricus*, which also derives from Greek analogs for experience, skilled, trial, and experiment. The term moves into adjectival form more noticeably in the 1600s. As an adjective, five inscriptions have been developed from 1600s to 1900s including: a physician who bases methods of practice on observation and experiment, not on scientific theory; a remedy that is successful in practice, with efficacy unknown; surgery without scientific knowledge and guilty of quackery; in matters of art or practice, being guided by mere experience; and in the disciplines, pertaining to or derived from experience, such as empirical psychology versus rational psychology.[3]

In accounts of the history of occidental philosophy, John Locke has been positioned as the father of empiricism, as well as the father of psychology and arguably of childcenteredness (Baker, 2001). Lockean epistemology stood in contradistinction to Cartesian versions, especially in regard to the role of Body (Locke 1692/1975). For Locke, Mind and Body (capitalized in his texts) stand on their own, each with unique mechanical laws of operation. The Body does not err as for Descartes, and is not a site of sin or illusion (Locke, 1692/1989). The Body senses facts through a variety of sensory portals, sensation thus becomes distantiated from reflection, while the density of the flesh operates as a new point of appeal in the veridical.

Density, as opposed to soul, aura, energy, sky, seasons, or exteriorized causalities of resemblance, changed where one looked for truth-production, with enormous ramifications in centuries to come. Theories of human being in the nineteenth century, for instance, forwarded a relation between faces, head shape, and skin in racializing, sexualizing, and ableizing projects—the social scientist must examine the density of the flesh and presume a relation to a buried or hidden depth. Like Alhazen, however, Locke did attribute a kind of animus to the object—objects have powers that leave imprints in the Mind, and power has two kinds, motivity and resistance. Lockean epistemology bequeaths, then, a different subject-ivity/object-ivity problematic that assumes an operational separation between subject and environment and establishes the way in which discourses of vision can operate in truth-production in terms now recognized as empiricist. The spatio-temporal definition of a subject-object distinction delimits humanity in new ways, then, and finds a special role for something called the self, launching somewhat discrete pathways of investigation in post-Cartesian epistemologies, of which Lockean empiricism was one popular version. The consistency of self-presence and World becomes shattered, however, over the following century. From Kantian ambiguity over whether mind maps the world or world maps the mind to a series of trials related to head injury, drug and alcohol consumption, magic shows and visual illusions, the discourse of vision/visuality and its role in veridicality changed dramatically.

By the twentieth century, confidence in the integrity of mental representation, its neutrality, had waned, while the mechanism of sight's formation had been transformed. For instance, maturity in the late 1800s debates over discourses of vision was considered a development away from thought in terms of pictorial imagery to thought in terms of word-based language, and in particular sentences. While some scholars have seen this as a broader Christian-based disciplining of the pictorial as the feminine, marking the turn away from iconography a turn away from domains of expertise historically associated with the feminine (Clark, 2007), others have posited that the separation of words from things generated complexities that included and exceeded concerns predicated on dual-sexed models of World (Foucault,

1970). In particular, it bequeathed an orientation to knowing that in refusing revelation as a pathway on the one hand (or at least modifying what were previously coded as revelations into being coded as egoic projections of an unconscious), accepted on the other hand the disturbance in the ontological continuity of the external object, the species, and the mental representation. A slough of post-Kantian psychologies of perception, attention, isolation, and selectivity in what was "seen" eventuated, and according to Crary (1999), attention especially becomes a specifically modern problem because of the obliteration of the possibility of obviousness or rather self-presence given in seeing. If we now "see" because of traveling photons between object and eye and if brains interpreted the traveling photons that hit the retina differently, then the eyewitness account loses its objectivity—the mental representation can be different in different people in regard to the objects perceived and the role of visuality in truth-production must subsequently be rethought.

The tactics developed in post-empirical inquiry thus refer to such discursive disjunctures.[2] In examining the tactics deployed to theorize whatever is taken as abjected during empiricism's reign, I am not claiming to be outside the discourses under consideration here, including ocularcentrism, modern geographical discourse, notions of linear time, etc. I am referring rather to a different range of transdisciplinary and transcontinental strategies that became part of social scientific thought, including:

- Reactions against linear mechanics of sight as totality of experience (e.g., phenomenology, psychoanalytics)
- Reactions against materialism as purely sensorial (e.g., romanticism, idealism)
- Efforts to resecure a relationship between an invisible depth, source, or forces and a visible surface or appearance (e.g., metaphysics, rationalism, religion)
- How what are now known as the social sciences reappropriated appeals to the empirical within new configurations of a modern episteme where the search for origins, separation of words from things, and their organization in orderly tables become central to what counts as knowledge and knowledge-production.

Last, for the purposes here, it is important to understand the relation to the term invisible. Invisible does not here remain synonymous with absence. Rather, the "it" of the invisible is still configured within a metaphysics of presence as identifiable as such. It refers more broadly, then, to what Diane Coole (2000) calls the politics of negativity and is related obliquely to what Michael Sells (1994) calls the ineffable and the strategies of performative apophasis that mark mystical languages of unsaying. The tactics crystallized across the nineteenth century to speak of or identify a presumed invisible we are still deploying. While this chapter does not claim to be beyond their play, it is pertinent and timely to think more deeply about the tools upon which we rely to make judgments about matters of concern, justice, quality, and equality. The three kinds of tactics that cross theoretical allegiances and academic disciplines which are considered here point to how something deeper seems to be at stake than simply educational policy, gatekeeping functions, or the definition of key terms.

## EXPLANATORY CONCEPTS: THE DISCOVERY OF THE UNCONSCIOUS

> We are not just criticizing psychoanalysis for having selected Oedipal statements exclusively. For such statements are to a certain extent part of a machinic assemblage, for which they could serve as correctional indexes, as in a calculation of errors. We are criticizing psychoanalysis for having used Oedipal enunciation to make patients believe they would produce individual, personal statements, and would finally speak in their own name. (Deleuze & Guattari, 1987, p. 38)

In the northern trans-Atlantic Republic of Scholars, studies of extraordinary behavior became a site of fascination in the late 1700s and new theories of mind-body-soul relation emerged. In some quarters, new theories pitted charges of a radical materialist atheism against charges of politically conservative naiveté. One long term outcome was a stricter scientization of mind especially. Mind was no longer subjected to consideration as to whether such a thing existed but now investigated in terms of it modalities of operation.

One new modality was appeal to an unconscious zone, domain, or operation. The term unconscious comes into English-language documents in the late 1700s and early 1800s in what is now referred to as Romantic literature, not as the opposite of the conscious *per se* but as reference to the habitual and the automatic. Henri Ellenberger (1970) goes so far as to name this a discovery. Integral to that naming well before Freud were a series of trials referred to initially as animal magnetism, and which long before psychoanalysis had led to a questioning of the discreteness of self, of the speaker, and of speaking in one's own name.

### Animal Magnetism, Mesmerism and Hypnosis

New possibilities for inspecting an interior posited as invisible arose in research and experimentation under a variety of labels, including animal magnetism, mesmerism, hypnosis, somnambulism, and magnetic slumber. In the late 1700s the therapeutic practices developed by Franz Anton Mesmer and popularized via his move to the Parisian salons led to an important federal investigation headed by Benjamin Franklin, which debunked the therapy as charlatan, just as *Empiriks* once had been. Mesmer had argued that a universal fluid, which is to be understood roughly as energetic rather than as wet, links all animate and inanimate objects, planets, and beings. This led to a monistic conception of problem and of cure. A blockage of the fluid's flow caused all illness and unrest and its release through a healing crisis would restore harmony and balance. After the dismissal in the French report of the late 1700s further trials reappeared in the 1820s and '30s UK and continental Europe, becoming popular again in the United States by the mid-century decades. Visiting and self-ordained Professor of Animal Magnetism, Charles Poyen St Sauveur observed how the population he engaged in the United States seemed unaware of the earlier controversies and took pains to describe what had been templated decades before:

> The Phenomena of somnambulism, which are to be subsequently described, may be arranged in the following order: Suspension, more or less complete, of the external sensibililty; intimate connexion with the magnetizer and with no other one; influence of the will; communication of thought [telepathy]; clairvoyance, or the faculty of seeing through various parts of the body, the eyes remaining closed; unusual development of sympathy, of memory, and of the power of imagination; faculty of appreciating and keeping time; faculty for seizing the symptoms of diseases and prescribing the proper remedies for them; entire forgetting, after awaking, of what has transpired during the state of somnambulism. (St Sauveur, 1837, p. 63)

The debates over the "invisible influence" of one mind upon another flowed into education and bamboozled observers there as elsewhere. As William Stone, Superintendent of New York Public Schools, wrote in a letter to his friend:

> The inference from your letter is, that I have suddenly become a convert to Animal Magnetism, to the whole extent claimed and practiced by Frederick Anthony Mesmer, the founder of the art, and contended for by Wolf art and Kluge, and the other German and French enthusiasts, who have written in explanation and support of the system. This is an error. I am not a positive believer in the system, because I know not what to believe; and yet, I am free to confess, that I have recently beheld phenomena, under circumstances where collusion, deception, fraud, and imposture, were alike out of the question, if not impossible, which have brought me from the position of a positive skeptic to a dead pause. From the evidence of my own senses, I have been compelled if not to relinquish, at least very essentially to modify, my disbelief; and I can no longer deny, although I cannot explain, the extraordinary phenomena pro-

duced by the exertion of the mental energy of one person upon the mind of another, while in a state of what is termed magnetic slumber. (Stone, 1837, p. 5)

In the perceived absence of frameworks through which to account for the extraordinary capacities and behaviors brought to view a slew of further templates dedicated to stylizing what are now called altered states arose. Three states were often identified. They were considered potentially mixed in form and could be displayed suddenly, originally or separately, they may or may not be produced in succession within a subject and the order could differ. However, for scholars such as Alfred Benet who developed the groundwork for the notion of IQ (intelligence quotient) and whose first area of training and expertise was hypnosis differing results will be obtained "if the patients are subjected to a different *modus operandi*; if, in other words, they do not receive the same hypnotic education [induction procedure]" (Binet & Féré, 1888, p. 160). This led to questions not just over technique and template but over ethical applications especially with confined populations such as soldiers and schoolchildren. Binet and Féré captured well these concerns in their comprehensive text *Animal Magnetism*: "The question arises how it should be possible for one person to exert over another the power of making him speak, act, think, and feel as it pleases the experimenter to dictate?" (Binet & Féré, 1888, p. 172). Binet and Féré noted further how the application beyond persons considered ill also raised questions about ethics: "It is possible not only to make suggestions to subjects in the waking state [after coming out of hypnosis], but also to persons who have not been hypnotized at all. Learned men have been agitated by these latter experiments, which have aroused in them doubt and dissatisfaction. They have no difficulty in admitting that suggestions may be made to hypnotized subjects, since they are not in normal health, but they cannot understand how they should be made to individuals who are awake, not under hypnotism, and that this should be done by modes of action in daily use in our relations to one another" (Binet & Féré, 1888, p. 178).

The multiple efforts to rethink the blurred lines of self-other, here-there, before-after and of governance, causality, criminality, and responsibility that such trials made available to the imagination impacted field-formation in education in ways that have largely been under-appreciated. The "discovery of the unconscious" prior to Freudian versions shaped education's domain along several vectors including: (a) behavior management strategies—hard and soft versions such as disability-treatment interventions and advice for citizen-production through behavior management of "the normals" respectively; (b) contouring of expertise and authority, such as determining how a particular trial was to be conducted and evaluated; (c) reintroducing the focus on Will in intelligence testing and child development theories—hypnotic suggestibility was initially taken as a sign of weakness because Will was seen as too easily bent by others, yet educability had to also go through Will if stimulus-response frameworks were to be contested; and (d) the redefinition of public and private via extending the domain of public inspection to a new area, the "psyche-" and "unconscious" (see Baker 2010a).

## Climbing Up Into Our Heads: The Veracity of an Unconscious?

The trials that followed from animal magnetism provided to education's emergent subjects-as-objects new strategies of racialization, sexualization, and development. The unconscious by the late 1800s had seeped into explanations for how children are and what they do, characterized as a hot or cold part of mind, as darkness and as Africa, and as threat and possibility. In the recesses of domestically grown mind, shaped prior to adulthood, an "un"conscious now lurked: chaotic, seething, tropical, and sex-laden in some accounts, while cold, automated, and ruthlessly efficient in others (Richardson, 2001), theorized either way as silently absorbing input from within and without, and servile—taking care of everything with which the conscious mind could not be bothered or attend to while, significantly, having the potential to undermine good intentions through surprising incursions into the castle of consciousness.

In turn of the twentieth century educational theories, such as Developmentalism, Recapitulation theories, and Culture-epoch philosophies, the more general shift in the scientization of mind away from unfolding faculties toward the chaotic and automatic—these were not mutually exclusive—play of irrational forces in an unconscious enabled the lodging of what Aravamudan (1999) calls Tropicopolitans at the center of the "normally developing child" of whiteness. The significance of such an "invisible" and "mental" construct to populational engineering strategies should not be underestimated, for it impacted diverse domains, from the theorization of memory/forgetting in testing and evaluation contexts (Baker, 2013) to the automation of muscular responses in physical education drills (Kirk, 1992).

It is important to note, then, the arbitrariness of the unconscious as an explanatory concept which accrued an incredible reach, not because someone held it in their hands and could verify its matter across laboratories, but because its existence was inferred from behavior that was initially thought to be extraordinary and/or supernatural. The arbitrariness of an unconscious is brought further into relief by observations that are exterior to its horizons of enactment.

In Western psychology . . . I think that there may be a tendency to overemphasize the role of the unconscious in looking for the source of one's problems.

I think that this stems from some basic assumptions that Western psychology starts with: for instance, it does not accept the idea of imprints being carried over from a past life. And at the same time there is an assumption that everything must be accounted for within this lifetime. So, when you can't explain what is causing certain behaviors or problems, the tendency is to always attribute it to the unconscious. It's a bit like you've lost something and you decide that the object is in this room. And once you have decided this, then you've already fixed your parameters, you've precluded the possibility of its being outside the room or in another room. So you keep on searching, but you are not finding it, yet you continue to assume that it is still hidden somewhere in the room. (HH Dalai Lama & Cutler, 1998, p. 7)

If explanatory concepts accrue a special reach based on the range of phenomena they can be marshaled to explain, even while blocking other possibilities, technicalizing instruments have operated to change the kinds of questions that can be asked and to delimit legitimation of the answers. The ways in which technicalizing instruments, such as transcripts, were deployed to mediate a visible/invisible horizon openly transformed debates regarding veridicality in the social sciences and constitute an instance of a new kind of tactic that emerged in relation to empiricism's reign and abjections.

## TECHNICALIZING INSTRUMENTS: TRANSCRIPTS, LIFE/DEATH, AND SPIRIT-RETURN

The work of Harvard professor of psychology and philosophy, William James (1842–1910) is informative here. James took it upon himself to decide whether the phenomena he was observing at the turn of the twentieth century could be attributed to this new thing called the unconscious or whether one would have to concede causations called superphysical and supernatural. The phenomena James was observing had already been classified by contemporaries as psychical research and sometimes as occult, which did not necessarily make them a low status study but which did make them controversial. James was involved in psychical research for twenty-five years, was part of a trans-Atlantic academic elite that conjoined Cambridge and Harvard universities around such investigations as mediumship, clairvoyance, telekinesis, and so forth, and himself considered such phenomena to fall within the domain of education (Baker, 2013).

When one of James best friends and secretary of the ASPR (American Society for Psychical Research which James helped to found), Richard Hodgson, passed over playing handball in New York, reports of his colleague being channeled were circulated rapidly thereafter. Both James and Hodgson had spent years studying a medium known as Mrs. Leonora Piper who had come to the ASPR's attention through James' wife, Alice and who had been paid a retainer for her services. In the first decade of the new century, James enters in upon the question of spirit-return more fully, trying to decide if this is really his friend Hodgson being channeled through Piper or whether there are more "naturalist explanations." He explains the set up early in his 1909 "Report on Mrs. Piper's Hodgson-control":

> Richard Hodgson died suddenly upon December 20th, 1905. On December 28th a message purporting to come from him was delivered in a trance of Mrs. Piper's, and she has hardly held a sitting since then without some manifestation of what professed to be Hodgson's spirit taking place. Hodgson had often during his lifetime laughingly said that if he ever passed over and Mrs. Piper was still officiating here below, he would 'control' her better than she had ever yet been controlled in her trances, because he was so thoroughly familiar with the difficulties and conditions on this side. Indeed he was; so that this would seem *prima facie* a particularly happy conjunction of 'spirit' with medium by which to test the question of spirit-return. (James, 1909a, p. 253)

Which conditions of proof to affirm in the test of such a thesis was part of a longer dispute. In publications and internal communications of participants in the ASPR the debate hinged on how what was visible to some was not visible to others and whether a lack of consensus around visibility meant unscientific (James, 1897, 1909b).

James notes that Hodgson jokingly agreed that should he pass over first he ought to try to return through Piper to clarify once and for all the spiritist thesis (James, 1909a). Eight days after Hodgson's heart attack, Leonora Piper reports channeling Hodgson. James explains the transcripts that he reviews in his final Report are from the American sittings collated from December 28th, 1905 to January 1st, 1908. William and sometimes Alice attended the Piper-Hodgson sittings. "Hodgson" was described as eventually speaking in his own name without the conduit of Rector (the spirit thought to control things on the other side), with his name suspended in quotes in the transcripts to indicate uncertainty over the status. James wrote up his review of the transcripts at the same time as his thoughts on pragmatism, radical empiricism, and pluralism. They were published a year before James passed over, at which point another series of claims regarding James being channeled were set off up until 1930 (Blum, 2006).

Crucial in James' approach to the transcripts produced is that they are not taken a priori as data, nor as evidentiary. Transcripts must be analyzed for incidences and events that could be seen as evidentiary, as good test cases, for deciding upon the spirit-return thesis. The second-order normativity embodied in the approach—that there are conditions of proof for what can count as genuine proof at all—places most of the transcribed sessions outside of detailed focus. Others remain, however, in the Report for instructive purposes:

**WJ:** Hodgson, what are you doing apart from Mrs. Piper?
**RH:** Why, I am working with the society, William, trying to reach other lights, trying to communicate, trying to get in touch with you all.
**WJ:** Why can't you tell me more about the other life?
**RH:** That is part of my work. I intend to give you a better idea of this life than has ever been given.
**WJ:** I hope so.
**AJ:** Hodgson, do you live as we do, as men do?
**RH:** What does she say?
**WJ:** Do you live as men do?
**AJ:** Do you wear clothing and live in houses?
**RH:** Oh yes, houses, but not clothing. No, that is absurd. Just wait a moment, I am going to get out.
**WJ:** You will come back again?
**RH:** Yes.
**Rector:** He has to go out and get his breath (James, 1909a, p. 330).

Besides the entertaining content, especially if one considers why clothing would be any more absurd than housing "on the other side," the role of the technicalizing instrument of the transcript is important to consider here. The nature of Alice and William's questions indicate something rather vague but significant about the commonsensical role of the visible and invisible in truth-production. They gesture toward different conditions of objectification and unique pathways to science-formation already aggravating the disconnect between what Chertok and Stengers (1992) call the theoretico-experimental and ethico-redemptive sciences, and the perceived need to develop a site around which to gather in order to generate the public consensus now thought necessary when ocular visibility of the "thing" being discussed is not available to all.

## Difficulties in Restoring the Cause–Effect Sequence Through a Different Mechanism

> Short-term memory includes forgetting as a process: it merges not with the instant but instead with the nervous, temporal, and collective rhizome. Long-term memory (family, race, society, or civilization) traces and translates, but what it translates continues to act in it, from a distance, off beat, in an "untimely" way, not instantaneously. (Deleuze & Guattari, 1987, p. 16)

Even if, though, as noted above ocularcentrism is dubiously flattened out as a singular historical category and rendered backwards as that which links medieval and early modern sciences in an "untimely" way, the task for James is not the same as for Alhazen, Galileo Galilei, or Isaac Newton. In postulating gravity as an invisible force that brings a discrete apple into contact with a discrete ground surface the question was not whether there was such a thing as apple or earth but rather what mediates their contact. For James, the first question in the spirit-return thesis arises at the level of legitimacy of the object, not simply of relations between a priori objects.

Moreover, because the discourse of visuality and its role in veridicality had changed dramatically by the twentieth century through appeal to traveling photons unevenly interpreted from observer to observer, a search to restore the cause-effect sequence through a different mechanism was required, that of public corroboration—of the match between the word and thing, of language as representation of representation. The difficulty in the spirit-return thesis, however, was the apparent absence of the thing to which to match the words. Compounding this is also, for James, the possibility of non-discreteness—a "spirit" either speaking through, inhabiting, being channeled, interpenetrating, or co-mingling with a subject already positioned as "medium" and "in a trance state" complicates any search for mechanical explanation if the object is legitimated. What would one say was Leonora Piper's "self" in such a circumstance? How would the medium that Hodgson claims to make use of on the other side be verified and tested? Where would the discrete locus of origin, and if not origin then cause, for the communication be placed?

## Implications

After a series of convoluted arguments in which James self-regulated his proximity to the term rational, he concluded, hesitantly, that the spirit-return thesis in this case could not be verified and that it was a question for posterity which may in due course overturn his conclusions if the mass of cognate evidence was to be considered rather than isolated transcripts or incidences. In the end, the breakdown of the transcripts suggests to James not that the models for vision and conditions of proof were inadequate to the specificity of the subject-matter but that the subject-matter did not exist. What is one to make of this, then, beyond seemingly internal disputes within a discipline or titillating fascination with "the occult" among a trans-Atlantic scholarly elite?

There is a broader (non-total) formation here that James' rigorous analyses open a window onto. Something else has to be both projected and protected in order for other kinds of status anxieties to be assuaged beyond disciplinary ones. At stake is a different kind of regionalization for which debate over a life/death border is but one possible index. In his genealogy of the terms religion and mysticism, for instance, King (2005) argues that the labeling of Christianity as a religion that attempts to dominate village life especially through the medieval period meant that Christianity had become the reference point for what constitutes a religion. *Religio* as tradition and as "to close" (such as to close eyes and ears for revelation or to close into secret initiations) in ancient Rome was transformed into *religio* as "to bind" in the medieval period—to a set text, a series of rituals, and presumption of shared beliefs that could be referred to systemically. That religion could become distinct at all, separated from other possibilities and treated as a category rather than as way of life suggests not a disciplining of Christianity for King but a move into a new colonizing mode of occupying the point of reference, for organizing all comparisons. For King secularization arises out of a public/private division in which the domination of the index of what counts as a religion is placed in association with the private, the irrational, the mystical, and the feminine. Hence, even when or where Christianity is pushed to the side, as it is in the later parts of the Jamesian oeuvre, it still dominates the criterion for determining what counts as public and what private. The nations that form the area known in the nineteenth century as Europe were dependent in part upon prior obsession with religious homogeneity—the belief in a shared essence emerges around "to bind" and especially but not only around Protestant and Catholic versions of what it meant to bind. More strongly, King posits that it was religious particularity as viewed through Christian theological templates that enabled the idea that nations could operate as enforced groupings with constitutional boundaries. With the Enlightenment, "the mystical" becomes relocated, ejected within the messy intersection of religion-nation-rationality, something that is separate from science and literature, attributed to the East, to the invisible, the personal, to that which cannot be publicly corroborated. At the same time, the mystical is posed as already existing within the West's story about itself, repressed as pagan or occult—by extension one might say that "the mystical" operates as the unconscious of the West, the unknowable and unfaceable alterity within and without.

The social sciences in the United States of James interpenetrated a unique nation-building project, however, that constitutionally rejected both monarchy and conflation of Church and State. It was a social experiment built out of slavery, reservation systems, and mass immigration. The above gestures at a different orientation, then, to the question of why it would matter whether there was such a thing as a ghost, opening onto all the problems of borders, territoriality, porousness, intersubjectivity, and suggestibility that mark social sciences, their inscription as Western, and the (un)availability of authenticity and purity in research. Such an apparent abyss as the after-life, unique models of causality, and the play of invisible objects would potentially threaten the attempted neat packaging of emergent disciplines as sciences, the presumption of a finite, this-worldly horizon, and the enforceability of boundaries around such entities as geopolitical territories, religions, and selves.

This was the uneasy dilemma within which James found himself located as adjudicator. It was uneasy because he sometimes critiqued borders between disciplines and concepts, borders that he saw as false abstractions of more fluid phenomena, and he did not always offer in his analyses at large the easy way out. He is (in)famous for complicating binaries, taking distance from dualisms, wanting things both ways, or refusing to resolve dilemma by coming down firmly on one side or another. However, if in 1909 the ghost is verified as a scientific object, not subjected to consideration of whether it exists but continuously analyzed for its attributes, then the reinforcement of a West/Orient division upon which James comments directly elsewhere (for example, in *Talks to Teachers* published in 1899) is also at stake. The borders around the stereotype of the Orient as mystical, as past-life oriented, as transcendentalist would become blurred, and the very privilege of Protestant-based institutions such as Harvard, amid the melting pot's other continuously present possibilities might be troubled as the twentieth century continued to unfold.

In the apparent absence of what could not be seen or agreed to by all, the relationship between rationality and empiricism was thus re-routed, seeded more deeply within a complex interplay between density, consciousness, and word-based expression. This was mediated by the transcript's new function as the technicalizing instrument for harnessing public consensus around a "visible" trace. Through James' rejection of the spirit-return thesis and the upholding of a veil between life and an after-life a twofold movement is then resecured: both the weightier role of density/the corporeal in veridicality is legitimated and at the same time the possibility is left open for "the mystical," "the supernatural," and/or "intuition" to inspire innovations in social scientific thinking indebted especially to Christian traditions—movements that today's educational research continues to embody through the encoded use of salvific signfiers, the overt use of discourses of redemption and rescue, and appeals to perfectibility.

### Veracity of the Ghost?

By introducing a meta-level distinction—that transcripts are not inherently evidence but that which one searches for evidentiary instances—the appeal to the technicalizing instrument effects a realignment of possible conclusions away from introspection, from individuality, and from revelation. While today an active ghost could be legitimated within a narrative under the heading of magical realism such as in postcolonial studies, in educational research this is largely not the case. Technicalizing instruments are more dedicated in educational research generally to trying to "capture reality," including the reality of things referred to as affect, emotion, feelings, motivation, or inspiration. Likert scales, interviews, photographs, or video footage of facial expressions constitute the toolkit for trying to give number and substance to things that seem to move through us that are sometimes difficult to explain to others outside of us.

The point here is not whether the ghost unilaterally exists, then, but to consider which not-fully-agreed upon quotidian "objects" become elevated to the level of scientific objects in social scientific thinking, and which not, and what the geopolitics and legacies of drawing and maintaining those distinctions might be. This requires thinking more deeply through how the divisions are made and sustained in contemporary circumstance: the ghost as moving "invisible" force being channeled through the likes of Leonora Piper remains at best under suspicion if not dismissed, while labels such as LD (learning disability) are readily applied to children in the absence of any consistent "visible" biophysiological markers or replicable photographs and images of their locus or origin (Tait, 2011). Such labels as LD are operationalized as veridical if not genetic, exposing how the differences here between the veracity attributed to one "invisible" thing relative to another remains an important part of interrogating the intellectual histories, spatializations, and regionalisms within which educationists work.

If technicalizing instruments change the way in which questions can be posed and in this case *preserve* the explanatory reach of mind and the unconscious as scientific concepts, however, strategies of stabilization act to *conserve* the relations and identity/difference schemata that lend context and meaning to such concepts and instruments. In particular, the strategy of nation-building, border-marking, and the making of the nation into a scientific object did not stand distinct from debates over mind science, life/death, and education but facilitated them and was facilitated by them.

## STRATEGIES OF STABILIZATION: THE GEO-BODY, THE NATION, AND PISA

A case can even be made to the effect that the rise of modern social theory... is intimately connected to the development of the nation-state and in some ways has been helpful to it. (Day & Thompson, 2004, p. x)

One of the major questions yet haunting the historians of early Southeast Asia concerns the formation of states. To be more specific, how one can talk about a state's formation without taking for granted what a state is—the criteria usually prescribed by social scientists, not by Southeast Asian peoples themselves. (Winichakul, 1994, p. 14)

In the twenty-first century, a variety of strategies of stabilization have become so taken-for-granted that they are worth stepping back from to consider the formation of such plateaus and their assumptions, too.[4] In particular the strategy of mapmaking, the borderline, and conception of a profane and material earth have been deployed to say who we are and where we are and to build policy and distributive logics on that basis. Here, Deleuze and Guattari are of little help, for despite the anti-Statist stance within the Nomadology, the preference for *mapping* over the *trace* in their work and their implicit adult-centrism elides another set of normativities, selective cosmological frames, and desires that need to be unpacked. In education, one of the most overt and obvious sites for mobilizing assumptions regarding mapping and distributive logics is PISA, Programme for International Student Assessment.

## PISA as a Social Project of Modernity/Nationalism

PISA is the offspring of the OECD, established in 1961, which "brings together the governments of countries committed to democracy and the market economy from around the world to:

- Support sustainable economic growth
- Boost employment
- Raise living standards
- Maintain financial stability
- Assist other countries' economic development
- Contribute to growth in world trade"

PISA was designed to answer the question of whether an increase in percent expenditure of GDP by national governments would correlate with an increase in the test scores of teenagers in public schools (Kallo, 2009). Held every three years and with a different focus each time, like math, science, etc, a series of league table-style outcomes is produced, with the subsequent circulation of results acting back on media and policy discourse regarding the quality of educational provision and funding.

## The Problem with State and Nation Theories

PISA employs a structural-functional logic to draw relations between quantitative units, which permit questions like the following: "Is there a correlation between number of hours spent per day at school and test outcomes?" Its basic structure assumes that education can be nothing but the nation and nothing but numerical. More silently and saliently, however, it assumes what a nation-state is altogether, even where this broad assumption has already been contested, such as in "non-European" cosmologies or in disciplines such as historical geography. As has already been argued in Baker (2010b), whereas Benedicte Anderson points to the new temporal consciousness that helps to formulate the sense of a new community in historical lineage, (as distinct from previous imagined communities), that is, how the new sense of homogeneous, linear time shaped the imagined community of the nation-state in Europe, Thongchai Winichakul focuses on another technology—the *geo-body*, describing the operations of technology of territoriality which created nationhood spatially. For Winichakul, the displacement of indigenous spatial concepts in what he calls premodern Siam by modern geographical ones *produced* social institutions and practices that *created* nationhood. In particular, the absence of the concept of physical boundaries in premodern Siam has been especially undertheorized or misplaced: "No study has been done on the relationships—either the transformation or shift or confrontation—between the premodern geographical discourse and the modern one. The absence of definite boundaries of the premodern realm of Siam is not taken seriously, as if it were due to some practical or technical reason" (Winichakul, 1994, p. 18).

Most studies of premodern Siam's concepts of space indicate that maps were not always conceived as travel aids but as ways of representing relations between sacred entities tied to Buddhist doxology. As noted in Baker's (2010b) analysis of Winichakul's historical geography:

> Such studies tend to focus on the Buddhist cosmography known as the *Traiphum* cosmography. *Traiphum*, literally meaning three worlds, was an important doctrinal tradition within Theravada Buddhism. The best-known text of this tradition is *Traiphum Phra Ruang*, believed to be the major treatise of the Sukhotahi kingdom in the upper Chao Phraya valley in the thirteenth century. There are thirty-one levels in the three worlds in which the human level is simply one and in this map, beings are classified by merit and designated to live in particular levels according to their store of merit. The store of merit can be accumulated or diminished by one's deeds and account for one's next birth. By this logic, one's present existence is the outcome of the previous one. While the surviving texts give concrete descriptions of the three worlds and especially the human one, as well as movements of the sun, moon, and seasonal changes, space is conceptualized in the *Traiphum* as a qualitative manifestation of existence, merit, and the relation between sacred entities. (Winichakul, 1994). (Baker, 2010b, p. 232)

In PISA, space is clearly not conceptualized as the relation between sacred entities but rather as objectivist territories marked by invisible borderlines encasing nations. Winichakul's analysis is dedicated, then, to a different question that unpacks such assumptions from the point of view of flashpoints. Rather than mobilizing simply one conception of space as obviously real and evidentiary above all others he asks: "what dramatic effects ensue when people stop imagining space in terms of orderly relations of sacred entities and start conceiving it with a whole new set of signs and rules?" (Winichakul, 1994, p. 36). As for the variety of premodern maps, modern geography for Winichakul is not objective but it has real effects and is a kind of mediator. Earth and modern maps are not given objects, just out there. Rather, modern geography is just one kind of knowledge, a conceptual abstraction of a supposedly objective reality, a systematic set of signs, a discourse. In analyzing premodern and modern discourses of space and detecting those moments when the new and the old collided issues of specificity in provincial form, in terms of measurement, accuracy, and empiricism arise.

PISA's economic foundationalist orientation also elides other latent possibilities that today would be called indigenous epistemologies and that would define the content of teaching quite differently from units called mathematics, literacy, science, etc. Winichakul notes, for instance, that the human world of the *Traiphum* has been treated as if it were the native's view of the planet earth, a distorted or primitive one, contaminated by false belief or lack of knowledge. It is doubtful, however, whether the symbolic representation was designed to represent the planet earth. That depictions are varied—square and flat and round—does not indicate the development of local knowledge of the earth or the lack of it. More probably, it suggests that the materiality of the human world can be imagined in more than one way, whereas the spiritual meaning of the three worlds must be obeyed. Under this view, the spiritual dimension is the reality of the *Traiphum* space, and the most important knowledge needed to be transmitted correctly. It constitutes more an immovable foundation, whereas the human material world is that which can be read off and into in a number of ways.

If one concedes that a map does not have to be a representation of the earth's surface, but can depict other relations, then it is easier to understand that different representations were developed for different purposes. Different maps with different ideas about spaces co-existed. The crucial point here is that this suggests that there was not simply one way to represent the world but that there was more than one world, *more than one imaginal domain* (Winichakul, 1994). In the standardization that the nation-state frame provides to popular surveys such as PISA, however, the contemporaneity of imaginal domains, their "substantive multiplicity" in Deleuzean and Guattarian (1992) terms, becomes abjected. A geographied and material sense of world and of curriculum is silently embedded in the design and enactment of such surveys, in their matters of concern and their allied conditions of proof, and they depend on an inherent restriction: the delimitation of what counts to what can be counted, to *mathesis*.

Crucial to this counting is divisibility of a presumed whole. In the case of modern map-making the invention of boundary lines especially created the units for sequencing national territoriality as though all were part of the same whole. Drawing lines was also the encoding of desire, the building of nations and ethnicities as political entities whose boundaries define "identity" and who must reproduce "within."

> Boundary lines are indispensable for a map of a nation to exist—or to put it another way, a map of a nation presupposes the existence of boundary lines. Logically, this inevitably means that boundary lines must exist before a map, since a medium simply records and refers to an existing reality. But in this case, the reality was a reversal of that logic. It is the concept of a nation in the modern geographical sense that requires the necessity of having boundary lines clearly demarcated. A map may not just function as a medium; it could well be the creator of the supposed reality... The boundary of a nation works in two ways at the same time. On the one hand, it sets a clear-cut limit on a sovereign unit; on the other, it imposes a sharp division between at least two units of space.... Consequently, many conceptions and practices of interstate relations must be changed to conform with the new geography of a country. The indigenous concepts must be displaced. (Winichakul, 1994, p. 56)

Significant here are the complexities and paradoxes around whatever is constituted as the visible/invisible in regard to the demand for empirical evidence: the importance of the shift into a "global" plane of reference is that the spatial reality that the modern map purports to present is never directly experienced in its totality—it is impossible to do so—no one under the auspices of scientific reasoning can *be* the earth, nor *see* all of it standing on a cliff, nor *hold it* in their hands. The modern map became an indispensable *mediator* in perceiving and conceptualizing such macrospace as though it was a totality, a function that none of the premodern maps ever performed.

On Winichakul accounts, then, it would not be enough to ask when does Thailand become Thailand or where do the borders fall in which period when inquiring into success or otherwise in PISA. Both questions remain within a Newtonian physics and modern conception of geography that presumes what should be explained—that is, the revolution into linear time, the assumption that space is only three dimensional, the presumption that there is only one world totality, and that Being can only be defined by understanding the self as one small part of macrospace.

## Implications: Reforming an Apollonian View as Globalism and All-Knowing

It is fruitful to understand PISA as one of the social projects of modernity/nationalism in which dispersal across a presumed earth and at the same time the desire to transcend co-habitate in the notion of performativity and instrumentality, in the reduction, that is, of education's purposes to the GDP. Denis Cosgrove argues that such efforts to transcend and to radiate, to secure an all-knowing, overarching view of place and to associate that with knowledge-production and dissemination has been a regular strategy in what is now called the West. In education, high-profile surveys including but not restricted to PISA, emerged right at that moment that a post-American and post-European world were suggested. In this context, authority is relocated into terms such as globalism and recognized via efforts to subordinate other "social" and "natural" worlds, other possibilities that are disciplined and ordered beneath the eagle-eye view. In attempting to obtain such an overarching view the strategy of ascent dedicated to the belief that there is nothing but the nation-state remains homologous to those in the human genome project and the contemporaneity of such projects is not a coincidence. In terms of radiation and dispersal, the effort to disseminate the results as the main way of seeing education—education can be nothing but measurement of test outcomes—tends toward another absolutist orientation in the name of documenting differences. Yet, for Cosgrove, both the absolutism of appealing to nations and borders and to quantification would not suggest entirely deterministic outcomes. Rather:

> Today, the globe continues to sustain richly varied and powerful imaginative associations. Globalization—economic, geopolitical, technological, and cultural—is widely recognized as a distinguishing feature of life at the second millennium, actualizing the Apollonian view across a networked, virtual surface. Resistance from the solid ground of earth, characteristically located at the spatial and social limits of Apollo's conventional purview, proclaims limitations of its male-centered Eurocentrism, a globalism hopelessly bound to exercising and legitimating authority over subordinate social and natural worlds. The criticism is well founded, both historically and morally. But the issue is by no means simple. The Apollonian perspective prompts ethical questions about individual and social life on the globe's surface that have disturbed as often as they have reassured a comfortable Western patriarchy. (Cosgrove, 2001, p. 3)

If PISA is to be understood as a new instance of an Apollonian eye and effort to reassert "Western values," then what has happened to discourses of vision and visuality in relation to such efforts? Delanty and O'Mahoney (2002) argue that the social projects of modernity were constituted through four key dynamics: state-formation, democratization, capitalism, and rationalization of culture. These dynamics crystallized at three levels: in specific historical trajectories; traveling ideals of modernity/nation-building as a cultural project; institutional formations and dynamics, and crucially, they all embodied a logic of perpetual differentiation-integration and dynamic renewal.

Perpetual differentiation-integration is particularly apposite in regard to current educational research and the "sensing" of phenomena or "something meaningful" that exceed available methods for recording that teachers, parents, students, and researchers have repeatedly noted. The current impossibility of placing educational policy outside of the sovereign nationalist frame, let alone Being, subjectivity, etc, remains in part indebted to the representational and mediating functions of the modern geographical map, which tend to restrict just how different differentiation can really be. Such visualizations can bring some conceptions of space into view as real and not others, primarily those conceptions whose foci are borderlines that are militarily defended, populations who are territorially governed, and who believe in an absolute imaginal domain, One World across which resources and logics are distributed.

Perhaps ironically, contemporary movements that challenge and eschew both nationalism and ethnicity as the origin of all explanation and that position formalized schooling as an act of colonization have not so much come from visual culture theory, but Deaf nationalism, Deaf Awareness, and Deaf Culturalist movements, which have in common the positioning of the rules of the Hearing as an aggressive act of subjugation of Deaf children (Wrigley, 1996). Such movements have contested anew the presumed liberatory potential of nationally- and linguistically-based schooling. The impossibility of surveys such as PISA to take on board such claims to a new Deaf nation that is not geographically bound or policed is obvious, but more subtle are the deeper questions this raises: of what education is, is for, and whose education surveys such as PISA take seriously and considers worth testing? If Deaf children are not tested in PISA but do participate in public schooling in some of the participating nations, then which students come to be seen as vessels and representatives of the nation construct? Which "subjects" cannot be considered part of the imaginal domain of GDP-relevance exposes the limits of the differentiation-integration dynamic of a modern episteme as it structures what becomes noticeable and agreeable to mainstream social scientific thought.

## The Veracity of the Nation and Geopolitical Borders?

Between Winichakul, Cosgrove, Delanty and O'Mahoney, and Wrigley the founding assumptions of PISA, and its coding and taxonomic project are brought out of a position of cultural neutrality and objectivity. The difficulty remains, though, because what can be "seen" even when it cannot be seen, the national border, cannot be fully challenged or easily made irrelevant in the perpetual logic of differentiation-integration when tied to a second-order normativity for Being and subjectivity grounded in the map. The strategies of stabilization indebted to a modern geographical discourse, to coding that privileges a profane and material surface of earth, thus crystallizes a foreground against a pluralized background of other possibilities, of multiple Worlds, of irreconcilable imaginal domains, and irreducible conceptions of life and death. This acts, then, to resecure the founding assumptions of the initial cosmological frame (in this case empiricism and materialism) and ensures the recalcitrance of nationalism as an organizational force.

Significantly, however, the kind of logocentrism at play in surveys such as PISA is perhaps more indebted to motion than to fixity: "Modern science rests on a 'dynamic' conception of the cosmos and nature (*physis*), one in sharp contrast to the static *Weltanschaung* of the Middle Ages. The very notions of earth moving in the celestial sphere, of the circulation of the blood, of the propagation of light, of the gravitational attraction of heavenly bodies are manifestations of this conception—just as modern social science was galvanized by Saint-Simon's and Marx's dynamic conception of social reality and Freud's dynamic conception of personality" (Tyriakian, 1974, pp. 11–12). If, as Tyriakian further suggests this ordering of things becomes the pivotal issue of what gets called modern societies and if simultaneously discourses of vision can no longer be purely associated with objectivity, yet some version of empiricism is required for public consensus and corroboration, then the "clash of civilizations" as much as of academic disciplines or regimes of truth will become central struggles: "To strike a balance between objectivity and subjectivity, that is a central problem of the modern period, a problem at the very core of the direction of modern society, and therefore a crucial sociological problem" (Tyriakian, 1974, pp. 11–12).

## CONCLUSION: TACTICS IN MODERN DISCOURSES OF VISION -IRRECONCILABLE RATIONALITIES OR MEANINGFUL "SOMETHING BEYOND"?

Theoretico-experimental sciences are distinguished by the practice of making their version of "reason" depend on the power to 'give reasons' for or to explain phenomena. This version of reason thus presumes the power of predicting outcomes, of controlling in order to replicate, or purifying to insure the implication of a theory—the power, in sum, to make a phenomenon "admit" its truth (Chertok & Stengers, 1992, p. xvi).

The enforcement of a subject/object division has had much energy dedicated to it and many further assumptions built around it, including the division of sciences and different conceptions of causality. Amid such possibilities and limits, the discipline of education in Anglophone-dominant contexts has always grappled with a kind of status anxiety relative to other disciplines. This is in part due to the ways in which evidence has been thought about in the theoretico-experimental sciences relative to the ethico-redemptive ones.[5] The former, as Chertok and Stengers have already argued, have been dedicated to a purification process—the search for a single, causal variable to explain an effect that is replicable across contexts. The latter have had to face the problem of intersubjectivity and suggestibility. Because "the infant's relations with its caretakers are already characterized by what we should recognize as a form of suggestion" (1992, p. xvii) the social sciences which focused on human relations could not so readily make a phenomenon admit its truth via a purification process: "suggestion puts 'truth' in question, that is, it problematizes the possibility of constructing a theory on the basis of experiment or experience. Suggestion is impure; it is the uncontrollable par excellence" (1992, p. xvi–xvii). The "heart" and "reason" dynamic that Chertok and Stengers identify as integral to the version of rationality produced within ethico-redemptive sciences at large also plays out in contemporary educational research.

The complexity of the dynamic and the tendency toward mimesis of higher status disciplines periodically spawns new efforts to reduce conditions of proof to particular forms that are regularity-oriented or pattern-obsessed. As Daston has already demonstrated in regard to the biography of scientific objects, the enduring Aristotelian belief that insists that "science ought to be about regularities—be they qualitative or quantitative, manifest to the senses or hidden beneath appearances, causal or statistical, taken from commonplace experience or created by specialized instruments in laboratories—has persisted long after the demise of Aristotelianism. Yet regularity alone seldom suffices to pick out scientific objects from the ordinary objects of quotidian experience . . . " (Daston, 2000, p. 17). As she notes further, sixteenth and seventeenth century studies, such as those of Bacon, focused on anomalies, yet still claimed to be science. Tactics developed for the theorization of "the invisible" stand as an index of that tension between mimicry of higher status disciplines, regularity-desire, and perceptions of unique subject matter or anomalous objects. The wavering between modern discourses of vision as central and untrustworthy, the imperative to appeal to "something empirical" in a variety of materialist terms, and the convoluted relation of both requirements to the formation of a heart-reason rationality in ethico-redemptive sciences elaborate rather than resolve more historic and still restrictive disputes.

This includes disputes over what Deleuze and Guattari (1987) might call Fake Multiplicities rather than substantive multiplicities, over spirit/matter, Divine/man, and mono/poly, suggesting that such debates, far from being settled, continue to have value without being continuous: Studies of extraordinary behavior and the unconscious repositioned "the invisible" as an embodied depth; studies of the life/death border and the spirit-return thesis repositioned "the invisible" as a possible disembodied transcendence; while studies of borders, nation-building, geographical mapping and PISA repositioned "the invisible" as scalar.

As noted at the outset, however, there is something greater at stake than simply truth-production, rationality, the political, political rationality, and/ or the protection of the humanist subject, discrete objects, and the allied definitional debates. The effort to theorize whatever was asserted as a visible/invisible horizon, sometimes in opposition, sometimes not, yet still significant, points toward the formation of non-totalizable but nonetheless potent plateaus regarding the very conceptualization of reality, of Being, and of place, reinforcing significant binaries between irreal/real, mad/sane, behind/developed, local/global that have marked what Foucault (1970) has called a modern episteme indicative of disciplinary societies. Such an episteme has worked to restrict how phenomena can appear and be experienced and explained, especially in relation to managing the politics of a broader savage/civilized division. The plateaus through which a modern episteme as rhizome takes shape and is given the ground to operate, however, includes the possibility for edifices *and* lines of flight. At a general level, this has meant that together the dominance of a discourse of empiricism in social science research *and* allied counter-moves that generated post-empirical tactics contributed to a broader onto-theo-philosophical regionalism (e.g., savage/civil, Third World/First World, irrational/rational, etc) and new logics of perception that "highlight some phenomena and occlude others" (Daston, 2000, p. 16), without necessarily becoming a totalizable or absolute regime in regard to the possibilities for thought.

At a more specific level of discipline-formation, the politics of this highlighting and occlusion changes the recognition of what gets to count as research, as an approach or method, and as a contribution. The politics of plateau-formation and lines of flight or seepage changes, for instance, the way in which contemporary debates in educational research might be framed, responded to, or opened out. First, debates over "empirical data," over quantitative/qualitative research versus conceptual/theoretical analyses arise as two sides of the same coin of the effort to maintain proximity to rationality (and by way of that "the human"), just rationalities of different kinds. Second, the marginal yet significant position of "the invisible" and allied marginalized research such as parapsychology can be understood beyond the usual framing—less in relation to other disciplines, their mastery of "empirical" conditions of proof, explanatory concepts, technicalizing instruments, and strategies of stabilization that render the (presumed) invisible visible, and more in relation to onto-theo-philosophical regionalism in which "the mystical" comes to be redefined, separated from science, from realism, from literature, and from the West, while operating from "within" the social sciences as a necessary yet subordinate, constitutively unstable node in the new logics of perception. And third, the active sublation of an invisible-mystical couplet, whose effects exceed disciplinary debates, subtly and "unconsciously" conjoins more than separates contemporary elevation of scientific-based research (such as EBE) in the discipline of education at large *and* today's repetitive critical and post-foundationalist critiques of evidence-based education as reductionist and inappropriate to its social scientific subject-matter.

In sum, currently abjected post-empricist tactics have been integral to the formation of social sciences, bequeathing an appeal to the importance and necessity of a consensual materialist empiricism *and* the sensibility that something significant or meaningful is not fully captured or honored by such perceptual and methodological restriction. As such, they have helped to mobilize a by-now fairly familiar oscillation: the question of the relation between perception, noticeability, and World/s in its Kantian (reason-based) and Comtean (experience-based) framing still endures, while the move beyond such ambiguities and a priori's into new plateaus and modalities of operation that exceed occidentalist references points simultaneously ensues. Such tactics open onto at least several potential reframings: a reframing of the relation between what gets to constitute the human, a discourse of vision, and veridicality; of existing and future possibilities that lie beyond the presumption of one shared World in which we are all just differently located; and a reframing of the vagaries and dilemma that arise amidst the logocentric instantiation of a human perceiver as the primary fountain of all knowledge.

The implications for educational philosophy and theory are profound, for the neatly sealed entities of nations, territories, religions, theoretical frameworks, and selves become open to dispute in ways that exceed appeal to linguistic, pictorial, and visual turns, disrupting easy processes of attribution in explanation and analysis, and requiring a deeper interrogation of not just the "clash of civilizations" thesis but of wider "Worlds" that are not reducible to the selective and repetitive focus on human-to-human interaction, power relations, and sentence-based expression. It may be such, then, that the waves of new research that emanate in the twenty-first century will be part of a proliferation of possibilities that social sciences have historically attempted to both generate legitimation for and simultaneously constrain.

### NOTES

1. I am not attending in this paper to Deleuzian conceptions of the empirical which arise in response to the broader heritages being traversed here.

2. I thank Bill Doll for pointing up the importance of the shift in terminology from research to inquiry, and the difference this makes also at federal levels.
3. Retrieved from OED online Jan 5, 2012: http://www.oed.com.ezproxy.library. wisc.edu/view/Entry/61344?redirectedFrom=empiricism#eid
4. Parts of this section draw upon a previous publication that generated a cross-reading between curriculum historical work and historical geography for the purposes of unpacking the conditions of possibility for subjectivity, including a subjectivity of globality. While this paper draws upon some content of this analysis it is for entirely different purposes and has thus been radically reduced and refocused. Readers interested in the earlier and longer historical argument can consult Baker (2010b, p. 63).
5. I view ethico-redemptive sciences and social sciences as interchangeable.

## REFERENCES

Aravamudan, S. (1999). *Tropicopolitans: Colonialism and agency, 1688–1804.* Durham, NC: Duke University Press.
Baker, B. (2001). *In perpetual motion: Theories of power, educational history, and the child.* New York, NY: Peter Lang.
Baker, B. (2010a). The unconscious of history? Mesmerism and the production of scientific objects for curriculum historical research. In E. Malewski (Ed.), *Curriculum studies handbook: The next moment* (pp. 341–364). New York, NY: Routledge.
Baker, B. (2010b). Provincializing curriculum? On the preparation of subjectivity for globality. *Curriculum Inquiry, 40*(2), 221–240.
Baker, B. (2013). *William James, sciences of mind, and anti-imperial discourse.* New York, NY: Cambridge University Press
Binet, A., & Féré, C. (1888). *Animal magnetism.* New York: D. Appleton & Co.
Blum, D. (2006). *Ghost hunters: William James and the search for scientific proof of life after death.* New York: Penguin Press HC.
Bynum, E. B. (1999). *The African unconscious: Roots of ancient mysticism and modern psychology.* New York: Teachers College Press.
Chertok, L., & Stengers, I. (1989/1992). *A critique of psychoanalytic reason: Hypnosis as a scientific problem from Lavoisier to Lacan.* Stanford, CA: Stanford University Press.
Clark, S. (2007). *Vanities of the eye: Vision in early modern European culture.* Oxford: Oxford University Press.
Coole, D. (2000). *Negativity and politics: Dionysus and dialectics from Kant to postructionalism.* New York: Routledge.
Cosgrove, D. (2001). *Apollo's eye: A cartographic genealogy of the earth in the Western imagination.* Baltimore, MD: Johns Hopkins University Press.
Crary, J. (1999). *Suspensions of perception: Attention, spectacle, and modern culture.* Cambridge, MA: MIT Press.
Dalai Lama, H. H., & Cutler, H. (1998). *The art of happiness.* New York, NY: Riverhead Books.

Daston, L. (Ed.) (2000). *Biographies of scientific objects.* Chicago: The University of Chicago Press.

Day, G., & Thompson, A. (2004). *Theorizing nationalism.* Houndsmill, UK: Palgrave Macmillan.

Delanty, G., & O'Mahoney, P. (2002). *Nationalism and social theory.* Thousand Oaks, CA: Sage.

Deleuze, G., & Guattari, F. (1987). *A thousand plateaus: Capitalism and schizophrenia.* Minneapolis: The University of Minnesota Press.

Ellenberger, H. (1970). *The discovery of the unconscious: The history and evolution of dynamic psychiatry.* New York: Basic Books Publishers, Inc.

Foucault, M. (1970). *The order of things: An archaeology of the human sciences.* New York: Vintage Books.

Füredi, F. (1998). *The silent war: Imperialism and the changing perception of race.* London: Pluto Press.

James, W. (1909a/1986). Report on Mrs. Piper's Hodgson-control. In G. Murphy & R. O. Ballou (Eds.), *The works of William James: Essays in psychical research* (pp. 253–260). Cambridge, MA: Harvard University Press.

James, W. (1909b/1986). Confidences of a "psychical researcher" In G. Murphy & R. O. Ballou (Eds.), *The works of William James: Essays in psychical research* (pp. 367–375). Cambridge, MA: Harvard University Press.

James, W. (1986). *Essays in psychical research (The works of William James).* Cambridge, MA: Harvard University Press.

Jay, M. (1994). *Downcast eyes: The denigration of vision in twentieth-century French thought.* Berkeley: University of California Press.

Kallo, J. (2009). *OECD education policy: A comparative and historical study focusing on the thematic reviews of tertiary education.* Helsinki: FERA.

King, R. (2005). *Orientalism and religion: Postcolonial theory, India, and "the mystic East".* London: Routledge.

Kirk, D. (1992). *Defining physical education: The social construction of a school subject in postwar Britain.* London: Falmer

Lather, P. (2007). *Getting lost: Feminist efforts toward a double(d) science.* Albany, NY: SUNY Press.

Latour, B. (2004, winter). Why critique has run out of steam: From matters of fact to matters of concern. *Critical Inquiry, 30,* 225–248.

Levin, D. M. (Ed.). (1997). *Sites of vision: The discursive construction of sight in the history of philosophy.* Cambridge: MIT Press.

Locke, J. (1692/1989). *Some thoughts concerning education* (edited with introduction, notes, and critical apparatus by J. W. & J. S. Yolton). Oxford: Clarendon Press.

Locke, J. (1692/1975). *Essay concerning human understanding* (Originally published 1692–1700 ed.). Oxford: Clarendon Press.

Poyen St. Sauveur, C. (1837). *Progress of animal magnetism in New England, being a collection of experiments, reports, and certificates from the most respectable sources. Preceded by a dissertation on the proofs of animal magnetism.* Boston: Boston, Weeks, Jordan & Co.

Richardson, A. (2001). *British romanticism and the science of the mind.* Cambridge: Cambridge University Press.

Scarborough, M. (2009). *Comparative theories of nonduality: The search for the middle way.* London: Continuum.

Sells, M. (1994). *The mystical languages of unsaying.* Chicago: University of Chicago Press.

Stone, W. L. (1837). *Letter to Doctor A. Brigham on animal magnetism, being an account of a remarkable interview between the author and Miss Loraina Brackett while in a state of somnambulism.* New York: George Dearborn & Co.

Tait, G. (2011). *Philosophy, behavior disorder, and the school.* Rotterdam: Sense.

Taubman, P. (2009). *Teaching by numbers: Deconstructing the discourse of standards and accountability in education.* New York: Routledge.

Tyriakian, E. (Ed.). (1974). *On the margin of the visible: Sociology, the esoteric, and the occult.* New York: Wiley.

Wrigley, O. (1996) *The politics of Deafness.* Washington, DC: Gallaudet University Press.

Winichakul, T. (1994). *Siam mapped: A history of the geo-body of a nation.* Honolulu: University of Hawaii Press.

CHAPTER 3

# INTERSECTIONALITY AND THE PRODUCTION OF SPACE

## Lefebvre, Rhythmanalysis and Social Justice in Education

**Pam Christie**
*University of Cape Town, South Africa*

This chapter brings intersectionality approaches into conversation with a particular analysis of space and its social production. Its purpose in doing so is to contribute to debates on how we might best understand the multiple social processes that produce educational inequalities, with a view to working towards greater social justice. As theoretical approaches, both intersectionality and spatial analysis involve multi-stranded and complex debates, and bringing them together runs the risk of theoretical confusion. Nonetheless, the conversation I propose is intended to supplement the research approaches of intersectionality through a specific engagement with spatial theory.

To begin the engagement, a comment about intersectionality is appropriate. The growing literature on intersectionality illustrates a wide range of theoretical and conceptual differences, as well as differences in research approaches. The

*Intersectionality and Urban Education*, pages 65–75
Copyright © 2014 by Information Age Publishing
All rights of reproduction in any form reserved.

literature shows contours of debates marked by different contexts at different times. In spite of this wide variation, this literature does, nonetheless, address a common problematic. It recognizes that social inequalities are seldom unitary in their causes, manifestations and consequences, and—crucially—it positions itself against these inequalities and their perpetuation. How to understand and work against social inequalities in their complex conjunctions, multiple interactions and relational forms, is the major challenge that intersectionality poses for educational researchers (see Grant & Sleeter, 1986; Grant & Zwier, 2011).

In picking up this challenge, it is important to acknowledge at the outset that educational research in different contexts over many decades has recognized the impact of social inequality reverberating through schooling. The effects of family background, of socioeconomic status, of race, gender, ethnicity, home language, and so on have been extensively studied and debated. As early as the 1960s, large-scale reports (notably the U.S. Coleman Report and the U.K. Plowden Report) provided governments with evidence that the outcomes of schooling were unequal and that students' home backgrounds had profound effects on their life chances. In academia, there is a rich tradition of research and debate on educational inequality and how to understand it. From banks of statistical information documenting the performances of different student groupings, to ethnographic studies of students' and teachers' experiences of schooling, there are multiple empirical studies and theoretical debates around the inequalities that are evident in schooling. Since much of this work addresses multiple forms of inequality, it could, in loose terms, be considered as 'intersectional'. And in a country like South Africa, where multiple structural inequalities are obvious to any researcher of the education system—the effects of poverty, race, gender and location being too stark to overlook—the claim could be made that almost all research is 'intersectional' anyway.

In other words, given the corpus of existing research on educational inequality in its multiple forms, and the polysemic nature of intersectionality as a concept, there is a real possibility that 'intersectionality' could be recruited as a fashionable term, without being used to provide new and different insights. (The 'spatial turn' faces a similar challenge, lending itself to being fashionably mapped onto existing work without new insights being generated.) The challenge, then, is to go beyond description and metaphor to explore the analytical insights that intersectionality affords. It is in this spirit that I bring intersectionality into conversation with work of Henri Lefebvre on the production of space.

## THE JOURNEY TO SCHOOL

Imagine three young people taking a journey to school in the city of Cape Town, South Africa. Imagine that all three are black girls attending the same

English medium school in one of the 'leafy suburbs' below Table Mountain. The school was once a white school, but with the end of apartheid, it now takes students of all races. Schools like this are colloquially referred to as 'Model Cs', a term which seems neutral enough to this generation of students, but in fact signals their status as former white schools under apartheid. The first girl lives in the neighbourhood of the school. The trip to school takes ten minutes in her mother's car. The shopping centre where she buys her school supplies (and hangs out with her friends) is ten minutes away in the opposite direction. It's relatively easy for her to stay on after school and in the evenings to participate in the many activities the school offers. She wears the insult of 'coconut' as a badge of privilege, for she is indeed an economically privileged child of the post-apartheid era. The second girl lives in one of Cape Town's older black townships, a long way from the school in the suburb. To get to school, she walks from home to the taxi rank, where she joins a group of other students who take a minibus taxi to the school gates. There is no major shopping centre where she lives, so she goes to the city for her stationery and books. It isn't easy for her to stay on at school after the time that the taxi leaves to go back to the township. Walking home in the dark isn't an option for her. Violent sexual assault is a daily event in the township; girls are not safe' and there are regular hate attacks against gay people too. Sometimes she feels that she's a coconut, but that can be quite dangerous where she lives. The third girl came to Cape Town about five years ago from the impoverished rural area of the Eastern Cape, and is very fortunate to be able to go to the 'Model C' school. Before coming to Cape Town, she had seldom heard people speaking in English, and when she first came to town, the kids in the squatter camp of shacks where she lived teased her for her old-fashioned way of speaking her home language. She still lives in an 'informal settlement' not far from the formal township, but she is the only person who journeys from there to a 'Model C' school in the suburbs. She walks with her mother to take the train to the city, where they separate to take different buses from the city to the suburbs. They meet in the city at the end of the day to travel home together. There is no street lighting where she lives, and in winter she travels in the dark. Sometimes, when her mother can't travel with her, she feels too frightened to take the public transport by herself. But she's managed to learn English and do well enough to get a place in the Model C school—which is highly unusual—and her family sees schooling as the only way to break out of poverty and forge a life in the city.

What would be different if the three black girls were white boys? What if they were disabled? What if one were a lesbian? What if the school were not a suburban school but a township or rural school? The journey from home to school takes many different forms. Clearly, intersectionality would enable an analysis of these differences—differences that attest to multiple configurations of privilege and disadvantage, resulting in students having different experiences of school, different chances of success at school, and different opportunities in life after school. What a Lefebvrean analysis offers is a means of understanding the multiple activities that produce the different and unequal configurations of social space. First, the journey to school may be viewed as a set of everyday practices for students as they move from home to school and back. Secondly, the journey may be understood in terms of representations of space, with the routes taken by cars and trains represented in the maps of town planners and the designs of engineers—alongside the tracks and informal shortcuts taken by those on foot. Thirdly, the journey may be viewed through the imaginaries of students in their daily experiences of getting to school and back, their stories about their journeys, and the impressions they form of the world as they look through their different vehicle windows on the way to and from school.

This sketch of the journey to school is intended as an introduction to the possibilities of spatial analysis in intersectional work. In the section that follows, Lefebvre's approach to spatial analysis is set out.[1] As will be shown, this approach enables both a historical materialist analysis and a phenomenological one, as the world is apprehended as a multiplicity of intersecting and colliding rhythms, movements of space, time and energy.

## RHYTHMANALYSIS AND THE SOCIAL PRODUCTION OF SPACE

In his work entitled *The Production of Space* (1991), Lefebvre sets out an analysis of space as socially produced. He suggests that conceptions of physical space as 'nature' and 'cosmos', and mental conceptions of Euclidian geometry or 'empty' space, are examples of abstractions that mystify the myriad social activities that make up space. For Lefebvre, space should not be conceived of as a container that could be filled with separate things, potentially empty and inert. Rather, space should be analysed in terms of the social relations embedded within it. Every society, argues Lefebvre, produces its own space in the process of developing its means of subsistence in place and time. Social space comprises multiple forms of human existence: the specificities of geography (site, climate), remnants and traces of history, a variety of natural and social objects, pathways and networks of exchanges, relationships of production, forms of regulation, symbolic forms, art forms and so on. Lefebvre's theoretical challenge is to analyse the social production of space and to set out a unitary account—but not a single or unifying one—that links mental, physical and social notions of space. His aim is to explain how societies generate their social space and time, how history resonates into the present, and how materiality shapes activities. In his words:

Every social space is the outcome of a process with many aspects and many contributing currents, signifying and non-signifying, perceived and directly experienced, practical and theoretical. In short, every social space has a history, one invariably grounded in nature, in natural conditions that are at once primordial and unique in the sense that they are always and everywhere endowed with specific characteristics (site, climate, etc.). (1991, p. 110)

In analysing social space, Lefebvre proposes a triadic approach. Space is socially produced through three realms of activities: spatial practices (the perceived space of daily actions and routines in their materiality); representations of practice (the conceptualized space of town planners and architects) and representational practices (the experienced space of everyday life and the images it evokes). This triad of perceived-conceived-lived (or practical, symbolic and imaginary) provides an analytical frame in which space is not abstract but concrete, and must be understood in relation to the practices that produce it. It is this framework that was used in the brief sketches provided above of the journey to school.

Lefebvre's analysis brings out the dynamic nature of social space. Social space consists of webs of relationships that are actively produced and reproduced in time. The notion of assemblage is one of simultaneity and encounter:

> But what assembles, or what is assembled? The answer is: everything that there is *in space*, everything that is produced either by nature or by society, either through their co-operation or through their conflicts. Everything: living beings, things, objects, works, signs and symbols. . . . (1991, p. 101)

All interactions of space, time and energy produce rhythms of different sorts. Social space is always traversed by myriad currents and rhythms which embrace 'individual entities and peculiarities, relatively fixed points, movements, and flows and waves—some interpenetrating, others in conflict and so on' (1991, p. 88). Spatial practices are polyrhythmic, and these rhythms may cut across, interrupt or be interrupted by each other in a hypercomplexity that is not simply random. The *places* of social space may be superimposed upon and intercalated, but the local never disappears even as regions and nations configure and reconfigure.

In *Rhythmanalysis* (1994), Lefebvre develops an account of the production of space through the interplay of multiple, simultaneous, intertwining and crosscutting rhythms. These are movements of repetition and difference, cyclical rhythms of the cosmos and linear rhythms of machines and production, intimate individual rhythms and state-political rhythms of public life. The rhythms of social space begin in the body—rhythms of breathing and heartbeat, sleeping and waking, eating and excreting, and so on. In close relation to the natural rhythms of seasons, tides and skies, rhythms of social life are experienced, conceived and represented, some easily identifiable, some hard to discern. These rhythms are lived and experienced subjectively and in the body, such that 'the body consists in a bundle of rhythms' (1994, p. 80). Each bundle of natural rhythms 'wraps itself in rhythms of social and mental function' (1994, p. 9) to produce the polyrhythms of daily life in particular place and time. Rhythmanalysis provides the methodology for 'opening and unwrapping' these bundles.

Rhythmanalysis entails, as its central activity, close ethnographic attention to everyday life. This is well illustrated in two evocative sections of *Rhythmanalysis* (2004), the Paris street 'Seen from the window', and 'The Rhythmanalysis of Mediterranean Cities'. These sections show how rhythmanalysis combines sensory with interpretive activity, seeking to listen not only to 'words, discourses, noises and sounds' but also 'to a house, a street, a town, as one listens to a symphony, an opera' (2004, p. 87). Ethnographic methods are accompanied by attention to rhythms and associations beyond the immediate, to patterns of historical geography, and to activities not necessarily evident in the moment. It is not hard to imagine, in reading these accounts, how schools would lend themselves to Lefebvrean analysis of the social production of space. Bundles of rhythms in patterns of repetition and difference, within and beyond the school, would provide rich terrain for investigating the social production of space.

## INTERSECTIONALITY AND THE PRODUCTION
## OF SPACE IN EDUCATION

In relation to intersectionality, Lefebvre's spatial analytic offers a number of points of engagement, three of which are addressed here. First, a spatial analysis brings particular perspectives on materiality to intersectional research. The different social activities that produce space are also activities that produce intersectional inequalities. Mapping these spatial inequalities may serve to supplement other analyses of social inequalities—though not necessarily to replace them (since it would be unhelpful to collapse everything into 'space'). Secondly, the particular triadic analytic that Lefebvre offers is a systematic approach to untangling the multiple activities that produce the inequalities of social space. Thirdly, an analysis of space using Lefebvre's approach enables different scales to be worked with simultaneously, without collapsing one into the other. Each of these three points will be expanded, in the context of intersectional inequalities in education.

## Mapping Spatial Inequalities

The notion of space as actively produced within social relations of production de-naturalises the inequalities of space and place, while also allowing the importance of historical geographies to be recognised. Cities with their wealthy suburbs and their ghettos, their industries and their market places, their rituals and symbols, are also specific places or sites where space is perceived, represented and experienced in distinctive ways. In rural areas, the carvings of land ownership and practices of exploitation and extraction are also distinctively produced in specific social relationships in time and place.

Schooling itself forms part of the production of space. Paying attention to the activities that produce schools in social space enables different considerations to be addressed and redressed. The location of schools in specific places, their differential levels of material resourcing, their architecture relating to their social status, their symbols and rituals, their patterns of teaching and learning, their regulation of bodily movements in differential ways—these may all be understood as aspects of the production of social space. Spatial materiality matters a great deal in explaining social inequalities, including inequalities in education. It is no coincidence that many 'disadvantaged schools' and 'poorly performing schools' are schools in poorer parts of towns or economically depressed parts of the countryside. These schools are socially produced along with the spaces in which they are located. The same is true of schools serving social elites. Tracing the spatial activities that produce inequalities in schooling enables a particular approach to understanding how intersectional inequalities are produced and how they may be worked against. The journey to school in Cape Town provides a small illustration of the effects of historical and contemporary geographies in the unequal social relations of contemporary South Africa. In South Africa, the location of schools, their specific architectures, their facilities and the conditions of their classrooms are obvious surface indicators of the depth of enduring historical inequalities. In urban areas, the desegregation of schooling has enabled social class to take over from race for some people in what remains a deeply unequal system. Rural schools remain the most poorly served on every score. And intersectional relations of gender are evident across all sites.

## Activities of Spatial Production

Turning to the second point above, Lefebvre's schema of activities that produce space offers a systematic framework for analysis of space as perceived, conceived, and experienced. Space as continuous encounter brings an unremitting materiality to be disentangled in its practical, symbolic and imaginary forms.

Again, the journey to school illustrates these different activities, providing an example of how Lefebvre's approach may be put to work in understanding the inequalities of schooling. As well as the activities of the daily journey, there are the specific routines that characterise the everyday activities of schools, evident particularly in the divisions and demarcations of time and place. There are the linear rhythms of the school year: the annual change of grade; term time interspersed with vacation time; weekly cycles; daily timetables. Routines of time and place bring bodies together and apart in formalised behaviour in demarcated spaces: classrooms, staffrooms, 'the office', 'the foyer', 'the playground'. Repetitive activities 'break in' the bodies of students so that they learn social rituals—a practice that Lefebvre (2004, p. 39) refers to as '*dressage*'. Predictable as these time-space activities are, they are also highly specific; each school has its own particular ways of doing things. Taken together, these may be understood as some of the perceived activities that produce schools as social spaces.

Then there are the representations of schooling: the recognizable architecture of schools, with variations reflecting resource levels; the planning of schools to fit their purposes and their environments; the representation of schools, teachers and students in policies of all sorts; the differential attention given to centres and margins. Then there are the everyday lived experiences of schools for teachers, students and parents; their experiences of familiarity or strangeness with what schools do; their memories and their aspirations; their bodily responses and their emotions; their knowledge of the nooks and crannies, shortcuts, sounds and smells of the school as a particular place. These three sets of activities (practical, symbolic and imaginary) produce the social spaces of schools in their specific sites, their local communities and their broader social relations. These activities are also intertwined with patterns of intersectional inequalities.

## Scales of Spatial Production

The third affordance of using Lefebvre's approach to engage with intersectionality is that it enables different scales to be worked with in a single framework. Space-as-encounter enables different rhythms and flows to be explored as simultaneous, interweaving, crosscutting, reinforcing and interrupting. Global, national, regional and local currents of activities may be understood as rhythms that match and clash in a complexity that is not simply random. In this approach, intersectionality is not a matter of structural determinism, sedimented in silos or layers; it is a matter of activities in the different rhythms and encounters of social space. Each scale or site of practice does not supersede another or eliminate it; multiple logics of different scales and sites coexist in complex interplays of encounter. These may be analysed, in Lefebvre's triadic approach, in terms of the particular activities, representations and experiences that make up the production of space at different scales or sites.

A triadic analysis of the production of spatial inequalities (including their historical geographies), how they are represented (mapped and charted), and the everyday experiences of spatial inequalities (including bodily, natural and social rhythms), brings a theoretical coherence across geography, political economy, society and culture in understanding the historical production of enduring social patterns of inequality. An analysis of social space may include historical forms and current practices in specific sites and climates, latent and dynamic forces, intimate experiences and state-political regulations, patterns of work and recreation, symbolic and material. This hypercomplexity of social space is rendered intelligible through an analysis of the activities that produce it.

## INTERSECTIONALITY, SPACE AND INEQUALITIES IN SCHOOLING

As mentioned at the start of this chapter, interest in intersectionality has burgeoned conceptually and methodologically in recent years. Within this literature, it is interesting to note several significant triadic frameworks that may be used alongside Lefebvre's. Notably, the praxeological approach of Gabriele Winker and Nina Degele (2011) proposes three levels for intersectional investigation: social structures at macro and meso levels, processes of identity construction, and cultural/representational processes. In a different theorization, Ina Kerner (2012) uses Foucault's analytics of power to differentiate heuristically between epistemic, institutional and personal dimensions of power/knowledge (in other words, discursive formations, institutional patterns and subject formation). These two approaches suggest the need for clear analytical frameworks—and frameworks of different sorts—to address the complexities of intersectionality in systematic ways.

A conversation with spatial analysis brings a particular set of concepts into play for intersectional consideration, notably concepts of materiality, place, assemblage and encounter (see Thrift, 2006). In this conversation, Lefebvre's work on the social production of space provides a particular form of engagement. As I have noted, the activities that produce social space are inevitably intersectional, and lend themselves to intersectional investigation. The engagement of intersectionality and spatial analysis may be beneficial in both directions, as theories developed in intersectional research are woven into spatial analysis, and intersectional inequalities are traced in the production of space.

In terms of educational inequalities and social justice, an intersectional analysis of the production of schools as social spaces has the potential to open up different agendas for consideration. In saying this, it is important to revisit the points made about existing research on educational inequality. First, in the face of much existing research, it would be unwise to assume that the knotty problems of social injustice are amenable to simple disentangling through intersectional approaches and spatial analysis. That said, the persistence of intersectional inequalities means that the ethical challenge of working for greater social justice remains. In recognizing this, Foucault's perspectives are useful: that power relations are inevitable, but their forms are not. Power generates resistance, and there are always cracks and fractures to push against. An understanding of the multiple activities that produce schools as social spaces—and spaces of intersectional inequality—provides particular opportunities for interrupting and working 'against the flow'. There are always opportunities to strive for greater social justice in education, and an analysis of the production of social space opens different possibilities in the broad intersectional research agenda in education.

## NOTE

1. As well as Lefebvre's own texts, this section is informed by the works of Elden (2004), Jacklin (2004), and Schmid (2008). In the South African context, Dixon (2011), Fataar (2007) and Jacklin (2004) have made important contributions to understanding space and education, while Christie (2012) provides an accompanying analysis.

## REFERENCES

Christie, P. (2012, July). *Framing the field of affordances: Space, place and social justice in education in South Africa.* Paper presented at the international seminar on Space, Place and Social Justice in Education, Manchester Metropolitan University, 13.

Dixon, K. (2011). *Literacy, power, and the schooled body: Learning in time and space.* New York: Routledge.

Elden, S. (2004). *Understanding Henri Lefebvre: Theory and the possible.* London: New York: Continuum.

Fataar, A. (2007). Educational renovation in a South African 'township on the move': A social-spatial analysis. *International Journal of Educational Development, 27,* 599–612.

Grant, C. A., & Sleeter, C. E. (1986). Race, class, and gender in education research. *Review of Educational Research, 56*(2), 195–211.

Grant, C. A., & Zwier, E. (2011). Intersectionality and student outcomes: Sharpening the struggle against racism, sexism, classism, ableism, heterosexism, nationalism, and linguistic, religious, and geographical discrimination in teaching and learning. *Multicultural Perspectives, 13*(4), 181–188.

Jacklin, H. (2004). *Repetition and difference: A rhythm analysis of pedagogic practice.* Unpublished doctoral thesis, University of the Witwatersrand.

Kerner, I. (2012). Questions of intersectionality: Reflections on the current debate in German gender studies. *European Journal of Women's Studies, 19*(2), 203–281.

Lefebvre, H. (1991). *The production of space.* (Trans. D. Nicholson-Smith.) Oxford: Blackwell.

Lefebvre, H. (2004). *Rhythmanalysis: Space, time and everyday life.* (Trans. S. Elden, & G. Moore.) London: Continuum.

Schmid, C. (2008). Henri Lefebvre's theory of the production of space: Towards a three-dimensional dialectic. In K. Goonewardena, S. Kipfer, R. Milgram, & C. Schmid (Eds.), *Space, difference, everyday life: Reading Henri Lefebvre* (pp. 27–45). New York: Routledge.

Thrift, N. (2006). Space. *Theory, culture and society, 23*(2–3), 139–155.

Winker, G., & Degele, N. (2011) Intersectionality as multi-level analysis: Dealing with social inequality. *European Journal of Women's Studies, 18*(1), 51–66.

# PART II

## EDUCATION IN URBAN SCHOOLS AND COMMUNITIES

CHAPTER 4

# INTERSECTIONALITY AND THE STATUS OF BLACK MALES

## Risk, Resilience, and Response

**Pedro A. Noguera**
**Tonya Leslie**
*New York University*

On February 26, 2012 an unarmed male teenager named Trayvon Martin was fatally shot by 28-year old George Zimmerman, a volunteer on neighborhood watch patrol. Trayvon Martin was Black, and George Zimmerman was initially described by police as "White" (Zimmerman is in fact half Latino). The killing, which generated a national wave of protests because Zimmerman had not been charged with a crime by the police or local prosecutors for over a month after the killing, fit into a well-established narrative in America's long troubled history of race relations (Legum, 2012). While the details of the incident are still emerging, and the trial of George Zimmerman will occur after this paper is published, it is clear is that Zimmerman deemed Martin's mere presence in his gated community as "suspicious."

*Intersectionality and Urban Education*, pages 79–96
Copyright © 2014 by Information Age Publishing
All rights of reproduction in any form reserved.

Zimmerman justified his pursuit of the teenager on the grounds that he posed a "threat." He followed the teen, even after he was instructed by the police not to do so, first in his vehicle, then on foot, and eventually confronted him. A physical conflict between Zimmerman and Martin ensued and resulted in the shooting death of the teen. Conflicting stories from witnesses made it difficult to determine exactly what had occurred; in the darkness, nothing was clear. However, in the aftermath the police determined that Martin had a right to be in the area (he was visiting his uncle) and was not involved in any criminal activity. In fact, the only items Martin carried were a can of Arizona Iced Tea, $40 and change, a red lighter, and a now iconic bag of skittles (Treyvon Martin Case, 2012). Surveillance video from the local convenience store shows Martin purchasing these items while wearing a gray hooded sweatshirt, also known as a "hoodie," shortly before his encounter with Zimmerman.

The killing of unarmed Black men is hardly a new or unusual phenomenon. Young Black men between the ages of 16 and 25 die in greater numbers, most often by violence and typically at the hands of other Black men, than any other segment of the US population (Greenberg & Schneider, 1994; Violence Poverty Center, 2007). The Trayvon Martin killing stood out because it followed another pattern: Black men killed by police or vigilantes because they are presumed to constitute a threat. In just the last few years, stories of unarmed Black men such as Oscar Grant in Oakland and Sean Bell in New York, being killed by police officers for "brandishing" items as banal as a cell phone, candy bar or wallet (Associated Press, 2007) have become all too common. The idea that Black men are inherently dangerous, pose a threat and must be controlled and contained has deep roots in American history (Fogel, 1989). Even now, as a Black man serves as president of the United States, images and stereotypes of Black men as thugs and predators are pervasive in American media and popular culture (Ford Foundation, 2007). Throughout America's history, Black males have been characterized and depicted as threats to the social order and the very personification of violence. Hundreds of Black men were lynched by White vigilantes in the aftermath of slavery, and that bloody record is perhaps the most vivid reminder that the Trayvon Martin killing has a very disturbing precedent in America's history (Brown, 2011).

The Treyvon Martin case compels us to consider how social identities tied to race, gender and class frame the ways in which Black men are "seen" and inform our national narratives about victims and victimization. Understanding the dynamic ways in which race, gender and class interact and intersect is important for examining the experience of Black males. No other segment of the U.S. population is as likely to be subject to incarceration, school failure, persistent unemployment, or an early death.[1] Nor is there any other group that is as likely to be castigated, shunned and vilified

(Gibbs 1988; Waters, 1990). Low-income Black males, constitute a pariah group in American society, and because of their status, relatively little public concern has been generated over their plight. Understanding why and how Black males have come to be so marginalized is important particularly for educators, who are charged with supporting and nurturing the intellectual and social development of Black males. More often than not, schools are the places where marginalization of Black males begins. Educators, policy makers and parents who are serious about finding solutions to the challenges confronting Black males must first understand how they, and Black males themselves, may be implicated in perpetuating these hardships.

In this paper, we examine how the educational and social experiences of Black males from low-income communities are shaped by structural and cultural forces that operate at the micro, meso and macro levels of interaction (Bronfenbrenner, 1975). Institutionalized racism, economic marginalization, mass incarceration and gender socialization within schools, families and communities, work in concert to perpetuate the status and the vulnerability of Black males in American society. Understanding how this occurs is critical if we are to figure out how to craft solutions to the broad array of challenges they face. Though in recent years there have been growing calls for action to be taken to address the plight of Black males (Fergus & Noguera, 2011), in many communities and schools throughout the United States, the failure of Black males is so pervasive and persistent that it has been normalized; it is increasingly accepted as a permanent part of the American social fabric. It is undoubtedly for this reason that the mass incarceration of Black males documented in such vivid detail by Michelle Alexander in her book, *The New Jim Crow* (2010), has generated so little of a response from policy makers (Noguera, 2003).

In this paper we present a conceptual framework for understanding the nature of the *risks* confronting Black males and the underlying causes of the problems that so frequently beset them. We also discuss why it is important that Black men not be framed merely as victims of injustice and indifferent institutions, and the social processes that contribute to *resilience* and success. Our purpose in presenting such an analysis is to assist educators, parents, policymakers and other potential "allies" who would like to develop measures to *respond* and counter the ominous trends that affect Black males to be equipped with a framework that will be useful in crafting programs and interventions. Such a framework must be capable of deconstructing the interlocking categories that Black males exist within—race, class and gender—so that we may achieve what Patricia Hill Collins (1989) calls new ways of thinking accompanied by new ways of acting. This will hopefully allow us to avoid static and simplistic representations of Blackness and lead us to more holistic solutions. As we will show, despite the broad array of hardships that beset Black men and boys, framing them either as victims or victimizers is too simplistic and one dimensional to explain why they occupy the particular status they hold in American society. It is only by fully embracing the complexity related to their social identities that interventions can be devised and the institutions that serve them, particularly schools, can be transformed. To begin to counter the formidable obstacles confronting them, sophisticated support systems must be put in place so that it will be possible for Black males to thrive and advance. We assert that an intersectional approach that acknowledges the complex dynamics between race, gender and social class, is essential to devising such supports.

## UNDERSTANDING THE RISKS

On all of the indicators of academic achievement, educational attainment and school success, Black males are distinguished from other segments of the American population by their consistent clustering in categories associated with failure (Schott Foundation, 2010). In most schools and districts throughout the United States, African American, and in many cases Latino males, are overrepresented in educational categories typically associated with failure and sub-par academic performance. Similarly, on those indicators that are associated with success—enrollment in honors or gifted classes, advanced placement courses, college enrollment and degree attainment, etc.—Black and Latino males are vastly under-represented. In cities across the United States, less than half of all African American males graduate from high school (47%), and those that do are less likely to go to college (Schott Foundation, 2010) than other students. Nationally, African American and Latino males are more likely than any other group to be suspended and expelled from school and more likely to rank at the bottom on most indicators of academic performance in most subjects. It is worth noting that Trayvon Martin, who has been described as likeable and kind by teachers and friends was suspended at the time of his shooting and had been suspended at least three previous times for incidents ranging from possible drug possession to lateness.[2]

Despite their importance and relevance to academic performance, risk variables and statistics do not by themselves explain these patterns much less individual behavior. The fact is, some Black males are at greater risk than others. While there is evidence that the achievement of middle class Black males typically lags behind that of their White middle class counterparts (Ferguson, 2001), in most cases, the privileges associated with class do accrue to middle class Black males and buttress them from the hardships that are more common among their lower class counter parts. Middle class Black males are more likely to come from families where fathers are present and are more likely to have strong relationships with caring adults who act as advocates and mentors (National Fatherhood Initiative, 2012). Research suggests that social capital generated through strong, positive relationships with family, friends, teachers and coaches can serve as protective factors that shield young Black men from the well known risks (Thomas & Stevenson, 2009). Black males from low-income households and communities are less likely to have access to such support systems and more likely to have opportunities for mobility and success denied to them early on. Consider the fact that low-income Black males have the highest infant mortality rates and are more likely than any other segment of the population to be categorized as mentally retarded in school (Office of Minority Health, 2010). Furthermore, failure rates for Black males (and females in many cases) are much higher in schools where poverty rates are high and resources are limited (Noguera & Wing, 2008).

One of the reasons why dropout and failure rates for low-income Black males is so high is because they are more likely to be concentrated in chronically under-performing schools located in neighborhoods where poverty is concentrated (Bowen, Bowen, & Ware, 2002). These are the schools that Education Secretary Arne Duncan has described as "dropout factories" and the neighborhoods that sociologist William Julius Wilson described as home to the "truly disadvantaged" (Wilson, 1987). Several researchers have documented how failure in such schools is often "normalized" by the indifference of the school districts that serve them and the dysfunctional cultures that too often are allowed to flourish there (Maeroff 1988; Payne 1984; Noguera, 2003). More often than not, such schools are characterized by strained relationships between educators and students, poor leadership due in part to high turnover among principals, an unwillingness among teachers to collaborate and to take responsibility for learning outcomes, a lack of discipline and motivation among students, and a lack of safety (Bauer, Guerino, Nolle, & Tang, 2008). While failure rates are understandably high for all students enrolled in such schools they tend to be highest for Black and in many cases Latino males (Mincy, Martin, Noguera, Zilanawala & Fergus, 2010; Karp, 2009). Understanding how school dysfunction contributes to the high rates of failure among Black males and the emergence of what several scholars have described as a "school to prison pipeline" (Losen & Orfield, 2002; Nolan, 2011), is critical for developing interventions.

In addition to the vulnerabilities associated with class status, empirical research also suggests that race and gender are equally important to understanding the problems that beset Black males. Black males are substantially more likely than Black females to be placed in special education (Losen & Orfield, 2002), to be suspended or expelled (Gregory, Skiba, & Noguera 2010; Krezmien, Leone, & Achilles, 2006), and to dropout or be pushed out of school (Meade, Gaytan, & Noguera,2009). They are also more likely than girls to express a sense of disaffection from school and from learning generally (Pollard, 1993).

Ethnographic research carried out within schools suggest that many of the behaviors that are more frequently associated with males, namely disruption, defiance and disengagement, are frequently cited by educators as the reason for Black males being subjected to a disproportionate number of negative sanctions (Pollack 2004; Carter, 2005; Noguera & Wing, 2008). This does not necessarily mean that other groups of students (e.g., Latinos, Whites, Asians, and girls generally) do not exhibit such behaviors. Rather, the research suggests that when challenging behaviors are exhibited by males of color they are more likely to result in a more severe response (Dance, 2002). In her important book entitled *Bad Boys* (2001), Ann Ferguson utilizes her extensive ethnographic research to demonstrate that the Black male students were more likely to be labeled as "slow," "unruly" or generally problematic by teachers and administrators. Rather than such labels resulting in greater support or the application of effective early interventions, Ferguson found that they were more likely to result in the labels being internalized by the students upon whom they had been affixed (Ferguson, 2001).

It is for these reasons that we argue that any effort to intervene to counter the negative trends associated with Black males must be rooted in an understanding of the ways in which race, class and gender interact to shape the nature of the risks that beset this group. Before we can take action to "save" Black males we have to understand what it is about being Black, male and low-income in America that places so many young men at risk. Without a clear and accurate understanding of the nature of the risks they confront the policies and interventions that are devised are not only unlikely to result in lasting solutions, they may even exacerbate the problem.

An example of how this may occur may be helpful to illustrate this point. About ten years ago, a middle school that we have worked with in northern California decided that it would create a separate classroom for its most difficult and troubled students in response to requests for assistance by teachers (Noguera, 2003). The teachers complained that their efforts to raise achievement levels were being thwarted by the misbehavior of a small but highly problematic group of students. In response to their request for help the superintendent asked the teachers to identify the most troubled students. Once identified, the students were placed in a separate classroom with a specially trained teacher. At the time the initiative was announced parents of the identified students were told that their children would be provided with additional resources in the form of tutors and mentors. They were also told that in order to be "helped" their children would be isolated from their peers, have a separate lunch period, and a different schedule so that they would not interfere with the rest the school.

The teachers proceeded to identify their "worst" students, and in this racially diverse school of six hundred students, a list of the twenty-four most difficult—all of whom were African American males—was generated. To meet their special needs a teacher was assigned to the school to work with the students. He too was a Black male but as it turned out, he was new and inexperienced. In fact, it appeared that the only qualification he had for doing this sort of work was that he was formerly a college football player who was quite large and physically intimidating. The students and their parents were told that the supports that were promised would eventually be made available to them.

Within a few days of being assigned to the classroom the behavior of the students took a turn for the worst. They quickly understood that their placement in this special room was not an opportunity but rather a means to isolate them from their peers. They took their resentment out on their teacher, and before long, serious conflicts ensued. However, the most interesting thing about this story is what occurred in the other classrooms. Rather than resulting in a safer and more orderly learning environment, teachers reported that the removal of the so-called troublemakers led to the emergence of new students who were equally as difficult to manage. Several teachers suggested that yet another classroom should be set up for troubled students to solve this problem.

What is most telling about this experience is how quickly all parties involved assumed that the cause of the problem was the individual students. Completely overlooked in their analysis of the problem was the fact that some of the teachers at the school had no trouble managing the behavior of the students who had been identified. In their desire to address the problem of classroom disorder they assumed that the problem resided in the students alone and not with their teachers or in the learning environment itself.

This example is important because there are undeniable parallels between the problems confronting young Black males within schools, and the problems confronting adult Black males in society. In response to the fear of crime, Black males have been incarcerated at a rate that far exceeds their percentage of the U.S. population (Alexander, 2010). While some of those incarcerated have been sentenced for committing violent crimes, the vast majority have been put away for drug related offenses, often for longer sentences than White males charged with similar offenses (Alexander, 2010). Even at a time when crime rates in many cities are at historically low levels, incarceration rates for Black males have barely begun to decline (Gopnik 2012).

Mass incarceration like the excessively high suspension rates meted out upon Black and in many cases Latino males, have been largely accepted as necessary (Losen, Martinez, & Gillespie, 2012). Because Black males are the embodiment of America's greatest fears, their arrest or suspension from school is often rationalized as necessary for the well-being of others. The consequences of this type of targeting are devastating for Black men and boys. Black males who dropout, or in many cases are pushed out (Fine, 1991) of school, are more likely to be unemployed or to be permanently relegated to low wage jobs. In most cities across the United States, Black males have the highest rates of unemployment (Moss, Phillip, & Tilly, 1993), even during periods of prosperity (Stoll, Holzer, & Ihlanfeldt, 2000). The prison population in the United States is not only made up of a disproportionate number of Black males, but the vast majority of those who are incarcerated have weak literacy skills, high rates of learning disabilities, and in many cases, their delinquency was first exhibited within school (Alexander, 2010). More often than not, we disproportionately incarcerate those we have failed to educate (Gregory, 1997). Researchers from John Jay School of Criminal Justice have coined the term "million dollar blocks" to describe neighborhoods in cities from which the vast majority of the prison population is drawn (Clear, 2007). In such neighborhoods, vast sums of public funds are expended to pay for the incarceration of Black men while other services—parks, libraries, health clinics, etc. are cut or inadequately funded. For these reasons, understanding how the U.S. economy and public institutions like schools influence the marginalization of Black males from low-income communities is essential. Black males are more likely than other segments of the U.S. population to experience a broad array of negative outcomes including a declining life expectancy (Office of Minority Health, 2010). Understanding why these risks exists and why so many Black males are vulnerable in so many ways is an essential first step that must be taken before strategies are devised that might begin to counter them.

Yet, it would be a mistake to frame Black males as merely victims of a racist and indifferent system. Many of the behaviors that get Black males into trouble in school—fighting , defying authority figures or selling drugs—are venerated in the popular media and often generate a sense of admiration and even envy from peers (Majors & Billson, 1992). To provide an example, a recent article appearing in the New York Times suggested that because the rapper known as Jay-Z (aka Shawn Carter) was a product of the Marcy Houses (a low-incoming housing project in Brooklyn) and had an early career as a drug dealer, his credibility as a new co-owner of the Nets basketball team was "indisputable" (Halbfinger, 2012). Jay-Z's collaborators in this business venture include Bruce Ratner, a multi-million dollar businessman, Mikhail Prokhorov a Russian businessman, and Robert Rubin, the former Secretary of the Treasury under President Bill Clinton. The fact that such prominent and powerful individuals are happy to be associated with Jay-Z because of the "street cred" he brings to their business venture speaks to the complexity of the images surrounding Black males.

Bad boys may get into trouble in school but bad boys are also looked up to if they are fighters like the boxer Mike Tyson (who is now appearing in a Broadway show about his life and was also from a public housing project in Brooklyn), a professional basketball player like Allen Iverson (who was arrested several times and raised by a single mother in Newport News, Virginia), or a rapper like Jay-Z, Lil' Wayne, and a host of others. They are not only looked up to by other Black males but by other segments of the broader society. When confined to familiar roles as athletes and entertainers, Black males and the stereotypes that might otherwise undermine them had they not achieved fame and fortune, are valorized and in some contexts, even idolized. Homi Bhaba, the well known cultural theorist, explains this phenomenon. He reminds us that in societies characterized by domination and oppression it is not uncommon for the subaltern, those who are shunned and treated as objects of fear and scorn, to also become objects of desire (Bhaba, 1983). Phobia and fetish exist in tandem as two sides of the same coin.

It is for this reason it would be a mistake to merely characterize Black males as victims. Like the working class lads in Paul Willis' important book *Learning to Labor*, some Black males embrace the stereotypes that have been foisted upon them and they becomes participants in self sabotage (Willis, 1981) and their own marginalization. As more information about Trayvon Martin is revealed the first image of the innocent boy taken when he was fourteen years old, the image that prompted President Obama to say that "If I had a son he would have looked like Trayvon" (Mackey, 2012), has been replaced by images of an older, angrier young man with a grill (the metallic frames often wore by rappers on their teeth). To the beholder, such images suggest that Trayvon may not have merely been an innocent victim after all but may in fact have been a person whose very presence might arouse fear and suspicion. The image does not change the facts of the case nor justify the killing, but it does introduce an element of complexity that cannot be ignored. If we are to fully understand how Black men are seen by others (including even other Black men) and how they in turn may see themselves in a society where being ordinary or even invisible (Ellison, 1995) is rarely possible for Black men, then we must be willing to acknowledge the ways in which the framing of Black masculinity has conditioned some Black males to accept the roles that society has assigned to them.

## FROM RISK TO RESILIENCE

What is missing from much of the research and many of the investigations on the status and academic orientations of Black male students is a critical analysis of the ways in which the subjective and objective dimensions of identity related to race, class and gender are constructed—within schools and society—and how these in turn influence academic performance and social behavior. Developmental psychologists who have carried out the bulk of the empirical and theoretical research in this area, have generally conceived of racial identity construction as a natural feature of human development; one that occurs through a series of stages (Phinney, 1989; Cross,1991). Missing from much of this of research is an awareness of the ways in which social context, social class and the cultural factors that give meaning to identity interact. Without a more complex, robust and nuanced understanding of the ways in which various social forces interact to construct social identities, we are less able to understand why certain individuals may be at greater risk than others.

For example, in his ground breaking study of openly gay, back male high school students, Lance McCready (2009) discovered that by violating social norms associated with sexuality, the individuals he studied were also more likely to violate and undermine the deeply entrenched stereotypes associated with Black males (McCready, 2009). McCready found that as they embrace a status related to their sexuality that places them at the margins of their peer groups, these individuals were more likely to open themselves up to engaging in activities that were at odds with the stereotypes associated with their status as Black males, such as modern dance and theater. McCready found that by subverting the tropes of Black male identity and participating in these unconventional activities, new possibilities for success were open to them. McCready makes it clear that Black males who defy narrowly constructed masculine identities place themselves at risk and frequently experience considerable stress as a result of the ostracism, bullying and harassment they endure. Sociologist Michael Kimmel reminds us that more often than not, masculinity is performed by males for males (Kimmel, 2009), and the hierarchies males create to establish dominance often have the effect of narrowing the types of identities men and boys can experience. McCready's research shows us that as Black males transcend the narrow confines of the Black male identity that are deeply entrenched within the schools they attend, new identities and unforeseen advantages, including a greater likelihood to succeed in school, become available.

In a similar vein, research on stereotype threats by Claude Steele and Joshua Aronson (1995) has shown how subjective awareness of the stereotypes and stigmas associated with particular social identities contributes to the under-performance of vulnerable individuals during periods when academic performance is being assessed, such as testing. The research on the prevalence of stereotype threats is extremely compelling. It shows that at an unconscious level, individuals are highly aware of the stereotypes associated with their group. It also shows that the effects of these stereotypes are context specific. Blacks are more likely to experience stereotype threats in predominantly White settings, while Whites are more likely to experience stereotype threats on math assessments when tested with large numbers of Asians. The interesting thing about this research is that both Steele and Aronson have found that the stress that tends to accompany stereotype threats and which often undermines academic performance can be countered by measures that offset the stigma associated with the stereotypes (Graham, & Lowery, 2004).

Recently, researcher Shaun Harper looked at the factors that contribute to Black male student success in higher education (Harper, 2012). His research identified the resources Black male college students draw upon to be successful such as: developing close ties with a mentor who knows and understands the institution, seeking assistance early before major academic problems develop, maintaining strong relationships with families and friends outside of the college who support emotional and psychological well-being. The findings from his research suggest that these students stand out from their less successful peers because of their ability to utilize their social networks. Harper has also found that these "achievers" also overwhelmingly subscribed to definitions of masculinity that—contrary to other literature about Black boys—did not focus on athletic ability or sexual attractiveness to women, but rather on leadership, achievement and personal responsibility (Harper, 2012). While the vast majority of Black males in Harper's research are from affluent backgrounds, understanding how they navigate the challenges they face within academia can help educators to have a clearer sense of the kinds of support systems that may be necessary for low-income Black males who have even less access to protective support systems.

These examples show us that the other side of risk and vulnerability can be well-being and resilience. Researchers who have studied the factors that contribute to resilience among students have found that they are more likely to have developed particular attitudinal and behavioral characteristics that distinguish them from others, namely: the ability to persist when confronted with adversity, the ability to seek help when needed, the ability to maintain a positive outlook, and the ability to defer gratification when pursuing long term goals (APA 2008; Tough 2012). The implications of this and the related research we have presented is clear: educators and service providers who adopt strategies for cultivating such traits within their Black male students are more likely to help Black males become resilient and successful.

However, while focusing on the needs of individual students is important, it is equally important to focus on transforming the schools and institutions that serve them. The two strategies must go hand in hand. It is not sufficient to provide mentoring, counseling and support aimed at cultivating the traits we have described if we are ignoring the pernicious effects of stereotypes that are present in the media, popular culture and society as a whole. If the environment they are socialized within remains hostile and toxic and continues to place many of them at risk, it is unlikely that more than just a few Black boys will have a chance to be successful in life.

In an important article on the factors contributing to the unusually high homicide rates of Black males, sociologists Greenberg and Schneider (1994) pose the provocative question: "Young Black men are the answer but what was the question?" Through their examination of the social conditions in neighborhoods in New Jersey where Black men are killed at the highest rates (most often by other Black men), the authors point out that the likelihood of being murdered is highly correlated with residing in areas where "jobs are scarce and the environment is toxic" (1994, p. 37). This example, like the case of the middle school in Northern California, reminds us that it is not sufficient to focus on the behavior of Black males, even when that behavior in question is extremely dangerous. Rather, we must be equally concerned about transforming the neighborhoods and schools where Black males are educated and raised so that positive relationships and opportunities are the norm rather than the exception. As we show in the final section of this paper, where this is being done it is possible to significantly increase the number of Black males who not only avoid the hardships and risks experienced by other Black males, but also to enhance their chance of experiencing success in school and in life. In the final section of this paper we begin to describe how this might be done.

## CRAFTING AN EFFECTIVE RESPONSE

As we have shown throughout this paper, structural and cultural forces work in complex and dynamic ways to influence the formation of individual and collective identities. Returning to the example of Trayvon Martin, his death at the hands of George Zimmerman appears to have been largely due to who he was in terms of race and gender, and not what he was wearing. Hoodies are an increasingly popular style of dress. It is hard to imagine that if a White teenager had been walking in the gated community on that fateful evening that his mere presence would have elicited a similar response from the shooter, George Zimmerman. Undoubtedly, it was who he thought Trayvon was as signified by his race, gender (and presumed class) that made him a suspect and placed him at risk.

There are of course numerous examples of individual Black males who have found ways to resist the stereotypes and stigmas associated with their status in America. There are also a small number of schools where this type of resistance goes well beyond the individual and entire groups of students benefit from being educated where a deliberate effort is made to avoid reinforcing narrow conceptions of identity. Such schools make it possible for Black males to subvert and react against the cultural and structural forces that would otherwise shape their social identities by providing safe spaces where they can develop and grow. The existence of such schools compels us to recognize that individual and collective choice agency can play a major role in countering the hardships that beset Black males.

In 2009, we conducted a study with several of our colleagues on dropout rates among Black and Latino males in New York City (Meade, et al., 2009). The results were disturbing but hardly surprising. In one of the few cities with a rising graduation rate (Official graduation rates in New York claim that graduation rates now over 65%), less than 40% of Black and Latino males were graduating, and fewer than 30% were graduating with a Regents diploma, the certificate used to determine college readiness. However, during the course of our study we also identified over twenty high schools in New York City where the graduation rate for Black and Latino males was over 80%. We were surprised both by the significant number of schools that were achieving at this level of attainment and by the fact that the knowledge they had gained was not being shared widely among schools throughout New York City.

Some of these were schools like Fredrick Douglass Academy and Thurgood Marshall in Harlem and Bedford Academy in Brooklyn; schools where high graduation rates had been the norm for several years. These schools serve students from low-income backgrounds who come from some of the most troubled and disadvantaged neighborhoods in the City, but unlike the other schools in their neighborhoods, they have found ways to create school cultures that counter the influence of gangs, promote strong relationships between teachers and students, and affirm the importance of learning. Our research in these schools showed us that strong, positive relationships between adults and Black male students are critical to their success. Equally important is the need to provide personalized learning environments where students have access to mentors, counselors and other supports that make it possible to intervene early and effectively when problems arise. Not surprisingly, these schools also have strong and effective school leaders, who are firm but not authoritarian or intimidating. On the contrary, in the surveys we carried out at these schools we learned that students regarded their principals as guardians and father figures. Most of all, these are schools where students experience a high level of physical and psychological safety. They report that they feel as though they can be themselves and that the peer culture reinforces the value of learning. These are schools where character, ethics and moral development are stressed rather than relying upon rigid discipline policies.

Some of these high performing schools are some of the new all male schools that have been created in the last few years, but not all of them. At co-ed schools like Thurgood Marshall, which is run through a partnership with the Abyssinian Development Corporation based in Harlem, a mentoring program was created specifically for male 9th graders who were paired with high performing female seniors. The school's principal implemented the program based on her realization that since girls were doing better at school than boys they could be utilized to model success for their younger peers. At Enterprise, Business and Technology High School in Williamsburg, Brooklyn, the school relied upon internships with local business to develop job opportunities for students to keep young men engaged.

Schools like these exist in small numbers throughout the United States. The Coalition of Schools Education Boys of Color (COSBOC), has developed a network of like-minded schools to make it possible for others to learn from the schools that have been most successful. It would make sense for policymakers to actively encourage these types of consortiums and exchanges rather than relying on pressure under the guise of accountability to force schools to improve. The evidence garnered from schools from over ten years of results under No Child Left Behind, the federal policy enacted in 2002, shows that not only are thousands of children still being left behind academically, but in the case of Black males, many are being relegated to a life of failure on the margins of society as a result.

## CONCLUSION

A central goal of this paper has been to make the case that research on identity must pay careful attention to the ways in which race, class and gender interact to frame the way in which Black males are seen in schools and society. Institutions such as schools play an important role in producing attitudes and behaviors that contribute to the risks and vulnerabilities experienced by Black males. Of course, schools do not act alone in shaping the identities of Black males. Families, communities, the media, the economy (local, regional, national and global), political institutions and their agents, also play a role in shaping the ways in which Black men and boys are seen and the identities they adopt and produce in reaction to these forces. However, schools may be the best place to look for new ways to challenge how Black boys are seen and how they see themselves. Writing on the general importance of identity to studies of schooling, Levinson, Foley, and Holland argue "student identity formation within school is a kind of social practice and cultural production which both responds to, and simultaneously constitutes, movements, structures, and discourses beyond school" (Levinson, Foley &Holland, 1996). As institutions that have been charged with the responsibility of preparing young people, both academically and socially, for adult roles in society, schools can be transformed in ways that make it possible for Black males to experience a degree of freedom from stereotype and stigma that may be more difficult to achieve elsewhere.

Examining the dynamics of identity construction may not get us any closer to knowing what really happened on February 26, 2012, the night when Trayvon Martin was killed, nor will it do much in the short term to prevent others like him from meeting a similar fate. However, if we can use this understanding to begin to design schools and programs where Black boys can be supported and nurtured, we may eventually reverse the trends that have led this group to be labeled an "endangered species" (Taylor-Gibbs, 1988), and begin to see greater numbers of Black men and boys who are able to grow, thrive and develop and contribute to the greater good of society.

## NOTES

1. For an extended discussion of the vulnerabilities experienced by Black males in American society see *The Trouble With Black Males: Race, Equity and the Future of Public Education* by Pedro A. Noguera (Wiley & Sons, 2008).
2. See Noguera and Fergus 2010 and Gregory, Skiba and Noguera 2010 for a discussion of racial disparities and school suspensions.

## REFERENCES

Alexander, M. (2010). *The new Jim Crow: Mass incarceration in the age of colorblindness.* New York, NY: New Press.

APA Task Force. (2008). *Task force on resiliency and strength in Black children and adolescents.* Adopted by APA council of representatives. Washington DC: American Psychological Association.

Associated Press (2007). When a candy bar, wallet or hairbrush leads to police gunfire. *The Cornell Daily Sun.* Retrieved from http://cornellsun.com/node/26276

Bauer, L., Guerino, P., Nolle, K. L., & Tang, S. (2008). *Student victimization in U.S. Schools: results from the 2005 school crime supplement to the national crime victimization survey* (NCES 2009–306). National Center for Education Statistics. Institute of Education Sciences, U.S. Department of Education, Washington DC.

Bronfenbrenner, U. (1975). *The ecology of human development in retrospect and prospect.* Invited address at the final plenary session of the Conference on Ecological Factors in Human Development held by the International Society for the Study of Behavioral Development, University of Surrey, Guildford, England, July 13–17.

Bowen, N. K., Bowen, G. L., & Ware, W. (2002). Neighborhood social disorganization, families, and the educational behavior of adolescents. *Journal of Adolescent Research, 17,* 468–489.

Brown, A. (2011). "Same old stories": The Black male in social science and educational literature, 1930s to the present. *Teachers College Record, 113*(9), 2047–2079

Carter, P. L. (2005). *Keepin' it real: Why school success has no color*. New York, NY: Oxford University Press.

Clear, T. (2007). *Imprisoning communities: How mass incarceration makes disadvantaged neighborhoods worse*. New York, NY: Oxford University Press.

Cross Jr., W. E. (1991). *Shades of Black: Diversity in African-American identity*. Philadelphia, PA: Temple University Press.

Dance, L. (2002). *Tough fronts: The impact of street culture on schooling*. London: Routledge.

Ellison, R. (1995). *Invisible man* (2nd ed.). New York, NY: Random House.

Fergus, E., & Noguera, P. (2011). Doing what it takes to prepare Black and Latino males in college. In C. Edley & J. Ruiz (Eds.), *Changing places: How communities will improve the health of boys of color*. Berkeley: University of California Press.

Ferguson, A. (2001). *Bad boys: Public schools in the making of Black masculinity*. Ann Arbor, MI: University of Michigan Press.

Fine, M. (1991) *Framing dropouts: Notes on the politics of an urban public high school*. Albany, NY: State University of New York Press.

Fogel, R. W. (1989). *Without consent or contract: The rise and fall of American slavery*. New York, NY: Norton.

Ford Foundation. (2007). *Why we can't wait: A case for philanthropic action: opportunities for improving the life outcomes for African American males*. New York, NY: Marcus Littles.

Gibbs, J. T. (1988). *Young, Black, and male in America: An endangered species*. Dover, MA: Auburn House Publishing Co.

Gopnik, A. (2012). The caging of America. *New Yorker Magazine*. Retrieved from http://www.newyorker.com/arts/critics/atlarge/2012/01/30/120130crat_atlarge_gopnik

Graham, S., & Lowery, B. S. (2004). Priming unconscious racial stereotypes about adolescent offenders. *Law and Human Behavior 28*, 483–504.

Greenberg, M., & Schneider, D. (1994). Violence in American cities: Young Black males is the answer, but what was the question? *Social Science Medicine, 39*(2).

Gregory, J. F. (1997). Three strikes and they're out: African American boys and American schools' responses to misbehavior. *International Journal of Adolescence and Youth, 7*(1), 25–34.

Gregory, A., Skiba, R. J., & Noguera, P. A. (2010). The achievement gap and the discipline gap. *Educational Researcher, 39*(1), 59–68.

Halbfinger, D. M. (2012). With Arena, Rapper Rewrites Celebrity Investor's Playbook. *The New York Times*. Retrieved from http://www.nytimes.com/2012/08/16/nyregion/with-the-nets-jay-z-rewrites-the-celebrity-investors-playbook.html?pagewanted=all

Harper, S. R. (2012). Black male student success in higher education: A report from the National Black Male College Achievement Study. Philadelphia: University of Pennsylvania, Center for the Study of Race and Equity in Education.

Hill Collins, P. (1989). *Toward a new vision: Race, class and gender as categories of analysis and connection*. The Research Clearinghouse and Curriculum Integration Project. Memphis, TN: The University of Memphis

Karp, S. (2009). *Black male conundrum*. Retrieved from www.catalyst-chicago.org

Kimmel, M. (2009). *Men, masculinity and violence.* Lexington, KY: University of Kentucky Press.

Krezmien, M. P., Leone, P. E., & Achilles, G. M. (2006). Suspension, race, and disability: Analysis of statewide practices and reporting. *Journal of Emotional and Behavioral Disorders, 14,* 217–226.

Legum, J. (2012). What everyone should know about Trayvon Martin (1995–2012). *Think Progress.* Retrieved from http://thinkprogress.org/justice/2012/03/18/446768/what-everyone-should-know-about-about-trayvon-martin-1995-2012/?mobile=nc

Levinson, B., Foley, D., & Holland, D. (1996). *The cultural production of the educated person.* Albany, NY: SUNY Press.

Losen, D., & G. Orfield (2002). *Racial inequality in special education.* Cambridge, MA: Harvard Education Press.

Losen, D., Martinez, T., & Gillespie, J. (2012). *Suspended education in California.* Retrieved from http://civilrightsproject.ucla.edu/resources/projects/center-for-civil-rights-remedies/school-to-prison-folder/summary-reports/suspended-education-in-california/SuspendedEd-final3.pdf

Mackey, R. (2012). 'If I had a son, he'd look like Trayvon,' Obama says. *The New York Times.* Retrieved from http://thelede.blogs.nytimes.com/2012/03/23/if-i-had-a-son-hed-look-like-trayvon-obama-says/

Maeroff, G. (1988). Withered hopes, stillborn dreams: The dismal panorama of urban schools. *Phi Delta Kappan, 69,* 632–638.

Majors, R., & Billson, M. (1992). *Cool pose. The dilemmas of Black manhood in America.* New York, NY: Simon and Schuster.

McCready, L. (2009). Understanding the marginalization of gay and gender nonconforming Black male students. *Theory into Practice, 43*(2) 136–143.

Meade, B., Gaytan, F., Fergus, E., & Noguera, P. (2009). *A close look at the dropout crisis examining Black and Latino males in New York City.* Retrieved from: http://steinhardt.nyu.edu/scmsAdmin/uploads/004/453/Dropout_Crisis.pdf

Mincy, R., Martin, M., Noguera, P., Zilanawala, A., & Fergus, E., (2010). *Understanding the education trajectories of young Black men in New York City: Elementary and Middle School Years.* Retrieved from: http://steinhardt.nyu.edu/scmsAdmin/media/users/eaf7/BMDC_Black_Male_Education_Trajectory_Report-FULL.pdf

Moss, P., &Tilly, C. (1993). *Raised hurdles for Black men: Evidence from interviews with employers,* (Working Paper, Department of Policy and Planning) University of Massachusetts-Lowell.

National Fatherhood Initiative (2012). Facts and Figures. Washington, D.C. retrieved from: http://www.fatherhood.org/media/consequences-of-father-absence-statistics

Noguera, P. (2003). *City schools and the American dream: Reclaiming the promise of public education.* New York, NY: Teachers College Press.

Noguera, P. (2008). *The trouble with Black boys and other reflections on race, equity and the future of public education.* San Francisco, CA: Wiley and Sons.

Noguera, P., & Wing, J. Y., (Eds.). (2008). *Unfinished business: Closing the racial achievement gap in our schools.* San Francisco, CA: Jossey-Bass.

Nolan, K. (2011). *Police in the hallways: Discipline in an urban high school.* Minneapolis, MN: University of Minnesota Press.

Office of Minority Health. (2010). Men's Health 101 Retrieved from: http://www.minorityhealth.hhs.gov/templates/content.aspx?ID=3733

Payne, C. (1984). *Getting what we ask for.* Westport, CT: Greenwood.

Phinney, J. S. (1989). Stages of ethnic identity development in minority group adolescents. *The Journal of Early Adolescence, 9*(1–2), 34–49.

Pollard. D. S. (1993). Gender, achievement and African American students' perceptions of their school experience. *Education Psychologist, 28*(4).

Pollack, M. (2004). *Colormute: Race talk dilemmas in an American school.* Princeton, NJ: Princeton University Press.

Schott Foundation. (2010). *Yes we can: The Schott 50 State Report on Public Education and Black Males.* Cambridge, MA.

Steele, C. M., & Aronson, J. (1995). Stereotype threat and the intellectual test performance of African Americans. *Journal of Personality and Social Psychology, 69*(5), 797–811.

Steele, C. (2010). *Whistling Vivaldi: And other clues to how stereotypes affect us.* New York, NY: W.W. Norton & Company.

Stoll, M., Holzer, H., & Ihlanfeldt, K. R, (2000). Within cities and suburbs: Racial residential concentration and the spatial distribution of employment opportunities across sub-metropolitan areas. *Journal of Policy Analysis and Management 19*(2) 207–231.

Taylor-Gibbs, J. (1988). *The Black male as an endangered species.* New York: Auburn House.

Thomas, D. E., & Stevenson, H. (2009). Gender risks and education: The particular classroom chanllenges for urban low-income African American boys. *Review of Research in Education, 33*(1) 160–180.

Tough, P. (2012). *How children succeed: Grit, curiosity, and the hidden power of character.* New York, NY: Houghton Mifflin Harcourt.

Treyvon Martin Case (2012). *The New York Times.* Retrieved from: http://topics.nytimes.com/top/reference/timestopics/people/m/trayvon_martin/index.html?8qa

Waters, M. C. (1990). *Ethnic options. Choosing identities in America.* Berkeley, CA: University of California Press.

Willis, P. (1981). *Learning to labor: How working class kids get working class jobs.* New York: NY: Columbia University Press.

Wilson, W. J. (1987). *The truly disadvantaged.* Chicago, IL: University of Chicago Press.

CHAPTER 5

# NEPANTLERAS IN THE NEW LATINO DIASPORA

## The Intersectional Experiences of Bi/multilingual Youth

Mariana Pacheco
*University of Wisconsin*

## ABSTRACT

The New Latino Diaspora has emerged across many Midwestern non-traditional gateway communities (Wortham, Murillo, & Hamann, 2002), bringing a unique set of linguistic and cultural resources, repertoires, and experiences that are shaping and being shaped by new demographic configurations. This chapter elaborates a line of analysis that conceptualizes the participation across in-school and out-of-school settings of one Latina bi/multilingual adolescent I call Sara as border-crossings. That is, like many Latina youth in the New Latino Diaspora, border-crossing *nepantleras* (Anzaldúa, 2002) live betwixt and between languages and cultures and traverse different spaces in ways that shape everyday practices—even as these youth are simultaneously being shaped in/through these practices. I argue that Sara's linguistic repertoire and identities were embraced and constrained in different but sig-

*Intersectionality and Urban Education*, pages 97–123

nificant ways across settings. In particular, I analyze how the intersections of difference across race/ethnicity, language, class, gender, and legal status affected the identities she enacted. I also examine the role her mother—and *mother–daughter pedagogies* (Villenas & Moreno, 2001)—played in Sara's educational and life experiences, as well as in her decision-making as a youth learning and growing in the shifting contexts of the New Latino Diaspora. This study has implications for understanding bi/multilingualism as a co-constructed process. It illustrates that individuals, peers, and co-participants make significant efforts, create opportunities and constraints, and instantiate sociocultural changes that affect identity-making and language-expanding processes.

## INTRODUCTION

The New Latino Diaspora has emerged across many Midwestern communities, bringing a unique set of linguistic and cultural resources, repertoires, and experiences that are shaping and being shaped by these new demographic configurations (Wortham, Murillo, & Hamann, 2002). States such as California, Texas, and New Mexico and large metropolitan communities such as Chicago, El Paso, and Miami have traditionally been home to both previous generations and new (im)migrants of Mexican and Latin American origin. In recent decades, however, Latinos have (im)migrated to nontraditional gateway communities in states such as North Carolina, Georgia, and Wisconsin and in rural communities throughout the United States for a variety of social, political, and economic reasons (Pew Hispanic Center, 2010). These rapid demographic shifts have created complex sociocultural dynamics, challenges, and opportunities for both the New Latino Diaspora as well as receiving communities.

For children and youth learning and growing in the New Latino Diaspora, Anzaldúa's (2002) notion of *nepantleras* captures the essence of life betwixt and between languages and cultures and the ways Latinas in particular must navigate, subvert, and re-imagine linguistic and cultural identities. As they confront circulating discourses about Latino families, Latino culture, and Latino (im)migrants in dominant-group communities, Latina youth must develop strategies for thriving and succeeding on their own terms in shifting linguistic and cultural landscapes. Perhaps the most noticeable conflicts, particularly in the educational arena, pertain to the Spanish discourses, varieties, and dialects Latino students enact. Thus, I have a specific interest in the ideologies about language, learning, and schooling that affect Latin@[1] students' active participation and sense making in the context of shifting landscapes.

This chapter draws from a larger ongoing ethnographic study that examines language learning and language-expanding opportunities as bi/multilingual youth accomplished various literacy tasks, in English and Spanish, across in-school, out-of-school, and on-line settings (e.g., classrooms, church groups, Facebook). Through an analytic focus on participation structures, discourses, language patterns, and interactional talk, I investigate how Latin@ bi/multilingual youth produced particular language forms that emerged as a by-product of their participation in different settings. I also examine the roles peers, teachers, and other adults (e.g., parents) played in the jointly accomplished participatory process, with a specific focus on the unique assistance they provided. For this chapter, I analyze the participation in/through English-Spanish language practices across in-school and out-of-school settings of one Latina[2] bi/multilingual adolescent I call Sara. Her experiences and perspectives as a *nepantlera* reveal that throughout her border-crossings in the New Latino Diaspora, her linguistic repertoire and identities were embraced and constrained in significant ways and that she, too, engaged in the process of enacting and embodying particular linguistic and cultural identities. I also examine the significant role her mother played in her educational and life circumstances and analyze how *mother–daughter pedagogies* (Villenas & Moreno, 2001) figured into Sara's decision-making processes.

This analysis has implications for how educational researchers and practitioners understand language and bi/multilingual practices as co-constructed processes rather than individual accomplishments and choices. It demonstrates the extent to which individuals, peers, and co-participants across settings make significant efforts, create opportunities and constraints, and shift normative practices that affect identity-making and language-expanding processes. Nevertheless, this process is fundamentally affected by the intersectionality of cultural and linguistic difference and their intersections with race/ethnicity, class, gender, legal status across contexts and settings for Latin@ bi/multilingual youth.

I begin first with a conceptualization of the significance of language practices for learning and development that occur in the context of (changing) cultural communities whose histories of oppression also afford opportunities for families to develop forms of resilience and resistance. I also discuss how an understanding of Latina youths' multi-dimensional, intersectional identities shapes their perceptions and experiences in the New Latino Diaspora—even as they are shaping these spaces.

## The Intersectionality of the Bi/multilingual Latina Experience

Bi/multilingual[3] adolescents—more commonly known as English Learners in public schools—are academically vulnerable in part because current assessment and accountability frameworks impose monolingual models on their learning and academic trajectories (Dworin, 2003; García & Kleifgen, 2010; Gutiérrez, Morales, & Martinez, 2009). These frameworks overemphasize academic competencies in English and ignore the distinct types of insights, knowledge, and understandings that bi/multilinguals develop through their participation in distinct social worlds in and across languages (Gutiérrez, 2008; Moll, Saez, & Dworin, 2001; Zentella, 2005). Further, these frameworks constrain what 'counts' as knowledge and competency and restrict ways teachers might come to recognize and leverage bi/multilingual students' sociocultural, intellectual, and linguistic resources in the classroom (González, Moll, & Amanti, 2005; Moschkovich, 2002; Orellana, 2009; Pacheco, 2009; Valdés, 2003).

To conceptualize how language practices have consequences for adolescent learning and development, this study employs cultural-historical perspectives on the relationship between language, culture, and cognition (Cole, 1985, 1996; Vygotsky, 1978). Specifically, these views conceptualize that everyday linguistic and cultural practices are fundamental to human learning and development as these practices provide essential mediational tools and artifacts co-participants employ as they participate in the valued but ongoing activities that constitute distinct cultural communities (Lave, 1996; Rogoff, 1995, 2003). Gutiérrez & Rogoff (2003) define cultural community as "a coordinated group of people with some traditions and understandings in common, extending across several generations, with varied roles and practices and continual change among participants as well as transformation in the community's practices" (p. 21). Thus, cultural communities are comprised of changing members who share some practices and views in common that change on an ongoing basis. Of relevance, this conceptualization shifts the focus away from monolithic—often deficit—views of racial/ethnic communities whose culture is located "within" its members (e.g., Asian Americans do X) to a cultural-historical view of dynamic, changing communities with common histories and shared experiences.

Adults and parents in particular play an important role in the learning and development process as they organize particular sociocultural activities and practices to prepare future generations to become full and meaningful members of their cultural communities (Cole, 1996; Rogoff, 2003). In this enculturation process, however, children are active and creative co-participants: they are not simply "recipients" of the learning and development process but instead engaged in deliberate meaning making in this bidirectional process. Thus, as individuals participate across cultural communities, they not only employ their available repertoire of linguistic, cultural, and intellectual resources but also acquire and amplify this repertoire as they appropriate resources within these communities (Gutiérrez & Rogoff, 2003).

Yet, while cultural communities are indeed dynamic, diverse, and changing, the shared experiences with oppression and marginalization experienced by cultural communities of color in the U.S., and women specifically, may be characterized as historically and structurally constituted (Lee, 2002; Crenshaw, 1991; Saldívar-Hull, 1991). In this regard, the notion of intersectionality provides insights for understanding how social experience is shaped not by a single-dimension such as socioeconomic class but by multiple intersecting dimensions of race, ethnicity, class, gender, religion, sexual orientation, and so on. Just as cultural communities do not transmit bounded single-dimension cultures from person to person across generations, no specific social category explains the extent and enduring ways communities of color have been discriminated against and marginalized in the United States. Their common histories and shared experiences, therefore, are better understood as the consequences of U.S. colonialism, expansionism, and imperialism.

For example, Latinos in the United States are a tremendously diverse group representing numerous nationalities, racial/ethnic backgrounds (e.g., African, mestizo, and Spanish ancestries), language varieties, educational backgrounds, etc. (Gándara & Contreras, 2009; Sánchez, 2002). Still, Latinos also share a common history of Spanish colonization and U.S. expansionism and imperialism that have created a particular sociohistorical context within which Latinos' race, ethnicity, class, gender, legal status, and language are situated (Solórzano & Delgado Bernal, 2001). Thus, while intersectionality illuminates the multiple factors that shape the Latino social experience, this multidimensional experience also operates within broader sociohistorical relations of oppression and discrimination that have material consequences for Latino communities across the United States.

This intersectionality has been famously conceptualized by Anzaldúa (1987) as a powerful dimension of everyday life in the physical and psychological borderlands, particularly for Chicana/o and Latina/o communities. She theorizes a *mestiza concsciousness* that fully embraces the multiplicity, contradictions, hybridity, and ambiguity of living betwixt and between sociocultural and linguistic worlds. Specifically, Anzaldúa articulates the notion of "linguistic terrorism" to capture the salient ways dominant Anglo society attempts to regulate, confine, and de-legitimize the language realities and material circumstances of Chicana/o and Latina/o communities. In her own words, she famously asserted, "If you want to really hurt me, talk badly about my language. Ethnic identity is twin skin to linguistic identity—I am my language. Until I can take pride in my language, I cannot take pride in myself" (Anzaldúa, 1987, p. 81). Thus, as a strategy of both individual and collective resistance and resilience among oppressed communities of color, *mestiza consciousness* reflects a rejection of oppositional cultural and linguistic categories that enhance these communities' vulnerabilities. Instead, it reflects a tolerance for being and living in *nepantla*—or the "land in the middle" located between shifting sociocultural landscapes and histories of colonization. As Anzaldúa (2002) elaborates:

> *Nepantla* is the site of transformation, the place where different perspectives come into conflict and where you question the basic ideas, tenets, and identities inherited from your family, your education, and your different cultures... Living between cultures results in "seeing" double, first from the perspective of one culture, then from the perspective of another. (p. 548)

Chicanas and Latinas, as *nepantleras*, navigate and traverse these borderlands with a consciousness that recognizes attempts to confine and silence cultural and linguistic hybridity and that simultaneously asserts the hybrid, multi-layered, and contested realities of their lived experiences. Anzaldúa's (1987, 2002) theorizations about everyday life in the borderlands and the necessarily hybrid, intersectional identities the borderlands engender provide useful ways to account for the consciousness developed by virtue of recurrently traversing these spaces.

The necessarily hybrid, mutually constituted cultural and linguistic forms enacted and embodied among bi/multilingual students have been documented in empirical literature that examines everyday practices related to codeswitching (Martinez, Orellana, Pacheco, & Carbone, 2008; Reyes, 2004; Wei & Wu, 2009), hybrid language practices (Gutiérrez, Baquedano-López, Alvarez, & Chiu, 1999), Spanglish (Martínez, 2010; Zentella, 1997), Chicano English (Fought, 2003), translanguaging (Creese & Blackledge, 2010; García, 2011), and translating and interpreting across languages (Orellana, 2009; Valdés, 2003). Furthermore, bi/multilinguals have been conceptualized as possessing repertoires of language (Gutiérrez, Morales, & Martinez, 2009) that include multimodal resources (Lam, 2009; Moshkovich, 2002; Skilton-Sylvester, 2002) as well as specialized discourses, registers, and dialects (Gee, 2005; Hornberger & Skilton-Sylvester, 2000). While bi/multilingual students whose lives in U.S. contexts are perhaps better understood as fundamentally hybrid and expansive in practice, examining their linguistic experiences as they intersect with constructions of race, ethnicity, class, gender, legal status, religion, and sexual orientation is central to understanding their marginalizing schooling experiences in more depth (Montoya, 1994; Solórzano & Delgado Bernal, 2001). That is, bi/multilingual students' rich cultural and linguistic experiences intersect inevitably with dominant ideologies about what *types* and *kinds* of students 'count' and are valued across everyday and educational contexts in ways that exacerbate the risks these youth face (González, 2001; Yosso, 2005).

Lee (2010) provides an alternative way to approach the material risks experienced by cultural communities of color, which includes (im)migrant communities. She argues compellingly that educational researchers and practitioners must seek to understand deeply both the multidimensionality of social experience across cultural communities as well as the ways in which these resilient communities generate adaptive mechanisms and responses. While an exclusive focus on the ways intersectional experiences exacerbate the risks experienced by students of color, she builds a persuasive case for the importance of examining resilience with equal attention. She explains that we must examine both risk and resilience and shift the focus away from homogenous and essentialized views of diversity to a focus on cultural and ecological frameworks:

> We need studies that examine how people who are Black, brown, and poor experience daily microaggressions (in school, in workplace settings, in neighborhoods) and uncover the range of resources (psychosocial and institutional) that buffer negative impacts...But such studies must avoid treating difference as deficit and cultural communities as static. We need longitudinal databases with variables that reflect the possibilities of plasticity and adaptation through multiple pathways. (Lee, 2010, p. 653)

My interpretation of Lee's proposition is that even though it is critical to examine individuals' intersectional, multidimensional lives as they are sociohistorically constituted, our studies must examine as well the resources their families and communities develop to help their children and youth thrive. Perhaps by virtue of teaching, learning, and living in oppressive contexts, modest-income cultural communities of color are forced to confront deliberately their exacerbated levels of risk and vulnerability in order to survive and thrive. I have made a similar argument about the importance of examining Latina/o families and communities' *everyday resistance* to social and education issues and the problem-solving resources they develop to address these issues, (Pacheco, 2012), including situated forms of *political-historical knowledge* (Pacheco, 2009), which could be used to develop responsive curriculum practices.

In my conceptualization of Latina bi/multilingual students' participation across settings and contexts, cultural-historical perspectives on teaching and learning help account for the cultural and linguistic resources individuals develop in changing cultural communities while notions of intersectionality illuminate the oppressive and discriminatory circumstances within which they develop these resources. Anzaldúa's (1987, 2002) theorizations of *mestiza consciousness* forefronts the consciousness individuals develop in the in-between spaces of *nepantla* characteristic of life in the physical and psychological borderlands. However, I agree with Lee (2010) that acts of resistance and resilience must be examined and documented as part of the broader ecologies of modest-income communities of color. In this chapter, I argue that Latina bi/multilingual youth participants are border-crossing *nepantleras* living between languages and cultures and traverse in- and out-of-school settings in ways that shape everyday practices—even as they are being shaped in/through these practices.

## The Larger Study

The following research questions guide the larger study, which is ongoing: (1) What are the normative English-Spanish language practices across out-of-school, in-school, and on-line settings? (2) How do bi/multilingual adolescents employ their English-Spanish bi/multilingualism in these settings? (3) What individual and institutional efforts, opportunities, constraints, and changes affect and shape these language practices? The goal of the study is to examine the language practices instantiated across a range of settings, how bi/multilingual adolescents employ their bi/multilingual repertoires, and the equally significant ways co-participants across particular institutions (e.g., schools) and organizations (e.g., church, after-school clubs) affect the language practices that characterized their joint activity. This multi-year ethnographic study relies on participant observations, formal and informal interviews, primary document sources, photographs, and audio recordings of ongoing social interactions across settings (Creswell, 1994; Marshall & Rossman, 1999).

The case presented here was developed through inductive analyses of field notes, transcripts of interactions and interviews, documents and photographs taken in different settings, and researcher memos (Miles & Huberman, 1994; Strauss, 1987). I specifically analyze the cultural and linguistic experiences of Sara and focus on her varied experiences of acceptance and marginalization, inclusion and exclusion, accommodation and positioning across contexts. I illuminate particular statements, practices, or critical incidents that reveal how socially constructed categories came to matter for Sara and her co-participants in these contexts.

Following Crenshaw (1991), "a large and continuing project for subordinated people...is thinking about the way power has clustered around certain categories and is exercised against others" (pp. 1296–1297). Thus, I analyze Sara's case to examine how power was employed in relation to particular social categories—adolescent, teen journalist, Catholic/Christian, friend, student, Mexicanas/Latinas, gang member—in ways that had consequences for Sara and other Latina bi/multilingual adolescents like her within and across settings. Additionally, I analyze Sara's *mestiza consciousness*, or her growing *awareness about* and *response to* how her fundamental differences mattered in distinct ways for the distinct individuals in her life (i.e., counselors, after-school program staff). To this end, I discuss some deliberate decisions Sara was making based on her emerging views and interpretations about who she was and how others saw her—"seeing and being seen"—and her simultaneous construction as subject and object (Anzaldúa, 1987). For example, I examine how Sara employed particular social categories to distinguish herself as 'American' in a way that revealed her uptake of circulating discourses about Mexican/Latino youth from modest-income families.

Finally, I analyze Sara's mother's beliefs, views, and decision-making based on her perceptions about her role in processes of socialization, language development, schooling, and education. Chicana feminist scholars have conceptualized the unique teaching and learning process between mothers and their daughters as *mother–daughter pedagogies* (Villenas & Moreno, 2001). Latina (im)migrant mothers in particular develop strategies for preparing their daughters to both succeed as well as develop resilience against systems and structures that exacerbate their vulnerabilities as (im)migrant women. These pedagogies are both reflective of mothers' critical understandings of their own racialized, classed, and gendered cultural experiences as *Mexicanas* of mixed legal status and their deliberate attempts to prepare their daughters for their yet unrealized futures. As such, mother–daughter pedagogies are "wrought with tensions and contradictions yet open with spaces of possibility" (Villenas & Moreno, 2001, p. 673). In what follows, I analyze how these pedagogies take on new significance as Sara and her mother navigate their intersectional betwixt -and-between experiences in the New Latino Diaspora where they seek to expand their educational opportunities and life chances.

## Community Context

Wisconsin is considered part of the New Latino Diaspora as it is in a non-traditional gateway region for Latino and Hispanic migrants and (im)migrants (Lowenhaupt & Camburn, 2011). While the state has had a history of Latinos and Hispanics in Milwaukee, it has only recently begun to experience significant increases in this distinct ethnolinguistic group throughout other parts of the state. Between 2000 and 2010, for example, Wisconsin's Latino/Hispanic demographic has increased by over 74% and currently comprises approximately 6% of the state's population (Applied Population Laboratory, 2011; U.S. Census Bureau, 2010). In this same decade, the state's overall growth was relatively slow, but Latinos/Hispanics accounted for slightly over 44% of its growth. Wisconsinites have at times responded with anti-(im)migrant policy initiatives—such as withdrawing state policies that allowed undocumented[4] students to pay in-state tuition— and data show that one-third of Latino/Hispanic adults in the state live in poverty (Pew Hispanic Center, 2009). Nonetheless, there is ample evidence that Latinos/Hispanics are integrating into the region's sociocultural, sociopolitical landscape (Benjamin-Alvarado, DeSipio, & Montoya, 2009; Pacheco, 2012). Demographic shifts in non-traditional gateway communities create dynamic cultural and linguistic contact zones whereby (im)migrant and receiving communities are mutually affected. Dritton[5] is one mid-sized city with a population of approximately 233,000 that has recently experienced significant demographic shifts. Despite its long-standing White Euro-American majority and African-American minority, the city had a Latino/Hispanic population of 6.8% in 2010 (U.S. Census Bureau, 2010). This shift, however, is most pronounced in the local school districts. Between the 2000–01 and 2011–12 school years, for example, the percentage of Latino/Hispanic students has more than doubled—from 6.9% to 17.9% (WINNS, 2012). Thus, school-aged Latino/Hispanic students are in a unique position to engage as cultural and linguistic brokers across (im)migrant home contexts, local community spaces, and classrooms and schools.

### Participants

Study participants currently include two male and four female U.S.-born Latina/o middle and high school students. I had met them previously through a multi-year study of a community-based teen newspaper, the *Maintown Gazette*, which documented students' developmental trajectories from novice to proficient journalists (Pacheco, 2010a). The majority of teen journalists at the community-based newspaper were English-only speakers but a quarter of them were native speakers of Spanish, Chinese, Nepali, Japanese, and Hindi. Given my particular interest in English-Spanish bi/multilingualism among adolescents, I recruited the six youth that were primary speakers of Spanish. Their families migrated from Mexico when these adolescents were very young. Like many (im)migrants, they migrated to the United States in search of economic opportunities and connected with networks of family, extended relatives, and friends from their Mexican hometowns to "make it" in the New Latino Diaspora of the upper Midwest.

While the larger study is ongoing, this chapter centers on a line of analysis pertaining to Sara who learned Spanish as a home language but who has been a proficient English-Spanish bi/multilingual since she started attending school. I developed a close relationship with Sara and her two cousins, Camila and Perlita during my time at the community-based newspaper and I occasionally treated them to dinner, the movies, or a play. This close relationship facilitated my communications with their mothers, who seemed to have a high level of trust for the *Maintown Gazette* staff and educators in general. My Spanish-speaking ability also played a key role as the mothers and I could communicate about a range of topics, including our (im)migrant narratives, our cultural backgrounds, their daughters' schooling, and our personal lives, especially since I was of a similar age. Still, their daughters were a common topic and they occasionally asked me for advice. These mothers' insights helped me understand their daughters' experiences from a different perspective.

In the following section, I briefly address some of the major findings of the larger study to provide a broader context for understanding Sara's border-crossings and the representativeness of her experiences. I then analyze Sara's participation across settings and contexts, highlighting the ways her multi-dimensional locations and experiences affected this participation, as well as her emerging consciousness and actions related to positionings that occurred in these spaces.

## FINDINGS

### The Broader Context

Three major findings emerged from my analysis of youths' participation across a range of settings and contexts but also my analysis of the ways in which intersections of race/ethnicity, class, gender, legal status, language, and religion factored into bi/multilingual Latina youth's lives. First, it became clear across youth that even though they participated in relatively similar settings (i.e., the *Maintown Gazette*, home), their intersectional and multi-dimensional lives mattered in nevertheless distinct ways that had social and material consequences, particularly in terms of educational access and opportunity.

Second, there seemed to be a mutually exclusive relationship between educational success and their ethnic-cultural identities, which these youth both understood and reified in their decision-making practices. In other words, they made deliberate decisions about what type and degree of the available—albeit imposed—ethnic-cultural identities of "Mexican," "(im)migrant," "gang member," and "ESL kid" they would enact and embody across these contexts. These enactments and embodiments also intersected with their co-participants' varied ideologies and views. In this regard, these youth were simultaneously 'seeing' and 'being seen' and hence revealing their "differential consciousness" (Anzaldúa, 1987). These deliberative practices can be conceptualized as the forms of resilience (and resistance) that their mothers, families, and communities have helped them develop to confront the vulnerabilities they might experience in particularly oppressive contexts. Finally, these youth had unique social experiences since their interpretations and perceptions—mother–daughter pedagogies for some—intersected distinctly with their social, cultural, and linguistic worlds. Sara's case is an illustrative and representative example of how these intersections shaped her everyday life even as she was simultaneously shaping the shifting linguistic and cultural spaces she navigated and negotiated.

## Sara: "I hang out with the White kids"

Sara's case highlights that even though she was a successful student, participated across several academic programs and extracurricular activities, and had a home environment that partly facilitated her successful participation in these contexts; this success seemed to align primarily with her views of being 'American.' It appeared that, from her point of view, success across contexts depended on her ability to embody and enact a White, American—and English-speaking—identity at the expense of her ethnic, linguistic, and cultural identities. While scholars have begun to challenge the 'acting white' approach to becoming academically successful (see Ogbu, 2008), Sara's case illustrates that her multi-dimensional experience pertaining to her language, culture, and Mexican (im)migrant background factored into her life. Significant tensions emerged for her (and her mother) as her attempts to realize a "good American student" persona clashed with the substantial challenges she faced at school.

Sara was in her freshman and sophomore years at the time of data collection and was a relatively successful student since she was enrolled in honors and college preparatory classes. In sixth grade, she was selected to participate in a university pre-college recruitment program for underrepresented students that awarded tuition scholarships to students who were admitted and chose to attend this university right after high school. Throughout middle and high school, the program provided weekly tutoring sessions, a summer academic enrichment program, academic advising, and assistance with the college application process. Her parents immigrated from Zacatecas, Mexico and moved to Dritton to join extended family members on the father's side. Sara and her younger brother, Adam, were born in Dritton.

Sara was often shy but was equally a determined, focused young woman who was willing to invest her time, energy, and efforts to achieve good grades and obtain a college degree with a tuition scholarship. As mentioned earlier, she was invested in maintaining an "American" identity, which she associated with being White and English-dominant, as captured in the following field note excerpt:

When we discussed school, Sara said she only speaks Spanish in her Spanish class and during "passing time" when she runs into other "Latin and Mexican people" in the hallways. She specified that she mostly speaks English at school and that even though she occasionally interacts with other Spanish speakers, she likes to "hang out with English-speaking people" because "the Mexican kids do bad stuff, like gangs and I don't wanna do that stuff so I hang out with the White kids." So, she knows Spanish speakers but chooses to hang out with English-only speakers. (Field note, September 23, 2010)

By the time she was in high school, Sara had already developed some clear distinctions between being Spanish-speaking Mexican and Latino who do "bad stuff" and may be in a gang as well as being White, English-speaking, and "good" and views about what cultural identities she would enact (Olsen, 1997; Pacheco, 2010b; Valdés, 1998). It seemed that despite being a fluent bi/multilingual of Mexican descent and brief interactions with students who shared her ethnolinguistic background, she made a conscious decision instead to "hang out with the English-speaking (White) people." She seemed to embody a "differential consciousness" about how dominant society and dominant groups perceived "the White kids" in positive ways as "good" students and people. Even though it is unclear how she developed her views about different groups, her views certainly aligned with negative stereotypes and images of Mexicans and Latinos in the popular media. Another way she enacted this "good" identity was by participating in mainstream extracurricular activities.

Sara spent most of her after-school time participating in cross-country practices and meets, attending required tutoring sessions for the university pre-college program twice per week, and "working" at the *Gazette*, which I discuss below. She was a member of her high school cross-country team though she acknowledged her marginal success. Still, she very much enjoyed running and went for long runs outdoors by herself when the weather permitted as a way to relax and have fun; in fact, her Facebook timeline poster was of a woman running outside in the countryside. Indeed, "runner" was a salient identity and relative to other aspects of her life.

## Participation in a Community-Based Newspaper

As mentioned earlier, Sara "worked" as a teen journalist at the *Maintown Gazette* for about two to four hours per week altogether where she received a small monthly stipend for every story she published in the monthly newspaper. Her older cousin Veronica, who had also been a teen journalist, had encouraged Sara and her two cousins to participate in the community-based newspaper. In many ways, Veronica was a role model for Sara and her two cousins. It was clear from these teens and their mothers that they were expected to follow Veronica's path since participation at the *Gazette* resulted in valuable sources of cultural capital. For example, the adult editorial staff helped facilitate the college application process, assisted youth with autobiographical statements, and provided excellent letters of recommendation for teen journalists. Since Sara's (im)migrant parents spoke very little English and had limited knowledge of schooling in the United States, they highly valued the assistance that the community-based organization and its staff could provide their daughter.

Typically, teen journalists received an original article source from both well-known hard copy and on-line publications and magazines (e.g., *Wisconsin State Journal*, cnn.com, *Discover*, etc.), which they then had to summarize within the journalism genre. The topics addressed in the *Gazette* newspaper reflected many of the same topics addressed in school: geography, history, physics, and health, for example. The editorial staff also assigned current events, technology, education, as well as oddities and "weird" news articles. In addition to its small staff, the organization relied on "teen editors" who had proven themselves as effective journalists, reliable and responsible, and positive mentors for novice teen journalists. Also, the program relied on numerous community volunteers such as retired journalists and teachers and occasionally, undergraduates from local universities.

Sara struggled a great deal with the everyday tasks and responsibilities related to journalistic writing in English, especially when she first started participating in the program as a novice teen journalist. During my observations in the newsroom, I documented her challenges with fully comprehending the article sources, deciding between major and minor details to include in her summaries, and writing with the use of journalism conventions (e.g., short sentences, succinct description, effective "hooks"). My analysis demonstrated, however, that Sara's ongoing challenges were significantly mediated by the spatial and temporal organization of human resources, material resources, and problem-solving resources in the newsroom. That is, teen journalists could access information, reference materials, and tips as their needs changed during the course of their journalism work. The newsroom, therefore, was spatially organized to allow free movement among program participants and to allow access to laptops with Internet access, reference materials, style and tip sheets, checklists, newspapers, and news magazines. Because teens completed most article summaries independently, the staff did not place rigid expectations about time-to-completion. Instead, teens could delve into an article to learn more about the topic or take advantage of working with available staff members and community volunteers on early drafts of their article summary. In this context, Sara thrived with the needed support from staff, teen editors, volunteers, and undergraduates to develop and hone a range of writing skills. She regularly completed summaries that were deemed worthy of publication in the newspaper and over time, she was assigned more complex topics and denser article sources.

When I asked Sara to reflect on her challenges with English writing, she understood they were quite unique to her own experience as a Mexican/

Latina who spoke English as a second language. She recognized that the challenges she faced at the *Gazette* were very similar to the challenges she faced at school. In a later interview, she reflected that White, native English-speaking students did not experience the same challenges she did as a "Mexican" student:

> I don't know if it's because they [White students] have parents to help them out or if they're just naturally gifted but, they're good. They could probably make it in the Senate or the House of Representatives! But I actually have to work hard to get a decent grade. They can slack off and get a decent grade. I wish I could do that, but I can't. (Interview, March 30, 2012)

It is evident that by this point in her educational career, she had developed clear ideas about the ease with which White students advanced through school, which she attributed possibly to being 'naturally' gifted and to assistance they received from their parents. She also seemed to hold some contradictory views about meritocracy. On one hand, she internalized the myth of meritocracy based on her view that White students' academic success meant they had the potential to succeed in government, for example, regardless of their "slacking off." On the other hand, despite the fact she really "worked hard," her inability to prosper academically meant that she would have limited opportunities in her future.

Additionally, she had developed awareness and a consciousness about the marginalizing effects of English and the language of school and textbooks for students like her. She understood that the content of her ideas, her communicative competence (Gumperz, 1972; Hymes, 1972; Philips, 2001), and her ability to express herself were undervalued because she did not speak the language of textbooks and school. She attributed her shortcomings to being Mexican, being from an (im)migrant family, and having responsibilities at home, as expressed here:

> You can *tell* I'm Mexican. [ ... ] I mean, my point's getting across. I think that's all that matters. Even if you have an accent, as long as your point gets across, that should be good enough. [ ... ] I'm not saying they [White students] don't [have difficulties]. But most of the kids are White and I guess it's kinda stereotypical—White people being smart. That's true. I don't know if it's cus they have parents that help them, they don't have other distractions, they don't come from another country, but they don't have to do chores. (Interview, March 30, 2012)

Based on her perceptions and interpretations, Sara seemed to recognize that language and its intersection with race/ethnicity, class, culture, and (im)migrant background put her at a disadvantage relative to the functioning and valuing of institutions such as the *Gazette* and school where language fares prominently.

Further, she took the stance that the *content* of what student say—regardless of accent, dialect, or non-'standard' forms—is ultimately more important than *how* they say it, "as long as your point gets across." She also seemed to have developed a sophisticated understanding that White students possess some highly valued language practices. It is evident from her doubtful posturing (i.e., "I don't know") and reasoning that even though she believed White people were "smart," she also believed they had several advantages (e.g., helpful parents, flexibility to focus on school, being U.S.-born). Thus, she seemed to implicitly critique the valuing of the *way* students speak rather than the valuing of *what* they say even as she continued to question and interrogate the reasons for White students' seemingly effortless accomplishments.

An important point here is that regardless of her challenges with 'standard' and academic English language and with honing her journalistic writing, she found a flexible, robust support network in the resource-laden newsroom at the *Gazette*. Her participation at the *Gazette*, then, was mediated and facilitated by her co-participants and the timely, relevant, and individualized help they provided on various articles about mammals, jellyfish, and bats as well as book reviews. My analysis of everyday newsroom practices demonstrated that the sociocultural organization of assistance, guidance, and support—rather than individual ability—affected Sara's successful participation and full inclusion as a novice (and later a teen editor) in the newsroom community. While *Gazette* staff members minimally discussed her Spanish-language background and life circumstances, the program was one context where her challenges were less consequential even though she was developing a sense of marginalization from and critique about the power of the English language. At home, Sara's mother was increasingly aware of the power of English, educational institutions, and American popular culture and engaged in calculated actions to mitigate their effects on her daughter.

## Mother–Daughter Pedagogies

Sara's mother, Señora Salazar, was determined and invested in her daughter's education: she sought as many educational opportunities as possible for her daughter, ensured she accomplished school tasks and assignments successfully, and maintained ongoing communications with her daughter's teachers and after-school program staff. Like many Latino (im)migrant parents, she enacted her own version of 'parent involvement' because she was unacquainted and unfamiliar with the U.S. public educational system and its formal and informal structures (Delgado-Gaitan, 1992; López, 2001; Valdes,

1996). As a homemaker raising young Adam, she was able to be highly involved in Sara's everyday life. Señor Salazar, worked as a Chinese restaurant chef to support the family. Sara bonded with her father over the Green Bay Packers and I observed them on several occasions discussing recent sports highlights, football statistics and rankings, and players' recent performances.

Señora Salazar had completed high school in Zacatecas and was highly literate in Spanish. She made concerted efforts to ensure that Sara had enough time to complete required schoolwork by making minimal demands of her within the home (e.g., chores). She respected her daughter's busy schedule pertaining to school and extracurricular activities but there were two areas where Señora Salazar asserted her parental authority: Sara's Spanish language maintenance as well as her Christian upbringing.

On most Sundays, the family attended a Christian church that, based on its growing Spanish-speaking congregation, had recently decided to provide Sunday services through simultaneous English-Spanish translation. Moreover, simultaneous translation was instituted to keep bi/multilingual youth "engaged with their parents" and to make religious content relevant for youth because " *no ponen atención*" [they don't pay attention] (Field note, October 10, 2010). In this setting, language backgrounds were accommodated and embraced, even though the church nevertheless maintained its typical religious routines and activities that had existed before their congregation's demographic profile began to change.

At home, Señora Salazar was forthcoming about the "mother–daughter pedagogies" she emphasized with her children, Sara in particular. First, she was adamant about the need for her children to speak and develop their home language. Thus, the parents spoke Spanish exclusively and the children were encouraged to speak Spanish as well, as captured in this memo excerpt:

> Señora Salazar elaborated that from a very early age, she created a rule for Sara that required her to use Spanish exclusively at home. She could speak English outside the home "*todo lo que quiera, pero en la casa tiene que hablar español*" [all she wants, but at home she must speak Spanish]. She says that it has really helped Sara develop as a bi/multilingual. Now that she's older, Sara tends to speak more English but the rule still stands. However, she uses a different strategy with Adam. She speaks to him in Spanish but attempts to translate everything to English so this translation has become a family endeavor. Just yesterday, for example, Adam asked about a noise and she responded, "Es un tambor" [It's a drum]. She then turned to Sara, who translated "tambor" into "drum." Though she is using different strategies with her children, she and her husband value both languages. (Memo, September 25, 2010)

Even though Sara was beginning to use English almost exclusively and was in English mainstream classes, Señora Salazar made concerted efforts to maintain and develop her home language. One particular activity she organized to promote Spanish language development was a weekly Bible reading. Oftentimes, mother and daughter read and discussed the Bible together. In her explanation about this routine practice, Señora Salazar referenced a television show about the importance of being bi/multilingual among recent university graduates looking for jobs.

Nevertheless, she was frustrated by the fact she could not help Sara with her homework for her Spanish classes because she did not know "*eso de la gramática y los acentos*" [things related to grammar and accents]. Additionally, she referenced occasional comments by Sara's Spanish teacher that "Spanish from Spain is the main and real Spanish" (Field note, December 5, 2010). Given these circumstances, it is clear that language ideologies about "correct" and substantive Spanish-language proficiency (Achugar, 2008; Valdés, González, García, & Márquez, 2003) factored into Sara's life experiences. On one hand, Sara's mother was deeply committed to Sara's Spanish-language maintenance through deliberately coordinated activities and tasks (e.g., home and church). On the other hand, Sara seemed to favor English and simultaneously received negative messages about the *kind* and *type* of Spanish—and Spanish speakers—that are valued.

Furthermore, Señora Salazar believed that Spanish was linked to Mexican culture. Whenever the opportunity arose, she made references to cultural traditions, beliefs, worldviews, and practices. For example, during one conversation between Sara, Señora Salazar, and I, we discussed the extent to which parents are honored and revered among Mexican families in the U.S. and Mexico. Specifically, Señora Salazar explained, "*Honrar a tus padres es una manera de honrar a Dios... En nuestra cultura se acostumbra que los padres se honran sobre todo*" [Honoring your parents is one way to honor God... In our culture, it is customary that parents are honored above all else] (Field note, October 10, 2010). Even though Señora Salazar was perhaps homogenizing an entire group's culture, she took advantage of opportunities to remind Sara "who we are" despite the circulating discourses about them as member of a Mexican/Latino ethnolinguistic group. Yet, Sara responded to her mother's assertion by proclaiming, "I love America!" in a loud and affirmative tone as if to shun her inclusion into "*nuestra cultura*" [our culture]. Because Sara identified as "American," she was clearly both aware and responsive to circulating discourses that devalued her home language (and her mother's efforts) and her Mexican cultural background even if it meant distinguishing herself from her mother.

Finally, Señora Salazar's mother–daughter pedagogies included sustained communications with Sara's classroom teachers and the *Maintown Gazette* staff as well as advocacy work on her daughter's behalf. To expand her knowledge about the U.S. educational system and the post-secondary pipeline, she gathered as much information and problem-solving strategies as possible from accessible teachers, *Gazette* staff, extended family, and educators (e.g., this author). When I first met her, for example, she asked me to share my educational narrative with her and Sara. She asked questions such as "*¿Come le hizo?*" and "*¿Como le ayudaron sus padres?*" [How did you do it? How did your parents help you?] (Field note, October 10, 2010).

During participant observations, Señora Salazar shared a critical incident she experienced with one of Sara's teachers. It pertained to an attempt she made to cooperate with one of Sara's teachers on her class grade, which I captured in a field note:

> The previous school year, Señora Salazar contacted Ms. Green, one of Sara's middle school teachers, about the fact Sara's grades were worsening. When contacted Ms. Green, she asked for some help monitoring Sara's schoolwork and grades. The teacher explained that Sara's low grades were due primarily to incomplete homework. Señora Salazar explained that she herself could not determine whether Sara completed her homework, did her assignments correctly, or fulfilled her teachers' expectations. Thus, she asked Ms. Green to notify her whenever Sara's homework was not submitted, incomplete, or incorrect. This suggestions angered Ms. Green—"*¡Se molestó mucho!*" [She got really bothered!]. Within the next week, Ms. Green forced Sara to call her mother about her homework during class, which Señora Salazar thought was humiliating. She also noticed that her daughter's attitude had started to change and decided she needed to be moved to another classroom. She contacted the assistant principal and school counselor to make the request. She also followed up with Ms. Green, who ignored her for two weeks. When they finally spoke, Señora Salazar demanded an explanation but the teacher instead proceeded to complain that she was the only parent who communicated with her—implying this was unfortunate. Although Señora Salazar threatened to complain to the district if Sara was not moved, the process took an entire semester so she decided to abandon the issue (Field note, December 5, 2010).

This particular incident illustrates that Señora Salazar was not only aware of the mechanisms used to rank students (i.e., grades, homework) but also that there were strategies she could employ to challenge teachers' practices, such as working closely with teachers to monitor students' schoolwork and performance. Importantly, it demonstrates the extent to which Señora Salazar was constrained in her ability to help Sara with her homework because assignments were in English and she did not know enough about U.S. schools to determine how, specifically, assignments needed to be completed.

Home-school misunderstandings and the subsequent marginalization of parents have been well documented, especially as these issues pertain to Chicano/Latino (im)migrant parents and mothers in particular (Lopez& Stoelting, 2010; Valdés, 1996; Villenas & Deyhle, 1999). In Wisconsin, researchers have documented that, for example, even when Latino migrant and (im)migrant parents have mobilized to advocate for their children, school administrators, teachers, and staff at times ignore these efforts (Cline & Necochea, 2006; Olivos, 2004). In Señora Salazar's case, she acted on her emergent knowledge of schooling systems and the spaces where particular policies and practices could be modified by administrators, teachers, students, and/or parents—individually or collectively. While Señora Salazar reached out to administrators, a teacher, and a counselor, her attempts to get Sara re-assigned to another classroom were at best ignored and at worst met with insults.

Here, the intersectionality of language, class, and (im)migrant status affected Señora Salazar's ability to facilitate Sara's educational success and ability to advocate changes in her daughter's education. That is, despite her high school education in Mexico, her status as a Spanish-speaking Latina (im)migrant might have affected the teacher's response to her as it has long been documented that mainstream teachers tend to hold negative views of non-dominant parents of color (Pacheco, 2010b; Ramirez, 2003; Souto-Manning & Swick, 2006). As a Spanish-dominant speaker with limited formal schooling because of her family's low socioeconomic status in her home country, Señora Salazar's multidimensional experiences factored into the ways she could potentially mitigate Sara's increasing vulnerability as a student. Though she possessed sufficient knowledge to understand her daughter's increasing level of risk in school, she did not possess the types of cultural capital upper- and middle-class dominant group parents transform into opportunities to advocate on behalf of their children in school settings (Auerbach, 2007; Jasis & Ordonez-Jasis, 2004; Lareau, 2000).

Mother–daughter pedagogies for Señora Salazar centered on promoting education and academic success, providing Sara plenty of time and space at home to complete her schoolwork and supporting her participation in after-school activities that were enjoyable and academically oriented (e.g., cross country, *Gazette*). She monitored Sara's educational progress and actively became involved when Sara's grades began to decline, talking with teachers and other adults familiar with schooling in the United States. Furthermore, it was evident that she was equally invested in her daughter's cultural identity. She made sure Sara attended church service on a weekly basis and required Sara to read and discuss the Bible in Spanish, which she also linked with being culturally Mexican—things *nosotros los mexicanos* [we Mexicans] do. Recall that, for example, Sara regularly made references about "loving America" and held negative albeit socially constructed perceptions about "Mexican kids who do bad stuff" at her school.

My ongoing analysis of these mother–daughter pedagogies reveals that through these practices, Señora Salazar simultaneously acknowledged that Sara needed to enact a "good student" identity associated with the highly valued opportunity provided by the U.S. public education system as well as a cultural identity linked to her parents, extended family, 'being' and 'doing' Mexican, and Christianity. In some ways, these practices reflected her fundamental dilemma. She had a keen perception about the type of views, dispositions, activities, and academic performance that is needed to succeed in education and in U.S. society. Drawing on her social location and experiences as a Spanish-dominant Latina (im)migrant in the New Latino Diaspora, she was still developing a nuanced understanding about the strategies and opportunities Sara actually needed to achieve educational and life success. On the contrary, Señora Salazar held strong beliefs about the particular cultural and religious practices, traditions, customs, and worldviews Sara needed to develop and maintain to succeed across her lifetime. In essence, she leveraged her growing knowledge about educational access and opportunity to help prepare her daughter for a still unknown future (Villenas, 2005; Villenas & Moreno, 2001), protecting her against still unknown risks and even as she helped her develop some resilience.

## Discussion

The case of Sara demonstrates that she was appropriating particular circulating discourses about Latino cultures and languages as well as developing sophisticated but nuanced perspectives about the power of the English language in educational settings as well as in society. She was questioning "the way things are" for her White counterparts and interrogating the underpinnings of meritocracy since her individual efforts were not resulting in similar levels of success. Nonetheless, she experienced relative success as a teen journalist with the robust assistance, guidance, and support from *Gazette* staff and volunteers. At the same time, Sara and Señora Salazar were developing strategies and pedagogies to enhance their life chances.

For Sara, the American and Mexican social worlds seemed mutually exclusive. For Señora Salazar, mother–daughter pedagogies attempted to resolve this tension. These pedagogies both encouraged Sara to embrace *nepantla*—the ambiguities, contradictions, multidimensionality, and intersectionality of life as a Latina Bi/multilingual adolescent in the New Latino Diaspora. They reflected Señora Salazar's trans-border lived experiences and emergent understandings about life in the New Latino Diaspora and the important need to retain and perpetuate some highly valued cultural practices and ideologies, despite its distinct challenges. Thus, in many ways, Sara was a *nepantlera*—living with ambiguity, traversing distinct social and linguistic worlds, enacting trans-border and trans-cultural identities (e.g., student, runner, teen journalist, English-speaking friend, Mexican), navigating ongoing contradictions and dilemmas, and resolving the process of 'seeing' and 'being seen' in particular ways in society. It was clear that Señora Salazar was deeply invested in Sara's educational and life future and that the consequences for Sara were still in process and being negotiated.

## Conclusion

Given that many Midwestern communities are experiencing significant increases in their Spanish-speaking Latino populations, this New Latino Diaspora represents a unique sociocultural, sociopolitical context for bi/multilingual adolescents. These spaces are not neutral, however, and reflect the unique albeit changing sociocultural, sociopolitical contexts that affect these youths' teaching and learning trajectories—as well as their identities. Thus, they provide important insights into bi/multilingual adolescents' ecologies of development. Latina bi/multilingual adolescents are in effect *nepantleras* (Anzaldúa, 2002). These *nepantleras* are betwixt and between linguistic and cultural worlds shaping and being shaped by these sociocultural, sociopolitical contexts where they experience divergent forms of acceptance, accommodation, and inclusion as well as marginalization, exclusion, and positioning.

This study has implications for educational researchers and practitioners, particularly those interested in bi/multilingual adolescents. First, it demonstrates that analyses of language must account for both the sociocultural and sociopolitical contexts of development for bi/multilingual youth, especially since assessment and accountability frameworks continue to narrow what it means to fully 'know' language. For example, despite her relative success in school, Sara felt increasingly marginalized based on her understanding about the way language practices interested with race/ethnicity, culture, class, (im)migrant background, and so on. Her growing critiques—and the critiques of other vulnerable students—deserve a more prominent place in the crafting of educational policy and practice.

Second, our theories of language, culture, learning, and development must recognize the everyday life of being betwixt and between for language minority and (im)migrant youth who are contending with multiplicity, contradictions, hybridity, and ambiguity (Anzaldúa, 1987, 2002). My point is that a more in-depth examination of the in-between spaces and the border-crossings reveal the extent to which youth—and those around them—are actively and creatively managing the fissures and crevices. Third, given these ecologies of development, educators might also consider the strategies, resources, and pedagogies for resilience and resistance youth, families, and communities develop to confront and overcome their distinct educational and life circumstances (Lee, 2010). These responses certainly would illuminate ways that educators can better assist, guide, and support language minority and (im)migrant youth, families, and communities with limited socioeconomic means as they navigate systems and institutions they are only beginning to fully comprehend. Finally, it seems that the power of *mother–daughter* and *home-community pedagogies* cannot be understated: Señora Salazar was deeply invested in the person Sara was *being* and *becoming*. Rather than continue to employ outdated modes and models of 'parent involvement,' educators are well positioned to learn from language minority and (im)migrant parents who are preparing their children for futures they can only imagine.

## NOTES

1. "Latin@" (with an at sign) is a combination of "Latino" and "Latina"—the masculine and feminine forms in Spanish that signify an individual of Latin American origin.
2. The terms "Latino" and "Hispanic" are used throughout this paper to characterize individuals of Mexican, Central American, and South American descent and who either speak Spanish as a home or were raised in Spanish-dominant homes. The term "(im)migrant" refers to first-generation individuals who migrated to the United States, as well as their children (the 1.5 generation).
3. For this paper, "bi/multilingual" refers to an individual who is relatively fluent using two languages—in this case, Spanish and English.
4. I recognize that use of the phrase "undocumented (im)migrant" poses many potentially problematic associations (e.g., dehumanizes them on the basis of U.S. policy). Still, the term is used commonly to describe the life experiences of individuals who did not enter the United States through a formalized process and yet contribute to its social and economic vitality.
5. All names are pseudonyms.

## REFERENCES

Achugar, M. (2008). Counter-hegemonic language practices and ideologies Creating a new space and value for Spanish in Southwest Texas. *Spanish in Context*, 5(1), 1–19.
Anzaldúa, G. (2002). Now let us shift...the path of conocimiento...: Inner work, public acts. In G. Anzaldua & A. Keating (Eds.), *This bridge we call home: Radical visions for transformation* (pp. 540–578). New York, NY: Routledge.
Auerbach, S. (2007). From moral supporters to struggling advocates reconceptualizing parent roles in education through the experience of working-class families of color. *Urban Education*, 42(3), 250–283.
Benjamin-Alvarado, J., DeSipio, L., & Montoya, C. (2009). Latino Mobilization in New Immigrant Destinations The Anti-HR 4437 Protest in Nebraska's Cities. *Urban Affairs Review*, 44(5), 718–735.

Cline, Z. & Necochea, J. (2006). Teacher dispositions for effective education in the borderlands. *The Educational Forum, 70*(3), p. 268–282.

Cole, M. (1985). The zone of proximal development: Where culture and cognition create each other. In J. Wertsch (Ed.), *Culture, communication, and cognition: Vygotskian perspectives* (pp. 146–160). New York, NY: Cambridge University Press.

Creese, A., & Blackledge, A. (2010). Translanguaging in the bilingual classroom: A pedagogy for learning and teaching? *The Modern Language Journal, 94*(1), 103–115.

Crenshaw, K. W. (1991). Mapping the margins: Intersectionality, identity, politics, and violence against women of color. *Stanford Law Review, 43*(6), 1241–1299.

Creswell, J. W. (1994). *Research design: Qualitative and quantitative approaches.* Thousand Oaks, CA: Sage.

Cruz, C. (2001). Toward an epistemology of a brown body. *International Journal of Qualitative Studies in Education, 14*(5), 657–669.

Delgado-Gaitan, C. (1992). School matters in the Mexican-American home: Socializing children to education. *American Educational Research Journal, 29*(3), 495–513.

Dworin, J. (2003). Inisights into biliteracy development: Toward a bidirectional theory of bi/multilingual pedagogy. *Journal of Hispanic Higher Education, 2*(2), 171–186.

Fought, C. (2003). *Chicano English in context.* New York, NY: Palgrave Macmillan.

Gándara, P., & Contreras, F. C. (2009). On being Latino or Latina in America. In *The Latino education crisis: The consequences of failed social policies* (pp. 54–85). Cambridge, MA: Harvard University Press.

García, O. (2011). *Bilingual education in the 21st century: A global perspective.* New York, NY: John Wiley & Sons.

García, O., & Kleifgen, J. A. (2010). Language and bi/multilingualism: Theoretical constructs and empirical evidence. In O. García & J. A. Kleifgen (Eds.), *Educating emergent bi/multilinguals: Policies, programs, and practices for English Learners* (pp. 37–52). New York, NY: Teachers College Press.

González, F. E. (2001). Haciendo que hacer—cultivating a Mestiza worldview and academic achievement: Braiding cultural knowledge into educational research, policy, practice. *International Journal of Qualitative Studies in Education, 14*(5), 641–656.

González, N., Moll, L. C., & Amanti, C. (Eds.). (2005). *Funds of knowledge: Theorizing practices in households, communities, and classrooms.* New York, NY: Routledge.

Gumperz, J. J. (1972). The communicative competence of bilinguals: Some hypotheses and suggestions for research. *Language in Society, 1*, 143–154.

Gutiérrez, K., Baquedano-Lopez, P., Alvarez, H., & Chiu, M. M. (1999). Building a culture of collaboration through hybrid language practices. *Theory Into Practice 38*(2), 87–93.

Gutiérrez, K., & Rogoff, B. (2003). Cultural ways of learning: Individual traits or repertoires of practice. *Educational Researcher, 32*(5), 19–25.

Gutiérrez, K. D. (2008). Developing a sociocritical literacy in the third space. *Reading Research Quarterly, 43*(2), 148–164.

Gutiérrez, K. D., Morales, P. Z., & Martinez, D. C. (2009). Re-mediating literacy: Culture, difference, and learning for students from nondominant communities. *Review of Research in Education, 33*(1), 212–245.

Hymes, D. H. (1972). On communicative competence. In Pride, J. B., & Holmes, J. (Eds.), *Sociolinguistics* (pp. 269–293). Baltimore, USA: Penguin Education, Penguin Books Ltd.

Jasis, P., & Ordonez-Jasis, R. (2004). Convivencia to empowerment: Latino parent organizing at La Familia. *The High School Journal, 88*(2), 32–42.

Lareau, A. (2000). *Home advantage: Social class and parental intervention in elementary education.* Rowman & Littlefield.

Lave, J. (1996). Teaching, as learning, in practice. *Mind, Culture, and Activity, 3*(3), 149–163.

Lee, C. (2002). Interrogating race and ethnicity as constructs in the examination of cultural processes in developmental research. *Human Development, 45*(4), 282–290.

Lee, C. D. (2010). Soaring above the clouds, delving the ocean's depths understanding the ecologies of human learning and the challenge for education science. *Educational Researcher, 39*(9), 643–655.

López, G. R. (2001). The value of hard work: Lessons on parent involvement from an (im) migrant household. *Harvard Educational Review, 71*(3), 416–438.

Lopez, G. R., & Stoelting, K. (2010). Disarticulating parent involvement in Latino-impacted schools in the Midwest. In M. M. Marsh & T. Turner-Vorbeck (Eds.), *(Mis)understanding families: Learning from real families in our schools* (p. 19–36). New York, NY: Teachers College Press.

Lowenhaupt, R., & Camburn, E. (2011). *Changing demographics in the schools: Wisconsin's New Latino Diaspora* (WCER Working Paper No. 2011-4). Retrieved from University of Wisconsin, Madison, Wisconsin Center for Education Research website: http://www.wcer.wisc.edu/publications/workingPapers/papers.php

Marshall, C., & Rossman, G. B. (1999). *Designing qualitative research* (3rd ed.). Thousand Oaks, CA: Sage Publications.

Martínez, R. A. (2010). Spanglish as literacy tool: Toward an understanding of the potential role of Spanish-English code-switching in the development of academic literacy. *Research in the Teaching of English, 45*(2), 124–149.

Martínez, R., Orellana, M. F., Pacheco, M., Carbone, P. (2008). Found in translation: Connecting translating experiences to academic writing. *Language Arts, 85*(6), 421–431.

Miles, M. B., & Huberman, A. M. (1994). *Qualitative data analysis: An expanded sourcebook.* Thousand Oaks, CA: Sage Publications.

Moll, L. C., Saez, R., & Dworin, J. (2001). Exploring biliteracy: Two student case examples of writing as a social practice. *The Elementary School Journal, 101*(4), 435–449.

Montoya, M. (1994) Mascaras, trenzas, y greñas: Un/masking the self while un/braiding Latina stories and legal discourse. *Chicano-Latino Law Review, 15*, 1–37.

Moschkovich, J. (2002). A situated and sociocultural perspective on bilingual mathematics learners. *Mathematical Thinking and Learning, 4*(2 & 3), 189–212.

Ogbu, J. U. (Ed.). (2008). *Minority status, oppositional culture, & schooling.* New York, NY: Routledge.

Olivos, E. M. (2004) Tensions, contradictions, and resistance: An activist's reflection of the struggles of Latino parents in the public school system. *The High School Journal, 87*(4), 25–35.

Olsen, L. (1997). *Made in America: Immigrant students in our public schools.* New York, NY: The New Press.

Orellana, M. F. (2009). *Translating childhoods: Immigrant youth, language, and culture.* Piscataway, NJ: Rutgers University Press.

Pacheco, M. (2009). Towards expansive learning: Examining Chicana/o and Latina/o students' political-historical knowledge. *Language Arts, 87*(1), 18–29.

Pacheco, M. (2010a). *Deadline!!!: Apprenticing adolescent writers at a community newspaper.* Paper presented at the annual meeting of the American Educational Research Association, Denver, CO.

Pacheco, M. (2010b). Performativity in the bilingual classroom: The plight of English Learners in the current reform context. *Anthropology & Education Quarterly, 41*(1), 75–93.

Pacheco, M. (2012). Learning in/through everyday resistance: A cultural-historical perspective on community 'resources' and curriculum. *Educational Researcher, 41*(4), 121–132.

Philips, S. U. (2001). Participant structures and communicative competence: Warm Springs children in community and classroom. In A. Duranti (Ed.), *Functions of language in the classroom* (pp. 329–342). Malden, MA: Blackwell Publishing Ltd.

Ramirez, A. Y. F. (2003). Dismay and disappointment: Parental involvement of Latino immigrant parents. *The Urban Review, 35*(2), 93–110.

Reyes, I. (2004). Functions of code switching in schoolchildren's conversations. *Bilingual Research Journal, 28*(1), 77–98.

Rogoff, B. (1990). *Apprenticeship in thinking: Cognitive development in social context.* New York, NY: Oxford University Press.

Rogoff, B. (1995). Observing sociocultural activity on three planes: Participatory appropriation, guided appropriation, and apprenticeship. In J. V. Wertsch, P. Del Rio, & A. Alvarez (Eds.), *Sociocultural studies of mind* (pp. 139–164). Cambridge: Cambridge University.

Rogoff, B. (2003). *The cultural nature of human development.* New York, NY: Oxford University Press.

Saldívar-Hull, S. (1991). Feminism on the border: From gender politics to geopolitics. In H. Calderón & R. D. Saldívar (Eds.), *Criticism in the borderlands: Studies in Chicano literature, culture, and ideology* (pp. 203–220). Durham, NC: Duke University Press.

Sánchez, G. J. (2002). ¿Y Tú Qué? (Y2k) Latino history in the new millennium. In M. M. Suárez-Orozco & M. M. Paez (Eds.), *Latinos: Remaking America* (pp. 50–56). Berkeley, CA: University of California Press.

Solórzano, D. G., & Delgado-Bernal, D. (2001). Examining transformational resistance through a critical race and LatCrit theory framework: Chicana and Chicano students in an urban context. *Urban Education, 36*(3), 308–342.

Strauss, A. (1987). *Qualitative analysis for social scientists.* Cambridge: Cambridge University Press.

Souto-Manning, M., & Swick, K. J. (2006). Teachers' beliefs about parent and family involvement: Rethinking our family involvement paradigm. *Early Childhood Education Journal, 34*(2), 187–193.

U.S. Census Bureau (2010). State and county quickfacts; Madison, Wisconsin. Retrieved November 5, 2013, from http://quickfacts.census.gov/qfd/states/55/5548000.html

Valdes, G. (1996). *Con respeto: Bridging the distances between culturally diverse families and schools.* New York, NY: Teachers College Press.

Valdés, G. (1998). The world outside and inside schools: Language and immigrant children. *Educational Researcher, 27*(6), 4–18.

Valdés, G. (2003). *Expanding definitions of giftedness: The case of young interpreters from (im)migrant communities.* New York, NY: Routledge.

Valdés, G., González, S. V., García, D. L., & Márquez, P. (2003). Language Ideology: The Case of Spanish in Departments of Foreign Languages. *Anthropology & Education Quarterly, 34*(1), 3–26.

Villenas, S. (2005). Between the telling and the told: Latina mothers negotiating education in new borderlands. In J. Phillion, M.F. He, & M. Connelly (Eds.), *Narrative and experience in multicultural education* (pp. 71–91). Thousand Oaks, CA: Sage.

Villenas, S., & Deyhle, D. (1999). Critical race theory and ethnographies challenging the stereotypes: Latino families, schooling, resilience and resistance. *Curriculum Inquiry, 29*(4), 413–445.

Villenas, S., & Moreno, M. (2001). To valerse por si misma between race, capitalism, and patriarchy: Latina mother-daughter pedagogies in North Carolina. *International Journal of Qualitative Studies in Education, 14*(5), 671–687.

Vygotsky, L. S. (1978). *Mind in society: The development of higher physchological processes.* In M. Cole, V. John-Steiner, S. Scriber, & E. Souberman (Eds.). Cambridge, MA: Harvard University Press.

Wei, L., & Wu, C-J. (2009). Polite Chinese children revisited: Creativity and the use of codeswitching in the Chinese complementary school classroom. *International Journal of Bilingual Education and Bilingualism, 12*(2), 193–211.

Wortham, S., Murillo, E. G., & Hamann, E. T. (Eds.). (2002). *Education in the new Latino diaspora: Policy and the politics of identity.* Westport, CT: Ablex Publishing.

Yosso, T. J. (2005). Whose culture has capital? A critical race theory discussion of community cultural wealth. *Race Ethnicity and Education, 8*(1), 69–91.

Zentella, A. C. (1997). *Growing up bilingual: Puerto Rican children in New York.* Malden, MA: Blackwell.

Zentella. (2005). *Building on strength: Language and literacy in Latino families and communities.* New York, NY: Teachers College Press.

CHAPTER 6

# STUDENTS OF COLOR IN MAJORITY WHITE SCHOOLS

## A Critical Race Theory Analysis of Race and Gender

**Thandeka Chapman**
*University of California, San Diego*

The literature focused on the racial identities of students of color has consistently attempted to answer questions concerning the impact of racial identity on student academic achievement and success. Conceptualizations of student identity have been framed through a number of theoretical positions such as cultural ecology, social reproduction, and social interactionism (Diamond, 2006). These theories have been used to explain the psychological processes and behaviors involved with how students craft their identities in racially homogenous and heterogeneous communities and school contexts. "Specifically, reproduction theories in their current academic deployment are deeply engaged in a project of 'racial myth-making' whereby racially explicit experiences and practices are recoded as cultural or social with little or no attention to the role of institutionalized racism in

*Intersectionality and Urban Education*, pages 125–146
Copyright © 2014 by Information Age Publishing
All rights of reproduction in any form reserved.

the construction of social inequality" (Akom, 200, p. 208) Moreover, little research has more directly focused on how racism, in school contexts, creates and maintains fissures in the identity development of students of color (Carter, 2008; Diamond 2006).

Through a critical race theory lens, the development of student identity is viewed as a hostile process in which students of color struggle against institutional and social structures that shape their identity development, and constrain their ability to be viewed as individuals. Using Crenshaw's framework of intersectionality to interrogate the identities of students of color in majority White suburban schools with inter-district busing programs, I posit that students of color identity development is a complex interaction between the constructs of race, class, and gender that affects their schooling experiences and prevents them from fully accessing an equitable education.

## CONTEXTS

Critical race theory is employed to depict the historical and current contexts of schooling in majority White suburbs. In 1974 the *Milliken vs. Bradley* decision was handed down from the Supreme Court. Chief Justice Berger decreed: "Where the schools of only one district have been affected, there is no constitutional power in the courts to decree relief balancing the racial composition of that district's schools with those of the surrounding district (Milliken vs. Bradley, 418 U.S. 717). This decision prevented urban districts from crossing district boundaries to alleviate racial segregation if the suburban district had no past culpability for segregation, therefore maintaining White spaces in suburban districts. Fearing court-interventions, several districts created inter-district busing programs before and after Milliken. This interest-convergence allowed the suburban districts to avoid litigation while a small number of urban students escaped their racially segregated schools. Many suburban cities followed Boston's Metco program model after *Milliken* because it allowed their district to control the number of students entering their schools.

These programs were not altruistic endeavors. Milwaukee's Chapter 220 program began in 1976 and became part of a federal court compromise between suburban districts and Milwaukee. In Milwaukee, the district per pupil spending money moves to the suburban district with the student. These funds, which are often greater than the per/pupil funds of the surrounding districts, help the districts financially. Currently 3% (2,250 of the 83,000 children) of Milwaukee students participate in the Chapter 220 program.

Competing with the old busing reforms is the movement of affluent families of color into suburban neighborhoods. The racial landscape of suburban schools has drastically changed in the past decade (see Table 6.1).

**TABLE 6.1   Racial Composition of Schools in the Study in 2009 (Wisconsin Department of Public Instruction)**

|  | Total # of Students | # Students of Color | % Students of Color |
|---|---|---|---|
| School A | 663 | 378 | 57% |
| School B | 1,490 | 194 | 13% |
| School C | 614 | 153 | 25% |
| School D | 1,143 | 267 | 23.4% |
| School E | 987 | 296 | 30% |
| School F | 890 | 160 | 18% |

As White families continue to move further from metropolitan areas, the nearby suburbs are becoming increasingly racially diverse, but not necessarily economically diverse. The current racial demographic changes, due to low interest loans and little money down in previously unaffordable suburban areas, are significantly affecting the racial landscape of suburban schools. Suburban districts find themselves dealing with more savvy, middle class, home owners of color who wield more cultural and social capital than previous low-income and middle-class parents whose students are seen as guests from the districts' minority busing programs (Burton, Bonilla-Silva, Ray, Buckelew, & Freeman, 2010). In demographics terms, these schools appear to be the multi-racial areas that proponents of desegregation strove to create.

Additionally, NCLB (2001) provided policy articulations that have highlighted current inequities in school and the schooling experiences of racial minority students. High achieving schools with racially mixed populations have a significant gap between the achievement of their students of color and their White students. As more middle-class, second generation college educated families of color and families with children of color move into these suburban enclaves, schools cannot blame family income and education levels for the gaps in achievement between students of color and White students. Under the 2001 federal mandate, schools can be penalized for maintaining academic gaps between White students and their minority populations. This is different from previous years where high achieving schools, which claimed to be integrated and thriving, used aggregated data to obfuscate their achievement gaps. School/ district reputations and funding are now vulnerable to sanctions based on a district's ability to meet the academic needs of all children. These potential sanctions make administrators take a new interest in the achievement patterns of their racial minority students.

## CURRENT RESEARCH ON STUDENT IDENTITY
## CONSTRUCTION

As racial demographics continue to shift, many scholars are researching the experiences of students of color in majority White high schools (Carter, 2007; Chapman, 2007; Diamond, 2006; Diamond, Lewis, Gordon, 2007; Huidor & Cooper, 2010; O'Connor, Mueller, Lewis, Rivas-Drake, 2011). An extensive review of students of color identity research is beyond the purview of the chapter, and also privileges particular authors whose work has received significant attention for "blaming the victim.[1]" Derrick Bell states that scholars of color who deny or temper claims of racism become the highlighted voice that is used to negate the legitimacy of racism and re-direct the discourse to cultural explanations of the achievements of racial groups (Bell, 1995, p. 908.) Diamond, Lewis and Gordon explain, "In fact, since the mid-1980s, the 'acting White' hypothesis and the related oppositional culture argument has captured the scholarly and popular imagination in discussions of educational achievement" (2007, p. 658). The contradicting perspectives on race and identity become entrenched battles that further instantiate discourses of cultural deficits and problematic communities by scholars being required to re-hash the scholarship of deficit before providing a counter discourse to explore the schooling experiences of students of color.

The scholarship reviewed for this chapter recounts those debates; therefore, I choose to focus on how the findings of recent scholarship move the conversations about student identity construction forward, and to disclose different ways to contemplate how students of color construct their identities. Huidor and Cooper (2010) state,

> Schooling experiences are not static but rather characterized by dynamic processes that can be understood in multiple conceptual ways. It is important to understand that as institutions of learning, both academic and life trajectories are developed within schools. (p. 143)

The authors reviewed in this article privilege the voices of students of color as a viable and necessary research strategy to demonstrate the various manifestations of race and racism within these settings and to better understand how students of color make academic choices that define their future academic success.

O'Connor, Mueller, Lewis, Rivas-Drake, and Rosenberg (2011) interviewed 44 Black students and conducted a more in-depth study of eight high-achievers to document the schooling experiences of high-achieving students of color in racially stratified accelerated courses. The researchers found that students maintained strong connections with their African American peers who were also in their less rigorous classes as a means to buffer them from acts of racism. The buffering system was unavailable to Black students in the upper-level AP and advanced courses, causing them to seek alliances with other racial groups such as Asian Americans. O'Connor et al. state that the students' resistance to stereotypes and their negotiation of the school contexts interacted with the contexts of the school as an unwelcoming space. The researchers also noted that some students were able to cross racial boundaries in classes by proving themselves as worthy academic partners. However, many of the high achieving Black students in the study espoused a negative view of Black low achievers, and connected these perceptions with negative stereotypes of race.

Similar to O'Connor et al., Diamond, Lewis, and Gordon (2007) found comparable results pertaining to issues of racial isolation and negative peer pressure in upper-level courses for Black students. For Black students in regular classes, there was a stronger support system among Black students. Diamond et al. also noted that the stress and racism of upper level classes caused Black students to doubt their academic abilities. Diamond et al. interviewed 70 Black and White high school students with a range of grade point averages. The researchers found that the majority of Black students felt that being Black would limit their life chances for success, while the White students did not believe that race was a factor in their success. However, the Black students' belief in racial stratifications of success did not impact their academic achievement and desire to be successful. In fact, Black students at every level of tracking hoped to attend college.

In her study of high-achieving Black students at a majority White suburban elite school, Carter (2007) also documented Black students' strategies of survival. She noted that Black students created homogenous racial enclaves to affirm racial identity and shield them from racism in the school. Carter conducted a series of three interviews with nine African American students in the 10–12th grades who accessed the school through a race-based, desegregation, busing program. Carter found that the students reinforced their Black identities through their forms of dress and informal language styles when socializing in certain areas of the school where Black students congregated. The students further supported each other through a formal association, the Black Leadership Advisory Council, which gave them the opportunity to meet and voice their frustrations. Carter asserts that formal and informal spaces for Black students help students maintain positive resistance to racism and a positive sense of self and academic achievement.

In a study of 12 Black students in a gifted program in a racially mixed school, Henfield, Moore, and Wood's (2008) themes resonate with the work of Carter (2007; 2008), Diamond et al. (2007), and O'Connor et al. (2011). Henfield et al. conducted a mixed-methods study of gifted African American high school students to explore how racial identity interacted with their academic identity. As with the previously mentioned researchers, they found that Black students maintain strong racial identities despite racism and isolation. Black students also were extremely cognizant of racist practices at the school and classroom levels. Interestingly, the gifted students combated issues of "acting White" and "nerd" by joining extra-curricular activities where they interacted with Black students who were outside of the gifted program.

Diamond (2006) and Chapman (2007) frame their analysis to describe the impact of racism in predominately White schools on students of color. Diamond (2006) interrogates the structural barriers, predicated upon implementations of desegregation that prevent Black students from fully engaging in White suburban high schools. Chapman (2007) explores how students of color, Black, Latino, and Asian American choose to participate or abstain from educational activities based on their levels of comfort and ability to negotiate the different circumstances. Both authors describe how the racial contexts of the school influence students' willingness to fully engage at all levels of schooling.

Huidor and Cooper (2010) explore the experiences of Black and Latino students through a quantitative lens. In their examination of 20 students of color who were bused to a predominately White school, the researchers documented the students' perceptions of their school experiences as significantly more rigorous and engaging than the school experiences afforded to them in their neighborhood schools. The students recognized the racial segregation in both academic and social components of the school, and mediated these issues by forming close bonds with their same race peers.

Although the study shares many of the conclusions of the previous studies, this paper closely aligns with the conceptual frameworks of Carter (2008), Diamond (2006), and Chapman (2007) to focus on how the institutional climate reproduces inequity and stratifies students' possibilities for identity development. The voices of students of color contradict the colorblind discourse articulated in White high schools, highlight the hypocrisy of colorblind discourses, and legitimate their "racially based feelings and viewpoints" (Bonilla-Silva, 2009, p. 11), by articulating the ways the students are racialized. The shift from focusing on internal identity formation to institutional instantiations of racism and oppression is an attempt to move the discourse from a focus on the racial group's reaction to racism to the public systems and actors that cause the conflict.

## Intersectionality and Students of Color in Majority White Schools

Critical Race Theory advocates for a complex articulation of how race is performed, understood, and manipulated primarily in the United States.

Race is the central tenet of CRT because of its pervasive nature and influence throughout various realms of social thought and behavior. Racism, or more specifically, White supremacy, has shaped the norm, values, and history of the United States through a system of binaries that continues to conflate good and moral with Whiteness and evil and immoral with Blackness.

> Historically, White supremacy has been premised upon various political, scientific, and religious theories, each of which relies on racial characterizations and stereotypes about Blacks that have coalesced into an extensive legitimating ideology. Today it *is* probably not controversial to say that these stereotypes were developed primarily to rationalize the oppression of Blacks. What is overlooked, however, is the extent to which these stereotypes serve a hegemonic function by perpetuating a mythology about both Blacks *and* Whites even today, reinforcing an illusion of a White community that cuts across ethnic, gender, and class lines. [author's italics] (Crenshaw, 1988, pp. 1370–1371)

It is the reliance on Blackness to solidify Whiteness that, in part, necessitates the need to maintain the ideology of race, and to justify systemic racism. "Racism helps to create an illusion of unity through the oppositional force of a symbolic 'other'" (Crenshaw, 1988, p. 1372) in a way, I would add, that is unique to this particular form of oppression and the sanctioning of policies that historically and presently privilege White citizens over citizens of color. Ladson-Billings and Tate (1995) recognize the importance of gender-and class based analyses; however, they assert that "the significance of race in the United States, and more specifically 'raced' education could not be explained with theories of gender or class" (1997, p. 196).

The centrality of race in CRT becomes the axel on which the wheels of U.S. society turn; the spokes holding that wheel to the axel are group memberships and forms of oppression that intersect with race and racism. To ignore the stratifications of race and racism that are caused by other group memberships would be to present an essentialist view of race. Indeed, one of the critiques of the theory is that, at times, CRT attempts to speak for a race of people without taking into consideration how these spokes of identity impact people's experiences as racialized subjects. When discussing the convergence of intersectionality with critical race theory, Scott explains that "together, culturally sensitive research approaches and CRT encourage scholars to center African Americans and other historically subordinated groups, their culture, knowledge, and experiences as valid rather than as marginalized deficiencies" (Scott, 2012, p. 626). Thus, the inter-dependence between issues of race, gender, class, and sexuality further complicates academic and practical understandings of how and why people are being oppressed, or have been oppressed in the past.

To address this interplay between the wheel, the spokes of identity, and the axel of race and racism for women of color, Crenshaw re-conceptualized a theory of intersectionality (1991). Crenshaw's concept is more complex than the initial wheel metaphor I employ because the spokes themselves cross each other even as they remain anchored in race and racism. Other scholars have used a critical race theoretical framework to explore how racial identity intersects with issues of class, gender, and heteronormativity in a range of fields of studies such as family studies (Few, 2007), criminal justice (Marchetti, 2008), psychology (Cole, 2009), and athletics (Anderson & McCormack, 2010).

Although Delgado (2011) suggests that critical race theorists confine their use of intersectionality to materialist projects, less it become a postmodern tool of nihilism to fracture racial groups and make coalition building for political solidarity an impossible task, other critical race theorists are concerned with the lack of interrogation of social forces of oppression that compound issues of racism (Bergers & Guidors, 2009; Grabham, Cooper, Krishnadas, & Herman, 2009). Covarrubias asserts,

> Intersectionality similarly challenges the notion that we live in a postcolonialist society in which these socially constructed divisions no longer impact or are impacted by power. Furthermore, it posits that institutions remain impacted by political projects that are guided by maintaining existing power relations at the expense of vulnerable populations along multiple intersecting continuums of difference (2011, p. 89).

Critical race theorists in education have used their scholarship to expose the multiple social axes of institutional and relational power differentials in schools and communities that marginalize people of color. Dixson (2003; with DeCuir-Gunby, 2008) has analyzed the confluence between gender and race with regard to Black women teachers as constricted professionals and student advocates. Lynn (2002, 2006, 2009) has explored the tensions between gender and race that Black male teachers experience in public schools. Other critical race scholars have documented the gendered experiences of Black boys (Berry, 2005, 2008; Brown & Donnor, 2011; Donnor, 2005; Duncan 2002; Howard 2008; Howard & Flennaugh, 2011; Muhammed, 2008; Vaught 2004), Black girls (Muhammed & Dixson, 2008), Chicanas (Malagon & Alzarez, 2010), and Latin@s (Munoz & Maldanado, 2012; Delgado-Bernal, 2002; Covarrubias, 2011) in racially homogenous and diverse school settings.

To share a nuanced, situational perspective of intersectionality, Crenshaw articulates her intersectional framework in three positions:

1. Structural intersectionality—the institutional subordination of women due to their gender roles, responsibilities, language, and job opportunities

2. Political intersectionality—the forced separation of women's multiple identities in political struggles and possible coalition building
3. Representational intersectionality—the presentation of public images that present narrow, stereotypes constructions of women (Crenshaw, 1995).

This intersectional framework critiques systems of oppression as well as discuss differences among, not just between, different groups.

In this analysis of the study, the three forms of intersectionality are applied to male and female students. Although most scholarship on intersectionality comes from the perspectives of women of color, issues of masculinity intersect with gender in schools in ways that specifically marginalize male students. Additionally, the construction of race intersects with issues of class in school settings to grant greater access and social capital to middle class students of color over working class students of color. While a comprehensive explanation of how social factors interact to maintain oppression is yet to be realized, the following data is used to unpack outstanding moments of intersectionality and racial oppression with specific regard for race and gender. Covarubias explains,

> Much of this work has effectively demonstrated that our lives and relationships to others, and institutions, are complicated. We experience these relationships through the simultaneity of our multiple political and social identities as mediated by external conditions and context. Hence, we live a life in which we are constantly recreating ourselves while the inertia of power continues to maintain itself and define us in ways that shape our opportunities. (2011, p. )

Because the "inertia of power" functions in complex dynamics, researchers can only provide a limited point of view of the different contexts where race and racism define people of color. Thus, the contexts of White suburban school settings as sites where race and gender intersect to promote structure opportunities for academic and social empowerment for students of color are examined in the following sections.

## Structural Intersectionality

In majority White suburban schools, structural racism is most blatantly represented through the tracking system. "For example, we know that in schools, most Chicanas and Chicanos are not tracked toward college readiness but rather relegated to under-resourced, overcrowded schools where they are taught by less experienced teachers and are often taught curricula that are the least valued" (Covarrubias, 91). In the case of majority White schools, students of color- Latin@s, Blacks and Hmong students are over-represented in the lower tracks of the school. In the study, high achieving students of color recognized that they were frequently the only Black or Brown bodies in their advanced placement or advanced subject classrooms. Those students of color in the high tracks could count the number of students of color in their classes.

**Student:** In AP Spanish there is only one other Black person in there. The rest of mine—no. They are all White.
**Student:** In my AP classes I have more Asian people.
**Student:** AP English there is one [Asian].
**Student:** My regular English classes, I have me, my brother, and two other Black people. The others are White. Or my Latin class, there are four Black people and the majority are White.
**Student:** Mostly all my classes are predominantly White. I only have one class with one Black person in my entire schedule.
**Student:** For my first time in high school, I had a class with two other Black kids and that was the most I ever had.

Conversely, students who were in lower tracked courses, could not give the number of students because there we too many to quickly count.

**Researcher:** So most [students of color] are in regular classes?
**Student:** Yeah
**Researcher:** Are they [students of color] in lower levels?
**Student 1:** Yes, math especially.
**Student 2:** Yes, I am in the lower level in every course.
**Researcher:** What is the representation in those courses?
**Student 1:** A lot.
**Researcher:** More than in regular?
**Student 3:** I have formal geometry, and there is only one White kid in there.

In White majority schools, higher tracks of curriculum serve as the property of White students in which few students of color are able to access these rigorous curricular experiences that lead to greater college access (Ladson-Billings & Tate, 1995; Ladson-Billings & Brown, 2008). These racial stratifications, created by teachers and counselors, reinforce the White supremacist ideology of students of color as intellectually inferior. Because most of the students of color have matriculated in these districts since kindergarten, their track positions cannot be dismissed as students of color transferring to suburban high schools from lower status urban high schools. Instead, the placement of students of color in lower tracks reflects forty-year conversations about how students are tracked into classes based on race and socio-economic status at an early age and unable to cross into upper tracks later in their schooling careers (Rist 1970, Oakes, 1985).

## Gendered Structural Intersectionality

The intersections of gender and race are demonstrated through more subtle forms of harassment. Female students describe incidents in which Black girls and Latinas are sent home for violating dress codes regarding leggings and short shorts, while White girls were not reprimanded. A Black female student explained,

> But we are students and we are here…and I disagree completely with the rules, because they are not consistent. They will tell one student one thing, the example being leggings. She walks around with leggings she going home within the first 30 minutes. Let a Caucasian come in with the leggings. She could wear them the whole week.

Female students of color are more likely to be judged by their appearance and clothing. Cruz explains that "we must ask how the Brown body is regulated and governed in schools and other social institutions. How does a regime of a given society become inscripted onto the bodies of our youth" (2001, 664)? In White majority suburban schools, the Brown body is a "messy text" (Cruz, 2001) that constantly must be contained and categorized. In the study, female students of color talk about the significant amount of attention they receive concerning their clothing. For female students, clothing represented a student's status as "ghetto" or "preppy"/ "academically inferior" or "acting White." For adults, the Brown body required strict surveillance in which girls of color could be sent home for not meeting the school dress code, while White girls were allowed to wear their gym clothes for the duration of the day. The emphasis on the Brown body creates a gendered context of racial oppression in which women of color are over-scrutinized for their appearance and hyper-sexualized. The realization that White girls maintain privilege through their ability to not be the focus of enforced dress codes and adult judgments of their attire creates an oppressive context in schools.

The surveillance of the Brown body functions differently for Black and Latino boys. More subtle representations such as the over-surveillance of Black boys further affects the schooling experiences of students of color and their ability to gain full access to the elite education offered by White suburban schools. Students described multiple instances where they were reprimanded, taken to the office, denied privileges, or harassed by adults based on their status as Black and Latino males.

**Black Male Student:** Do not hang outside of this school. Once you go
here, go home.
**Researcher:** Why is that?
**Black Male Student:** For a month straight, I go to lunch and you got
punks [policemen questioning you].... I guarantee it be
three weeks in a month per week, somebody calling you
names, for real.
**Researcher:** Racial profiles. They don't call you by first names? You
haven't committed any crime. You haven't done anything
that was suspicious.
**Black Male Student:** The police was sitting by my car when I leave
[school].
**Black Male Student:** One time I was sitting outside waiting for a ride after
school, then the police pulled up by me and questioned
me about sitting out here for too long or something like
that. [city] police pulled me over, and it was something like
[gang] rivalry or something. They pulled me over for that.
**Researcher:** If you are African American you have a high chance of being
pulled over? So you don't really hang out here?
**Student:** Between here, school, and basketball. Even on Fridays, when
I get out of school, I be ready to go.

Male students are keenly aware of the stereotypes concerning men of color,
and how these perceptions restrict their behavior in schools and society.
Akom explains that, "In the context of racism the negative status determining characteris- tics of race, skin color, and gender assigned to Black males
undermines our ability to be taken for granted as law-abiding and civic participants" (p. 220). Males of color do not receive the benefit of the doubt
when accused of disobedience, violence, harassment, or other criminal or
unethical behavior. Howard, Flennaugh, and Terry state,

> We operate from the position that large numbers of Black males experience
> education in a manner unlike most groups in the U.S. and that these experi-
> ences are rooted in a historical construction of what it means to be Black and
> male. These experiences, we assert, are often guided by a less than flattering
> account of the aca- demic potential, intellectual disposition, and social and
> cultural capital possessed by Black males. Moreover, our contention is that
> not only do these notions of Black males shape their schooling experiences,
> but may severely influence their life chances at a time where educational ac-
> cess is vital to competing in an increasingly global society. (2011, p. 87)

In an off the recorded conversation, a Latino student described an incident
in which he and several other Black and Brown students were lined up,
frisked, and forced to open their backpacks in the cafeteria when another

student's Ipod went missing at lunch. He was further enraged to find out that the culprit was a White male student who was not subjugated to the interrogation. Black and Latino male students report that incidents such as adult harassment and over-surveillance in and outside the classroom are inescapable, frequent events.

The consistent harassment of Black and Brown males serves as reinforcement of their precarious position in these schools. Students who are viewed as physically threatening or morally corrupt can be expelled from the school. In order to avoid the label of physically threatening, Black and Brown males discussed how they purposely held their tempers, lowered their eyes, remained still, and lowered their voices to demonstrate respect for teachers and administrators. These actions connote White middle class norms of behavior that place these students in subjugated positions in ways reminiscent of slaves and field workers speaking to their masters or bosses. Thus, Black and Brown males are expressly aware of their powerless position in the schools.

## Political Intersectionality

Stratifications of race permeated the school in forms that were less delineated than the structural issues of tracking and surveillance. As a formal part of the study, students were asked to self-designate their race. Many of the students questioned the researchers about the extent of categories they were able to list. The researchers replied that there was no limit. This resulted in our receiving several diverse racial constructions that would not have been accessed by pre-structured categories. Political intersectionality, when identities compete against each other, is highlighted through the Black-White binary that prevents bi-racial students from being able to acknowledge both racial backgrounds or requires students with inter-racial family structures to defend their parents' choices. The following White and Black bi-racial student's quote demonstrates the complexities of race that are invisible to her friends and teachers.

**Bi-racial Female Student:** If you say like a big word or something, they will say you are so White. I admit that I am a cracker. I was raised that way. People think it is cool to be ghetto and stuff but it is not. My mom is White and she was raised in the ghetto. She went through foster home and went through a whole bunch of stuff. Her parents were on drugs and all that stuff. She was raised in the ghetto on the east. So she has been through it all. She has been through a lot of stuff. She has been held at gunpoint before down on 20th and Center.

And she is White. But the thing is that we are where we are now because she got away from the ghetto. People act like they are cool because they live in the ghetto or they are cool because they have a—You are not cool. Get away from me.

This student rejects notions of White privilege because she was recently poor and her mother's history is riddle with events that are associated with people of color living in urban communities. While most of her friends are Black, she is constantly reminded of her limited affiliation by comments about her speech and her new middle-income status.

Other bi-racial students, such as the following student, became frustrated from the ignorance displayed by students regarding his family structure.

**Multi-Racial Male Student:** I might not look like Black, Brown, I am Black, White, Indian. When I first came here I had a tan, a darker complexion. People would ask are you Mexican or this or that. They would ask that constantly. My brothers come off as Black. This group of girls come up to me like is that your real brother. And I looked at them and said why wouldn't it be. They were like you have a darker complexion. When my mom walks in, they assume that my mom is like Mexican. My mom is thoroughly White. They said that can't be your mom or your brothers or sisters [brother]. They constantly just ask what are you again, what color are you again. [they say] I wish I was that color. My hair is curly. And they would say that is the Black side of you or something like that. That is just how my hair is.

In these school settings, the student is raced as Black, Latin@, or Asian even if he/she has a White parent. Crenshaw poses political intersectionality as "two subordinate groups that frequently pursue conflicting political agendas" (1991, p. 1252). However, in racialized school settings, where race becomes a primary avenue of academic and social stratification, bi-racial students suffer from having one group representing the majority and one group representing a minority population contesting each other, or two minority population groups.

Given the politics of race as phenotype appearance, they are most often labeled by skin color or facial structure. The bi-racial identity serves as a double-edged sword for many of these students in which they may receive power and privilege for their racial identity in some instances, and may be outcast for the very same identity in other situations. One bi-racial student stated, "I don't let people know that I am Native American. I look White. I have White skin so it is not really a big deal. Some people know I am Native

American, but no one really cares." Clearly, her decision to hide half of her identity and pass for White demonstrates the extreme levels of "care" exhibited by the student. Howard et al. state. "Moreover, the contingencies, or the things that one has to deal with because of his or her group member-ship, can take a tremendous toll on stigmatized groups" (2011, p. 93).

Similarly, students who had inter-racial families displayed a secondary affiliation to more than one racial group. These students felt maligned and torn when the race of their family members were verbally attacked.

> People say I am not racist but like at the basketball game my dad married a White woman and I have two step-sisters who are White. I live with them on the weekdays. She [step-sister] came with me to the basketball game and she ended up meeting up with her other friends and they watched the game. I was with my friends. I was with them and she came up to me and [my friend] asked me a question like who is she. I said she is my step-sister and [my friend] started laughing and making fun of me. I literally cussed her out because there is nothing wrong with being with family. My great-grandmother was White. I have White in me. It made me so mad.

**Latino Student:** Actually I can actually relate to that point really well because the reason I can get along with a lot of different persons. But I personally look at people as people because I grew up in an all White family and I am adopted from a different country. So I have to I can go between, like, I have like friends that I grew up within intercity—and I don't look at them as kids who grew up in intercity —. I look at them as my old friend I grew up with. And like here. I see kids, and they talk about [me]. Like, I have been called all different sorts of names. I think they called me just about anything you can possibly call me.

Students of color who have inter-racial families are forced to defend their families because they do not fit the Black/ White binary of relationships. Similar to children from interracial families in Australia, students of color in the United States struggle to "establish their 'sameness' in discriminatory environments of schools and workplaces where there was little public dis-course on or about difference that was not couched in discriminatory and racist stereotypes" (Luke & Luke, 1998, p. 736). The bi-racial students often are required to prove themselves as belonging to a chosen racial group, if phenotype does not deny their choice; while students of one race must balance their allegiance to their racial group and alliance with their family members from another race.

## Representational Intersectionality

Students of color were keenly aware of the media/ TV stereotypes they battled in their school settings. Students explain,

**Black Female Student:** Because there is such a small percentage of Black people here and because the White students here may not have the opportunity to interact with Black people. When they see something negative, they are just saying oh this perpetuates what I feel on TV, the stereotypes or the negative images that I may see. It solidifies it for them in their mind.

**Black Female Student:** They think that we are the girls on the videos that they see on BET, that we are the people who they see on TV rolling their neck and having lipgloss on and wearing big hoops and having like plenty of babies. They think that that is who we are- that we are from [urban city], and that we live around people who go to [urban school district] and women are having babies and doing wild stuff like that. But that is not who we are.

Students recognize the social media discourses that they are exposed to in their everyday lives; however, they may not know about the academic discourses that do them the same disservice when educating adults to work in schools. In schools, representational intersectionality, the ways in which students of color are marginalized by pathological discourses that reinstantiate negative stereotypes, is propagated through the academic literature on students of color that characterizes them and their families through deficit lenses of analysis. Howard et al. adds, "The challenge of making meaning of an imposed identity, which does not reflect on one favorably, and then fighting to debunk that image raises serious concerns about how school performance plays out" (2011, p. 92). These deficit lenses pose high achieving students of color as disconnected from their peers and communities of color. Low achieving students of color are often constructed through the lenses of cultural deficiency and limited intellectual ability. Academic conversations further construct a false dichotomy between high and low achieving students of color as "acting White" and "unmotivated." Howard et al. explain that "... inaccurate portrayals of groups can contribute to the development and maintenance of deeply ingrained ideas and beliefs about groups that can profoundly shape their experiences in a given society" (2011, p. 91). The inaccurate portrayals of students of color shape the perceptions and practices of teachers, administrators, and students, and result in various forms of treatment that mold their experiences in schools.

The academic stereotypes force students to develop a response to perceptions of them as under-achievers, less motivated, or low intelligence. Students in the study discussed how they counter deficit discourses of student achievement.

**Black Female Student:** You are a Black female and no one is going to take pity on you. No one is going to feel sorry for you. You have to work twice as hard as a White female and that is the way it is. Every time a grade comes in a C, maybe a D she [pointing to friend] don't like. She [Black friend] is working twice as hard.

**Black Female Student:** Talking as a Black male, I would say that you would always have to fight the stereotype. If you make one small mistake, they are going to hold it against you.

The burden of performing race causes the students to want to disappear racially in order to smoothly matriculate through school. However, they realize this is not a rational expectation. Instead, students tried to minimize their presence as much as possible by remaining quiet and unobtrusive, not drawing attention to themselves, and getting good grades. Carter explains, "It is a resistance for survival in that these Black students' psyches are constantly under attack in a learning environment in which their racial group membership is often associated with anti-intellectualism and/ or intellectual inferiority" (2008, p. 478). The racialized contexts of the school push the students of color to bracket their race in order to focus on learning.

Over time, these microaggressions prove to be racially fatiguing and endanger students of color' academic success and experience in high school. Students struggled to craft an authentic identity in the face of racial stereotypes and socially pervasive perceptions of them as raced and gendered subjects. These incidents prevented students from creating authentic relationships with school staff members and White peers as a means to foster greater student engagement. The cumulative effect of racial microaggressions takes a considerable toll on the students' of color identity formation and their level of engagement (Chapman, 2007; O'Connor et al., 2011; Huidor & Cooper, 2010; Carter, 2007).

## CONCLUSION

Two Black female students summed up the experiences of students of color in majority White high schools.

It is sometimes hard. Just sometimes being here can be challenging for us because they [White adults and students] don't seem to understand what we go through.

Every day, like you really feel like you are carrying around this burden. Like I don't belong here, I don't fit it.

Scholars have begun to document how students of color in majority White high schools experience significant institutional racism and social stratification based on race (Diamond, 2006; Carter, 2008). However, the intersections of gender provide a more detailed understanding of how male and female students experience racism, and what prevents them from fully interacting in these academic environments.

Rather than attempting to obscure the racial realities of majority White high school settings, administrators, teachers, and staff must understand how race is consistently and newly constructed in schooling environments.

School leaders must be prepared to work with individuals who are culturally different and help create learning environments that foster respect, tolerance, and intercultural understanding. They must also have an awareness of the effect of racism and how it intersects with other areas of difference such as gender, sexual orientation, disability, and class oppression. (Lopez, 2003, p. 71)

These constructions of race must be interrogated to acknowledge how institutional policies and practices reinstantiate White supremacy and support inequitable systems. Moreover, Carter noted that, "schools and educators need to be counter-hegemonic in their practices, challenging traditional dominant discourses and paradigms about what it means to be successful and who is successful" (208, p. 494).

For researchers, the task to unpack identity in a meaningful way that reflect the structural, political, and representational aspects of students' lived experiences requires researchers to employ an intersectional framework to fully embrace the racialized human experience. Akom asserts,

As it stands now, the challenge for future scholars will be to continue to recognize the ways in which race and merit shift across time and space and intersect with other axes of social difference as well as to continue to illuminate the ways in which past and contemporary global White supremacy can be challenged and overcome instead of reproduced and maintained. (Akom, 2008, 224)

Critical race theorists have called for a more nuanced approach to researching race that challenges stock stories of deficit behaviors and morals with the complexities of intersectionality and structural oppression (Burton, Bonilla-Silva, Ray, Buckelew, Freeman, 2010; Akom, 2008; Howard et al., 2011). While Delgado caution critical race theorists to avoid splintering groups, other critical race theorists believe that an intersectional approach is necessary to disclose the myriad ways race and racism interact with other forms of oppression to deny coalition building and support barriers to racial empowerment.

For students of color in White majority schools, the structural barriers are both obvious and elusive when issues of gender and class intersect with race. With regard to Black boys, Howard et al. states,

> We contend that a more critical analysis of Black male outcomes in schools should be linked to structural conditions and arrangements in the schools and society that produce such alarming numbers. Part of *depathologizing* Black males and reconstructing another type of social imagery is to place appropriate scrutiny on institutional practices, structural arrangements, cultural practices, and ideologies which create the conditions that may stifle the intellectual, academic, and social growth and development of Black males. (2012, p. 87)

From this analysis, it is clear that students of color, in general, and both boys and girls require a more critical analysis. Only through a continued interrogation into the pervasive nature of race and racism will we discover ways to help students of color fully access a quality and equitable education.

## NOTE

1. See the scholarship of John Ogbu (1978; 1987; 2004; with Fordham, 1986) for an articulation on original constructions of the identity development of students of color. In the 1990s, a group of prominent scholars evolved presenting more complex accounts of students of color identity development include Davidson (1996), Aisnworth-Darnell and Downey (1998), and Carla O'Connor (1997, 1999).

## REFERENCES

Akom, A. A. (2008). Ameritocracy and infra-racial racism: Racializing social and cultural reproduction theory in the twenty-first century, *Race Ethnicity and Education, 11*(3), 205–230.

Ainsworth-Darnell, J., & Downey, D. (1998). Assessing the oppositional culture explanation for racial/ethnic differences in school performance. *American Sociological Review, 63*, 536–553.

Anderson, E., & McCormack, M. (2010). Intersectionality, Critical Race Theory, and American sporting oppression: Examining Black and Gay male athletes. *Journal of Homosexuality, 57*(8), 949–967.

Bell, D. A. (1995). Who's afraid of critical race theory? *University of Illinois Law Review*, (4), 893–910.

Berger, M. T., & Guidroz, K. (Eds.). (2009). *The intersectional approach: Transforming the Academy through race, class, and gender.* University of North Carolina Press.

Berry III, R. Q. (2005). Voices of success: Descriptive portraits of two successful African American male middle school mathematics students. *Journal of African American Studies, 8*(4), 46–62.

Berry III, R. Q. (2008). Access to upper-level mathematics: The Stories of successful African American middle school boys. *Journal for Research in Mathematics Education, 39*(5), 464–488.

Bonilla Silva, E. (2009). *Racism without racists. Colorblind racism and the persistence of racial inequality in America* (3rd ed.). Roman & Littlefield Publishers: New York.

Brown, A. L., & Donnor, J. K. (2011). Toward a new narrative on Black males, education, and public policy. *Race, Ethnicity & Education, 14*(1), 17–32.

Burton, L. M., Bonilla-Silva, E., Ray, V., Buckelew, R., & Freeman, E. (2010). Critical race theories, colorism, and the decade's research on families of color. *Journal Of Marriage & Family, 72*(3), 440–459.

Carter, D. J. (2007). Why the Black kids sit together at the stairs: The Role of identity-affirming counter-spaces in a predominantly White high school. *Journal of Negro Education, 76*(4), 542–554.

Carter, D. J. (2008). Achievement as resistance: The development of a critical race achievement ideology among Black achievers. *Harvard Educational Review, 78*(3), 466–497.

Chapman, T. K. (2007). The power of contexts: Teaching and learning in recently desegregated schools. *Anthropology & Education Quarterly, 38*(3), 297–315.

Cole, E. R. (2009). Intersectionality and research in psychology. *American Psychologist, 64*(3), 170–180. doi:10.1037/a0014564

Covarrubias, A. (2011). Quantitative intersectionality: A critical race analysis of the Chicana/o educational pipeline. *Journal of Latinos & Education, 10*(2), 86–105.

Crenshaw, K. W. (1991). Mapping the margins: Intersectionality, identity politics, and violence against women of color. *Stanford Law Review, 43*(6), 1241–1299.

Crenshaw, K. W. (1995). Mapping the margins: Intersectionality, identity politics, and violence against women of color. In K. Thomas (Ed.), *Critical race theory: The key writings that formed a movement* (pp. 357–383). New York, NY: The New Press.

Delgado, R. (2011). Rodrigo's Reconsideration: Intersectionality and the Future of Critical Race Theory. *Iowa Law Review, 96*(4), 1247–1288.

Delgado Bernal, D. (2002). Critical Race Theory, Latino Critical Theory, and Critical Raced-gendered epistemologies: Recognizing students of color as holders and creators of knowledge. *Qualitative Inquiry, 8*(1), 105.

Diamond, J. B. (2006). Still separate and unequal: Examining race, opportunity, and school achievement in "Integrated" Suburbs. *Journal of Negro Education, 75*(3), 495–505.

Diamond, J. B., Lewis, A., & Gordon, L. (2007). Race and school achievement in a desegregated suburb: Reconsidering the oppositional culture explanation. *International Journal of Qualitative Studies, 20*(6), 655–679.

Dixson, A. D. (2003). 'LET'S DO THIS!' Black women preachers' politics and pedagogy. *Urban Education, 38*(2), 217.

Dixson, A. D., & Dingus, J. E. (2008). In search of our mothers' gardens: Black women teachers and professional socialization. *Teachers College Record, 110*(4), 805–837.

Donnor, J. (2005). Towards an interest-convergence in the education of African-American football student athletes in major college sports. *Race, Ethnicity & Education, 8*(1), 45–67.

Duncan, G. A. (2002) Beyond love: A critical race ethnography of the schooling of adolescent Black males, *Equity and Excellence in Education, 35*(2), 131–143.

Few, A. L. (2007). Integrating Black consciousness and Critical Race feminism into family studies research. *Journal of Family Issues, 28*(4), 452–473.

Fordham, S., & Ogbu, J.(1986). Black students' scholl success: Coping with the burden of 'acting White.' *Urban Review, 18,* 176–206

Grabham, E., Cooper, D., Krishnadas, J., & Herman, D. (Eds.). (2009). *Intersectionality and beyond: Law, power, and the politics of location.* New York, NY: Routledge-Cavendish.

Howard, T. C. (2008). Who really cares? The disenfranchisement of African American males in preK-12 schools: A Critical Race Theory perspective. *Teachers College Record, 110*(5), 954–985.

Howard, T., Flennaugh, T., & Terry Sr., C. (2012). Black males, social imagery, and the disruption of pathological identities: Implications for research and teaching. *Educational Foundations, 26*(1/2), 85–102.

Huidor, O., & Cooper, R. (2010). Examining the socio-cultural dimension of schooling in a racially integrated school. *Education and Urban Society, 42*(2), 143–167.

Ladson-Billings, & Brown, K. (2008). Curriculum and cultural diversity. In F. M. Connelly, F. H. Ming, & J. Phillion (Eds.), *The Sage handbook of curriculum and instruction* (pp. 153–175). Los Angeles: Sage.

Ladson-Billings, G., & Tate, W. F. (1995). Toward a critical race theory of education. *Teachers College Record, 97*(1), 47–68.

Lopez, G. R. (2003). The (racially neutral) politics of education: A Critical Race Theory perspective. *Educational Administration Quarterly, 39*(1), 68–94.

Luke, C., & Luke, A. (1998). Interracial families: difference within difference. Ethnic & Racial Studies, 21(4), 728–754.

Lynn, M. (2002). Critical Race Theory and the perspectives of Black men teachers in the Los Angeles public schools. *Equity & Excellence in Education, 35*(2), 119.

Lynn, M. (2006). Dancing between two worlds: A portrait of the life of a Black male teacher in South Central LA. *International Journal of Qualitative Studies in Education, 19*(2), 221–242.

Lynn, M., & Jennings, M. E. (2009). Power, politics, and critical race pedagogy: a critical race analysis of Black male teachers' pedagogy. *Race, Ethnicity & Education, 12*(2), 173–196.

Malagon, M. C., & Alvarez, C. R. (2010). Scholarship girls aren't the only Chicanas who go to college: Former Chicana continuation high school students disrupting the educational achievement binary. *Harvard Educational Review, 80*(2), 149–173.

Milliken vs. Bradley, 418 U.S. 717

Muhammad, C., & Dixson, A. D. (2008). Black females in high school: A statistical educational profile. *Negro Educational Review, 59*(3/4), 163–180.

Oakes, J. (1985). *Keeping track: How schools structure inequality.* New Haven: Yale University Press.

O'Connor, C. (1997). Dispositions toward (collective) struggle and educational resilience in the inner city: A case analysis of six African American high school students. *American Educational Research Journal, 34*(4), 593–629.

O'Connor, C. (1999). Race, class, gender in America: Narratives of opportunity among low-income African American youth, *Sociology of Education, 72*(3), 131–157.

O'Connor, C., Mueller, J., Lewis, R., Rivas-Drake, D., & Rosenberg, S. (2011). "Being" Black and strategizing for excellence in a racially stratified academic hierarchy. *American Educational Research Journal, 48*(6), 1232–1257.

Rist, R. (1970). Student social class and teacher expectations: The self-fulfilling prophecy in ghetto education. *Harvard Educational Review, 40*(3), 411–451.

Scott, K. (2012). Lessons learned: Research within an urban, African American district. *International Journal of Qualitative Studies In Education, 25*(5), 625–643.

Vaught, S. (2004). The talented tenth: Gay Black boys and the racial politics of Southern schooling. *Journal of Gay & Lesbian Issues In Education, 2*(2), 5–26.

CHAPTER 7

# DE AQUÍ Y DE ALLÁ
## Latino Borderland Identities

**Lorena Mancilla**
**Tim Boals**
**Mariana Castro**
*University of Wisconsin-Madison*

Because I, a *mestiza,*
continually walk out of one culture
and into another,
because I am in all cultures at the same time,
*alma entre dos mundos, tres, cuatro,*
*me zumba la cabeza con lo contradictorio.*
*Estoy norteada por todas las voces que me hablan*
*simultáneamente*

—Gloria Anzaldúa (1987)

...I think [my identity] is linked to partly my culture, partly my upbringing, partly the people I'm surrounded with...I take pride in knowing that I have all these things that I contributed to my identity versus feeling like...I'm just one thing or one square when I check a box...I'm more than that. I'm not just a race or culture. (Interview with Diana[1])

*Intersectionality and Urban Education,* pages 147–168
Copyright © 2014 by Information Age Publishing
All rights of reproduction in any form reserved.

**147**

## INTRODUCTION

In the quote above, Diana, a 32 year old female born in Mexico who self-identifies as Latina, describes the feeling of agency she has in the development of her identity while at the same time describing external factors that contributed to her Latina identity. *I'm not just a race or culture.* For Diana, it was the intersections of multiple identity markers, such as her ethnicity, her use of language, and the communities in which she has lived, that led her to self-identify specifically as Latina. Diana's words reflect the complexity of Latino identity—a complexity that cannot be captured in checkboxes on a demographic questionnaire that simply asks for one to identify their ethnicity and race. With the growing number of Latinos in the country, and in U.S. schools, there is a need to better understand Latino identity.

This chapter discusses the findings of an exploratory study that examined how the intersections of multiple identity markers, or identity axes, influenced the K–12 schooling experiences of Latinos in the United States and the role of these intersections in Latino identity development. While recognizing that Latinos represent diverse racial and ethnic backgrounds, we chose to focus our study specifically on the intersections of linguistic identity (language), geographic identity (*comunidad*), and citizenship identity (*raíces*). We use the term language as an identity marker to capture how participants' identify their linguistic abilities, and describe their use of language varieties in both formal (e.g., school classroom) and informal (e.g., family interaction) settings. *Comunidad* is used to refer to the types of communities (e.g., urban, suburban, rural) participants grew up in, went to school in, and/or currently live and work in. Lastly, *raíces* is used to refer to participants' family history and origins in the United States. For the purposes of this study, *raíces* does not refer to legal citizenship status, therefore, participants were not asked to disclose information about their legal status during the interviews.

Our exploratory study was guided by the following questions: (1) How do the intersections of language, *comunidad,* and *raíces* influence the K–12 schooling experiences of Latinos in the United States? (2) What role do these intersections play in Latino identity development? As former classroom teachers and advocates for culturally and linguistically diverse students, we were driven to do this work because of our belief that there is a need to better understand Latino identity and schooling experiences in order to improve the education of Latinos in U.S. schools. It is our hope that these findings provide a voice to the *riqueza* and complexity of Latino identity and experience.

### Why Study Latino Identity?

At over 50 million strong, Latinos are the fastest growing population in the United States. In the last decade, the Latino population grew by 43%, accounting for more than half of the nation's total population growth (U.S. Census Bureau, 2011). Contrary to popular belief, a majority of Latinos, roughly 60%, are U.S. born (Pew Hispanic Center, 2012). Among all children ages 17 and younger in the nation, Latinos represent almost a quarter of this population with a growth of 39% between 2000 and 2010 (Pew Hispanic Center, 2011). Mexicans continue to be the largest ethnic group followed by Puerto Ricans and Cubans (U.S. Census Bureau, 2011). More than half of the nation's Latinos identify their race as white while almost 37% of Latinos identify their race as "some other race" (Pew Hispanic Center, 2011). In terms of geographic distribution, Latino communities have long-standing roots in Arizona, California, Colorado, Florida, Illinois, New Mexico, New Jersey, New York and Texas, however, current data shows large Latino communities are now being established beyond the borders of these nine states (Hamann & Harklau, 2010; Pew Hispanic Center, 2011). The geographic distribution and the rapid growth of the Latino population, particularly the growth of the Latino school-age population, are changing the American landscape and American classrooms.

Policy makers and educators must identify ways to best meet the needs of K–12 Latino students. The U.S. school system has historically failed to meet the needs of Latinos and the result has been persistently low educational attainment levels in comparison to other groups. For instance, Latinos have the highest high school dropout rate in comparison to other racial and ethnic groups and roughly only 11% of Latinos over the age of 25 hold a bachelor's degree (U.S. Department of Education, 2011). In his analysis of the Chicano/a educational pipeline, Covarrubias (2011) found that Latinos of Mexican descent, the nation's largest Latino ethnic group, are the group that is the most poorly served by American schools. Gándara and Contreras (2009) refer to the current state of Latino education as a "crisis" and urge a call for action in order to improve the educational outcomes of Latino students. Historically, the blame for this academic underperformance, viewed through a deficit lens, has been laid solidly at the feet of Latino students, their families and culture, their communities, immigration and citizenship status, and the use and influence of the Spanish language (Valencia, 2010). More recently, however, scholars and advocates for Latinos are calling for research that examines the education of Latinos through a more asset-based lens that recognizes and values the cultural and linguistic resources, and lived experiences, that Latinos bring to their education (Borrero, 2011; Elenes & Delgado Bernal, 2010; Irizarry & Nieto, 2010; Zarate & Conchas, 2010). Some scholars argue that the nation's future is linked to the academic success of Latino youth (Gándara & Contreras, 2009; Hurtado, Cervantez, & Eccleston, 2010). If this is the case, then educators must gain a better understanding of the Latino students in their schools.

Part of the problem in trying to accomplish this task is the rich diversity that is often hidden beneath pan-ethnic labels like Latino and Hispanic—two demographic labels commonly used to identify students by ethnicity with little to no regard for the many other factors that contribute to Latino identity. The Pew Hispanic Center, in a recent national survey, collected data to better understand how Latinos perceive their identity. Key findings of this survey show that although 60% of Latinos are U.S.-born and over 60% of Latinos are of Mexican descent, 69% of Latinos do not see a shared common culture among U.S. Latinos and 51% of Latinos prefer to identify with their country of origin rather than with pan-ethnic labels (Pew Hispanic Center, 2012). This finding has several implications for educators that may operate under the false assumption that all Latinos share a common culture. The survey also found that 87% of Latinos indicated that learning English is important, but 95% indicated that the ability to speak Spanish is very important for future generations (Pew Hispanic Center, 2012). Thus, the Spanish language is a strong uniting force for U.S. Latinos, and this calls into question monolingual ideologies that permeate our nation's language policies.

Latino identity has been described by scholars as complex, dynamic, hybrid and malleable. Anzaldúa (1987), in her seminal work, writes about hybrid, or *mestiza*, identities and about the constant tension *mestizas* experience as they negotiate life in the metaphorical borderlands of their multiple cultures. Bejarno (2005) and Valenzuela (1999), in their studies of urban Chicano/Latino youth, discuss the complexity of the role of language, citizenship status and ethnicity in identity development. Flores-González (1999) examined external school-related factors that contribute to the development of a positive academic identity in urban Puerto Rican youth. To further demonstrate the complexity of identity, Matute-Bianchi (1986) identified five categories of Mexican-descent identity in her ethnographic study of Mexican and Japanese-descent youth. Lastly, in his study of urban Latino youth, Irizarry (2007) highlights the importance of recognizing the influence of peer urban youth culture on Latino identity.

The scholarship on Latino identity and the findings of the survey by the Pew Hispanic Center are significant to our study because they support our motivation to undertake this work. We believe there is a strong need for educators to look beyond the pan-ethnic labels of Latino and Hispanic in order to see every student as a dynamic individual with infinite possibilities for a bright future. We do not believe it is possible to capture the diversity and complexity of the Latino population with a mere check in a demographic box. Identity is not static—it is in a constant state of transition and it is shaped by many factors. It is our hope to contribute to the work of scholars who have examined the intersectionality of Latino identity

(Achinstein & Aguirre, 2008; Briscoe, 2009; Camarrota, 2007; Covarrubias, 2011; Irizarry, 2007).

## Conceptual Framework

> Borders are set up to define the places that are safe and unsafe, to distinguish us from them. A border is a dividing line, a narrow strip along a steep edge. A borderland is a vague and undetermined place created by the emotional residue of an unnatural boundary. It is in a constant state of transition. (Anzaldúa, 1987, p. 25)

Citizenship, language use, and geography have been used as units of analysis in studies examining factors that affect the academic achievement of Latinos. Across the literature that examined citizenship, we identified the following themes: immigrant students tend to outperform their U.S.-born counterparts; lack of resources available to immigrant students; subsequent generations of Latinos do not perform better academically than previous generations (Ariza, 2010; Covarrubias, 2010; Crosnoe & Turley, 2011; Harper, 2011; Jimenez et al., 2009; Lutz, 2007; Valenzuela, 1999). In literature focused on the language use of Latinos, we found an emphasis on the role a child's first language plays in academic achievement and the benefits of bilingualism to the academic achievement (de Jong, 2002; Hoff, 2013; Garcia-Vazquez et al., 1997; Ochoa & Cadiero-Kaplan, 2004). Lastly, many studies that examine the academic achievement of Latinos are set in large, urban contexts and schools (Antrop-González, Vélez, & Garrett, 2005; Borrero, 2011; Fernandez, 2002; Flores-González, 1999).

But what about the lived realities and identities of Latinos who are U.S.-born bilinguals living in the suburbs? What do monolingual English-speaking Latinos in rural communities experience and how do they perceive their identity? Without considering the intersections of multiple identity axes and the lived experiences that result from these intersections, we feel that we cannot truly or fully understand the experiences of individuals. Therefore, in order to reflect the complexity of Latino identity, we sought theoretical frameworks that afford opportunities to examine the multiple axes that inform Latino identity and also provide a lens to examine the axes as fluid and hybrid. Thus this study draws from conceptual frameworks in intersectionality (Crenshaw, 1989, 1991; Grant & Zwier, 2011), transcultural repositioning (Guerra, 2004), and borderlands or border-crossing (Anzaldúa, 1987; Elenes, 2011).

Intersectionality is a theoretical framework born out of the discontent with the analysis of the experiences of oppressed individuals using single markers, or axes, of identity. Crenshaw (1989, 1991) critiqued "single-axis" frameworks and proposed using intersectionality as a lens to consider the meaning and consequences of multiple categories of identity, difference and disadvantage and to avoid focusing on the most privileged member of oppressed groups. Grant & Zwier (2011) argue for the use of intersectionality to examine student achievement stating that the intersections of various identity markers and their inter-dependence create systems of oppression and privilege that can easily be missed if one only considers each category, or axis, independently. For instance, Covarrubias (2011) applied an intersectional lens and found that there were diverse patterns of achievement depending on the intersections of distinct social, economic, political, and legal conditions (citizenship) of the individuals of Mexican descent reported in the Chicano/a educational pipeline. In our work, we used intersectionality as a starting point to think about how the intersections of language, *comunidad*, and *raíces* influence Latino identity and schooling experiences.

Another theory we drew upon was transcultural repositioning. The term transcultural repositioning has been used to describe the practices of changing the rhetorical abilities of disenfranchised individuals to move in and out of spaces, languages, social classes, and ways of thinking and seeing the world (Guerra, 2004, 2007). Transcultural repositioning is useful in examining multiple discourses that inform our everyday lives and is often used to describe the cultural, linguistic and intellectual shift of individuals. Transcultural repositioning provides an asset-based lens to describe the unique experiences and skills of oppressed individuals. This repositioning from a deficit lens to an asset-based lens was one of the goals of our study. The participants in our study embodied Guerra's "shape-shifters" (2004) as they recounted their experiences of shift in discourses and identities to negotiate the world around them.

Borderlands theory is based on the work of scholars like Anzaldúa (1987), who used the theory to represent how race, ethnicity, language, class, citizenship, gender and sexuality create systems of constant border-crossing. These borderlands do not represent fixed places where border-crossing occurs, but instead an undetermined place in a constant state of transition. Further, Anzaldúa theorized that in this malleable place, individuals become hybrid and form "a racial, ideological, cultural and biological cross-pollinization (p. 25)." Individuals develop a consciousness of the borderlands, what she called "mestiza consciousness." It is this consciousness that provides individuals with the malleability, hybridity, and resilience to contest hegemonic practices and cross borders and systems of oppression and opportunity. Elenes (2011) defines the existing discourse in these borderlands as the discourse of people who live between different worlds and which speak against dualism, oversimplification, and essentialism. Our team understood the stories from our participants as multiple examples of this border-crossing across languages, spaces, and identities. Through their stories, participants' embodied the hybrid identities of border-crossers navigating, contesting, and adapting to the different environments they inhabited in various, and sometimes, contradicting manners.

Similar to intersectionality, borderlands focuses on the impact of multiple identity axes on individuals' identities. However, borderlands is a theory developed by Latinos to represent Latino experiences. It has been used extensively to explore the unique circumstances of Latinos as border-crossers metaphorically in the political, racial, social and cultural senses of the word. In our work, we chose to use borderlands theory because it affords us a critical look at the role of language, *comunidad,* and *raíces* in the experiences of Latinos in K–12 systems and the inter-dependence between the three axes. Borderlands also allowed us to focus on the movement across borders and the change in borders themselves. By situating our participants in the roles of border-crossers, we are able to focus on their agency and their fluid identities rather than on them as hybrid individuals being changed by their reality while themselves changing that reality.

Like transcultural repositioning, borderlands seeks to explore the shift in discourse. However, borderlands theory moves the discussion to the state of shifting, to the bridge rather than the two sides the bridge brings together. The *nepantla* state (Anzaldúa, 1987), or the in-between state, is as important as the shifting from one identity to the next. In our study, we sought to go beyond the various identities of our participants or their border-crossing between different languages and contexts. Our goal was to understand our participants as individuals embodying the shift, the border, and the intersections of how they identify themselves and the worlds in which they live.

## Description of the Study

This exploratory study used a narrative inquiry approach. Data was collected through semi-structured interviews. Our goal was to hear directly from Latinos about their experiences in U.S. schools and how they perceive their identity. Narrative inquiry is an approach that has historically been used to give voice to members of marginalized groups in order to understand their lived experiences (Merriam, 2009). Although our interview protocol identified themes to discuss, it allowed participants, and our research team, the flexibility to navigate the interview in a way that was conducive to the topics shared by the participants. The one-time interviews, which lasted up to ninety minutes, explored the community, or communities, in which participants lived while attending K–12 schools (*comunidad*); the use of language at home, work, and school (language); the participant's family history in the U.S. (*raíces*); and how they identify themselves. Interviews were audio recorded, transcribed, and coded for themes. Participants were recruited from two Midwestern cities, one of which has a large Latino population with longstanding roots and the other has a more recent and growing Latino population. Recruitment was done through the use of social media sites (e.g., Facebook) and snowball sampling utilizing the research team's personal contacts with Latino social networks and professional organizations. We looked for participants that were Latino adults, both male and female, that are 18 years or older and have experience with K–12 schools in the United States. A total of eight participants were recruited—four males and four females—between the ages of 19 and 45. Table 7.1 below summarizes the demographic information of the participants, but it is important to note that although they all identified as "bilingual," they represent a variety of different language practices and abilities in both English and Spanish. Appendix A provides narrative profiles of each participant.

## Findings

Findings from the study highlight the agency, resilience, and deeply-rooted family values of all eight participants'. Three core themes emerged from the interview data about participants' intersectional identities and their K–12 schooling experiences: *querer es poder*, taming a wild tongue, and *nahuales*. We discuss these themes in detail in the sections below and present excerpts from the interviews to support our findings. Similarly to Borrero (2011), by presenting these excerpts from our exploratory study, we do not intend to make broad generalizations that can be applied to all Latinos. Rather, we present them to give voice to the participants of our study and to highlight the complexity of their identities.

**TABLE 7.1  Participant Demographics**

| Participant[a] | Age | Ethnicity | Language[b] | Birthplace |
|---|---|---|---|---|
| Diana | 32 | Mexican | Bilingual | Foreign-born |
| Henry | 44 | Salvadoran | Bilingual | Foreign-born |
| Jaqueline | 30 | Mexican & Puerto Rican | Bilingual | U.S.-born |
| Jasmin | 19 | Mexican | Bilingual | U.S.-born |
| Jessica | 19 | Mexican | Bilingual | U.S.-born |
| Pablo | 42 | Mexican | Bilingual | U.S.-born |
| Saul | 31 | Mexican | Bilingual | U.S.-born |
| Sergio | 47 | Mexican | Bilingual | Foreign-born |

[a] All names are pseudonyms to protect the identity of participants
[b] Participants indicated they spoke English and Spanish

## *Querer es poder*

*'¡Si se puede!'*—*Cesar Chavez*

The spirit of perseverance and resilience is a theme that emerged from our data and one that we believe reflects a sense of *querer es poder*. *Querer es poder* is a commonly known or proverb in Spanish that translates to "where there's a will there's a way." As in English, *querer es poder* is used to speak about someone's level of determination to accomplish a task or goal regardless of the obstacles or challenges in one's path. Several participants spoke about their determination to overcome obstacles and challenges they faced, and/or the desire to persevere in order to serve as a role model for their families and communities.

Participants shared stories about challenges they faced in school, such as discrimination or inequitable access to rigorous curriculum, and instead of letting these challenges or experiences hinder their progress, they served to fuel their motivation to succeed. For instance, in the passage below, Sergio speaks about his determination to succeed academically and overcome challenges in order to serve as an example not only for his immediate family, but also for future generations of his family:

> I think of myself as an example for my own family members and second generation because there hasn't been that in my family, and so it's that personal interest, in proving to myself that I can do it and proving to others that it's a possibility... I had attempted to take more advanced classes in math and science, but I didn't have the support of the school counselors and staff... the counselor would constantly say why do you want to take higher level English or why do you want to take algebra when you don't even speak English?... My school literally placed me in my courses based on the fact that they asked me what my parents did and I said they worked in the fields and they said OK, and they assigned me the classes and they were all very basic courses, including ESL, basic math, basic English, science... if you look at the spectrum of academic rigor, I was literally at the bottom. And once you are tracked into one level it's very difficult to get out...

During his interview, Sergio spoke about being born in a small, rural village in Mexico and coming to the United States when he was 12 years old. His parents were migrant farm workers and his family settled in a migrant camp. He began his experience with U.S. schools as an eighth grader and was identified as an English language learner. No consideration was given to his academic abilities when his counselor selected his courses. As he states in the quote above, he was placed in the lower track due to the simple fact that his parents "worked in the fields." Sergio eventually moved out of the lower track. He completed high school and went on to U.C. Berkeley.

He is currently completing a doctorate degree and speaks four languages: Spanish, English, Portuguese, and Italian. Sergio's story reflects the spirit of *querer es poder*. As a result of his language (labeled as an English learner), his *raíces* (foreign-born, son of migrants), and *comunidad* (urban school near a migrant camp), Sergio faced unique challenges that he was able to overcome. Although Sergio identifies as a Latino, and was identified as such by his school, it is clear that the challenges he faced in school were not simply because of his ethnicity, a single axis of identity, but because of the intersections of multiple identity axis.

Jasmin is another participant that reflects *querer es poder*. Jasmin is an English speaking, U.S.-born Latina of Mexican descent and the challenges she faced in school also fueled her motivation to be successful and persevere. In the passage below, Jasmin talks about racial and ethnic slurs against Mexicans that she frequently heard in her predominantly White, suburban middle-school:

> ...there was always Mexican jokes being said and stuff like that. It was all about being dirty and stealing jobs. I hated that. I was just like, I'm not stealing any jobs...if anything, I don't even have a job. I was like, I'm just as American as you are...I was born here too... Just because I speak Spanish? I barely even speak it.

In the following passage, Jasmin goes on to talk about how much she values her ability to set her mind on something and simply do it despite of the challenges that she has faced because of her identity:

> I value the fact that despite everything that I've gone through...despite how many times...people have told me that Mexicans are stupid...I proved them wrong, you know? I remember some of the white kids used to call me . . . stupid and all that stuff...if I'm really stupid how come you're the one failing the class and I'm not, you know? You know, if I'm so bad at English, how come I'm the one...getting straight A's in English and you're passing with a D?... If you want me to stop speaking Spanish how come you can't speak English better than I can?

In the above passages, Jasmin speaks about the challenges she faced in her suburban school because she is of Mexican-descent and bilingual. During her interview, she expressed that the first time she encountered incidents of racial and ethnic slurs was during middle school. Jasmin is a first-generation Mexican-American whose family moved to the suburbs when she was in third grade. Prior to the move, Jasmin attended a more diverse school and recalled having several Spanish-speaking classmates. At home, she primarily uses Spanish to communicate with her mother because her mother was born and raised in Mexico and speaks very little English. Jasmin uses

English to communicate with her father, who grew up in the U.S., and her siblings. However, Jasmin feels that she "lost her Spanish" because she speaks mostly in English now and at times she struggles to communicate with her mother. During her interview she expressed that at times she walks away from conversations with her mother feeling frustrated because she struggles to communicate in Spanish, but yet she was the victim of ethnic slurs at school because she was Mexican and it was assumed that she was a proficient Spanish speaker. Jasmin describes herself as a "genius," "nerd," and "geek" because she has been a straight A student since middle school. She recently completed her first semester of college with straight A's. Like Sergio, Jasmin faced unique challenges because of her intersectional identity and these challenges fueled her determination to succeed. While only two participants were highlighted in this theme, it is important to note that their stories and experiences are similar to those of the other participants.

*Taming a Wild Tongue*

> Until I am free to write bilingually and to switch codes without having always to translate, while I still have to speak English or Spanish when I would rather speak Spanglish...my tongue will be illegitimate. (Anzaldúa, 1987, p. 81)

We used the words of Anzaldúa (1987), *taming a wild tongue*, to describe the fluidity and hybrid nature of language use by participants and their deliberate use of language, and their bilingualism, as a tool for linguistic border-crossings, or navigating different spaces. We also want to recognize participants' agency for their choice of language use. A common thread among all participants was that they identified as bilingual and they consider bilingualism to be an important aspect of who they are regardless of their level of Spanish proficiency. This feeling is supported by a national survey conducted by the Pew Hispanic Center (2012), in which 95% of Latinos responded that future generations of Latinos should speak Spanish. According to the same source, even across generations, while English use among Latinos is higher in later generations and Spanish use is lower, Spanish use persists among the third generation in daily activities such as listening to music or watching television (Pew Hispanic Center, 2012). In a way, the Spanish language is one of the strongest ties among the Latino population.

In the excerpt below, Pablo shares his perspective on the importance of his children maintaining their ability to communicate in Spanish:

> I speak to my kids in English and Spanish, but mostly English...my wife speaks to our kids in Spanish...[My kids] have been taking English classes their entire life so once they get to high school...even though they speak Spanish, they have that little accent...You know, you can speak ghetto Spanish, or the rancho Spanish, or you can speak professional [Spanish] and that

will get you places. So, I have made it a priority to have my kids take Spanish in high school...when you get out into the real world and you're...dark-skinned and you don't speak Spanish and you have a Hispanic name...you're gonna get in trouble...

Pablo understands that language is not only a tool for communication, but an asset for him and his children. Further, he expresses how language use provides bilingual individuals not only opportunities, but potentially, safety. With respect to opportunities, Pablo believes that one can "get places," by the sole fact of speaking multiple languages. However, he also warns about getting "into trouble" because a person's looks in certain communities may be a marker for belonging, but not speaking the language can automatically exclude you from the same community.

An example of a linguistic border-crossing experience for all of our participants occurred when communicating with different people in their lives (e.g., family members). Many of them reported speaking to older relatives in Spanish and to younger siblings or relatives in English. For most of them, the language shift across their life experiences was tied to changes in *comunidad* (e.g., moving from the city to the suburbs). The way in which language use changed across time, location, and audiences is exemplified in Jessica's recount of her language journey:

My father speaks more Spanish to me, so my instinct is just to respond to him in Spanish whereas my mother speaks more English to me so I respond to her in English. When I lived in the city, I think I spoke more Spanish. That's where I learned the majority of my Spanish that I know now, whereas in the suburbs, I stopped using it unless I spoke to my grandparents or my dad, or in my Spanish classroom.

Jessica remembers speaking Spanish first and later crossing to English. She attributed her early learning and use of Spanish to her family and their *raíces*. As we established earlier in this chapter, we are using *raíces* to describe participants' family journeys and/or histories in the United States. Jessica's father is Mexican and he speaks mostly Spanish. When Jessica was little, she spent a lot of time with her father's family. She also connected her historical geography (i.e., growing up in the city), with speaking Spanish. During her interview, she spoke about her memories of living in a Spanish-speaking community in the city, the bilingual kindergarten program at her school, and her father's family providing her opportunities to speak in Spanish. Her move to the suburbs and to suburban schools, where most people spoke English, did not provide her the same opportunities for using her Spanish and her language use eventually shifted to English. Jessica's wild tongue, her ability to cross linguistic borderlands, and her strong ties to her family history, contributed to her ability to relate to others and to step in and out of different contexts.

### Nahuales

> Without anyone ever saying a word, I learned right away that if I were going to thrive and not merely survive in such an environment, I was going to have to learn to engage in the practice of transcultural repositioning, of shape-shifting in cultural, linguistic, and intellectual terms. (Guerra, 2004, p. 15)

Our third and last theme relates to the shape-shifting identities of our participants, which we refer to as *nahuales*. Through our analysis of the data, we recognized participants' skills at adapting to their environments and life situations. We wanted to highlight this as an asset to be recognized and celebrated, and which seems to be a common thread to the different histories our participants shared.

Saul provides an excellent example of *nahuales*, of how one learns from experiences to adapt to new geographical and cultural settings. In the quote below, Saul speaks about his transition from a suburban elementary school where he was a minority Latino among mostly White students, to a junior high that was majority Latino; then two years later he attends a high school with many of the same White students from the elementary school setting.

> The junior high I went to was very different than everything else I experienced up to that time: Lower middle class families went to that junior high, a lot of Latino immigrants... I was the Latino kid in elementary school and I didn't have to do anything to show I was a Latino kid, but now I'm in this junior high with a lot of Latino kids that are, safe to say, more Latino than me and now I have to turn on the Latino to fit in. So I was wearing clothes with Mexican flags on them... hanging out with all the Latinos instead of the White students like I used to... So then I go to the high school with all the students I went to elementary school with and I pretty much conform back to what I was in elementary school... growing my hair out, I'm playing guitar, I'm trying to start a band, I'm wearing Metallica t-shirts and it's like junior high never happened.

In elementary school Saul is seen as Latino by virtue of skin color and last name. But now he is in an environment where being Latino requires a more complex identity as it is based on more than how the White kids perceive him. He must dress a certain way, talk in the appropriate register, join the right group, and behave in accordance with the norms expected, even if that means getting in trouble. A change in school, or *comunidad*, requires returning to the cultural norms of the group with which he attended elementary school. Saul goes on to say that he always identified as a Latino but being Latino had a different connotation with each stage of his life. Saul later talks about being like a "social chameleon" and how this adaptability trait has served him well as he negotiates relationships using language as a tool. For instance, he uses his Spanish, which he claims to fake proficiency in surprising well, and English in registers appropriate to changing professional and social situations.

Jacqueline is proud of her mix of ethnicity and unique multicultural and linguistic experiences, and considers herself to be a "balanced" bilingual, bicultural individual. She has a Puerto Rican father and Mexican mother. In terms of her *comunidad*, her multiethnic extended family experiences took place in an urban U.S. setting, in a neighborhood that was predominantly Puerto Rican with summer trips to Mexico. One can sense her pride throughout the interview in her abilities to adapt and interact linguistically and culturally with fluency. This is, in fact, who she is as a person and she seeks to affirm that rich, complex identity. Referring to her knowledge of Spanish dialects and English registers as a trait that allows her to communicate broadly, Jacqueline talks of navigating linguistic and cultural borders:

> Yeah, I'm good with that, you know, if they're like, oh, I want a *naranja*, or a *china*... I know what they are referring to. They want an orange. It's not difficult for me... I think [being bilingual has] opened doors to a lot of different opportunities... In school it was predominantly English and I just spoke Spanish with my family and Spanish, English and Spanglish [with friends]... I never felt like, oh I have to pretend that I'm something I'm not, or deny the fact that I'm Mexican or Puerto Rican or that I speak Spanish. I never had to hide that. So actually that motivated me... it's okay to be Latina, it's okay to speak Spanish...

Jacqueline is aware that the broader U.S. society is not necessarily supportive of her linguistic and cultural identity, nor do people necessarily comprehend or appreciate the cultural and linguistic borders she crosses with ease. She talks about how caring individuals and Latino support groups have helped her along the way to maintain her sense of pride and a positive self identity. This was particularly important to her when she transitioned from high school into college:

> Like I've always had a good sense of who I am... but the transition from high school to college, it was just a different world to me. [College] opened my eyes to different things... about race and ethnicity. I knew you had your Latinos, your Asians, your Blacks ... and I knew there were class issues 'cause I knew there were people with less work and people with more money, more privilege. But it wasn't as plain as when I actually went to college and I was like, oh wow... it is a tougher life out there ... I'm amongst more, um, Whites. We were in the majority [before college] and I'm in the minority [now] so I had to deal with that issue.

Jacqueline appreciates that her family and support networks have imbued her with resilience, pride and the ability to be a *nahual* in a world of constant border crossings. Where society may see deficits, Jacqueline has learned to see personal and professional assets. Today, in her position as a social worker she uses her linguistic and cultural capital to reach out more effectively to the individuals and families she serves.

## Complex Identities

The eight participants of this study support our argument that there is a need to look beyond the pan-ethnic labels of Latino and Hispanic in order to see the rich complexity that lies beneath. For instance, although on the surface, the eight participants of this study could be identified as Latinos, only two of the participants self-identified as "Latina." According to Jaqueline, the term "Latina," in her opinion, is more inclusive and since she is of Mexican and Puerto Rican descent, she feels it is a term she identifies with. In fact, she started her interview by saying, "I'm a 30 year old Latina." On the other hand, Diana, who was born in Mexico and came to the United States at the age of 13, identifies as Latina because after living in the United States for almost 20 years, she no longer identifies as "Mexican." According to Diana, her experiences in the United States and her relationships with Latinos of diverse cultural and linguistic backgrounds have influenced her own cultural and linguistic practices and she feels she is no longer "Mexican" but more "Latina."

Three participants expressed primary identities that were not tied to their ethnicity at all, but were more associated with other identity axes. For instance, Jasmin identifies as an artist because art is her passion. Henry expressed that although he was born in El Salvador, if he had to identify with an ethnic label, he would identify as Hispanic, because of the Hispanic community in the city he currently lives in, however he felt stronger towards identifying as a member of the community in which he lived rather than with the ethnic label. Pablo identifies primarily as a parent and expressed he is okay with people referring to him or labeling him as Latino, Hispanic, Mexican, or Mexican American because according to Pablo, these terms are "just labels" and he has no real preference. What is of importance to him is his identity as a father. Jessica is a U.S.-born female of Mexican-descent yet she strongly identifies as "Mexican." This is largely due to her family's cultural practices and the fact that several of her family members speak Spanish at home. Even though Jessica herself mostly speaks in English and has lived in the United States all of her life, it is her family's roots and origins, her *raíces*, that drive her to identify as "Mexican."

Lastly, Saul and Sergio both identify as "American," however, Sergio specifically identifies as "American with a Mexican in me." During his interview, Sergio spoke about the many labels that were imposed on him (e.g., minority, migrant, ELL, Hispanic) and how these labels negatively affected him. He identifies as an American with a Mexican inside because he wants to first and foremost be seen as an individual and a complex human being rather than being seen as a minority first. On the other hand, Saul identifies as American because he feels that his diverse background reflects the diverse background of the United States. He recognizes that his choice of identifying as American is controversial to some, but he also feels that since he was born in the United States and has lived here his whole life, he is an American and identifies as such. According to Saul, "I'm able to live my dreams in this country...exactly as my parents thought...it's the American dream...I am an American citizen." In conclusion, all eight participants expressed very diverse and unique ways of identifying themselves. Their identities were shaped by their unique experiences living in the United States. These findings support our argument that there is a need to better understand the complex identities of Latinos in our schools.

## Conclusion

Latino identity is shaped and influenced by both internal and external factors. It is complex and constantly changing. The dynamic nature of identity can be lost when blanketed with pan-ethnic labels like Latino and Hispanic. In order to better understand how to support Latino students and how to maximize opportunities for academic achievement in U.S. schools, we must begin by recognizing the diversity of experiences and realities of those individuals who share the label of Latino. For instance, we need to understand the critical role that Spanish plays in Latino identity. Our exploratory study focused on the intersections of linguistic identity (language), geographic identity (*comunidad*), and citizenship identity (*raíces*) and our findings confirmed the inability of current practices used in institutions (e.g., schools) to capture the experiences of subgroups through the use of labels that only consider ethnicity and/or race. Instead, our findings celebrated the diversity of individuals who will guide the direction of what learning and achieving in American schools may look like in the twenty-first century.

We identified three core themes in our data. First, we conceptualized *querer es poder* to represent the resiliency and perseverance of participants. As a result of their complex identities and the intersections of multiple axes, participants in the study often faced challenges that there were driven to overcome. Next, borrowing from Anzaldúa (1987), we conceptualized *taming a wild tongue* to represent participants' linguistic hybridity and flexibility as they employ their bilingualism as a tool or resource. Finally, we conceptualized *nahuales* to represent participants' ability to adapt and navigate multiple contexts.

We hope that by sharing the findings of this study, we can emphasize the need for more research using intersectionality and borderlands theories rather than isolated axes that do not represent the complex reality and identity of Latinos in the U.S. We also hope that our work will help educators across the country think of their Latino students as individuals with complex histories and resources that cannot be lumped into a group without losing the opportunity to leverage the resources and richness in experiences that they bring with them to school.

## APPENDIX A: PARTICIPANT PROFILES

*Diana*

Diana is a 32 year old, foreign-born female from Mexico. She came to the United States as a teenager with her family and did not speak English. Her family settled in a large, urban Midwestern city and she was enrolled in a public high school. She was identified as an English language learner and was placed in an ESL program. Diana was in ESL for three years and was exited from the program in twelfth grade. She always considered herself to be a high achieving student and currently holds a bachelor's degree in education. She is bilingual and uses both Spanish on a daily basis at work and to communicate with her family. Diana identifies herself as a Latina because she believes the term Latina encompasses the cultural and linguistic diversity she has been exposed to since her arrival in the United States. According to Diana, identifying as Latina, rather than Mexican, is a better reflection of her hybrid identity.

*Henry*

Henry is a 44 year old, foreign-born male from El Salvador. He came to the United States with this family at the age of fifteen and spoke little to no English. His family settled in a mid-sized Midwestern city and he was enrolled in a public high school. He was identified as an English language learner and received ESL services in school, but Henry struggled with the language barriers. He dropped out of school but completed his GED. He currently works at the same school district he attended as a teenager. He uses Spanish to communicate with his parents and when he travels back to El Salvador, but English is the primary language he uses to communicate with his children and at work. Henry identifies himself as a resident of the city where he lives because he has lived there most of his life and does not see himself as an active member in the Hispanic community.

## Jaqueline

Jaqueline is a 30 year old, U.S.-born female of Mexican and Puerto Rican descent. She grew up and lives in a large, urban Midwestern city with her family and attended public schools. Jaqueline is proud of her ethnicity and feels that her experiences growing up in a predominantly Latino community contributed to this sense of ethnic pride. She holds a master's degree and attributes her academic success to her participation in a variety of Latino organizations. In elementary school, Jaqueline was in a bilingual program but she eventually transitioned out. She uses Spanish to communicate with her family and at times to serve as a translator at work. Jaqueline identifies as Latina because she feels this terms is more inclusive than the term Hispanic.

## Jasmin

Jasmin is a 19 year old, U.S.-born female of Mexican descent. She currently lives in small suburban community in the Midwest with her family and she attended public schools. Her family moved to the suburbs when Jasmin was in third grade. Jasmin has been academically successful throughout her K–12 experience. She is currently enrolled at a community college and hopes to transfer to a four-year institution soon. Although Jasmin grew up speaking both Spanish and English, her father did not want her to be placed in a bilingual program because he feared it would hold her back academically. She was placed in general education classrooms and received all of her instruction in English. Currently, she mainly uses Spanish to communicate with her mother and grandparents but she often feels frustrated at her limited proficiency in Spanish. She is an artist and identifies as such. She does not like pan-ethnic labels such as Latina or Hispanic because she believes they do not apply to her.

## Jessica

Jessica is a 19 year old, U.S.-born female of Mexican descent. Jessica and her family moved from a large, urban Midwestern city to a mid-sized suburban community when she was in third grade. While living in the city, she attended Catholic school and once they moved to the suburbs, she attended public schools. Jessica always felt that school was challenging for her. She is currently enrolled at a community college and hopes to transfer to a four year institution soon. Although Jessica grew up speaking both Spanish and English at home, she was never placed in a bilingual program and has always received instruction in English. Jessica uses Spanish mostly to communicate with her father's family and English is used at school, work, and at home with her mother and siblings. Jessica identifies as Mexican because she feels this reflects the cultural and linguistic practices, and origins, of her family.

*Pablo*

Pablo is a 42 year old, U.S.-born male of Mexican descent. Pablo grew up and lives in a large, urban Midwestern city where he attended public schools for most of his K–12 experience. Pablo was in a bilingual program in elementary school, and used Spanish to communicate with his parents. He completed high school in Mexico and remembers experiencing culture shock during the time he spent in Mexico because he realized that he spoke Spanish with an accent. Pablo holds a high school degree and believes that had his family had access to more resources to help him in school that he could have achieved much more. He is the father of five children and is actively involved with their education. He identifies himself primarily as a parent, and he feels that terms like Hispanic and Latino are just labels, thus he has no preference for them.

*Saul*

Saul is a 31 year old, U.S.-born male of Mexican descent. He was born in a large, urban Midwestern city, but his family moved to a suburban community when he was very young. He attended public schools and holds a law degree. Saul was enrolled in a bilingual PreK program, but remembers not being able to understand or communicate with the other children because he was English dominant. He was then placed in general education classes for K–12 and received all of his instruction in English. He primarily uses Spanish to communicate with family members and at times must use Spanish at work. He prefers to communicate in English. Saul identifies as American because he feels his experiences reflect the diversity of the United States and the ideals the nation was founded on.

*Sergio*

Sergio is a 47 year old, foreign-born male from Mexico. He was the seventh of 11 children in a family of migrant workers who eventually settled in a state that borders with Mexico. Sergio attended public schools and although his parents supported him, they did not completely understand his need to continue his studies beyond high school. With little resources or information, Sergio was not aware of the possibility to go to college until a teacher encouraged him to take college prep classes which eventually led to him having the opportunity to apply and go on to obtain a Bachelor's degree in Spanish, becoming the first in his family to obtain a college degree. Sergio eventually moved to a mid-size Midwestern city, where he attended graduate school and started a family. He currently works for the state as a grant manager and migrant officer while at the same time, pursuing an EdD. Sergio identifies himself as an "American with a Mexican inside" recognizing the opportunities that the US has offered him while maintaining strong roots to his family, the Mexican community, his ethnicity and cultural heritage, and Spanish.

## NOTE

1. Pseudonyms are used throughout to protect the identity of participants.

## REFERENCES

Achinstein, B., & Aguirre, J. (2008). Cultural match or culturally suspect: How new teachers of color negotiate sociocultural challenges in the classroom. *Teachers College Record, 110*(8), 1505–1540.

Antrop-González, R., Vélez, W., & Garrett, T. (2005). ¿Dónde Están los Estudiantes Puertorriqueños/os Exitosos? [Where are the academically successful Puerto Rican students?]: Success factors of high-achieving Puerto Rican high school students. *Journal of Latinos & Education, 4*(2), 77–94.

Anzaldúa, G. (1987). *Borderlands/La Frontera: The new mestiza.* San Francisco: Aunt Lute Books.

Ariza, D. (2010). Puerto Rican youth in Central Florida: Adaptation and identity. *Centro Journal, 22*(1), 129–153.

Bejarno, C. L. (2005). *¿Qué onda? Urban youth culture and border identity.* Tuscon, AZ: The University of Arizona Press.

Borrero, N. (2011). Shared success. *Multicultural Education, 18*(4), 24–30.

Briscoe, F. M. (2009). "They make you invisible:" Negotiating power at the academic intersections of ethnicity, gender, and class. *Equity & Excellence in Education, 42*(2), 233–248.

Camarrota, J. (2007). A social justice approach to achievement: Guiding Latina/o students toward educational attainment with a challenging, socially relevant curriculum. *Equity & Excellence in Education, 40,* 87–96.

Covarrubias, A. (2011). Quantitative Intersectionality: A critical race analysis of the Chicana/o educational pipeline. *Journal of Latinos & Education, 10*(2), 86–105.

Crenshaw, K. (1989). Demarginalizing the intersection of race and sex: A Black feminist critique of antidiscrimination doctrine, feminist theory and antiracist politics. *University of Chicago Legal Forum:* 139–167.

Crenshaw, K. (1991). Mapping the margins: Intersectionality, identity politics, and violence against women of color. *Stanford Law Review, 43,* 1241–1252.

Crosnoe, R., & Turley, R. (2011). K–12 educational outcomes of immigrant youth. *Future Of Children, 21*(1), 129–152.

de Jong, E. (2002). Effective bilingual education: From theory to academic achievement in a two-way bilingual program. *Bilingual Research Journal, 26*(1), 65–84.

Elenes, C. A. (2011). *Transforming borders: Chicana/o popular culture and pedagogy.* Lanham, MD: Lexington Books.

Elenes, C. A., & Delgado Bernal, D. (2010). Latina/o Education and the reciprocal relationship between theory and practice: Four theories informed by the experiential knowledge of marginalized communities. In E. G. Murillo, Jr., Villenas, S. A., Galván, R. T., Muñoz, J. S., Martinez, C., & Machado-Casas, M. (Eds.), *Handbook of Latinos and education: Theory, research, and practice* (pp. 157–169). New York: Routledge.

Fernandez, L. (2002). Telling stories about school: Using critical race and Latino critical theories to document Latina/Latino education and resistance. *Qualitative Inquiry, 8*(1), 45–65.

Flores-González, N. (1999). Puerto Rican high achievers: An example of ethnic and academic identity compatibility. *Anthropology & Education Quarterly, 30*(3), 343–362.

Gándara, P., & Contreras, F. (2009). *The Latino education crisis: The consequences of failed social policies.* Cambridge, MA: Harvard University Press.

Garcia-Vazquez, E., Vazquez, L., Lopez, I., & Ward, W. (1997). Language proficiency and academic success: Relationships between proficiency in two languages and achievement among Mexican American students. *Bilingual Research Journal, 21*(4), 395–408.

Grant, C. A., & Zwier, E. (2011). Intersectionality and student outcomes: Sharpening the struggle against racism, sexism, classism, ableism, heterosexism, nationalism, and linguistic, religious, and geographical discrimination in teaching and learning. *Multicultural Perspectives, 13*(4), 181–188.

Guerra, J. C. (2004). Emerging representations, situated literacies, and the practice of transcultural repositioning. In M. H. Kells, V. Balester, & V. Villanueva (Eds.), *Latino/a discourses: On language, identity, and literacy education* (pp. 7–23). Portsmouth, NH: Boynton/Cook Publishers.

Guerra, J.C. (2007). Out of the valley: Transcultural repositioning as a rhetorical practice in ethnographic research and other aspects of everyday life. In C. Lewis, P. Enciso, & E. B. Moje (Eds.), *Reframing sociocultural research on literacy: Identity, agency, and power* (pp. 137–162). New York: Routledge.

Harper, C. E. (2011), Identity, intersectionality, and mixed-methods approaches. *New Directions for Institutional Research,* 103–115. doi: 10.1002/ir.402

Hamann, E. T., & Harklau, L. (2010). Education in the New Latino Diaspora. In E. G. Murillo, Jr., Villenas, S. A., Galván, R. T., Muñoz, J. S., Martinez, C., & Machado-Casas, M. (Eds.), *Handbook of Latinos and education: Theory, research, and practice* (pp. 157–169). New York: Routledge.

Hoff, E. (2013). Interpreting the early language trajectories of children from low-ses and language minority homes: Implications for closing achievement gaps. *Developmental Psychology, 49*(1), 4–14.

Hurtado, A., Cervantez, K., & Eccleston, M. (2010). Infinite possibilities, many obstacles: Language, culture, identity and Latino/a educational achievement. In E. G. Murillo, Jr., S. A. Villenas, R. T. Galván, J. S. Muñoz, C. Martinez, & M. Machado-Casas (Eds.), *Handbook of Latinos and education: Theory, research, and practice* (pp. 157–169). New York: Routledge.

Irizarry, J. G. (2007). Ethnic and urban intersections in the classroom: Latino students, hybrid identities and culturally responsive pedagogy. *Multicultural Perspectives, 9*(3), 21–28.

Irizarry, J. G., & Nieto, S. (2010). Latino/a theoretical contributions to educational praxis: Abriendo Caminos. In E. G. Murillo, Jr., S. A. Villenas, R. T. Galván, J. S. Muñoz, C. Martinez, & M. Machado-Casas (Eds.), *Handbook of Latinos and education: Theory, research, and practice* (pp. 108–124). New York: Routledge.

Jimenez-Silva, M., Hernandez, N. V. J., Luevanos, R., Jimenez, D., & Jimenez, A. (2009). Results not typical: One Latino family's experiences in higher education. *Harvard Educational Review, 79*(4), 730–744.

Lutz, A. (2007). Barriers to high-school completion among immigrant and later-generation Latinos in the USA: Language, ethnicity and socioeconomic status. *Ethnicities, 7*(3), 323–342.

Matute-Bianchi, M. E. (1986). Ethnic identities and patterns of school success and failure among Mexican-descent and Japanese-American students in a California high school: An ethnographic analysis. *American Journal of Education, 95*(1), 233–255.

Merriam, S. (2009). *Qualitative research: A guide to design and implementation.* San Francisco: Jossey-Bass.

Ochoa, A., & Cadiero-Kaplan, K. (2004). Towards promoting biliteracy and academic achievement: Educational programs for high school latino english language learners. *The High School Journal, 87*(3), 27–43.

Pew Hispanic Center. (2011). *Census 2010: 50 Million Latinos Hispanics account for more than half of nation's growth in past decade.* March 2011. Retrieved November 27, 2012, from http://www.pewhispanic.org/files/reports/140.pdf

Pew Hispanic Center. (2012). *When labels don't fit: Hispanics and their views of identity.* April 2012. Retrieved February 2, 2012 from http://www.pewhispanic.org/files/2012/04/PHC-Hispanic-Identity.pdf

U.S. Census Bureau. (2011). *The Hispanic Population: 2010.* Retrieved February 11, 2013 from http://www.census.gov/prod/cen2010/briefs/c2010br-04.pdf

U.S. Department of Education. (2011). *Winning the future: Improving education for the Latino community.* Retrieved February 11, 2013 from http://www.whitehouse.gov/sites/default/files/rss_viewer/WinningTheFutureImprovingLatinoEducation.pdf

Valencia, R. (2010). *Dismantling contemporary deficit thinking: Educational thought and practice.* New York: Routledge.

Valenzuela, A. (1999). *Subtractive schooling: U.S.–Mexican youth and the politics of caring.* Albany, NY: State University of New York Press.

Zarate, M. E., & Conchas, G.Q. (2010). Contemporary and critical methodological shifts in research on Latino education. In E. G. Murillo, Jr., S. A. Villenas, R. T. Galván, J. S. Muñoz, C. Martinez, & M. Machado-Casas (Eds.), *Handbook of Latinos and education: Theory, research, and practice* (pp. 157–169). New York: Routledge.

# PART III

## THINKING INTERSECTIONALLY
## IN TEACHER EDUCATION AND HIGHER EDUCATION

# CHAPTER 8

# INTERSECTIONAL IMAGINATION

## Arts-Based Strategies for Teaching Critical Sociocultural Knowledge

**Amelia M. Kraehe**
*University of North Texas*

**Keffrelyn D. Brown**
*The University of Texas at Austin*

The scholarly literature on diversity studies in teaching and teacher education supports the argument that, in addition to knowledge of subject matter
content and content-specific pedagogies (Shulman, 1986, 1987), teachers
need to acquire knowledge of the history of social and educational inequality, sociocultural differences, and the various processes by which inequities
are maintained in schooling (Sleeter & Grant, 2006). Research suggests
that teachers who understand and care about students' cultural assets and
the sociopolitical context of students' lives often mobilize this knowledge as
a part of their pedagogy, particularly when teaching students from histori-

*Intersectionality and Urban Education*, pages 171–191
Copyright © 2014 by Information Age Publishing
All rights of reproduction in any form reserved.

cally marginalized communities (Beauboeuf-Lafontant, 2005; Dilworth & Brown, 2008; Hollins, King & Hayman, 1994; Irvine, 2002; Ladson-Billings, 1994; Valenzuela, 1999; Villegas & Davis, 2008). Since critical perspectives are often omitted from the K–12 curriculum, teacher education courses become the places where many teachers are first introduced to this sociocultural knowledge (Brown, 2011; Milner, 2006, 2010).

It is tempting to think of sociocultural knowledge in the context of a single factor that serves as the primary organizing principle to explain persistent educational inequalities and exclusion. Though various sociocultural factors, such as race, gender, class, and sexuality, do impact schooling and society in distinct ways, it is important that teachers (and teacher educators) understand and be able to analyze these constructs intersectionally, that is, in relation to and in interaction with each other rather than in isolation (Choo & Ferree, 2009; Collins, 1990; Crenshaw, 1991; Dhamoon, 2011; Glenn, 1999; Hancock, 2007; McCall; 2005). Despite the complexity this entails, such complexity is vital in teachers' developing deeper understandings of culture (Pollock, 2008) and creating relationships of solidarity and well-being within and across differences (Gaztambide-Fernández, 2012; Hancock, 2011).

This chapter emerges from a larger stream of research wherein, for several years, we have examined the construction of sociocultural knowledge of teachers and teaching. This research takes place in the context of teaching multiple instantiations of an undergraduate education foundations course. We have documented how, in teaching critical sociocultural knowledge, broadening our repertoire to include an eclectic use of arts-based and other embodied aesthetic modalities has helped to stir beginning teachers' "imaginative capacities" (Greene, 1995) and expand their receptivity to critical sociocultural knowledge (Brown & Kraehe, 2010a; Kraehe & Brown, 2011). By critical sociocultural knowledge we mean the social, cultural, economic, political and historical knowledge that informs how societies and schools operate (Brown & Kraehe, 2010b). These studies have taught us that using art-based inquiries as a creative mode of classroom engagement is potentially very powerful in aiding students' perceptivity and recognition of normalizing processes as well as reimagining possibilities for more just conditions and group relations in schools and society (Brown & Kraehe, 2010b; Kraehe & Brown, 2011). We, therefore, consider the imagination to be a generative point of focus for rethinking pedagogy in critical teacher education.

In this chapter, we address the need for pedagogic strategies and modalities for cultivating an intersectional imagination for teaching. First, we briefly review the difficulties of pre-service teachers' development of more complex understandings of difference and a commitment to equity. This review draws from theories of teacher learning as well as scholarship generally termed critical, multicultural, anti-oppressive, and social justice education. Then, we consider the relevance of intersectionality theory to the development of a more expansive imagination for teaching and, from this, conceptualize what teaching toward an intersectional imagination entails. In the final part of the chapter, we illustrate the complementarity of arts-based inquiries and intersectionality. We detail the arts-based teaching practices we have employed that have been most fruitful in supporting students in making sense of key concepts and promoting an intersectional orientation. Our intent here is to attend to the manner of instruction and, in doing so, make a contribution to the understudied problem of a critical teacher education pedagogy (Sleeter, 2001). We conclude this chapter with a discussion of the challenges and limitations of teaching toward an intersectional imagination, particularly in the context of introductory level education courses.

## LITERATURE ON TEACHING CRITICAL KNOWLEDGE IN TEACHER EDUCATION

Education programs commonly use a combination of interventions to help pre-service teachers acquire critical sociocultural knowledge. These include lectures and discussion around selected theoretical texts and case studies in order to expand student understanding of the history of inequality in schools, ideologies of schooling, and cross-cultural interactions. Many programs have added service-learning and field immersion experiences (Melnick & Zeichner, 1995; Sleeter, 2001; Wiest, 1998). These "hands-on" experiences often serve as a context for developing reflective practice while increasing teachers' contact with different sociocultural groups. Reflection that is done in conjunction with these field experiences is intended to help prospective teachers closely examine how their knowledge of teaching gained from their years as students shape their assumptions about teaching (Britzman, 2003; Lortie, 1975). Journaling and writing autobiographies are common activities used for reflection, yet they can succumb to a confessional mode (Fendler, 2003) that is not necessarily useful in bringing about "informed reflection—that is, rumination couched in an understanding of issues of culture" (Smagorinsky, Cook & Jackson, 2003, p. 1426). Much teacher reflection lacks a critical sociocultural framework with which to frame how one thinks about teaching and learning (Milner, 2006). Simply looking back at one's biography in schools or recounting a cross-cultural experience may not aid pre-service teachers' insights and, instead, be miseducative. Britzman (1998) explains:

> While initially the learner attaches to the experience of the other by way of wondering what she or he would have done had such an event occurred in her or his own life, this is not yet an implication. For this experiment in empathy

actually may provoke defenses and resistance to insight. This is so because what tends to be projected is the learner's undisturbed present and not the way the learner's life has become her present. But just as significantly, the learner's strategy of projection impedes an understanding of the differences between the learner's knowledge and the knowledge of the other. (pp. 117–118)

Britzman's (1998) psychoanalytic perspective suggests that in helping teachers to make sense of "difficult knowledge" we must recognize and account for the deeply intimate, often painful affective disturbances such learning imposes on one's sense of self and personhood. Left untroubled, teacher reflection can be a self-legitimating, reproductive process that foments a tendency to make assumptions and generalizations based on their own experiences.

While the research literature suggests that some of these efforts at critical teacher education can be effective (Ladson-Billings, 2001), it is also clear that for many students, negative stereotypes and deficit perceptions of minoritized groups are reinforced by teacher education pedagogies (Banks, 2001; Gomez, 1996; Haberman & Post, 1992; Sleeter, 1995; Terrill & Mark, 2000). Teacher educators have documented their experiences with student frustration, denial, guilt, resentment, resistance, paralysis, silence, and silencing of others (Amos, 2010; Asher, 2007; Brown, 2004; Ellsworth, 1992; King, 1991; Ladson-Billings, 1996; Solomona, Portelli, Daniel & Campbell, 2005). This literature has spurred criticism of the way it positions preservice teachers as lacking, in particularly white teachers (Laughter, 2011; Lowenstein, 2009). At the same time, the scholarship's overemphasis on the issue of preparing White monolingual (and usually female) students for diversity is yet another instance of White dominance and privilege (Leonardo & Porter, 2010). The insights of Leonardo and Zembylas (2013) illuminate the contradictions inherent in privileging White students' experiences:

Turning to whiteness in education means that the subjects who are least individually prepared and collectively underdeveloped for race dialogue occupy a central place at the table..., retain the luxury to leave a dialogue when it becomes too arduous..., and...benefit from the pretense of invisibility. (p. 155)

A consequence of centering the perceived needs of White pre-service teachers is that teacher education programs ignore the potential cultural, experiential assets that students from minoritized groups bring to teacher education (Banks et al., 2005; Villegas & Davis, 2008). These potential contributions are the basis of arguments for recruiting more students of color and bilingual students into teacher education and developing coursework that values and proceeds to build from the foundation provided by these students' cultural knowledge and other assets (Sleeter, 2001).

While some see an intersectional understanding of difference and inequality as a desireable outcome of preparing teachers to teach in equitable and just ways (Grant & Zwier, 2011), there is a large void in the scholarly literature that addresses how to promote teachers' development of an intersectional perspective. As a teacher education framework, intersectionality is helpful for moving beyond an us/them binary. It provides a ground on which to consider identities and epistemologies as formed in the simultaneity and interaction of multiple forces of differentiation. It is based on the assumption that boundaries that categorize and inscribe our identities and epistemologies with differential power, privilege and status are not fixed; rather, these boundaries are contingent and require negotiation from one situation to the next (Beltran, 2004; Hancock, 2011). This "context- and time-contingent nature of intersectionality and interlocking oppressions" (Hulko, 2009, p. 45) makes the goal of providing an intersectional understanding of difference and inequality very complex.

Here it is constructive to distinguish between employing intersectionality as a pedagogical stance that addresses all teachers, regardless of their social location, as capable learners, and a recognition that, because of their social locations, there is a need for pedagogic strategies that account for the hermeneutic barriers imposed by the common terms and concepts many teachers have internalized (often as part of their teacher education) for talking about and making sense of their experiences with difference and inequality. The challenge educators face is when and how to employ intersectionality. Intersectionality offers a level of complexity that, if introduced too soon, may hinder students in understanding in how to apply key theoretical concepts around race, class, gender and sexuality (Jones & Wijeyesinghe, 2011) and can lead to thinking that reinscribes existing power relations (Brown & Kraehe, 2010b). For those who are just beginning to acquire a new language for understanding race, class, gender and sexuality, focusing on their intersections prematurely can conceal their differential discursive and material effects (Harris, 1996) and produce what Collins (1998) calls a "new myth of equivalent oppressions" (p. 211). Arguing for a tactical use of singularity, Luft (2009) questions the wisdom of a "universally applied, uncritical practice of intersectionality" (p. 101). She suggests that, depending upon the cultural and political milieu, strategically adopting a single-issue approach can be more effective as a short-term intervention at the beginning phases of consciousness-raising interactions, such contexts as introductory level university classrooms. The basis for this pedagogic tactic is to circumvent the prevailing evasive and negating maneuvers individuals employ particularly when asked to talk about race and racism. Often bringing up issues of gender and class serves to "refute the notion of race' ubiquity, and thereby to remove the speaker from accountability to whiteness or racial privilege" (Luft, 2009, p. 111).

Taking a step back for a moment, we see that the challenge of teachers' concept development is not unique to the domain of diversity studies. Drawing from sociohistorical theory, Smagorinsky, Cook and Jackson (2003) explain that teacher development is hardly straight-forward or predictable. Development proceeds from opportunities to learn how to use conceptual tools of teaching. They state that the "interplay between formal knowledge of principles and knowledge gained through activity enables people to think about problems beyond their range of experience" (p. 1405). Looking across teacher education programs, these authors found that novice teachers routinely struggled to develop coherent understandings of theoretical concepts because of different and at times contradictory meanings of concepts as well as institutional constraints and inconsistencies. The authors noted that most students gained only knowledge of terms without understanding when and how to apply them in schools and classrooms. Students graduating from teacher education programs, therefore, often began teaching without the conceptual practices needed to discern, critique, and respond to dilemmas of curricula and learning. The researchers conclude that "instruction in principles alone will not result in the development of a concept; rather, knowledge of abstracted governing rules must come in conjunction with empirical demonstration, observation, or activity" (p. 1404). The premise here is that in order to adopt and integrate concepts—both common sense and academic knowledge—learners need multiple opportunities to try out and practice using these concepts in a variety of situations. Within situated practice, concepts can be sharpened into a more finely nuanced set of cultural tools with which to make sense of experience.

## TEACHING TOWARD AN INTERSECTIONAL IMAGINATION: A THEORETICAL FRAMEWORK

Intersectionality is a multidimensional model for producing knowledge of difference and inequality. The term intersectionality emerged from legal scholar Kimberlé Crenshaw (1991). It is a term that has been taken up by many in the discipline of sociology and political science, and as a concept, it has been cross-pollinated by multiracial and feminist scholarship from various fields, including the arts, cultural criticism, philosophy, and social movements (e.g., Combahee River Collective; 1977; DuBois in Hancock, 2005; hooks, 1995; Moraga & Anzaldúa, 1981). Intersectionality encompasses a combination of practices—advocacy, analysis, theorizing, and pedagogy (Dill & Zambrana, 2009)—that provide a basis for justice-oriented education and broad-based solidarity in anti-oppressive social movements.

Choo and Ferree (2010) outline three approaches to an intersectional methodology. The first is the group-centered strategy that focuses on inclusive analysis of marginalized intersecting identities and giving voice. As an example, a group-centered approach would seek greater recognition under the law and in policy for ways in which Black women's experiences of injustice differ from those of Black men or White women. One drawback of this focus on inclusion is that it can fetishize difference. A second strategy is process-centered. The focus here is on the multiplicity and interaction of effects. Separate processes are understood as interacting and mutually constituting whereby the totality of their effects produces more than the sum of their individual parts. This moves away from analyses that look at race, gender, class, sexuality and other categories of difference in isolation and generally engages a multi-level, comparative analysis. The third strategy is systems-centered intersectionality. Here race, gender, class and sexuality are not merely descriptors. They are conceptualized as interpenetrating social structures that operate through institutions to produce and maintain inequalities. For example this strategy looks at race and gender as broad systems that not only intersect and reinforce each other but serve integral economic functions as well. Familiarity with these strategies is important as each one has its strengths, and no single approach will suffice all situations (Choo & Ferree, 2010; Luft, 2009).

A methodological challenge for educators is in designing learning conditions wherein students may actively develop analytic concepts that enable them to engage in these intersectional strategies. This is a question of how to cultivate an intersectional imagination, that is, the ability to read the world intersectionally. Borrowing from C. Wright Mills' (1959) concept of the "sociological imagination" and its essential combination of "playfulness of mind … as well as a truly fierce drive to make sense of the world" (pp. 232–233), our notion of intersectional imagination similarly emphasizes the capacity to "shift from one perspective to another—from the political to the psychological; … from the most impersonal and remote of transformations to the most intimate features of the human self—and to see the relations between the two" (p. 4). We submit that an unyielding commitment to the collective struggles against oppression sets the intersectional imagination apart from Mills' emphasis on the ability to view phenomena from multiple vantage points. Pastrana (2006) echoes this important distinction when he states that an intersectional imagination is

> an outlook embedded in, and informed by, histories and experiences of oppression. While acknowledging the particularities of oppression and discrimination, the intersectional imagination also helps to locate these in a larger field of social injustice, thereby calling attention to the ways in which oppression and discrimination systematically affect everyone—not just those who witness or experience oppression. (p. 220)

Thus, in teaching toward an intersectional imagination, attention must be given to the problems and process by which learners (mis)apprehend, (mis)interpret, and (mis)represent experiences of difference, structural inequalities, and the relationship between them.

In order to cultivate an intersectional perspective, it is not enough simply to add to prior understandings. Learners need support in developing "inter-standing" (Taylor & Saarinen, 1994) by unfixing, complicating, and transgressing prior knowledge and relations of self/other (hooks, 1994). Developing inter-standing is to access a transitional or in-between space wherein we can "exceed what everyday thoughts tolerate as normal" (Britzman, 1998, p. 61). This is not, to use Matsuda's (1996) words, "a random ability to see all points of view but a deliberate choice to see the world from the standpoint of the oppressed ... in its concrete particulars" (p. 8). An intersectional imagination recasts oppressive material conditions and sociocultural differences as historical, political, and "unnatural," rather than normal or "natural." This recasting is a creative process of identifying relations of domination as human-made artifacts (Greene, 1988) and posing them as barriers to freedom (Freire, 1970). The most generative imaginative practices facilitate as well as complicate how we perceive difference and when difference matters. Matsuda (1991) complicates difference through a method called "ask the other question." She describes the process this way:

> When I see something that looks racist, I ask, "Where is the patriarchy in this?" When I see something that looks sexist, I ask, "Where is the heterosexism in this?" When I see something that looks homophobic, I ask, "Where are the class interests in this?" Working in coalition forces us to look for both the obvious and the non-obvious relationships of domination, helping us to realize that no form of subordination ever stands alone. (p. 1189)

Complicating strategies such at this mean that an intersectional imagination inculpates everyone. It "requires one to acknowledge one's intersecting identities, both marginalized and privileged, and then employ self-reflexivity, which moves one beyond self-reflection to the often uncomfortable level of self-implication" (Jones, 2010, p. 122). Arriving at a place of inter-standing implies a form of imagination that is committed to and capable of achieving empathic response-ability.

Conceptions of empathy and empathic response are often framed around the idea of caring for others, such as Noddings' (1984) notion of engrossment within an authentically caring relationship. If, however, empathy is framed within a pathologizing orientation toward marginalized groups, it can impede the development of the kind of imagination necessary for justice-oriented teaching (e.g., Valenzuela, 1999). Empathic responsiveness is not an atomized conception of empathy as an individual capacity. After all, empathy is always already shaped by unjust societal divisions and hierarchies of knowledge (Duncan, 2002). These power dynamics mean that empathy for the non-dominant "other" can be a deleterious form of appropriation where feelings of unfamiliarity and difference are made "less strange, less threatening, less out of control by reading it through one's own cultural positions and interests" (Ellsworth, 1992, p. 7).

Teaching that relies purely on cognitive transmission of abstract, distant theoretical principles of caring, morality, and justice are inadequate to the task of stimulating the intersectional imagination. As Matsuda suggests, "Moral abstraction and detachment are ways out of discomfort of direct confrontation with the ugliness of oppression. Abstraction, . . . is the method that allows theorists to discuss liberty, property, and rights in the aspirational mode of liberalism with no connection to what those concepts mean in real people's lives" (1996, pp. 8–9). In order to dislodge deep-seated liberal ideologies and logic of dysconscious racism, heteronormativity, patriarchy, and individualism, it is not enough to instill the merits educational equity and social justice. The "cool" academic discourse is incapable of stimulating learners' emotional reaches/compass because it lacks "hot affection" that is the basis of indignation toward all manner of unjust conditions and unfair treatment of others (Kristjánsson, 2004).

Recent work in curriculum studies takes up the task of theorizing creative strategies for ethical relations with others and within difference (Chappell, Craft, Rolfe, & Jobbins, 2012; Gaztambide-Fernández, 2012). Creative strategies often call for embodied practices of "touch" (Springgay, 2008) or being-with the other. This is a departure from notions of creativity associated with individual genius, cognition, and self-expression (Banaji & Burn, 2007). Gaztambide-Fernández (2012) envisions creativity as a mode of solidarity that "places difference rather than commonality at the center" and "assumes the intersection of social categories of race, class, gender, and sexuality as a source of strength" (pp. 88–89). This form of solidarity is "premised on the relationship between difference and interdependency, rather than similarity and a rational calculation of self-interests" (p. 49). For Villenas (2013), interdependency and coexistence (*convivencia*) entail an active orientation to others, wherein "I recreate myself in other people's company as they recreate themselves in my company." In this formulation, an intersectional imagination sets a foundation for solidary relations with others/Others and decolonizing, anti-oppressive pedagogy (Hancock, 2011).

According to Gaztambide-Fernández (2012), a "pedagogy of solidarity requires a profound faith in the creative possibilities that become available when we recognize each other (and each 'Other')" (p. 61). This creative aspect of solidarity is "concerned with the multiplicity of cultural practices that might evolve in such encounters [with difference], as a way of countering the versions of "culture" and "identity" that are imposed by the colonial project of modernity" (p. 57). Moreover, "all encounters are encounters with difference that are always already hierarchical" (p. 57) and intersectional as human experience is produced within interlocking dynamics of inequality. In teacher education, we routinely ask students to explore "unspoken, subjugated, and embodied knowledges" (Lewis, 2011, p. 54) in order to encourage new possibilities for how they might understand and participate in encounters with difference. This is experienced as emotionally risky and often threatening proposition for many of our students (Leonardo & Porter, 2010; Leonardo & Zembylas, 2013). In justice-oriented teacher education, the pedagogic intent behind such deliberate encounters with difference is to enable "more creative and productively defiant approaches to identity and subjectivity" (Beltran, 2004, p. 596). We believe that teaching toward an intersectional imagination can help to buttress these encounters by providing multiple points of entry for students with widely varying experiences and ideological leanings.

Our discussion now turns to fruitful teaching strategies we have employed in our classes and our pedagogic decision-making around their use. These strategies incorporate creative practices that are often found within the arts. Our instructional approach is decidedly eclectic and open-ended, much in keeping with arts-based inquiry methods (Rolling, 2010). We have found that this approach can engender critical aesthetic learning experiences (Kraehe & Brown, 2011) that open up pathways for students to develop complex knowledge of sociocultural influences on schools that connect macro-level structures and social processes with micro-level interactions (Brown & Kraehe, 2010). These critical approaches to arts practices in the teacher education classroom provide students a creative mode of engagement with each other and the Other. They can be used to generate a space and time for learning from histories of oppression and discrimination

## READING THE WORLD INTERSECTIONALLY THROUGH CRITICAL ARTS-BASED INQUIRIES

There are a growing number of educational texts outlining concepts teachers need to know and be able to apply in various teaching contexts. These resources generally provide theories and examples of differentiation, social inequality, equity, critical multiculturalism, and social justice education (Adams et al., 2010; Banks & Banks, 2010; Milner, 2010; Nieto & Bode, 2012; Sensoy & DiAngelo, 2012). This work is drawn from multiple disciplines, often incorporating concepts from ethnic studies, sexuality and gender studies, sociology, anthropology, social psychology, philosophy, history, cultural studies, legal studies, and curriculum studies. The perspectives and critical orientation contained in these concepts are commonly marginalized to a single class in a teacher education program (Cochran-Smith, Davis & Fries, 2003), making it difficult for students to acquire a deep understanding of and commitment to diversity and educational equity. These problems are compounded when teacher educators do not have the practical experiences or theoretical knowledge to teach about difference and inequality (Melnick & Zeichner, 1995).

There is also evidence to suggest that it may be the teaching strategy itself that turns off many learners, leaving them bored and listless (Brown, 2004). We have learned from our own encounters with students that traditional classroom strategies that rely heavily upon the disembodied transmission of knowledge, typically enacted as monological lectures and pedantic texts, can turn what is for many beginning students already a foreign academic discourse into a self-alienating body of knowledge to acquire (Kraehe & Brown, 2011; see also, Leitch, 2006). A number of educators have turned to the visual and performing arts specifically looking for more creative and flexible alternatives to text-driven pedagogies (Belliveau, 2006; Berghoff, Borgmann & Parr, 2005; Dillon, 2008; Ellsworth, 1992; Lee, 2012; Maguire & Lenihan, 2010; McDermott, 2002; Mullen, 1999; Osei-Kofi, 2013; Shelton & McDermott, 2010). McDermott, Shelton and Mogge (2012) explain that they employ children's literature and performance activities to augment their teaching because it is "not through 'talking at' preservice teachers, or in handing them statistics, but by throwing their bodies and their hearts into experiential processes which reorient the senses toward those of the 'Other'" (p. 15). It is a sentiment that is widely shared across this emerging scholarship and suggests that the arts offer a fundamentally different kind of experience that affectively "reorient" one's perceptions and conceptions of the social world.

The idea that the arts enable new ways of sensing and knowing proliferates in current curriculum studies and qualitative inquiry (Gaztambide-Fernández, 2002). Given the media saturation of contemporary societies, Desai, Hamlin, and Mattson (2010) suggest that humans "no longer represent ideas, feelings, thoughts, and experiences primarily through oral and written means. Rather, multi-modal ways of representing human experience are now commonplace" (p. 5). For these authors, arts practices have relevance for engaging learners in cultural modes of signification and resignification with which they are already familiar. Arts practices can become powerful pedagogical strategies when they involve learners "in the sensations and emotions of historical knowledge" (p. 11) and "critically open-ended conversations" (p. 6). Though the arts can be practiced in ways that destabilize routine thinking and relations with others, as with any cultural practice, there is no guarantee that an encounter with the arts will "enlarge human understanding" (p. 553) as Eisner (1991) contends. Learning experiences that engage in arts practices are not inherently, nor uniformly transformative (Ellsworth,

1992). We agree with Gaztambide-Fernández (2010) who cautions that the arts should be taken up with a "deep awareness and critical stance toward itself and its own potential short-comings" (p. 83).

## INTERSECTIONALITY AND THE ARTS AS ALLIED PRACTICES FOR TEACHER EDUCATION

Our approach is to use critical arts-based inquiry methods as a way to design possible entry points through which students can encounter difference and develop concepts of educational inequality. We describe here how, in the context of a course designed and revised by Keffrelyn over time, intersectionality and the arts were interwoven as allied practices for critical teacher education.[1] The purpose of the course was to help students move towards more complex understandings of the sociocultural knowledge related to schooling and teaching. One of the immediate challenges that Keffrelyn encountered when teaching the course during its early instantiation was moving students to a deeper understanding of sociocultural knowledge. Based on students' responses on class assignments and to interview questions Keffrelyn posed in a larger research study she designed to examine what understandings students had about sociocultural knowledge after taking her course, she found that students generally left the course with shallow knowledge.

To address this problem she spent a semester critically reflecting on the course. This included outlining the specific learning goals she had for students taking the course. She identified four goals. The first was to help students recognize the power and limitations of their own personal experiences with schooling (Britzman, 2003; Lortie, 1975). The second goal was to increase students' content and theoretical knowledge related to critical sociocultural competence. Another goal of the course was to help students recognize and accept the role and responsibility that teachers hold for ensuring that all of their students succeed academically (Ladson-Billings, 1994). Finally, the fourth goal was to help students acknowledge the problems related to holding and drawing from deficit-oriented views of their students and the families and communities from which they come (Valencia, 1997). Ultimately Keffrelyn recognized that if students were going to acquire a complex and critical sociocultural knowledge base for schooling and teaching they would need to have access to a learning experience that was critical and engaging, while also theoretical and creative. Clarifying the key critical theoretical constructs that students needed to know in order to reach the learning goals of the course was the first step. The second was providing students with pedagogic activities that would open the students' minds and allow them to enter into the often unfamiliar and contentious content terrain explored in the course around race, social class and gender.

## Organization of the Course

Pedagogically the revised course that Keffrelyn developed and that Amelia later taught, drew heavily from insights related to both sociocultural approaches to learning (Tharp & Gallimore 1988; Vygotsky 1986, 1978; Wertsch 1991) and visual culture (Mirzoeff, 2002, 1998; Tavin, 2003) approaches. The course also relied on case-based pedagogy. Keffrelyn moved from the perspective that learning is a social process in which students learn from their engagement with self, others and cultural tools that are organized to elicit first engagement and then new knowledge and understandings. Visual culture is comprised of popular culture, media technologies and of works of art (Tavin, 2005) and offers a way to "open up an entire world of intertextuality in which images, sounds and spatial dimensions are read onto and through one another" (Rogoff, 1998, p. 14). This would include using methods that allowed students to view and interpret images and text as found in film, television clips, documentaries, music videos, magazines and arts works, along with research based educational texts. Case-based pedagogy (Sykes & Bird, 1992), coupled with sociocultural approaches to learning and teaching that value and include visual cultural methods ask students to engage with realistic scenarios that both illuminate and ask students to create, in visual ways, how sociocultural content knowledge.

In the revised course students read and engaged with many different kinds of cases. By cases we refer to broad notion of cases as assemblages that "embody expert knowledge, captured wisdom, and critical aspects of the domain under study" (Kim & Hannifin, 2008, p. 1838). Leaving the definition of a case open to a variety of media was purposeful, as to not prematurely occlude learning from cases that might take multiple forms. Student read and commented on both textual and visual cases that examined how race, social class, gender, sexuality, culture and teaching operate in society and in schools. The textual cases comprised both ethnographic research studies and vignette cases of a realistic, but fictional scenarios focused on how race, class, gender, culture and teaching exist with a sociocultural context of schooling. Visual/film cases explored topics such as race, the struggle for equality and equity in school, the social construction of gender and the role of social class in U.S. society and in K–12 schooling. Class discussion and activities asked students to draw from and create visual materials (e.g., drawings, collages).

## Course Content

The content of the course fell into several categories. The first section of the course focused on helping students understand the concepts of othering, norming and deviance. The second section explored the history of schooling, particularly as it played out of various marginalized student populations (i.e., African Americans; Chinese Americans; Disabled Students; European American immigrants and Latinos). The third section considered some of the contemporary issues facing schools including tracking, issues related to the opportunity/achievement gap and the pervasiveness of deficit-oriented thinking. The fourth section targeted how race, social class, gender, culture and language respectively operate in schools to help create inequitable opportunities for all students to learn. The fifth and final section explored the role of teaching and curriculum in the schooling process.

To help students understand this material, each week they were provided a collective list of over 50 key terms that outlined important concepts and frameworks that students needed to understand and gain competence in applying. To help students understand these terms, various collaborative arts-based activities were employed such as drawings, collages, and the creation of a video case project. These terms were taken from education scholarship in the social foundations area and included: academic achievement, meritocracy, social reproduction, social/cultural/economic/symbolic capital, privilege, racism, color-blind ideologies, gender performativity, approaches to curriculum and culturally responsive/relevant pedagogy. These terms, along with the required course readings allowed students to first understand the underlying sociocultural construct and then how they often operate together in social/school practice to create educational inequities. This approach was taken to the course because most students taking the class begin either completely unfamiliar with or lacking a deep understanding of each of the key sociocultural factors (e.g., social class; race; gender). Acquiring an intersectional analysis of how these factors occur represents a complex understanding of sociocultural factors, that pedagogically we have found, students best learn when introduced to each factor separately and then in an intersectional way.

## CONCLUSION

In our experience of teaching with arts-based methods, we have found that they afford generative processes through which students can interact, improvise, and construct unexpectedly complex knowledge over time (Brown & Kraehe, 2010b; Kraehe & Brown, 2011). Many of our university students come into our classrooms with few experiences of talking about race, class, gender and sexuality and little knowledge of how to navigate a provocative dialogue in mixed groups settings. For dominant and non-dominant group students, classes such as ours are potentially very threatening, and learning can feel uncomfortable, even dangerous. We utilize arts-based inquiries to provide what we hope will be a more creative and constructive context for practice and participation in the difficult, disjunctive, and perhaps trauma-inducing work of unsettling habitual categories and their normalizing logics (Britzman, 1998; Luke, 2004). Arts-based inquiries become a vehicle through which students seem to more readily contest dominant meanings through alternate discourses (asking "what if...?") and provisional identities (becoming "as if..."). As a transitional space (Ellsworth, 2005), the arts can be used to activate a spirit of play, experimentation, and ambiguity that can enhance conditions for imagination and insight (Gude, 2010; Mills, 1959). We also acknowledge that this unpredictability also demands that we, as teacher educators, take risks as there is always the possibility that learning may fall short of or surpass the pedagogic encounter for which we have prepared ourselves.

## NOTE

1. As an assistant professor, Keffrelyn developed and taught a section of this foundations course every semester as a part of the teacher education program at a large research university. A doctoral student with a background and research interest in arts education, Amelia approached Keffrelyn about observing the course for a semester. Amelia subsequently taught two sections of the course over a year using the course design developed by Keffrelyn. The two conducted a collaborative research based on four sections of this course. Their study illuminated how students' sociocultural knowledge was shaped by the course and the pedagogic affordances of the arts-based practices they used in the course.

## REFERENCES

Adams, M., Blumenfeld, W., Castañeda, C., Hackman, H. W., Peters, M. L., & Zúñiga, X. (Eds.). (2010). *Readings for diversity and social justice* (2nd ed.). New York, NY: Routledge.

Amos, Y. T. (2010). "They don't want to get it!": Interaction between minority and White pre-service teachers in a multicultural education class. *Multicultural Education, 17*4), 31–37.

Asher, N. (2007). Made in the (multicultural) U.S.A.: Unpacking tensions of race, culture, gender, and sexuality in education. *Educational Researcher, 36*(2), 65–73.

Banaji, S., & Burn, A. (2007). Creativity through a rhetorical lens: Implications for schooling, literacy and media education. *Literacy, 41*(2), 62–70.

Banks, J. A. (2001). *Cultural diversity and education: Foundations, curriculum, and teaching* (4th ed.). Boston: Allyn & Bacon.

Banks, J. A., & Banks, C. A. M. (Eds.). (2010). *Multicultural education: Issues and perspectives* (7th ed.). Hoboken, NJ: Wiley.

Banks, J. A., Cochran-Smith, M., Moll, L., Richert, A., Zeichner, K., LePage, P., et al. (2005). Teaching diverse learners. In L. Darling-Hammons & J. Bransford (Eds.), *Preparing teachers for a changing world: What teachers should learn and be able to do* (pp. 232–276). San Francisco: Jossey-Bass.

Beauboeuf-Lafontant, T. (2005). Womanist lessons for reinventing teaching. *Journal of Teacher Education, 56*(5), 436–445.

Belliveau, G. (2006). Engaging in drama: Using arts-based research to explore a social justice project in teacher education. *International Journal of Education and the Arts, 7*(5), 1–16.

Beltran, C. (2004). Patrolling borders: Hybrids, hierarchies and the challenge of *mestizaje. Political Research Quarterly, 57*, 595–607.

Berghoff, B., Borgmann, C. B., & Parr, N. C. (2005). *Arts together: Steps toward transformative teacher education.* Reston, VA: National Art Education Association.

Britzman, D. (1998). *Lost subjects, contested objects: Toward a psychoanalytic inquiry of learning.* Albany: State University of New York Press.

Britzman, D. (2003). *Practice makes practice: A critical study of learning to teach* (2nd ed.). Albany: State University of New York Press.

Brown, E. L. (2004). What precipitates change in cultural diversity awareness during a multicultural course—The message or the method? *Journal of Teacher Education, 55*(4), 325–340.

Brown, E. L. (2005). Using photography to explore hidden realities and raise cross-cultural sensitivity in future teachers. *The Urban Review, 37*(2), 149–171.

Brown, K. D. (2011). Breaking the cycle of Sisyphus: Social education and the acquisition of critical sociocultural knowledge about race and racism in the U.S. *The Social Studies, 102*(6), 1–6.

Brown, K. D., & Kraehe, A. M. (2010a). When you've only got one class, one chance: Acquiring sociocultural knowledge using eclectic case pedagogy. *Teaching Education, 21*(3), 313–328.

Brown, K. D., & Kraehe, A. M. (2010b). The complexities of teaching the complex: Examining how future educators construct understandings of sociocultural knowledge and schooling. *Educational Studies, 46*(1), 91–115.

Chappell, K., Craft, A., Rolfe, L. M., & Jobbins, V. (2012). Humanizing creativity: Valuing our journeys of becoming. *International Journal of Education and the Arts, 13*(8), 1–35.

Choo, H. Y., & Ferree, M. M. (2010). Practicing intersectionality in sociological research: A critical analysis of inclusions, interactions, and institutions in the study of inequalities. *Sociological Theory, 28*(2), 129–149.

Cochran-Smith, M., Davis, D., & Fries, K. (2004). Multicultural teacher education: Research, practice, and policy. In J. A. Banks & C. A. M. Banks (Eds.), *Handbook of research on multicultural education* (2nd ed., pp. 931–978). San Francisco: Jossey-Bass.

Collins, P. H. (1990). *Black feminist thought: Knowledge, consciousness, and the politics of empowerment.* Boston: Unwin Hyman.

Collins, P. H. (1998). *Fighting words: Black women and the search for justice.* Minneapolis: University of Minnesota.

Combahee River Collective. (1983). The Combahee River statement. In B. Smith (Ed.), *Home girls: A black feminist anthology* (pp. 272–282). New York, NY: Kitchen Table/Women of Color Press.

Crenshaw, K. (1991). Mapping the margins: Intersectionality, identity politics and violence against women of color. *Stanford Law Review, 43*(6), 1241–1299.

Desai, D., Hamlin, J., & Mattson, R. (2010). *History as art, art as history: Contemporary art and social studies education.* New York and London: Routledge.

Dhamoon, R. K. (2011). Considerations on mainstreaming intersectionality. *Political Research Quarterly, 64*(1), 230–243.

Dill, B. T., & Zambrana, R. E. (2009). *Emerging intersections: Race, class, and gender in theory, policy and practice.* New Brunswick, NJ: Rutgers University Press.

Dillon, D. (2008). Theatre and critical consciousness in teacher education. *LEARNing Landscapes, 2*(1), 179–194.

Dilworth, M. E., & Brown, A. L. (2008). Teachers of color. In M. Cochran-Smith, S. Feiman-Nemser, & D. J. McIntyre (Eds.), *Handbook of research on teacher education: Enduring questions in changing contexts* (3rd ed., pp. 424–444). New York, NY: Routledge.

Duncan, G. A., (2002). Critical race theory and method: Rendering race in urban ethnographic research. *Qualitative Inquiry, 8*(1), 85–104.

Eisner, E. (1991). Art, music, and literature within the social studies. In J. P. Shaver, *Handbook of research on social studies teaching and learning* (pp. 551–558). New York, NY: Macmillan.

Ellsworth, E. (1992). Teaching to support unassimilated difference. *Radical Teacher, 42*, 4–9.

Ellsworth, E. (2005). *Places of learning: Media, architecture, pedagogy.* New York, NY: RoutledgeFalmer.

Fendler, L. (2003). Teacher reflection in a hall of mirrors: Historical influences and political reverberations. *Educational Researcher, 32*(3), 16–25.

Gaztambide-Fernández, R. (2002). (De)constructing art as a model / (re)constructing art as a possibility: An interactive essay exploring the possibilities of the arts in relationship to education. In T. Poetter, K. Wilson Baptist, C. Higgins, C. Haerr, & M. Hayes, (Eds.), *In(ex)clusion: (Re)visioning the democratic ideal—Selected papers from the 2001 Curriculum and Pedagogy annual conference* (pp. 83–107). Troy, NY: Educator's International Press.

Gaztambide-Fernández, R. (2010). Toward creative solidarity in the "next" moment of curriculum work. In E. Malewski (Ed.), *Curriculum studies handbook—the next moment* (pp. 78–94). New York, NY: Routledge.

Gaztambide-Fernández, R. (2012). Decolonization and the pedagogy of solidarity. *Decolonization: Indigeneity, Education & Society, 1*(1), 41–67.

Glenn, E. N. (1999). The social construction and institutionalization of gender and race: An integrative framework. In M. M. Ferree, J. Lorber, & B. B. Hess (Eds.), *Revisioning gender* (pp. 3–43). New York, NY: Sage.

Gomez, M. L. (1996). Prospective teachers' perspectives on teaching "other people's children." In K. Zeichner, S. Melnick, & M. L. Gomez (Eds.), *Currents of reform in preservice teacher education* (pp. 109–132). New York, NY: Teachers College Press.

Grant, C., & Zwier, E. (2011). Intersectionality and student outcomes: Sharpening the struggle against racism, sexism, classism, ableism, heterosexism, nationalism, and linguistic, religious, and geographical discrimination in teaching and learning. *Multicultural Perspectives, 13*(4), 181–188.

Greene, M. (1988). *The dialectic of freedom.* New York, NY: Teachers College Press.

Greene, M. (1995). *Releasing the imagination: Essays on education, the arts, and social change.* San Francisco: Jossey-Bass.

Gude, O. (2010). Playing, creativity, possibility. *Art Education, 63*(2), 31–37.

Haberman, M., & Post, L. (1992). Does direct experience change education students' perceptions of low-income minority children? *Midwestern Educational Researcher, 5*(2), 29–31.

Hancock, A. (2005). W. E. B. DuBois: Intellectual forefather of intersectionality? *Souls, 7*(3–4), 74–84.

Hancock, A. (2007). When multiplication doesn't equal quick addition: Examining intersectionality as a research paradigm. *Perspectives on Politics, 5*(1), 63–79.

Hancock, A. (2011). *Solidarity politics for millennials: A guide to ending the oppression Olympics.* New York, NY: Palgrave Macmillan.

Harris, C. I. (1996). Finding Sojourner's truth: Race, gender, and the institution of property. *Cardozo Law Review, 18,* 309.

Hollins, E. R., King, J. E., & Hayman, W. C. (1994). *Teaching diverse populations: Formulating a knowledge base.* Albany: State University of New York Press.

hooks, b. (1994). *Teaching to transgress: Education as the practice of freedom.* New York, NY: Routledge.

hooks, b. (1995). *Art on my mind: Visual politics.* New York, NY: The New Press.

Hulko, W. (2009). The time- and context-contingent nature of intersectionality and interlocking oppressions. *Affilia: Journal of Women and Social Work, 24*(1), 44–55.

Irvine, J. J. (Ed.). (2002). *In search of wholeness: African American teachers and their culturally specific classroom practices.* New York, NY: Palgrave.

Jones, R. G. (2010). Putting privilege into practice through "intersectional reflexivity": Ruminations, interventions, and possibilities. *Reflections: Narratives of Professional Helping, 16,* 122–125.

Jones, S. R., & Wijeyesinghe, C. L. (2011). The promises and challenges of teaching from an intersectional perspective: Core components and applied strategies. In M. L. Ouellett (Ed.), *An integrative analysis approach to diversity in the college classroom* (vol. 125, pp. 11–20). San Francisco, CA: Jossey-Bass.

Kim, H., & Hannafin, M. J. (2008). Situated case-based knowledge: An emerging framework for prospective teacher learning. *Teaching and Teacher Education, 24,* 1837–1845.

King, J. (1991). Dysconcious racism: Ideology, identity, and the miseducation of the teachers. *Journal of Negro Education, 60*(2), 133–146.

Kraehe, A. M., & Brown, K. D. (2011). Awakening teachers' capacities for social justice with/in arts-based inquiries. *Equity and Excellence in Education, 44*(4), 37–41.

Kristjánsson, K. (2004). Empathy, sympathy, justice and the child. *Journal of Moral Education, 33*(3), 291–305.

Ladson-Billings, G. (1994). *The dreamkeepers: Successful teachers of African American children.* San Francisco, CA: John Wiley & Sons.

Ladson-Billings, G. (1996). Silences as weapons: Challenges of a Black professor teaching White students. *Theory into Practice, 35*(2), 79–85.

Ladson-Billings, G. (2001). *Crossing over to Canaan: The journey of new teachers in diverse classrooms.* San Francisco, CA: Jossey-Bass.

Laughter, J. C. (2011). Rethinking assumptions of demographic privilege: Diversity among White preservice teachers. *Teaching and Teacher Education, 27*(1), 43–50.

Lee, N. (2012). Culturally responsive teaching for 21st-Century art education: Examining race in a studio art experience. *Art Education, 65*(5), 48–53.

Leitch, R. (2006). Limitations of language: Developing arts-based creative narrative in stories of teachers' identities. *Teachers and Teaching: Theory and Practice, 12*(5), 549–569.

Leonardo, Z., & Porter, R. K. (2010). Pedagogy of fear: Toward a Fanonian theory of "safety" in race dialogue. *Race Ethnicity and Education, 13*(2), 139–157.

Leonardo, Z., & Zembylas, M. (2013). Whiteness as technology of affect: Implications for educational praxis. *Equity & Excellence in Education, 46*(1), 150–165.

Lewis, M. M. (2011). Body of knowledge: Black queer feminist pedagogy, praxis, and embodied text. *Journal of Lesbian Studies, 15*(1), 49–57.

Lortie, D. C. (1975). *Schoolteacher: A sociological study.* Chicago: University of Chicago Press.

Lowenstein, K. (2009). The work of multicultural teacher education: Reconceptualizing white teacher candidates as learners. *Review of Educational Research, 79*(1), 163–196.

Luft, R. E. (2009). Intersectionality and the risk of flattening difference: Gender and race logics, and the strategic use of antiracist singularity. In M. T. Berger & K. Guidroz (Eds.), *The intersectional approach: Transforming the academy through race, class, and gender* (pp. 100–117). Chapel Hill: The University of North Carolina Press.

Luke, A. (2004). Two takes on the critical. In B. Norton & K. Toohey (Eds.), *Critical pedagogies and language learning* (pp. 21–29). Cambridge, UK: Cambridge University Press.

Maguire, C., & Lenihan, T. (2010). Fostering capabilities toward social justice in art education. *Journal of Cultural Research in Art Education, 28*, 39–53.

Matsuda, M. (1991). Beside my sister, facing the enemy: Legal theory out of coalition. *Stanford Law Review, 43*(6), 1183–1192.

Matsuda, M. (1996). *Where is your body? And other essays on race, gender, and the law.* Boston: Beacon Press.

McCall, L. (2005). The complexity of intersectionality. *Signs: Journal of Women in Culture and Society, 30*(3), 1771–1800.

McDermott, M. (2002). Collaging preservice teacher identity. *Teacher Education Quarterly, 29*(4), 53–68.

McDermott, M. Shelton. N. R., & Mogge, S. G. (2012). Preservice teachers' perceptions of immigrants and possibilities of transformative pedagogy: Recommendations for a praxis of "critical aesthetics. *International Journal of Multicultural Education, 14*(2), 1–22.

Melnick, S. L., & Zeichner, K. M. (1995). *Teacher education for cultural diversity: Enhancing the capacity of teacher education institutions to address diversity issues.* East Lansing, MI: National Center for Research on Teacher Learning, Michigan State University.

Mills, C. W. (1959). *The sociological imagination.* Harmondsworth, Middlesex: Penguin.

Milner, R. (2006). Preservice teachers' learning about cultural and racial diversity: Implications for urban education. *Urban Education, 41*(4), 343–375.

Milner, R. (2010). What does teacher education have to do with teaching? Implications for diversity studies. *Journal of Teacher Education, 61*(1–2), 118–131.

Moraga, C. L., & Anzaldúa, G. E. (1981). *This bridge called my back: Writings by radical women of color.* Watertown, MA: Persephone Press.

Mullen, C. A. (1999).Whiteness, cracks, and ink-stains: Making cultural identity with Euroamerican preservice teachers. In C. T. P. Diamond & C. A. Mullen (Eds.), *The postmodern educator: Arts-based inquiries and teacher development* (pp. 147–190). New York, NY: Lang.

Nieto, S., & Bode, P. (2012). *Affirming diversity: The sociopolitical context of multicultural education* (6th ed.). Boston, MA: Pearson Education.

Noddings, N. (1984). *Caring: A feminine approach to ethics and moral education.* Berkeley and Los Angeles: University of California Press.

Osei-Kofi, N. (2013). The emancipatory potential of arts-based research for social justice. *Equity & Excellence in Education, 46*(1), 135–149.

Pastrana, A. (2006). The intersectional imagination: What do lesbian and gay leaders of color have to do with it? *Race, Gender & Class, 13*(3/4), 218–238.

Pollock, M. (2008). From shallow to deep: Toward a thorough cultural analysis of school achievement patterns. *Anthropology & Education Quarterly, 39*(4), 369–380.

Rogoff, I. (1998). Studying visual culture. In N. Mirzoeff (Ed.), *Visual culture reader* (pp. 14–26). New York, NY: Routledge.

Rolling, J. H. (2010). A paradigm analysis of arts-based research and implications for education. *Studies in Art Education, 51*(2), 102–114.

Shelton, N. R., & McDermott, M. (2010). Using literature and drama to understand social justice. *Teacher Development, 14*(1), 123–135.

Shulman, L. (1986). Those who understand: Knowledge growth in teaching. *Educational Researcher, 15*(2), 4–14.

Shulman, L. (1987). Knowledge and teaching: Foundations of the new reform. *Harvard Educational Review, 57*(1), 1–22.

Sleeter, C. E. (1995). White preservice students and multicultural education course work. In J. M. Larkin & C. E. Sleeter (Eds.), *Developing multicultural teacher education curriculum* (pp. 17–30). Albany: State University of New York.

Sleeter, C. E. (2001). Preparing teachers for culturally diverse schools: Research and the overwhelming presence of Whiteness. *Journal of Teacher Education, 52*(2), 94–106.

Sleeter, C. E., & Grant, C. A. (2006). *Making choices for multicultural education: Five approaches to race, class and gender* (5th ed.). New York, NY: John Wiley & Sons.

Smagorinsky, P., Cook, L. S., & Jackson, T. S. (2003). The twisting path of concept development in learning to teach. *Teachers College Record, 105*(8), 1399–1436.

Solomona, P., Portelli, J. P., Daniel, B., & Campbell, A. (2005). The discourse of denial: How white teacher candidates construct race, racism and 'white privilege'. *Race Ethnicity and Education, 8*(2), 147–169.

Springgay, S. (2008). *Body knowledge and curriculum: Pedagogies of touch in youth and visual culture.* New York, NY: Peter Lang.

Sykes, G., & Bird, T. (1992). Teacher education and the case idea. *Review of Research in Education,* 18, 457–521.

Tavin, K. (2003). Wrestling with angels, searching for ghosts: Toward a critical pedagogy of visual culture. *Studies in Art Education, 44*(3), 197–213.

Tavin, K. M. (2005). Hauntological shifts: Fear and loathing of popular (visual) culture. *Studies in Art Education, 46*(2), 101–117.

Taylor, M., & Saarinen, E. (1994). *Imagologies: Media philosophy.* London: Routledge.

Terrill, M. M., & Mark, D. L. H. (2000). Preservice teachers' expectations for schools with children of color and second-language learners. *Journal of Teacher Education, 51*(2), 149–155.

Tharp, R. G., & Gallimore, R. (1988). *Rousing minds to life: Teaching, learning, and schooling in social context.* New York, NY: Cambridge University Press.

Valencia, R. R. (1997). Genetic pathology model of deficit thinking. In R. R. Valencia (Ed.), *The evolution of deficit thinking: Educational thought and practice* (pp. 41–112). London: Falmer.

Valenzuela, A. (1999). *Subtractive schooling: U.S.-Mexican youth and the politics of caring.* Albany, NY: State University of New York Press.

Villegas, A. M., & Davis, D. E. (2008). Preparing teachers of color to confront racial/ethnic disparities in educational outcomes. In M. Cochran-Smith, S. Feiman-Nemser, & D. J. McIntyre (Eds.), *Handbook of research on teacher education: Enduring questions in changing contexts* (3rd ed., pp. 583–605). New York, NY: Routledge.

Villenas, S. (2013, March). *Civic agency as community building and social movement: Thinking with Latina/Chicana feminisms in diverse communities.* Paper presented at La Collectiva Lecture Series, Denton, TX.

Vygotsky, L. (1978). *Mind in society: The development of higher psychological processes.* Cambridge, MA: Harvard University Press.

Vygotsky, L. (1986). *Thought and language.* Cambridge, MA: MIT Press.

Wertsch, J. V. (1991). *Voices of the mind: A sociocultural approach to mediated action.* Cambridge, MA: Harvard University Press.

Wiest, L. R. (1998). Using immersion experiences to shake up preservice teachers' views about cultural differences. *Journal of Teacher Education, 49*(5), 358–365.

CHAPTER 9

# TEACHER IDENTITIES AND INTERSECTIONALITY

## A Case Study
## from Aotearoa New Zealand

**Anne Hynds**
*Victoria University of Wellington*

### ABSTRACT

This chapter uses intersectionality as an analytical tool (Grant & Zwier, 2011) to re-analyze research findings from a case study of collaborative work between Indigenous Māori and non-Māori teachers within two mainstream schools in Aotearoa New Zealand. In an attempt to redress the damaging and ongoing effects of colonization and institutional racism, recent government supported initiatives have focused on improving classroom practice and outcomes for Māori learners. A case study of one such initiative highlighted the influence of multiple identity markers on teacher engagement within culturally responsive school reform work. Teacher identity markers included relational connections which were place and community based, and highlighted identity territories and membership collectives which enabled or disrupted a teacher's sense of acceptance or belonging. 'Forced identities' (McIntosh,

*Intersectionality and Urban Education*, pages 193–211
Copyright © 2014 by Information Age Publishing
All rights of reproduction in any form reserved.

2005) also emerged from the data. These identities were located across intersections of power and privilege related to social constructions of race/ethnicity, sexuality and gender. All of these identity markers, whilst influencing teacher engagement in collaborative work, remained unexamined within the context of culturally responsive school reform. Intersections of difference within hegemonic schooling processes of colonization and assimilation are discussed along with recommendations to promote social justice and solidarity across diverse school communities.

## INTRODUCTION

Across the world, particularly in Western style democracies, schools are tasked with ensuring culturally responsive schooling for Indigenous and other non-dominant culture students. Yet in my own country of Aotearoa New Zealand, there is evidence that schools are saturated with the dominant worldviews, curricula, and structures reflecting the cultural capital of the colonizers—Pākehā New Zealand Europeans (Bishop & Glynn, 1999; Penetito, 2010).

Our colonial history has left a number of intergenerational legacies, including educational failure and unequal employment patterns for Māori. The issue of Māori student underachievement is usually framed within a cultural deficit explanation rather than in the enacted racism embedded within the New Zealand schooling system (Penetito, 2010). The deficit explanation locates the problem of educational failure with the child and/or the child's home background rather than in the mono-cultural practices of teachers (Shields, Bishop, & Mazawi, 2005; Sleeter, 2011). Ministry of Education statistics indicate that in 2010, 74% of teachers identified as Pākehā (New Zealand European). In contrast, only 9% of teachers employed were Māori. Sleeter (2011) warns that teachers with limited cross-cultural experiences and knowledge are unable to utilize the rich resources of children and families from diverse backgrounds.

In Aotearoa New Zealand the government has invested in a number of school-based initiatives to improve the quality of teaching for Māori students within mainstream English Medium schools. Bishop and Glynn (1999) have argued that change can occur when teachers re-position themselves as co-learners or facilitators of learning experiences as they learn to connect with, and value, Māori students and their Māori tanga (Māori culture and ways of living). Relationship-based professional development initiatives such as Te Kotahitanga (Bishop, Berryman, Cavanagh, & Teddy, 2009) and Te Kauhua (Tuuta, Bradnam, Hynds, Higgins, & Broughton, 2004) promote the development of unity between Māori and non-Māori teachers, students and community members in order to create a shared vision of change in schools. In such contexts, culturally responsive teachers seek to critically examine their own and others' cultural practices and assumptions about teaching and learning within collaborative inquiry contexts (Bishop & Glynn, 1999). This is important because teachers bring their own unique identities and positions into relationship-based professional learning contexts (Hynds, 2007).

Identity formation is not a process that any individual constructs by themselves (Fine & Weiss, 2005; McIntosh, 2005): "Identities are co-constructed between individuals and society at large" (Alejandra Elenes, 2003, p. 191). Teacher identities are not static (Vähäsantanen, Hökkä, Eteläpelto Rasku-Puttonen, & Littleton, 2008) as they develop over a teacher's career (Beijaard, Meifer, & Verloop, 2004). Teacher identity has been described as the teacher's perception of them self as a professional actor (Beauchamp & Thomas, 2009). Identity formation for teachers is often linked to an ongoing development process of practical knowledge-building, an integration and exchange of collective and individual beliefs about what is considered relevant to learning and teaching (Beijaard et al., 2004). Professional identity formation is closely associated with an individual's personal motivations, which in turn are influenced by a sense of meaning and commitment to others in teaching work (Beijaard et al., 2004; Vähäsantanen et al., 2008). However, it can also be argued that in Aotearoa New Zealand, teacher identities are constructed and influenced through power relationships, since the overwhelming majority of teachers are from the dominant cultural group of Pākehā (New Zealand Europeans), reflecting culturally mediated and preferred practices of this group. Therefore, it can be assumed that Māori and non-Māori teacher identity in relationship-based professional development initiatives that seek to make a difference to the teaching practice and learning outcomes of Māori students are also influenced by "a territorialized politics of belonging" (Kidman, 2012, p. 189). In researching Māori youth identities, Kidman cites the work of Yuval-Davis (2006) in arguing that "the politics of belonging extends beyond a familiarity or affinity with particular places and centers on membership of a particular collective" (p. 191).

While there is acknowledgement about the influence of context in the shaping of teacher identity (Beauchamp & Thomas, 2009), I found a lack of research literature that identifies the identity territories and membership collectives that teachers bring into the collaborative dynamic, when Indigenous (Māori) and non-Indigenous (non-Māori) teachers work together on culturally responsive reform. Such gaps within our knowledge base mean we may fail in our ability to truly understand how to care for students as culturally located individuals (Bishop et al., 2009) in our quest to create more responsive and inclusive learning environments for all.

## Theoretical Framework

In this chapter I have used "intersectionality" as an analytical tool (Grant & Zwier, 2011) to critically reexamine culturally diverse teacher engagement in culturally responsive relationship-based reform contexts. I have adopted Grant and Zwier's stance that intersectionality "can be used to reframe educators' thinking and subsequent actions in the classroom" (p. 16). I agree with Artiles (1998) that difference is socially constructed and that privilege and oppression work in multiple and often unexamined ways. I have focused my attention on teachers, as I believe teacher identity plays a major role in professional learning and that a focus on teacher collective work is needed to "cultivate individual and collective consciousness of oppressive practices" (Grant & Zwier, 2011, p. 186). Intersectionality also supports more inclusive and responsive pedagogies "through teachers' counter-stories and counter-practices and complicates the idea of a teacher-student cultural match" (Grant & Zwier, 2011, p. 186). In their analysis of analytic intersectionality, Choo and Ferree (2010) highlight different types of intersectional practices, with one being a focus on being process centered whereby "interaction effects come to the fore" (p. 133). Comparative analysis, through process-centered approaches, "places attention on context and comparison at the intersections" as being "sensitive to the issues of identities or social locations", whilst understanding identity formation as being a "contested process of self-creation in a field of power relations" (Choo & Ferree, 2010, p. 134).

## Background to the Research Context

The first stage of the professional development initiative, Te Kauhua, was launched by the Ministry of Education across Aotearoa New Zealand in 2001. A number of schools volunteered to be part of this exploratory pilot project. Schools used action research to gather baseline data on Māori student achievement and develop new forms of teacher professional learning activities in partnership with local Māori communities. In-school facilitators established school clusters and worked with school and community leaders to develop and implement partnership plans, observe and record changes on student achievement, and assess the impact. I was part of a bicultural (Māori and non-Māori) research team contracted by the Ministry of Education to evaluate the impact of this first phase. Evaluation findings indicated evidence of initial partnership processes and progress towards reframing the mainstream school experience for Māori students within several schools (Tuuta et al., 2004). However, it was also noted that further research was needed on partnership processes in schools between Māori and non-Māori participants (students, teachers and family members).

After this first phase of the contract evaluation process for the Ministry project was completed and the final report written, I set up a group of Māori cultural advisors and approached the Ministry of Education and school communities for permission to use the action research initiative as a context for further study. This second evaluation (Hynds, 2007) was conducted in two school communities that had been independently identified as making progress with partnership and relationship-based reform work. My initial research questions were:

- What are the experiences of participants in relation to Māori and non-Māori teachers' collaborative partnership work?
- What are the beliefs of participants, in relation to these experiences? And
- What are participants' perceptions of the impact of these experiences?

Although these were my starting points, more appropriate research questions developed over the course of data analysis and included:

**What are the identities that those involved bring into the collaborative dynamic, when Māori and non-Māori teachers work together on a school reform project?**

My first unit of analysis was partnership work between Māori and non-Māori teachers. I utilized Māori centered research methodology (Bishop & Glynn, 1999) in order to develop appropriate research relationships across diverse communities. Research involving Māori and their knowledge must be conducted in culturally responsive ways (McFarlane, 2004) and promote transformative action and critical consciousness (G. Smith, 2002; L. T. Smith, 1999). Bishop and Glynn (1999) call for non-Māori researchers to engage in research ensuring their inquiry is guided by Māori-centered research protocols such as:

1. Initiation (describing how the research was initiated)
2. Benefits (identifying the benefits that will come from the research)
3. Representation (identifying whose voice is heard within the text)
4. Legitimation (explaining the authority of the text)
5. Accountability (identifying who the researcher is accountable to)

**Ko wai au? Who am I?**

As a Pākehā researcher, I acknowledge and support the status of Te Tiriti o Waitangi (Treaty of Waitangi) and Māori as tangata whenua (people of the land). The Treaty was signed in 1840, by a number of Māori chiefs and representatives of the British Crown. It was supposed to establish a partnership that acknowledged the Crown's role and responsibility to protect Māori cultural interests. However, in practice this has not occurred. As a Pākehā, I acknowledge that debt alongside an understanding that I am also part of a privileged White group.

My motivation to conduct this research in culturally responsive ways meant an adherence to whakawhanaungatanga (relationship building). A series of invitations was extended to me to talk about the possibilities of this second research process, which required me to front up to people, kanohi te kanohi (face-to-face). Some invitations were afforded me, giving an opportunity to speak about this new stage of research and to answer any questions people had. The process of invitation was particular to different school community contexts and occurred over several months, with specific groups or individuals acting as gatekeepers to other possible participant groups. The research spanned two years after the initial evaluation. I spent time on site at the two schools, in participant homes, and at community events, attending staff meetings and whānau (family) hui (meetings). Semi-structured interviews were conducted over two years with 77 participants (Māori and non-Māori teachers, students and their parents/caregivers, other school community members). I used inductive analysis (Janesick, 2000) to ensure that codes, themes and patterns emerged from interview data as well as comparative analysis. Participants were also asked to comment on the trustworthiness of emerging results through a process of on-going member checks.

**Context**

It is also important to acknowledge the wider context (Choo & Ferree, 2010), as it had a bearing on study findings. During my second year of conducting interviews (2004) and subsequent member checks (2005), national debates on race relations stormed across Aotearoa New Zealand. These related to the status of the Treaty of Waitangi, the Foreshore and Seabed legislation, the subsequent hikoi (march) to Parliament and the unifying protest against this legislation, the formation of the Māori Party as a new political force, and Don Brash's[1] infamous Orewa Speech. 'Kiwi verses Iwi (Tribe)' was a contentious political billboard fuelled by perceived Māori privilege as 2005 was an election year. During the research process, I collected Letters to the Editor from national newspapers as they revealed the macro-political context against which participant identities were framed.

## Limitations

I found it was easier to connect with some participants than others. Some opened up and wanted to reveal their own stories of teachers' collaborative work, and others did not. Initially, I did not gather information related to participants' socio-economic status, country of birth, iwi or hapu connections, or sexuality. This is a real weakness in my work, revealing my own naivety and ignorance at the time of designing the research. At first I did not think that participant identities would be so important to teacher engagement in relationship-based school reform work, or know how power relationships influenced teacher identity, as there is little within the professional development literature about this. I found that in the process of interviewing participants, some opened up and were happy to reveal aspects of their identities to me. For example, two participants wanted me to know that they identified as Queer. Through the process of interviewing participants over time, I became aware of the diversity of participants' identities and the influence of power relationships that saturate collaborative work when Māori and non-Māori teachers work together to improve practice and outcomes for Māori learners.

As I conducted member checks, some participants challenged me to rethink my analysis by emphasizing the diversity of identity and the interplay of context. However, I found there was also a discomfort associated with checking back with some participants, particularly in relation to comparing the visible and less visible beliefs, values, and activities that preceded teachers' collaborative partnership work. Not all participants, particularly parents/caregivers of non-Māori children and young people, welcomed my analysis especially that associated with the issues of deficit thinking and 'forced identities' (McIntosh, 2005). I found myself confronted with messy text, "...where multiple voices speak....often in conflict and where readers are left to sort out which experiences speak to their personal lives" (Lincoln & Denzin, 2000, p. 1050).

## Findings

As I have explained in other publications (Hynds, 2008, 2010), initially the signs of culturally responsive reform looked good. The first round of data analysis highlighted the development of new collaborative practices that were perceived by Māori and non-Māori participants to have had an impact on the beliefs and practices of many teachers across both schools:

> There have been changes since our mahi (work) on our vision....I think every teacher had to go through that. As I said before, it was like a healing

process to come out the other side, and it's made big changes for some teach-ers and I talked about myself before. I've noticed we're more considerate, we respect one another a lot more, we share a lot more and we're not afraid to challenge each other. Because the way we look at things now is different to what it was before. And it was like cleansing, it's getting rid of the staleness, and for me reconnecting to my wairua (spirituality), like that's how I felt. I had got to this point in my teaching which was like just, 'Do it, turn it over, turn it over', but I wasn't really doing anything for my own growth and I cer-tainly wasn't doing anything for my children's growth. (Māori female teacher)

But having listened to the commentaries, the voices of Māori students and realising now that my whole teaching delivery was uncomfortable, suddenly the problem was there for me, and I haven't got solutions I know, but at least I see it. I couldn't see the problem before. My eyes have been opened to that, I don't think I am alone, and we haven't solved it yet, it is huge. But let's start identifying what the problem is, and the problem doesn't necessarily sit out there . . . , it sits here within us as teachers. (non-Māori male teacher)

Teachers described a growing sense of kotahitanga (unity) and collective agency towards the work of change. They became involved in new and dif-ferent professional learning activities with a focus on teachers developing culturally responsive practices (Bishop et al., 2009). There was an empha-sis on teachers depriviatizing classroom practice through reciprocal peer observation and feedback and review of data related to Māori students' learning and achievement. Teachers were challenged to think about their expectations and beliefs about Māori students, and develop an understand-ing of the negative impact of deficit theorizing. This was not an easy or comfortable process, according to some participants:

Some of that was really tough data . . . data coming from teachers and particu-larly from their Māori students. Teachers confessing that it was all on top of them and they couldn't do it, teachers believing one thing about their teach-ing and then having students giving data that absolutely opposed their beliefs, and teachers having to confront that gap. (Māori female in-school facilitator)

New teacher partnership approaches included a focus on involving whānau, and creating more welcoming classroom and school environments. There was an increased use and valuing of te reo me ona tikanga (Māori language and customs). Participants described changes such as increased teacher experimentation with co-construction approaches whereby students had a voice in decision-making in the classroom. Other pedagogical changes in-cluded experimentation with feedback-feedforward and related assessment strategies. Teachers also engaged in new collaborative planning approaches in order to draw on Māori students' lives outside of the classroom and to ensure relevance of classroom learning activities.

Over time my analysis revealed inter-cultural differences (across groups) as well as intra-cultural differences (within groups). Teacher identity markers were linked to participants' perceptions of trust with colleagues in collaborative work. Māori teacher identity markers included relational connections which were place and community based (Penetito, 2010). These emphasized the individual's connection to community and the importance of mana (leadership and status), gender, place of training, age and whānau background. These identity markers emerged as key factors that influenced these Māori teachers' engagement in collaborative work over time. There was also a glimpse of territory politics (Kidman, 2012) associated with belonging to particular collectives, legitimacy, and acceptance of particular teacher identities. One Māori teacher believed she was the victim of discrimination because of her sexuality and her outspoken views. Other non-Māori teachers indicated that their sense of engagement in collaborative work was also influenced by perceptions of psychological safety and acceptance by peers.

Teacher identity markers also included 'forced identities' (McIntosh, 2005) associated with negative stereotypes of Māori and existing prejudices across both communities. During participant interviews with many non-Māori participants particular negative stereotypes of Māori were shared. These were related to participant beliefs that Māori were 'lazy' and 'greedy'. McIntosh has argued that forced identities are "formed under conditions of deprivation, distorted by the realities of living on the margins". Such identities are largely stereotypes based on the perceptions of "outsider groups" (p. 48). These negative stereotypes are social constructions, and an identity formation was forced on Māori with damaging results—low expectations, racism, prejudice and alienation (McIntosh, 2005).

However, it was not just teacher identities that influenced collaborative work within schools, as dominant community discourses related to 'Identity as Sameness' and resistance emerged over time. Whilst influencing teacher engagement in collaborative work, these identity markers remained unexamined within the context of culturally responsive school reform.

## Teacher Identity Markers and Trust

I first became aware of teacher identity markers as participants described their interactions with peers as being influenced by perceptions of trust and psychological safety:

> There has got to be trust when you work with colleagues really closely... that we can freely talk about my shortcomings or the shortcomings of the method

that I had chosen that day and why it didn't work for certain students and there has to be quite a bit of trust... to broach that. (non-Māori male teacher)

So to be critically supportive involves a colleague looking at what I do and examining ways in which it can be done better, but at the same time it doesn't belittle my whole methodology and that's why that trust thing comes in. If I am working with somebody that I can trust, that is generally supportive of the thrust of what I am trying to do, then we can happily criticise or tweak the bits that need to be tweaked. So I think it actually again comes down to trust. I always come back to that. (non-Māori male teacher)

Using intersectionality to reframe my original analysis of interview material, I located teacher identity markers that stressed similarities and differences as well as group and territory boundaries. These interactions heightened my awareness to particular contradictions. One of these was that teachers spoke of valuing and respecting differences and diversity and yet their activities highlighted that teachers trusted 'sameness'. They spoke about the importance of selecting a peer whom they trusted, of trusting their professional judgment and knowing that they were a suitable role-model:

In our department there's a couple of teachers who are really strong teachers and who I think are good role models in terms of what I would like to have in my classroom or how I would like to be as a teacher so I'd really value their contributions, and there are teachers who aren't as strong or who might do certain things that I might not necessarily want to model my teaching on and so you'd put less value on their contributions... so that's important in... choosing your peer. (Māori female teacher)

Although teachers highlighted how important it was to trust their peers, different teacher identity markers emerged related to institutional territories, such as where teachers were trained:

You need to find someone who is going to challenge you... so I chose (teacher's name)... there are other Māori teachers here (she mentions them by name), One.... I would not be able to have a challenging discussion with her, if you know what I mean.... She trained through Māori immersion... [and] she is not my idea of a trained teacher. She hasn't, well, been to Teachers' College, maybe that's why I like [this other person] because (she) and I went to Teachers' College together and teachers who came out of there were always very well equipped, they were good teachers, they just had that sort of reputation and when (the teacher) mentioned it, I said, 'Yeah, I trained there too', and so, 'What year?', and we talked about that. Whereas the other teacher, I think she hasn't been given that type of training. (Māori female teacher)

Others explained that their decisions to engage in collaborative professional development activities and discussions were influenced by the availability of peer mentors. This Māori teacher believed it was important to have another Māori male mentor who had the necessary status, mana and leadership:

> I came under (Māori teacher's name)...and he mentored me just in the basics, yeah, which I hadn't had before. Organising your day, time management skills, your planning, making sure it's all there and is systematic, and that you're following it, making sure that you deliver, and that you're organised. And...he's been one of the key people who has been instrumental in changing this school around because of his professionalism, his mana. He came here wanting to improve himself as a teacher, he had a goal and he knew where he was going and how he could help the school. A lot of us were just here and bumbling on but he came with purpose and, yeah, he's pretty much kept to that, and he's done a tremendous job in lifting the standards of teaching and maintaining that professional integrity. (Māori male teacher)

## Teacher Identity, Honesty and Relational Factors

Over time, individual teachers had concerns about the way the collaborative process was developing within their school community. Analysis highlighted that some teachers may not raise concerns for different reasons. One teacher wanted to raise questions about what he perceived to be tokenistic partnership work; however, he had chosen not to talk about these concerns with colleagues because he did not want people to think ill of him:

> When the whole...project started, just like any new activity, everyone just embarked on it and there was a bit of a hoohaa about it and then I've kind of had the impression that the dust is settling and teachers are getting back to their old habits.... To be honest, I haven't shared these ideas [with my colleagues] probably because I don't want people to think badly of me. (non-Māori male teacher)

Other teachers had concerns. One young female Māori teacher was also concerned that over time the collaborative process had deteriorated and was not being implemented in the way that it had initially been designed. She believed though that it was not her place to raise important issues within professional development discussions. Her decisions were influenced by her own cultural beliefs, related to her status and position as a young female Māori teacher, which had also been shaped through her own whānau experiences:

> I feel uneasy with myself about it because of the way that I have been brought up...we don't talk back to our elders...it would be a bit like back-chatting to my Nan or something.... I'm the junior of this place and I already have enough to say and...that's the role of senior staff and I respect the other people that are already here.... I'm young and...I don't feel it's my place to

intrude... it sort of goes against my upbringing. It's like talking back to your elders, it's the whole sort of values and morals that you're used to. (Māori female teacher)

Another teacher told me that she had become frustrated by some of her colleagues' inability to "talk straight". She believed that some of her teaching peers found it hard to be honest and to debate issues due to their upbringing:

> We're raised to be nice. You know, how when a little kid says, 'Oh Mummy, look at that lady's dress', and we all say, 'Ssh, don't say that, it's not very nice'. But it's actually the truth, that dress looks dreadful on the woman and she'd be much better off in a different colour and different style ... but we shut the child up and go away thinking, 'Yeah, she looks pretty gross', so people can't talk straight because we have to be nice. (Māori female teacher)

Alton-Lee (2003) has highlighted gender and class issues associated with teacher niceness as reflecting Pākehā, gendered, middle class values. Such niceness, she argues, inhibits teachers' ability to work in critically, constructive ways, work that is needed to unmask the hidden curriculum within schools. Initially on the marae (meeting house) teachers had been encouraged to discuss issues openly, honestly and critically in safe and productive learning environments. Another teacher also believed that such partnership processes that had been established early on with the professional learning initiative were no longer being followed. When I asked her if she would raise these issues openly with colleagues, she said she was afraid of potential conflict and again related this to her own family upbringing:

> I think being honest can be problematic in staff-rooms actually.... Conflict can be upsetting ... I just don't feel comfortable about it. ... I don't think it achieves anything (and later) In my own family ... there was a focus for the girls, we were brought up to keep the peace ... so I don't feel comfortable about bringing up things which I think will be controversial. (non-Māori female teacher)

Intersectional analysis emphasized teacher identities as being influenced by values and beliefs associated with relational factors (such as cultural groupings). The presence of dominant cultural elites and associated power relationships also emerged.

## 'Forced' Teacher Identities (Stereotypes)

Analysis of teacher engagement in new collaborative activities revealed negative stereotypes and images of Māori. These were "lazy" and "greedy":

I... have seen teachers... being basically racist and that troubles me... at that school... there was a general consensus among some of the non-Māori teachers that the Māori teachers didn't work as hard, like they were really laid back, and... these teachers hoped the Māori teachers would come up to everyone else's standard, not the other way around. (non-Māori female teacher aide)

One Māori teacher described how she was shocked and upset by a colleague's comments in the staffroom, and while she wanted to confront her colleague, she had felt unable to do so:

We were talking in the staffroom, I can't exactly remember what the topic was, but we were talking about equal rights and the Treaty and bits and pieces and there was something in the paper about Māori,... but the comment she made was, 'Oh, that's just typical... they want everything!', and... it just blew me away. (Māori female teacher)

Such constructions of Māori contradicted other interview evidence that indicated the majority of Māori teachers were giving up their own time after school to support non-Māori colleagues in te reo (Māori language) lessons and/or facilitating extra and additional whānau hui (family-school meetings) to support the work of reform. Messages within participant stories emphasised a lack of respect amongst some for Māori teachers' views, as well as a lack of openness and honesty about personal attitudes:

I know that the teachers were really encouraged to think about their attitudes and how their attitudes could impact on kids, Māori kids particularly. And to look at the whole picture and to look at the perspective of the students and that they did have different cultural values... but some staff were just blaming the kids and seeing them as the problem.... I was sitting at a table with some teachers and we were predominantly Pākehā, and there was a blackboard and there was a chart with Pros and Cons and attitudes written on it and the teacher that I was sitting next to, when a question was asked, 'When a kid comes to school without their lunch, what do you think?', and her attitude was extremely negative, and she was blaming the kids and the family and being just really negative in the group, yet she didn't raise these issues when the facilitator asked for comment. (Māori female parent/caregiver)

Of course, these negative stereotypes of Māori were not limited to staffrooms and were present across both school communities (Hynds, 2010):

The teachers, the Māori teachers and the non-Māori teachers at the school have accepted more stuff than they should have and let more stuff go. I think it's not good if there's too much of a Māori influence in the school... I think there needs to be a stricter discipline in the school, and that's because the discipline has broken down at home and the teachers are expected to do more of that. I think the kids that come into school now are more needier than they were, there's more theft in the area, there's more direct disobedience towards their elders and a lot of that has to do with the kids and where they come from. The lives that their parents have had. I mean, you might have a Māori woman who has five or six kids from different fathers and they're all in or out of jail. And the kids are living with their grandparents and they're swapped around and they don't have good role models. (non-Māori female parent/caregiver)

Analysis of interviews revealed other stereotypes or 'forced identities' that were not limited to constructions of race. Interviews highlighted other prejudices across both school communities (Hynds, 2007):

> We had set that up; (she) had asked me to observe her and then she'd observe me, because of our commitment to the project that we wanted to include both classes in it and as best we can . . . as is typical with a few female teachers, maths doesn't tend to be a hell of a strong point with her. (non-Māori male teacher)

> In another class with a . . . teacher, . . . she actually said to the kids that homosexuals shouldn't be allowed to marry in New Zealand and that homosexuality was wrong. . . . I think she felt quite comfortable saying that to the kids. I was quite shocked at what she said. (non-Māori female teacher aide)

Other interviews across both schools also highlighted participant prejudices towards those who were perceived as different. Derogatory names, such as *'fag'* and *'special needs'* were used freely to describe those perceived as different (Hynds, 2007, 2012). Intersectional analysis emphasized the influence of power and power relationships in the construction of those identities perceived to be 'similar' (safe and trusted) and 'diverse' (unsafe and untrustworthy).

### 'Identity as Sameness'

Resistance to teacher partnership emerged over time and was related to a dominant discourse of 'sameness'. This was most evident as parents and caregivers of non-Māori children reacted negatively to the increased Māori presence and use of Māori language and customs. A delegation of non-Māori parents confronted one school principal and demanded that the partnership work cease immediately, threatening withdrawal of their own children (Hynds, 2008). I interviewed many of these participants. They expressed beliefs that *'focusing on cultural differences is wrong and divisive'* and that *'We are all the same'*. Other views expressed were *'We're all New Zealanders'*, *'we're all given the same opportunities in life'* and that teachers' use of Māori language and customs threatened their own child's identity and educational chances. Many expressed the view that the work was *'racist'* and consisted of *'special treatment'*.

Interview analysis also highlighted that individual teacher (Māori and non-Māori) identity could threaten others and that individuals could experience peer pressure to conform to what was seen as acceptable to the majority. Individual teachers expressed their concerns about other teachers' behaviour, describing peer pressure and personal vendettas. One Māori teacher had chosen to work with a male Pākehā colleague, whom she trusted. She believed she had a *'radical'* identity within her school community and that this had influenced the way some colleagues chose to view and/or engage with her. She described herself as a "*staunch Māori teacher*", committed to working to improve practice for Māori pupils most at risk who were involved in local street gangs. She explained that she had previously taught in kura kaupapa (Māori Immersion) schools and that she was a passionate advocate for power-sharing approaches with students "*who struggle*". She believed her outspoken beliefs had caused some problems at her school. A few of her colleagues (Māori and non-Māori) had written a letter of complaint to the principal about her behaviour and her conduct with students, in particular her behaviour towards Māori students:

> I've been described as a radical and accused of deficit theorising by my some of my colleagues, which is actually bull-shit.... I'm interested in our kids who struggle to get to school.... Teachers need to get off their pedestal, you know, and get into the role of their students more.... Does it really matter what language the kids use (swearing) if they're turning up to class and getting their work done? I mean, for me, it's about working with them, the students first and stepping into their world and then when you have their trust and some credibility with them, because for a lot of our young people their experience of adults is that they shit on them and just want to disempower them all the time, so if teachers, we get off our pedestals and work alongside our students and really build that relationship and our understanding of them as people... but that means letting go of the power... and teachers like power. (Māori female teacher)

In my final member check with her, this teacher also disclosed she was Queer and proud of it. She believed that there was a group of Māori and non-Māori teachers at her school who "*were out to get her*" because of her sexuality:

> No one came and saw me or talked through their concerns directly with me.... Another staff member came to me at assembly actually and very quietly said, 'Watch your back', and I said, 'What?', and she said, 'Oh, because there are some people gunning for you', and I said, 'Oh, what have I done?' And she said it was just a personal vendetta. (Māori female teacher)

Another teacher also expressed concern about peer pressure that he had experienced. He believed it was important *'not to stand out'* and that the underlying message was conformity to particular dominant groups:

> I have learned not to say some things to my colleagues... I got told by a colleague to 'Shut up', and, 'Who the fuck do you think you are?'... [and later] things like that. I was just trying to do my job as well as I can.... So whatever you do, you are always stepping on someone's values.... I have found through past experience that there is [teacher] peer pressure not to stand out, because if you stand out, then you bring a shadow on the other teachers. Sad, but that is a reality. I know it is the main hindrance to raising academic achievement amongst our kids in school. (male non-Māori teacher)

An intersectional analysis of teacher interactions again highlighted the pressure to 'be the same'.

## Discussion and Recommendations

Study results revealed that teachers' cultural and professional identity markers were intertwined and strongly connected to socio-cultural and socio-political influences such as power relationships, community, and territory. They were associated with race/ethnicity, age, gender, status, place of training, and sexuality as well as community membership or territory boundaries. These identity markers and intersectional factors influenced teachers' engagement in partnership work as well as their perceptions of inclusion, psychological safety, and acceptance by peers within and across Māori and non-Māori groups. Identity markers emphasized teacher beliefs about the legitimacy and inclusion of voice and whether participants felt it was their place to raise important issues or concerns within and across school communities. Study findings also revealed forced identities (McIntosh, 2005) and relationships of power and privilege (Choo & Ferree, 2010). Many teachers who were interviewed for this study talked initially about the power, pain and turbulence in exploring contradictions of practice (Hynds, 2008). However, these activities, which had initially 'opened' teachers' eyes to previously hidden aspects of their work, were not sustained as they challenged the implicit norms, power, and authority of dominant cultural elites across both school communities. Research findings indicated that culturally responsive practice, which privileged particular groups, was alive and well fuelled by hegemonic schooling processes of colonization and assimilation. In hindsight, teachers seemed inadequately prepared to sustain such work on their own and there are ethical implications here for how we create the necessary solidarity for needed transformation across institutional boundaries.

Findings highlighted the importance of bringing participant identities to the surface in collaborative work; however, simply uncovering is not enough. Participants must be engaged in critical collective analysis, which enables all teachers, students and their parents/caregivers to understand that difference is socially constructed, and is linked to pathologizing practices and White supremacy identities (Artiles, 1998; Shields et al., 2005). In this way we can address the concerns raised by Choo and Ferree (2010) within intersectionality work, which capture "the agency of individuals . . . " as well as "the enabling and constraining forces" that have the power to influence (p. 134).

This means we need to pay far more attention to the complex intersections and territories inherent in teachers' collaborative work and the acceptance or rejection of particular teacher identities. I have found an invisibility and silence in much of the research work on the complexity, influence, and intersectionality of teacher professional and cultural identities within school reform contexts, which are saturated with power, White privilege, and inequalities. I agree with Grant and Zwier (2011) that we "risk reproducing patterns of privilege and oppression, and perpetuating stereotypes" and are failing at the task we most care about: supporting all students' learning across a holistic range of academic, personal, and justice-orientated outcomes (p. 187). Such learning communities will not be comfortable, certain, or particularly safe places. Teachers, and those who support their work, need to be prepared to disrupt hegemonic schooling processes of colonization and assimilation, as left unchallenged they prevent the sustainability of transformational work. It is therefore recommended that more attention is placed on disrupting the silence and invisibility of difference, particularly within teacher professional development, whilst preparing and sustaining partners for contested collaboration within social justice work. This means we need to prepare and support participants within school learning communities to work together in ways that facilitate solidarity across complicated territories of cultural identity, difference, and power (Hynds, 2012). There is much potential and opportunity for new collaborative, political work which reveals transformative participant identities and the relationship territories that facilitate and sustain them.

## ACKNOWLEDGEMENTS

Kia ora tātou, I wish to thank and acknowledge Susan Faircloth, Joanna Kidman and the editors, Elisabeth Zwier and Carl Grant, for their thoughtful and constructive feedback in preparing this chapter.

# NOTE

1. At this time, Don Brash was the Leader of the Opposition Party: the National Party. In his Orewa speech he accused the government of employing 'racist policies', which targeted particular ethnic groups (such as Māori) in an attempt to close disparities between Māori and non-Māori groups in such areas as health and education.

# REFERENCES

Alejandra Elenes, A. (2003). Reclaiming the borderlands: Chicana/o identity, difference and critical pedagogy. In A. Darder, M. Baltodano, & R. Torres (Eds.), *The critical pedagogy reader.* London: Routledge Falmer.

Alton-Lee, A. (2003). *Quality teaching for diverse students in schooling: Best evidence synthesis.* Wellington: Ministry of Education.

Artiles, A. J. (1998). The dilemma of difference: Enriching the disproportionality discourse with theory and context. *The Journal of Special Education, 32*(1), 32–36. doi.org/10.1177/002246699803200105

Beauchamp, C., & Thomas, L. (2009). Understanding teacher identity: An overview of issues in the literature and implications for teacher education. *Cambridge Journal of Education, 39*(2), 175–189. doi.org/10.1080/03057640902902252

Beijaard, D., Meifer, P. C., & Verloop, N. (2004). Reconsidering research on teachers' professional identity. *Journal of Teaching and Teacher Education, 20*, 107–128. doi.org/10.1016/j.tate.2003.07.001

Bishop, R., & Glynn, T. (1999). *Culture counts: Changing power relations in education.* Palmerston North: Dunmore Press.

Bishop, R., Berryman, M., Cavanagh, T., & Teddy, L. (2009). Te Kotahitanga: Addressing educational disparities facing Māori students in New Zealand. *Journal of Teaching and Teacher Education, 25*(5), 734–742. doi.org/10.1016/j.tate.2009.01.009

Choo, H. Y., & Ferree, M. M. (2010). Practicing intersectionality in sociological research: A critical analysis of inclusions, interactions and institutions in the study of inequalities. *Journal of Sociological Theory, 28*(2), 129–149. doi.org/10.1111/j.1467-9558.2010.01370.x

Fine, M., & Weiss, L. (2005). Introduction. In L. Weiss & M. Fine (Eds.), *Beyond silenced voices: Class, race and gender in United States schools.* New York: State University of New York Press.

Grant, A. C., & Zwier, E. (2011). Intersectionality and student outcomes: Sharpening the struggle against racism, sexism, classism, ableism, heterosexism, nationalism, and linguistic, religious, and geographical discrimination. *Journal of Teaching and Learning, Multicultural Perspectives, 13*(4), 181–188. doi.org/10.1080/15210960.2011.616813

Hynds, A. S. (2007). *Navigating the collaborative dynamic: Teachers collaborating across difference* (Unpublished PhD thesis). Victoria University of Wellington, New Zealand.

Hynds, A. S. (2008). Developing and sustaining open communication in action research initiatives: A response to Kemmis (2006). *Journal of Educational Action Research, 16*(2), 149–162. doi.org/10.1080/09650790802011445

Hynds, A. S. (2010). Unpacking resistance to change within school reform programs with a social justice orientation. *International Journal of Leadership in Education, 13*(4), 377–392. i.org/10.1080/13603124.2010.503282

Hynds, A. S. (2012). Challenges to the development of solidarity: Working across intersections of power and privilege in New Zealand (pp. 163–180). In C. E. Sleeter & E. Soriano (Eds.), *Creating solidarity across diverse communities: International perspectives in education.* New York: Teachers' College Press.

Janesick, V. (2000). The choreography of qualitative research design. Minuets, improvisions and crystallisation. In N. K. Denzin & Y. S. Lincoln (Eds.), *Handbook of qualitative research* (2nd ed.). London: Sage.

Kidman, J. (2012). The land remains: Māori youth and the politics of belonging. *AlterNative: An International Journal of Indigenous Peoples, 8*(2), 189–202.

Lincoln, Y., & Denzin, N. (2000). The seventh moment. Out of the past. In N. K. Denzin and Y. S. Lincoln (Eds.), *The handbook of qualitative research* (2nd ed.). London: Sage.

McIntosh, T. (2005). Māori identities: Fixed, fluid, forced. In J. Liu, T. McCreanor, T. McIntosh, & T. Teaiwa (Eds.), *New Zealand identities: Departures and destinations* (pp. 38–51). Wellington, NZ: Victoria University Press.

Ministry of Education. (2010). Education counts: Teaching staff. Retrieved February 15, 2011 from http://www.educationcounts.givt.nz/statistics/schooling/ts/teaching_staff

Penetito, W. (2010). *What's Māori about Māori education?* Wellington, NZ: Victoria University Press.

Shields, C., Bishop, R., & Mazawi, A. (2005). *Pathologizing practices: The impact of deficit thinking on education.* New York: Peter Lang.

Sleeter, C. (2011). The quest for social justice in the education of minoritised students. In C. E. Sleeter (Ed.), *Professional development for culturally responsive and relationship-based pedagogy* (pp. 1–22). New York: Peter Lang.

Smith, G. (2002). *Kaupapa Māori theory: Transformative praxis and new formations of conscientisation.* Paper presented at the Second International Conference on Cultural Policy Research, Te Papa, Wellington.

Smith, L. T. (1999). *Decolonising methodologies: Research and indigenous peoples.* Dunedin: University of Otago Press.

Tuuta, M., Bradnam, L., Hynds, A., Higgins, J., & Broughton, R. (2004). *Evaluation of the Te Kauhua Māori mainstream pilot project: Report to the Ministry of Education.* Wellington, NZ: Ministry of Education.

Vähäsantanen, K., Hökkä, P., Eteläpelto, A., Rasku-Puttonen, H., & Littleton, K. (2008). Teachers' professional identity negotiations in two different work organisations. *Vocations and Learning: Studies in Vocational and Professional Education, 1*(2), 131–148. doi.org/10.1007/s12186-008-9008-z

# ACADEMIC PERFORMANCE AND INTERSECTIONALITY BETWEEN ATYPICAL SUB-DIMENSIONS IN KOREA

**HeeMin Kim**
**Hyunah Lee**
*Seoul National University, Korea*

## ABSTRACT

Factors affecting students' access to higher education and academic performance have been studied extensively in various sub-fields of education research. For whatever reason, however, this vast literature rarely touches on the
notion of intersectionality. In this chapter, we examine students' academic performance in the country of Korea. We have already done extensive research on
the determinants of student performance in the three subjects areas of Korean,
mathematics, and English (Kim 2012). In this chapter, we briefly introduce our
previous findings. We then use multivariate regression models to investigate the
intersectionality among the factors affecting student performance on the national standardized exam for college entrance in Korea. Our interaction model
shows that intersectionality exists between mother's education and family income for the subjects of Korean and English, but not for mathematics. Another

*Intersectionality and Urban Education*, pages 213–228
Copyright © 2014 by Information Age Publishing
**213**

interaction model shows that intersectionality exists between place of residence and OSL expenses for the subjects of mathematics and English, but not for the Korean language. With only two examples, however, we can make several conclusions about the applicability of intersectionality theory in non-race related, non-gender related, issues/sub-dimensions in education outside of the United States. Our interaction models also raise the question that many of our previous findings could have been based on underspecified models—and we have made biased conclusions about the factors determining educational access and academic performance.

Presented at the 7th annual International Alliance of Leading Economic Institutes meeting and conference held at the Beijing Normal University, China, 2013. This research was supported by a research grant from the College of Education, Seoul National University. The usual disclaimer applies.

## INTRODUCTION

Factors that affect students' access to higher education and academic performance have been studied extensively in various sub-fields of education research (e.g., Baker & Stevenson 1986; Campbell & Mandel, 1990; Carey, 1958; Crane 1996, Deslandes, R. et al., 1997; Fan 2001; Georgiou, 1999; Gordon, 1996; Jeynes, 2005; Hansford & Hattie, 1982; Milton, 1957; Paulson, 1994). This area of research can be linked to what education specialists call "educational disadvantage."[1] Whatever factors promote students' academic performance, those who do not have the benefit of those factors can face significant educational disadvantage. For whatever reason, however, this vast literature rarely touches on the notion of intersectionality.

Intersectionality is a methodology of studying "the relationships among multiple dimensions and modalities of social relationships and subject formations" (McCall 2005). The theory suggests—and seeks to examine how—various biological, social and cultural categories such as gender, race, class, ability, sexual orientation, and other axes of identity interact on multiple and often simultaneous levels, contributing to systematic social inequality (http://en.wikipedia.org/wiki/Intersectionality). Although there are many ways it can impact social interactions, the notion of "intersectuality", when applied to higher education, primarily affect access and academic performance.

The intersectionality, a feminist sociological theory first highlighted by Kimberlé Crenshaw (1989), holds that the classical conceptualizations of oppression within society, such as racism, sexism, homophobia, and religion-based bigotry, do not act independently of one another; instead, these forms of oppression interrelate, creating a system of oppression that reflects the "intersection" of multiple forms of discrimination (Knudsen, 2006).

From the little documentation that exists, it is understood that the concept of intersectionality came to the forefront of sociological circles in the late 1960s and early 1970s in conjunction with the multiracial feminist movement. The movement led by women of color disputed the idea that women were a homogeneous category sharing essentially the same life experiences. This argument stemmed from the realization that White middle-class women did not serve as an accurate representation of the feminist movement as a whole. Recognizing that the forms of oppression experienced by White middle-class women were different from those experienced by Black, poor, or disabled women, feminists sought to understand the ways in which gender, race, and class combined to "determine the female destiny." (DeFrancisco & Palczewski, 2007). The term gained prominence in the 1990s when sociologist Patricia Hill Collins reintroduced the idea as part of her discussion on Black feminism. This term increased the general applicability of her theory from African American women to all women" (Mann & Huffman, 2005, p.61). Much like her predecessor Crenshaw, Collins argued that cultural patterns of oppression are not only interrelated, but are bound together and influenced by the intersectional systems of society, such as race, gender, class, and ethnicity (Collins, 2000, p. 42). So, by this time, the term, intersectionality is not just about Black women in the United States.

A standard textbook example of intersectionality theory might be "the view that women experience oppression in varying configurations and in varying degrees of intensity" (Ritzer, 2007, p. 204). Intersectionality is an important paradigm not only for sociological and cultural studies, but there have been many challenges in utilizing it to its fullest capacity. While the theory began as an exploration of the oppression of women within society, today sociologists strive to apply it to all people and to many different intersections of group membership. That is, now the term, intersectionality, applies to much more dimensions of groups of people sharing identity.

Now the term, "intersectionality," is being adopted in many disciplines and to explain many different events, such as social work, psychology, studies of labor market (e.g., Browne & Misra, 2003), and pollitics and violence (for instance, Collins, 1998).

In this paper, we examine students' academic performance in the country of Korea. We do so by applying the method of intersectionality. At first, high school students' academic performance in Korea and intersectionality may look as unrelated as they can ever be. But by the end of this chapter, we hope to show that (i) the theory of intersectionality can be extended to analyze many different aspects of human behavior, including academic performance; and (ii) by creatively applying the theory, we can improve many existing analyses in education research.

The Korean educational system is perceived to be high-performing partly because of Korean students' performance in widely accepted international academic tests/competitions (see below). Further, many believe that Korea's educational system is at least partly responsible for the country's rapid economic development. As we will see below, Korea is also unique in the sense that admission to certain types of universities can largely determine the course of one's life. This may be true in many countries, but the situation is extreme in Korea. Given the high stakes involved, Korean high school students endeavor to get into a handful of elite universities. In this chapter, we first review the factors that affect the academic performance of Korean high school graduates, which in turn determine what universities they enter. Then we analyze the intersectionality of these performance-determining factors. This study will be unique as social and cultural categories and axes of identity that create social inequality are not identical to those examined in previous studies.

## FACTORS AFFECTING ACADEMIC PERFORMANCE IN KOREA

Most Korean high school graduates (and their parents) want (their children) to go to the *best* universities, rather than just any university, in Korea, and for good reason. I showed elsewhere that the top positions in both public and private sectors are dominated by the graduates of only three schools in Korea, Seoul National University, Korea University, and Yonsei University, the so-called SKY schools, despite there are currently 347 four-year universities and two-year community colleges in Korea (Kim, 2012). It is clear, therefore, why most Korean high-schoolers want to go to a handful of top schools and why Korean parents are so willing to go to great lengths to ensure their children can attend the most elite universities.

Now that such a large proportion of high school graduates go on to college (according to Korean government statistics, 81.5% of high school graduates went on to study at universities in 2012 (http://www.schoolinfo.go.kr/index.jsp)) and most of them understandably want to go to elite schools, a logical question is "who has access to the best universities in Korea?"

The type of universities individual students enter is largely determined by their performance on the national standardized aptitude test implemented by the Korean government. By investigating the factors that determine individual students' performance on this exam, then, we can understand the factors that determine where they will end up.

Individual students can choose to be tested in the subjects of Korean language, mathematics, English, social sciences, natural sciences, vocational education, and a second foreign language. Almost all universities require test scores from Korean, mathematics, and English. Thus, almost all high school seniors take tests in these three subjects, with fewer numbers of them taking tests in extra subjects. We have already done extensive research on the determinants of student performance in the three subjects areas of Korean, mathematics, and English (Kim 2012). In this chapter, we briefly introduce our previous findings. We will then investigate if intersectionality exists among different dimensions/factors we have identified.

There are certain elements that affect student performance on the national standardized test that are not necessarily disadvantages. Because they do affect test scores significantly, though, we need to control for their impact in our analysis. Otherwise our model will be underspecified. When we report our previous findings, we go over those elements first.

**Finding 1:** *Eating breakfast regularly has a positive impact on student performance.*

This appears to be stemming from lifestyle and habits rather than from economic disadvantage in Korea.

**Finding 2:** *The arts, music, and physical education majors perform below average.*

Those who apply to music, art, and physical education programs in college take the same national standardized tests but they tend to have lower test scores than others because the university admissions criteria for them are different in nature from those of other disciplines. That is, these students take their own performance tests, be they in singing, playing musical instruments, drawing, and so on. As a result of that, they focus much of their time practicing whatever they perform in as opposed to traditional academic subjects, so their academic achievements tend to be lower.

**Finding 3:** *The amount of time that a student spends studying by himself makes a difference in performance.*

We next discuss gender differences. Education is reserved for male, and females do not have access to it in some cultures. Overt or covert discriminations exist against women in others. As we will find out below, it is not the case in Korea, and there is no discrimination against women as far as educational access is concerned. Then the next question is potential disadvantage with regard to performance.

**Finding 4:** *There is a clear performance gap between male and female students, with girls performing better in Korean and English language. There is no clear difference in math between the two genders.*

We are not so sure if this has anything to do with a systemic disadvantage that male students face. Rather, it may have more to do with behavioral patterns of different genders in that age cohort.

Now we enter the realm of what can be regarded as socioeconomic factors. As we find out below, there are many different dimensions of socioeconomic factors, which can "intersect" among themselves. We discuss factors that are relevant to educational performance in Korea one by one.

**Finding 5:** *"The place of residence" variable behaves differently across disciplines. The size of the community the student is living in does not make a difference in her performance in Korean language. But it does clearly in English, and its impact hovers around statistical significance in mathematics.*

**Finding 6:** *The students whose mothers are well educated perform better than those whose mothers are not. On the other hand, the father's education level seems to have little to no impact on the performance of the student.*

In Korea, a large proportion of high school students and their parents believe that a regular high school education curriculum is inadequate to prepare for the national test. Students tend to get even busier *after* school, which is quite an odd phenomenon. We will collectively call students' learning activities before or after regular school hours "Out-of-School Learning" (hereinafter, "OSL"). These activities range from relatively inexpensive options, such as long-distance learning, to very expensive alternatives such as one-on-one tutoring with a tutor of national repute.

**Finding 7:** *Students who take more expensive (whose parents spend more money on) OSL supplements perform better.*

It appears that more expensive tutors track the national standardized exam scheme better than less expensive ones. According to the OECD report (2004), the level of attachment to their regular schools is lowest in Korea among OECD countries. At the same time, Korean students achieved top scores in the Program for International Student Assessment (PISA) (OECD and UNESCO 2003). We believe that this strange combination (low level of attachment to schools—high level of performance) is indirectly caused by students' OSL experiences in Korea, which we discuss extensively below. Simply put, Korean students' heavy reliance on OSLs explains both their good performance on PISA and their low level of attachment to regular schools.

**Finding 8:** *The level of household wealth makes a difference in test performance.*

That is, *all other things being equal,* the greater the household income, the better the student performed on the national standardized exam. This is the case while controlling for any money spent on the OSL experience. This is a troublesome trend.

## THE DATA

To investigate the factors influencing students' performance on the national standardized test in our previous work and potential intersectionality among them in this current chapter, we use(d) the Korean Education and Employment Panel (KEEP) data (2004-2009) collected by the Korea Research Institute for Vocational Education & Training (KRIVET), a government-created think-tank. The collection of these data started in 2004 to study the educational experiences, college selections, and career patterns of Korean youth. Since 2004, the same sample of young people has been surveyed to develop meaningful panel data. 2009 was the sixth year of the study and when the data were made public.

In 2004, a random sample of 2000 students of: (1) the graduating class of middle schools (9th graders in the U.S. system); (2) the graduating classes of regular high schools; and (3) graduating classes of vocational schools (12th graders in the U.S. system) was selected. These 6000 students and their household members have been surveyed every year since then. In 2007, those students who were in the 9th grade in 2004 reached 12th grade, but the size of the sample of 12th graders was half the size of that of 2004, so a new sample of 12th graders was collected.

The KEEP data were collected based on one-on-one interviews using PDAs and notebooks. We choose to use the KEEP data set, because it contains many survey items we can use to investigate the factors affecting student performance on the national standardized exam. Further, all 12th graders' survey responses were matched with their actual scores on the test.

## SELECTED INTERSECTIONALITY ANALYSES

We use multivariate regression models to investigate the intersectionality among the factors affecting student performance on the national standardized exam for college entrance in Korea. The individual variables we use in our models are described in detail in the Appendix.

Of the three issues identified by intersectionality theory most frequently, gender, race, and class, race is not a big issue in Korea. Korea has been one of the most racially homogenous countries in the world. Only recently some Southeast Asian workers are migrating to Korea to fill the blue color jobs in Korea, and women from the same area are being married to Korean male living in the countryside. As we mentioned, this is a recent phenomenon, the number of foreigners living in Korea is not high, and long-term data about their personal characteristics and educational choices have not been collected. Thus, we do not include them in our study.

So, we do not check if intersectionality exists among race and gender dimensions, two of the most cited cases of intersectionality, because the race and gender-driven discrimination hardly exists in Korea as far as educational access and performance are concerned (see *Finding 4* above). Instead, we investigate the potential intersectionality among sub-dimensions comprising big dimensions such as class. So, the main difference between the previous studies of intersectionality and our piece is that the former primarily look at the intersectionality between or among big and known discrimination-inducing dimensions (e.g., experiences of Black women vs. White women), while ours investigate the potential intersectionality among small sub-dimensions within the major dimensions such as race, gender, and class. We believe this has rarely been done in the past, and view it to be our major contribution to the study of intersectionality in education. To save space, though, we will show only two examples where intersectionality seems to exist between two different variables.

We first report the findings from the model including all of the variables we discussed in the previous section plus an interaction term between mother's education and family income for 2005. The reader will notice that there are two columns under each subject heading, Korea, mathematics, and English in Table 10.1. The column on the left contain what we call a baseline model. The one on the right contains the baseline model plus an interaction term (testing intersectionality). The baseline models in Table 10.1 show that all of the variables behave as we expected; the interaction model shows that intersectionality exists between mother's education and family income for the subjects of Korean and English, but not for mathematics. The same models involving the same variables exhibit the almost same results for the year 2008.

To help the readers see the intersectionality clearly, we show more detailed graphic analyses of the interactions. We first test how the family income conditions the effect of mother's education on the students' performance in English (Figure 10.1). Simply put, mother's education level has a positive impact on the students' performance in English regardless of the level of family income (both the graph and the 95% confidence interval are above the horizontal axis). Further its impact increases as the family income grows, that is, the same level of mother's education (say, a college graduation) has greater impact on the students' performance in an affluent family (the graph is a monotonically increasing function). We ran the same test, and the result is nearly identical for Korean language.

**TABLE 10.1  An Intersectionality Model, 2005**

| Variables | Korean | | Mathematics | | English | |
|---|---|---|---|---|---|---|
| Breakfast | 0.2811 (0.0575)*** | 0.2776 (0.0575)*** | 0.3117 (0.0624)*** | 0.3080 (0.0625)*** | 0.2989 (0.0561)*** | 0.2935 (0.0560)*** |
| AMPE Majors | -0.7556 (0.1396)*** | -0.7500 (0.1396)*** | -0.9238 (0.1744)*** | -0.9170 (0.1744)*** | -1.1665 (0.1373)*** | -1.1561 (0.1371)*** |
| ATSSBO | 0.1417 (0.0180)*** | 0.1416 (0.0180)*** | 0.1542 (0.0189)*** | 0.1546 (0.0189)*** | 0.1813 (0.0175)*** | 0.1813 (0.0175)*** |
| Gender | -0.2081 (0.0805)*** | -0.2090 (0.0804)*** | 0.0286 (0.0854) | 0.0289 (0.0854) | -0.2408 (0.0784)*** | -0.2418 (0.0783)*** |
| OSL Expenses | 0.0014 (0.0009) | 0.0015 (0.0009) | 0.0019 (0.0010)* | 0.0019 (0.0010)* | 0.0019 (0.0009)** | 0.0020 (0.0009)** |
| Family Income | 0.0000 (0.0002) | -0.0011 (0.0008) | 0.0004 (0.0003) | -0.0006 (0.0009) | 0.0004 (0.0002) | -0.0015 (0.0007)* |
| Mother's Education | 0.2127 (0.0340)*** | 0.1518 (0.0523)*** | 0.1404 (0.0361)*** | 0.0873 (0.0558) | 0.2665 (0.0332)*** | 0.1629 (0.0510)*** |
| Mother's Education*Family Income | | 0.0003 (0.0001)* | | 0.0002 (0.0001) | | 0.0003 (0.0001)*** |
| Constant | 2.8275 (0.2151)*** | 3.1497 (0.3009)*** | 2.6960 (0.2302)*** | 2.9828 (0.3254)*** | 2.2583 (0.2098)*** | 2.8049 (0.2928)*** |
| $R^2$ | 0.12 | 0.13 | 0.12 | 0.12 | 0.20 | 0.21 |
| N | 1,653 | 1,653 | 1,503 | 1,503 | 1,649 | 1,649 |

* $p < 0.1$; ** $p < 0.05$; *** $p < 0.01$

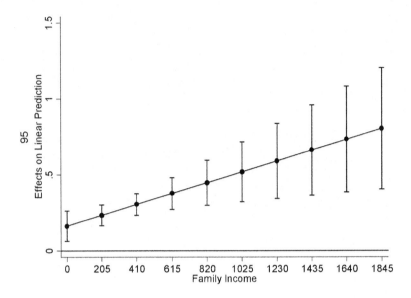

**Figure 10.1** Average marginal effects of mothers education on students' performance in English with 95% confidence intervals.

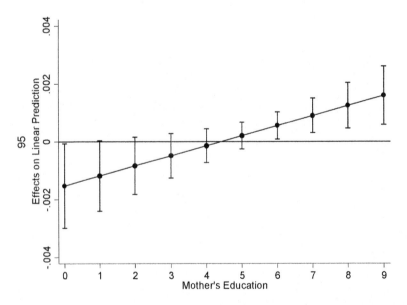

**Figure 10.2** Average marginal effects of family income on students' performance in English with 95% confidence intervals.

Next, we examine how the mother's education level conditions the impact of family income on the students' performance in English (Figure 10.2). Again, the result is nearly identical for the Korean language. Figure 10.2 shows that the increase in family income does not necessarily lead to better performance of students in English (the graph intersects with the horizontal axis). The family income has positive impact only when the mother's education level is high. Surprisingly the growing family income has negative impact on the students' performance in English when the mother's education level is very low. So, mothers with college degree and above find ways to improve their children's academic performance when the family income grows; mothers with no education or only elementary school education find a way to hurt their children's academic performance when the family income grows.

Second, we report the findings from the model including all of the basic variables we discussed above plus an interaction term between place of residence and OSL expenses for 2008. The columns on the left under each subject headings in Table 10.2 show that all of the variables behave as we expected; and the columns on the right show that the intersectionality exists between place of residence and OSL expenses for the subjects of mathematics and English, but not for the Korean language. The results of the same models involving the same variables exhibit the almost same results for the year 2005.

As before, we perform more detailed graphic analyses of the interaction terms. We describe how the place of residence conditions the effect of OSL expenses on the students' performance in mathematics (Figure 10.3) and English (Figure 10.4), which show nearly identical patterns. Simply put, the OSL expenses have a positive impact on the students' performance in math and English regardless of the place of residence (both the graphs and the 95% confidence intervals are above the horizontal axis). The only exception is that an increase in the OSL expense does not seem to have any effect in math in large metropolitan area (Figure 10.3). In both math and English the impacts of OSL expenses decrease as we move from the countryside (1) to the metropolitan area (4). That is, one unit increase in OSL expenses has greater impact on the students' performance in the countryside than larger cities (the graphs are monotonically decreasing functions).

This result simply means that "one unit increase in OSL expenses" (whatever that means) buy more OSL in the countryside than large cities. However, all the good expensive OSL tutors do business in large cities, and a large proportion of Korean parents are willing to spend more than "one unit" of money to buy more expensive OSL. This type of behavior creates inefficiency in the OSL market, in such a way that "one-unit purchase" of math OSL does not mean anything in metropolitan areas.

**TABLE 10.2  An Intersectionality Model, 2008**

| Variables | Korean | | Mathematics | | English | |
|---|---|---|---|---|---|---|
| Breakfast | 0.1516 (0.0396)*** | 0.1494 (0.0397)*** | 0.2152 (0.0386)*** | 0.2111 (0.0385)*** | 0.1876 (0.0383)*** | 0.1845 (0.0383)*** |
| AMPE Majors | -1.1220 (0.2534)*** | -1.1091 (0.2535)*** | -1.7304 (0.2652)*** | -1.7231 (0.2642)*** | -1.2006 (0.2452)*** | -1.1830 (0.2452)*** |
| ATSSBO | 0.0370 (0.0036)*** | 0.0371 (0.0036)*** | 0.0362 (0.0035)*** | 0.0363 (0.0035)*** | 0.0400 (0.0035)*** | 0.0401 (0.0035)*** |
| Gender | -0.4753 (0.1169)*** | -0.4763 (0.1169)*** | -0.1648 (0.1134) | -0.1653 (0.1130) | -0.3946 (0.1127)*** | -0.3958 (0.1126)*** |
| Family Income | 0.0005 (0.0002)** | 0.0005 (0.0002)** | 0.0008 (0.0002)*** | 0.0007 (0.0002)*** | 0.0007 (0.0002)*** | 0.0006 (0.0002)*** |
| Mother's Education | 0.1166 (0.0290)*** | 0.1170 (0.0290)*** | 0.0917 (0.0281)*** | 0.0926 (0.0280)*** | 0.1361 (0.0279)*** | 0.1365 (0.0279)*** |
| Place of Residence | 0.0957 (0.0622) | 0.1480 (0.0732)** | 0.1123 (0.0605)* | 0.2199 (0.0710)*** | 0.1371 (0.0599)** | 0.2051 (0.0705)*** |
| OSL Expenses | 0.0024 (0.0015) | 0.0083 (0.0047)* | 0.0042 (0.0015)*** | 0.0164 (0.0045)*** | 0.0058 (0.0015)*** | 0.0136 (0.0045)*** |
| Place of Residence*OSL Expenses | | -0.0019 (0.0014) | | -0.0039 (0.0014)*** | | -0.0025 (0.0014)* |
| Constant | 3.3605 (0.2600)*** | 3.2309 (0.2771)*** | 2.8834 (0.2535)*** | 2.6149 (0.2694)*** | 2.7454 (0.2506)*** | 2.5784 (0.2665)*** |
| $R^2$ | 0.21 | 0.21 | 0.25 | 0.26 | 0.28 | 0.28 |
| N | 1,031 | 1,031 | 1,004 | 1,004 | 1,022 | 1,022 |

* $p < 0.1$; ** $p < 0.05$; *** $p < 0.01$

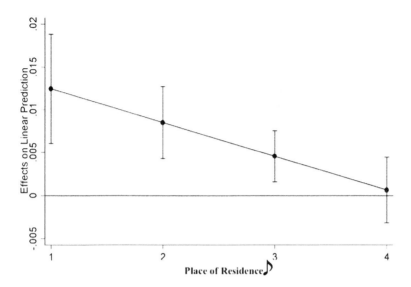

**Figure 10.3** Average marginal effects of the OSL expenses on math performance with 95% confidence intervals.

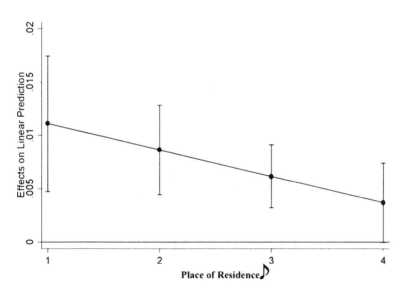

**Figure 10.4** Average marginal effects of OSL expenses on English performance with 95% confidence intervals.

## DISCUSSION

In this chapter, we just show two examples of intersectionality among the explanatory variables of student performance in the standardized national test in Korea. We could have shown many more cases of intersectionality among different variables but did not to save space. With only two examples, however, we can make several observations.

As we discussed in the introduction of this chapter, Collins increased the general applicability of intersectionality theory from African American women to all women" (Mann & Huffman, 2005, p. 61). She argued that cultural patterns of oppression are not only interrelated, but are bound together and influenced by the intersectional systems of society, such as race, gender, class, and ethnicity (Collins, 2000, p. 42). So, by this time, the term, intersectionality is not just about Black women in the United States. Our study in this chapter is a testimony that the notion of intersectionality can be applied to non-race or gender related issues outside of the United States.

As we also discussed in the beginning, today sociologists strive to apply intersectionality to all people and to many different intersections of group membership. That is, now the term, intersectionality, applies to much more dimensions of groups of people sharing identity. Our study takes full advantage of different identities, be they sub-dimensions of women's education level or the size of the community the students live in.

Now the term, "intersectionality," is being adopted in many disciplines and to explain many different events. Our chapter and all other chapters in this book are testimony that the notion is relevant to the access and performance in education theory in various countries.

Finally, and most importantly for our chapter, intersectionality does not need to be about race, gender, and class, or any other "big" dimensions of identity. We applied intersectionality theory to sub-dimensions that can be part of larger dimensions such as class, and any other dimensions. Further, our study finds interaction models statistically significant. We show only two cases of intersectionality in this chapter. But we could have found many more cases of statistically significant interaction terms. What this means in our understanding of access to higher learning and academic performance is that many of the previous findings were based on underspecified models—and scholars have made biased conclusions about the factors determining educational access and academic performance. This is a scary thought.

Given our findings, however, it is inevitable for us to revisit some of the previous work, and the study of educational access and academic performance may turn out to be much more complicated thing than we have previously assumed.

## NOTE

1. Educational disadvantage takes many different forms, but globally is a major barrier to the well-being of individuals and communities and the prosperity of nations. What represents "disadvantage" will differ from country to country (OECD 2007).

## APPENDIX

We describe individual variables used in our analyses here.

**Breakfast:** This is a categorical variable with a value of 1 meaning "I do not eat breakfast" and 5 meaning "I eat breakfast everyday."

**AMPE Majors:** This is a dummy variable indicating those who ended up majoring in arts, music, or physical education in college.

**AMPE Majors:** This is a dummy variable indicating those who ended up majoring in arts, music, or physical education in college.

**AMPE Majors:** This is a dummy variable indicating those who ended up majoring in arts, music, or physical education in college.

**Amount of Time Spent Studying By Oneself (ATSSBO):** the average weekly amount of time the student studied by himself.

**Gender:** This is a dummy variable with male student coded as 1 and female student as 0.

**Place of Residence:** A categorical variable that shows the place of residence as one of a large municipality (4), a city, a township, and a rural area (1).

**Mother's Education:** A 10-point categorical variable ranging from no education (with the value of 0) to holding a Ph.D. (with the value of 9)

**OSL Expenses:** The average monthly OSL expenses for the student for the previous year. Out-of-school learning experience includes all types of learning other than a student's regular high school curriculum in a particular subject area. It includes private tutoring, group tutoring, paid long-distance learning, and so on.

**Household Income:** Average monthly household income for the previous year.

## REFERENCES

Baker, D. P., & Stevenson, D. L. (1986). Mother's strategies for children's school achievement: Managing the transition to high school. *Sociology of Education, 59,* 156–166.

Browne, I., & Misra, J. (2003).The intersection of gender and race in the labor market. *Annual Review of Sociology,* 487–513.

Campbell, J. R., & Mandel, F. (1990). Connecting math achievement to parental influences. *Contemporary Educational Psychology, 15,* 64–74.

Carey, G. L. (1958). Sex differences in problem-solving performance as a function of attitude differences. *Journal of Abnormal and Social Psychology 56,* 256–260.

Collins, P. H. (1998). The tie that binds: Race, gender, and U.S. violence. *Ethnic and Racial Studies, 21*(5).

Collins, P. H. (2000). Gender, Black feminism, and Black political economy. *Annals of the American Academy of Political and Social Scienc, 568,* 41–53.

Crane, J. (1996). Effects of home environment, SES, and maternal test scores on mathematics achievement. *Journal of Education Research, 89,* 305–314.

Crenshaw, K. W. (1989). Demarginalizing the intersection of race and sex: A Black feminist critique of antidiscrimination doctrine, feminist theory and antiracist politics. *University of Chicago Legal Forum,* 139–167.

DeFrancisco, V. P., & Palczewski, C. H. (2007). *Communicating gender diversity: A critical approach.* Los Angeles: Sage Publications.

Deslandes, R. et al. (1997). School achievement at the secondary level: Influence of parenting style and parent involvement in schooling. *McGill Journal of Education, 32,* 191–207.

Fan, X. (2001). Parental involvement and students' academic achievement: A growth modeling analysis. *Journal of Experimental Education, 70,* 27–61.

Georgiou, S. N. (1999). Parental attributions as predictors of involvement and influences on child achievement. *British Journal of Educational Psychology, 69,* 409–429.

Gordon, I. (1996). Family structure, educational achievement and the inner city. *Urban Studies, 33,* 407–423.

Hansford, B. C., & Hattie, J. A. (1982). The relationship between self and achievement/ performance measures. *Review of Educational Research, 52,* 123–142.

Jeynes, W. H. (2005). A meta-analysis of the relation of parental involvement to urban elementary school academic achievement. *Urban Education, 40,* 237–269.

Kim, H. M. (2012). Educational disadvantage and access to the best universities in Korea." Presented at the 6th annual International Alliance of Leading Economic Institutes meeting and conference held at the University of Melbourne, Australia, August 2012.

Knudsen, S. (2006). Intersectionality—A theoretical inspiration in the analysis of minority cultures and identities in textbooks. *Caught in the Web or Lost in the Textbook* http://www.caen.iufm.fr/colloque_iartem/pdf/knudsen.pdf

Korea Education and Employment Panel, Korea Research Institute for Vocational Education & Training, 2004.

Mann, S. A., & Huffman, D. J. (2005). The decentering of second wave feminism and the rise of the third wave. *Science and Society, 69,* 56–91.

McCall, L. (2005). The complexity of intersectionality. *Journal of Women in Culture and Society, 30*(3), 1771–1800.

Paulson, S. E. (1994). Relations of parenting style and parental involvement with ninth-grade students' achievement. *Journal of Early Adolescence, 14,* 250–267.

Ritzer, G. (2007). *Contemporary sociological theory and its classical roots: The basics.* Boston: McGraw-Hill.

# CHAPTER 11

# INTERSECTIONALITIES OF DIFFERENCE

## Asian Women's Experiences of Religion, "Race," Class, and Gender in Higher Education in the United Kingdom

**Kalwant Bhopal**
*University of Southampton, United Kingdom*

### INTRODUCTION

This paper will explore issues of intersectionality and 'race' with a focus on theorising difference. There is little research which has explored issues of intersectionality in the United Kingdom. The research that does exist has examined issues of class and gender (Skeggs, 1997; Reay, et al., 2001) or 'race' and gender (Bhopal, 2008; Gillborn & Mirza, 2000; Mirza, 2009; Shain, 2003) but has failed to engage with debates around the intersections of difference particularly in relation to 'race', class and gender as interlocking systems of oppression. Discourses around 'race', diversity and inclusion have tended to be analysed as disparate issues. 'Race' has been

*Intersectionality and Urban Education*, pages 229–245
Copyright © 2014 by Information Age Publishing
**229**

compartmentalised (in racial, ethnic or area studies), or has been empha-sised as the defining characteristic of identity (in studies of national identity or in some versions of critical race theory) (see Gillborn, 2009) rather than as one aspect of a complex web of intersections, oppressions and identity formations (Bhopal, 2010). In much of the research which has explored issues of difference, discourses around 'race', diversity and inclusion have tended to be analysed as disparate issues. This chapter uses empirical re-search with Asian women (British born third generation Indian, Pakistani and Bangladeshi women) in the United Kingdom who were studying at one particular university in the South East of England, to explore how wom-en's experiences of higher education are affected by their diverse identi-ties which in turn, position them as 'other' within the White space of the Academy. It will focus on women's experiences of religion, 'race', class, and gender and draw upon the work of Beck (1992) and Giddens (1993) to analyse how such differences interweave and intersect upon women's lives in modern day 'risk' society. The chapter argues that Asian women's experi-ences in the White space of the Academy are characterised by risk, racism and Islamaphobia in which their marginal status continues to be 'othered'.

In this chapter, I am particularly concerned with examining *theorising* intersectionalites and difference. In recent years, the concept of intersec-tionality has taken centre stage and become a dominant model with which to engage in how differences such as 'race', gender, class, sexuality, age, disability and religion interweave and intersect upon individual lives in a modern 'risk' society (Beck, 1992). Intersectionality has become a model upon which to understand, analyse and engage with difference in which difference itself becomes a defining feature of 'otherness'. Otherness is re-lated to the notion that identity itself is fragmented, fragile even, yet con-stantly evolving through multiple engagements and relationships in soci-ety and through this complexity, intersectionality helps us to engage with understanding outsiders and what it means to be a 'stranger' in modern society. Intersectionality then is to be understood as a dynamic, rather than a static process. It is based on the premise that understanding *identities* is a journey, one that changes through different times in history and transforms through different spaces. Current discourses around threats to identity and the categorisation of individuals is related to macro forces, even the 'war on terror', particularly when such identities are seen as a threat to the Brit-ish way of life and notions of British identity. In writing and thinking about 'race', I contend that 'race' is a contested concept and is not only problem-atic but also controversial.

## BACKGROUND AND CONTEXT

Whilst there is considerable literature on social inequality and exclusion (particularly in relation to education), there is little which explores notions of *intersectionality* and how such difference is theorised. Given the gap in the literature on theorising difference it becomes all the more important to address the specificity of difference. Intersectionality has been used by feminists to address essentialist models of social theory by acknowledging that not all women's experiences are the same. Black feminist theory arose from the need for Black women and women of colour to question discourses of the concept 'woman', particularly to address the absence of Black women's experiences in relation to feminist struggles. The focus for Black feminism was to challenge White Eurocentric knowledge which was taken as the norm. There was a need to understand and deconstruct the concept of 'woman' and analyse this in relation to 'race', class, gender and sexuality (hooks, 1990; Bhavnani & Phoenix, 1994). In Britain, these discussions centred around women's political position and how they defined themselves in relation to being 'Black' (Grewal et al., 1988; Anthias & Yuval-Davis, 1992; Brah, 1996), this took place through challenges around the essentialist assumptions of racism (such as through employment, domestic violence and reproductive technologies). In discussing the everyday struggles of Black women, recent work on intersectionality has acknowledged the, 'recognition that 'race', social class and sexuality differentiated women's experiences has disrupted notions of a homogenous category 'woman' with its attendant assumptions of universality that served to maintain the status quo in relation to 'race', social class and sexuality, while challenging gendered assumptions' (Brah & Phoenix, 2004, p. 82). This has also been emphasised by Collins (2005, p. 11) who views intersectional paradigms as mutually constructing systems of power which permeate all social relations and Seidman (1994) who analyses the different facets of intersectionality through the multiple axes of social hierarchy. What is clear about this work is the need to focus on the *multiplicities* of identity and to acknowledge that experiences cannot be taken in isolation, 'We need to be more aware of how all of our experiences intersect and merge with one another' (Brock, 1991, p. 14).

The pioneering work of Crenshaw (1989; 1994) in the United States addressed the flawed essentialist model by arguing that a single axis analysis of 'race' or gender did not acknowledge the true experiences of Black women. Through legal cases of discrimination, Crenshaw argued that the one dimensional approach did not take into consideration the multi dimensions of an individual's experiences.

Black women can experience discrimination in a number of ways and that contradiction arises from our assumptions that their claims of exclusion must be unidirectional. Consider an analogy to traffic in an intersection, coming and going in all four directions. Discrimination, like traffic through an intersection, may flow in one direction; it may flow in another. (1989, p. 321)

More recent work in the United Kingdom by Floya Anthias has attempted to move away from the idea that certain groups or categories (of 'race' or gender for instance) intersect, instead she explores the influence of social locations and processes through the concept of *translocational positionality*. 'The concept of translocational positionality addresses issues of identity in terms of locations which are not fixed but are context meaning, and time related and which therefore involve shifts and contradictions' (Anthias, 2008, p. 5). Anthias argues that translocations are not just about people moving to different locations (either spatially or culturally), rather they are about crossing borders and defining and redefining boundaries associated within them. 'The notion of translocation references the idea of 'location' as a social space which is produced within contextual, spatial, temporal and hierarchal relations around the 'intersections' of social divisions and identities of class, ethnicity and gender (amongst others)' (2008, p. 9).

Post structuralism has also attempted to analyse the concept of intersectionality. Crudely speaking, poststructuralists aim to deconstruct perceptions of the world and to challenge what appears to be 'normal' or 'natural'. The perspective of post structuralism is grounded in different types of analyses such as discourse theory, psychoanalysis and postcolonial theory. Consequently, the focus is on examining questions of intersectionality through historical relationships which are embedded in contesting fields of discourses and multiple subject positions. Here, the concepts of 'agency' and 'power' (Foucault, 1972; Derrida, 1974) are central. As a result, new ways of examining how difference is understood within the realms of intersectionality have developed (Butler, 1990; Weedon, 1996; Spivak, 1999). Postcolonial studies for example have been used to examine the processes around colonial and postcolonial discourses surrounding the category 'woman'. In developing such approaches, some researchers have attempted to use the analysis of 'border theory' to explore how intersectionality works through time and place and the crossing of specific boundaries (Lewis, 2000). 'Borders' here are addressed in the geographical and analytical sense. The concept of 'deterritorialisation' proposed by Deleuze and Guattari (1986) has been used to examine 'border writing' (Hicks, 1991; Calderon & Salvidar, 1991).

Other theorists have used the concept of space to refer to diasporic identities. Brah (1996) uses the concept of 'diaspora space' to analyse how identity is configured when individuals move from space to space through particular historic moments.

Diaspora space is the intersectionality of diaspora, border and dis/location as a point of confluence of economic, political, cultural and psychic processes. It is where multiple subject positions are juxtaposed, contested, proclaimed or disavowed; where the permitted and the prohibited perpetually interrogate; and where the accepted and the transgressive imperceptibly mingle even while these syncretic forms may be disclaimed in the name of purity and tradition. (1996, p. 208)

According to Brah then, difference is conceptualised as part of an experience, that of subjectivity, identity and location. The concept of diaspora is about relations of power, 'that similarise and differentiate between and across changing diasporic constellations' (p. 183). An understanding of diaspora involves different processes of 'multi-locationality across geographical, cultural and psychi boundaries' (p. 194). So diaspora and the identities associated with it cut across several different boundaries at one time. Within this, combinations of the local and global aspects are an important part of different diasporic identities. In further analysing the concept of diaspora, Brah further examines how the concept of racism can be categorised in relation to diaspora in which she argues that different racisms do not exist in parallel, rather they exist as, 'intersecting modalities of *differential racialisations marking positionality across articulating fields of power*' (p. 186 original emphasis).

More recently McCall (2005) has questioned the methodologies that are used to examine intersectionality and the difficulties associated with this. She outlines three approaches for the study of intersectionality; anticategorical complexity, intercategorical complexity and intracategorical complexity. McCall states, that, 'Interest in intersectionality arose out of a critique of a gender-based and race-based research for failing to account for lived experience at neglected points of intersection—ones that tended to reflect multiple subordinate locations as opposed to dominant or mixed locations' (2005, p. 1780). She argues that the study of intersectionality has in fact in its analysis introduced new methodological problems which as a consequence have in fact limited the range of methodologies that can be used to study or analyse it as a concept. There is no one particular approach that can manage the complexity of intersectionality and its analysis.

Other approaches such as, Critical Race Theory (CRT), and in particular, Critical Race Feminism (CRF), frequently adopt intersectional theories to understand the dynamics of racial oppression. Despite the emphasis in CRT on the endemic nature of racism and White supremacy as a 'conspiracy' of White interests (Gillborn, 2005; 2006; Leonardo, 2005) it has been sensitive to the interactions of other modes of oppression with racial oppression. Firstly, CRT has been nuanced by the specific dynamics of racial oppression in various cultural contexts giving rise to offshoots such as Asian American CRT (AsianCrit), Latino CRT (LatCrit) and American Indian

CRT (TribalCrit). These derivatives of CRT show how different racial oppressions are experienced and resisted by various 'racial' groups and point towards the specificity of intersectional racialised experience. Secondly, and particularly through CRF the specificity of racialised and gendered experience and 'voice' is fore grounded.

## The Research

The empirical research for this paper is based on research carried out with Asian women in England who were studying at one particular university in the South East of England. The main piece of research was based on in-depth interviews with 45 women. All of the women were studying for a Social Sciences or Education Studies degree. Case study semi-structured interviews were carried out on university premises in private. Women were recruited via year group announcements and advertisements placed on notice boards around the campus. Initially, very few women came forward to participate in the study, but once several women participated, other women on the course also agreed to take part. I am aware of the issues associated with snowball sampling and discuss this elsewhere (see Bhopal, 2010). Other researchers have also highlighted the difficulties of gaining access to minority ethnic groups and the use of snowball sampling (Eghraveba, 2001; Phoenix, 2001). As a British Asian female academic I explicitly decided *not* to conduct the research in my own academic institution hence creating a 'distance' between myself and the respondents. However, given my own status as an academic, issues of power differentials existed between myself and the respondents. In my role as researcher I revealed personal aspects of my own life (such as my own views and those of my family on arranged marriages and Asian cultural experiences) which encouraged respondents to open up and gain my trust. The interviews became 'conversations with a purpose' (McCracken, 1988) rather than a formal structured question and answer session. After the interview, many of the women expressed how they had enjoyed participating in the interview and were glad that *their* views were heard.

All of the women who participated in the research were born in the UK and all had parents and/or grandparents who were born in India, Pakistan or Bangladesh. The women were aged between 20 and 25. Thirty seven women were single and eight were married. Thirty four were from backgrounds in which their parents were employed in traditional middle class occupations (such as solicitors, accountants, teachers and lecturers). All other women had parents who were employed in traditional working class backgrounds (such as factory workers, shop assistants and cab drivers). The interviews were tape-recorded and the data transcribed. The data was analysed using methods of grounded theory (Strauss & Corbin, 1990). It was based upon examining the views of women and analysing these in relation to particular themes. The themes were coded and indexed in relation to their responses on their views on marriage. Grounded theory was used so that systematic qualitative analysis could be used to generate and develop explanatory theoretical frameworks to analyse the experiences of Indian women. I wanted to examine how women made sense of the meanings of their lives and how a theoretical analysis could provide a way of exploring the differing meanings women gave to their experiences.

For this chapter, I will focus on the women in the study who defined themselves as Muslim women. Thirteen women in the study defined themselves as Muslim; other women defined themselves as Sikh and Hindu. The focus of the chapter on Muslim women is based on their emphasis on the importance and effects of religion on their lives. For these women, religion was a significant factor in their lives in how they defined themselves and how others defined them. The data for this chapter is based on the responses of thirteen women, this is not a representative sample and I do not intend to generalise the experiences of all Muslim women, but will particularly examine how the respondents expressed their views with an attempt to analyse this through understandings of intersectionality; such as the women's 'race', class and gender in relation to their religion.

## Identity

Women were specifically asked how they saw their identities in relation to their experiences in higher education and also in their everyday lives. Many of the Muslim women spoke about different aspects of their *identities*, rather than their one identity. The majority of women defined themselves primarily in terms of their religious identity as Muslim and many said that since 9/11 and 7/7[1] they were more inclined to be proud of their religious identity rather than to hide it.

> When someone asks me how I define myself I would say I am a Muslim woman. My religion is very important to me; it's how I live my life and the way that I have been brought up.

Farah said that she was aware since the 'war on terror' Muslims were treated badly by everyone: by the press, the politicians and by society in general. Since the major attacks in the United States and in London, she felt that she was seen very differently by British and also non-British Asians, as being 'one of them'.

> As a Muslim when you go out and you dress like a Muslim, people always look at you and they do think about terrorism. I don't think that our identity as Muslims has been helped by what has been going on in the world. In a way, the anti-Muslim attitudes of people make us feel bad, but at the same time we think that we have as much right as other people to be proud of who we are—and we are Muslims and we are proud of that.

When asked about issues of 'race', class and gender in terms of their identity, many of the women emphasised that being a Muslim woman had different connotations attached to it, specifically when compared to Muslim men. Furthermore, there was always an assumption that Muslim women were uneducated and from a working class background. Meena was from a traditional middle class background (both her parents were teachers) and all her siblings had been to university. She spoke about how it was always assumed by her teachers and her non-Muslim friends that she would leave school at 16 and have an 'arranged marriage'.

> I think being a Muslim woman people do make assumptions about you, about what you do and about your education. At school they would think that because I was Muslim I was going to leave at 16 and get married. They always thought I was going to be shipped back home to Pakistan to get married to an old man. Just because I am a Muslim it doesn't mean that I'm like that. My parents don't want me to get married until *I want to* and the most important thing they want for me is to get a good education [original emphasis].

Farzana also spoke about the racist stereotypes she encountered whilst at school and also from her own neighbours.

> When I was at school, there were lots of assumptions made about what I was going to do with my life just because I am a Muslim. There some statements made which I think were just ignorant and racist. Even our neighbours who are White have changed towards us since the terrorist attacks; they [White people] just don't trust Muslims anymore and equate Muslim with being a terrorist. That is simply wrong and I think it is racist.

However, some of the women spoke about how when they went to university, things were slightly (but not entirely) better, there seemed to be more of an accepting attitude and one of openness and tolerance towards others. Farah was very aware of this.

> At University, it was different because people were more accepting and seem to be more open minded and didn't make assumptions about what you were going to do. They don't seem to be that ignorant because they speak to you and get to know you as a person and so accept you more. But of course, there

are some people who will always be a bit ignorant and not understand other cultures.

Shinaz agreed with this and articulately related how her own experiences would affect others and their future lives.

> I think because this university is very mixed and there are lots of Asian people and people from different backgrounds, that makes it more accepting and it makes it more like people try to understand you and they try to understand your culture and your religion. They don't just dismiss it and that is what should happen, because we are all here to learn about each other and that will help you later on in your life, particularly in education. If you want to be a teacher then you have to be able to understand that child and not make judgements about him or her or their family. You have to take that child as an individual.

Many of the Muslim women spoke about gender and how the situation of being seen as an 'outsider' and as 'othered' was much harder for Muslim men than it was for Muslim women.

> It is harder for Muslim men than women because men would get a harder time and it all depends how they are seen. If they have a beard and wear traditional dress, then immediately assumptions are made about them and these are usually negative. One of my uncles is very traditional in what he looks like and we laugh sometimes and say he looks like a serious cleric, but he is only young. He always gets harassed wherever he goes; people shout abuse at him and insult him. He is just a kind, devout person. But to society he is not seen like that, he is seen as a threat, as a terrorist and that is so unfair.

Both Muslim women and men were seen as a threat to the social order of acceptable notions of British society and particularly when this non-acceptance is seen as a threat to the British way of life, to notions of acceptability citizenship and identity. The 'presentation of self' (Goffman, 1959) was crucial to how Muslim women (and men) were seen in the educational milieu; either in schools or universities. Within the predominantly 'White space' of the Academy, Muslim women felt that they were outsiders but at the same time they felt accepted by others (such as students) because many of the women felt that the university was a more liberal environment from which they could emphasise their sense of 'being' and in some respects their sense of 'belonging'.

Recent research has suggested that second and third generation British born Pakistanis and Bangladeshis are more likely to assert their Muslim identities (Archer, 2003; Shain, 2011). Much of the research suggests that is a response to the 'demonisation of Muslims' in the current climate based on the 'war on terror' and the past Rushdie affair, for example an identification for Muslim males with a global collective notion of Muslim brotherhood is a form of empowerment for them. For many Muslim women there is the notion that Islam is used to counter patriarchal assumptions based on marriage and educational achievement. More recent research suggests that young Pakistani and Bangladeshi boys define themselves as 'Muslim first' and as British second (Shain, 2011). In her study, Shain found that, Pakistani and Bangladeshi boys felt, 'Britishness is more a legal entitlement for ethnic minorities than a statement of ethnicity or identity' (2011, p. 56).

## Communities of Belonging

Within their sense of self, for many of the women their sense of community was critical to their notions of identity (of how they defined themselves and of how others also defined them). Community and an adaptation to notions of community provided women with a sense of security from which their identities were able to manifest themselves. Their sense of community took different forms; there was the sense of community to which they belonged to as part of their religious cultural identity, this also included members of their own extended family and there was also the community to which they were attached in the university; this consisted of their friends and people like them with whom they could identify and with whom they felt confident with. Farzana described this as,

> There are people that I identify with me that make me feel safe. I suppose you could say they are members of my community who share similar things to me. Our first identity of being a Muslim is what brings us together as a community and then there are other connections, like if you're a woman you will tend to speak to other women. We are able to have these connections that bring us together and almost make us felt that we have allies, or people that would be on your side or people that understand where you're coming from.

She went on to speak about her sense of belonging which she received from her being a member of her community in the White space of the Academy.

> Universities tend to be dominated by White men I think. Most of the lecturers are men and all of the professors are men and they are White. There are a few Black women, but they tend not to be in positions of power. I do find that some of them [lecturers] though not all of them don't really understand the situation for us that much so we tend to stick to other Muslims or Asians who understand us. But that's not to say that I don't have friends who are non-Asian or non-Muslim because I do, it's just because the level of understanding you get from someone who is like you is different.

For many of the women a sense of community was a significant part of their lives in how they identified themselves and in terms of their acceptance. Community enabled women to feel accepted, to be a sense of something in which they were not afraid to express their views and to be open about their sense of religious difference. Community made women feel valued, and gave them a sense of belonging. The concept of community has been widely discussed in academic discourse; it is a concept which has a variety of means. In my analysis of community I agree with Redfield (1971) who suggests that community marks out clear membership, it is clear who is 'one of us' and who is 'one of them'. Members of a community know where they stand and there is no cause for confusion or ambiguity about belonging or not belonging. A community is distinct from other groups (it is clear where it begins and where it ends); it is generally small (the members know who is and who is not a part of it) and it tends to be self-sufficient (it provides for its members). The distinctiveness of the community is translated in the clarity of who belongs and who does not (Bhopal, 2010). In a modern sense, particularly in relation to the experiences of Muslim women, community can develop around shared interests and goals rather than a particular place or territory. Many of the women spoke about their relationships with other Muslim women which were centred on a shared identity, but also seemed to focus in the space of the Academy. In this sense, community formed part of a shared identity and a shared common space. Part of the belonging to the community for Muslim women was based on, '... a feeling that members have of belonging, a feeling that members matter to one another and to the group, and a shared faith that members' needs will be met through their commitment to be together. So members work together to achieve and develop strategies which increase their sense of community. Many of the Muslim women did this by supporting one another whilst at university, particularly when they may have experienced some form of racism from others or support through help with assignments, and a general sense of 'being there for each other' which was apparent. So the notion of community had a positive effect on group mobilisation to solve problems that members may have been experiencing and with a focus on the development of positive relationships between its members. As Crow and Allan state, 'Community plays a crucial symbolic role in generating people's sense of belonging'. Cohen on the other hand argues that the reality of community is based on an individual's perception of the vitality of its culture, 'People construct community symbolically, making it a resource and repository of meaning, and a referent of their identity' (1985, p. 118). Frazer (2000) discusses the 'pay of' of community. She states that when individuals engage in shared exchanges and share personal experiences and from this a sense of community is achieved and because of this she states, 'Here I think we have the 'pay-off' of community... in the relation of community concrete patterns of material social relationships are felt to be transcended. The aspiration to community is an aspiration to a kind of connectedness that transcends the mundane and concrete tangle of social relationships' (2000, p. 83). Many of the Muslim women in the study felt a strong sense of belonging to other women with whom they could identify. Their sense of belonging was based on a mutual acceptance and understanding which came with a sense of sharing similar religious and cultural beliefs, but these were not entirely exclusive. The security of acceptance of the community enabled women to gain a sense of their identity in an environment in which they felt safe and one in which they felt they could belong.

Benedict Andersen's (1983) sense of community as 'imagined' is important here. He explores how the nation is imagined as limited, as sovereign and imagined as a community because of the inequalities and exploitations that exist within it. Andersen explores the ways in which communities share membership through their language and how knowledge of language affects whether one can become a member of the community. For Muslim women, this language was based on a shared commonality of understanding affiliated to their religious identity and their sense of being a Muslim woman in British society. From this perspective, in Andersen's 'imagined community', the strength of it is largely that it copes with change by *imagining* a structure, the nation state, to replace the lost communities. In many respects the sense of community for Muslim women takes on a more 'real' sense, particularly in relation to their status of 'outsiders'. They are members of a minority ethnic group, a religious and cultural group which remains demonised because of its association with the 'war on terror', consequently their sense of community (whether real or imagined) provided them with a sense of security and identity in the White space of the Academy.

## The Effects of Living in a 'Risk Society'

Ulrick Beck (1992) in his work discusses the effects of modern day 'risk' society associated with modern living which is marked by insecurity and instability in a changing world. However, many of the Muslim women spoke about 'risk' in a different way; they spoke about risk in relation to their own identities. On the one hand, they suggested the world had changed since 9/11 and 7/7 and consequently everyone (regardless of their religious background) was seen as being associated with 'risk' in one form or another. But on the other hand, they associated the 'risk' with their own identities, particularly their religious identity. As a Muslim woman, they identified how their aspect of 'risk' was heightened and consequently their position of the 'other' was further manifested in them being marginalised. Shinaz said,

We are not seen in the same way as other people and I don't think we are seen in the same ways as other Asian people because we are religious and mainly because we are Muslim. I don't think we can ever get away from that aspect of our identities.

Shinaz emphasised how being a Muslim was associated with different types of 'risk'.

We have to think about our own identities as Muslims, how people see us and what they think about us. But we also have to think about the fact that if there was another bomb attack, we would be included. We could also be those innocent people who are killed in terror attacks, but why is that not thought about? Just because we are Muslim we are not all the same. And to think that we are, is wrong.

Shinaz spoke about how she would sometimes hide her identity if she was concerned that she would experience negative reactions from others.

There are times that I don't tell people about my religion. There are times when I don't tell them that me and all my family are Muslims and that my parents take it very seriously. Unless they understand, then they might think differently about me. I don't tell lies to them; I just don't want to talk about it. Most of my friends [non-Muslim] know that I am a Muslim and they respect that and it can be a good thing as it means we can have open and frank discussion whilst still respecting the other person.

Giddens in his work (1999, p. 3) states that a risk society is 'a society increasingly preoccupied with the future (and also with safety) which generates the notion of risk'. Beck (1992, p. 21) on the other hand defines it as a systematic way of dealing with hazards and insecurities induced and introduced by modernisation itself. Both Giddens and Beck use the term modernity and reflexivity, in which modernity is seen as 'a shorthand term for modern society or industrial civilisation ... modernity is vastly more dynamic than any previous type of social order. It is a society ... which unlike any preceding culture lives in the future rather than the past'. (Giddens, 1990, p. 4). The idea of reflexivity is based on the notion that society should examine itself, particularly how it changes during this process of modernity. Although both Giddens and Beck explore the concept of risk in terms of natural disasters which may be seen as a result of the modernisation process itself. For many of the Muslim women it was the risk associated with inequalities which reinforced their difference in British society, but it was also how the concept of risk society interacted with social divisions in society (such as their gender and religion).

Beck argues that risk in the form of wealth can lead to inequalities in society in which wealth is not distributed equally in society which will influence how people are treated and furthermore how they fit in with society. Beck argues that those who occupy certain social positions in society will be risk averse. 'In some of their dimensions these follow the inequalities of class and strata positions, but they bring a fundamentally different distribution logic into play' (1992, p. 23). But at the same time all individuals will be exposed to risk regardless of their social class background. Giddens on the other hand argues that older forms of class structure maintain a stronger role in risk society, defined 'in terms of differential access to forms of self-actualisation and empowerment' (1991, p. 6).

## Conclusions

This chapter has argued that when examining the lives of Muslim women in the White space of the Academy, it is crucial to explore how women define themselves and how they are in turn defined by society—which in some sense reinforces their status as 'others' and 'outsiders'. Women's identities are based not only on their intersections of 'race', class and gender but their religious identity played a significant impact on how women defined who they are and how they were in turn, defined by others. Their intersecting identities are based on how they are further defined in a society characterised by risk, by racism and by Islamaphobia. In such a society, they will continue to be othered and their marginal status within the White space of the Academy and within society more general will be seen as 'outsiders'. Shain in her study found a distinction between an 'us and them' identity which was similar to my findings with Muslim women above. For the boys in Shain's study they '. . . drew specifically on *Muslim* 'we' identities which were constructed in relation to a collective 'they' composed of 'Whites', 'Europeans' and 'Americans' sometimes collapsed into a single entity and at other times referenced interchangeably. Collectively, 'they' at one level, were imbued with the power to judge Muslims in collusion with a powerful and highly partial media that also represented imperial interests' (p. 63). My research also supports that of Shain (2011) which argues that individuals adopt a range of strategies to counter dominant discourses on the 'war on terror' which positions Muslims as a problem. Also as Shain shows the boys in her study countered these dominant discourses through the strength of their families which were seen as providing security and were seen as having stronger moral values than non-Muslim families. The women in my study also valued their family and the strength of their communities in providing them with a strong sense of identity and security in relation to how they were construed by non-Muslims, particularly in relation to public stereotypes portrayed in the media and public discourses.

For the Muslim women in my study the traditional structures and under-standings of their 'race', gender, class and religion played a significant part in their lives, both in how they defined themselves and also how they were defined by others. Their identities played a significant part in their relationships with their communities, both by providing a secure identity but also by providing a sense of acceptance and legitimacy in a world in which they were often marginalised because of their identities; those of being an Asian female Muslim.

## NOTE

1. The 9/11 attacks took place on 11 September 2001 when a series of four coordinated suicide attacks took place in the United States in New York. The hijackers crashed two planes into the Twin Towers of the World Trade Centre in New York with attempted simultaneous attacks in Virginia Pennsylvania. 3000 people died in the attacks. The 7/7 attacks took place in London on 7 July 2005. Four terrorist detonated four bombs on the London underground and on a London bus. Fifty two people were killed in the attacks and over 700 injured. The Islamist militant group, Al-Qaeda claimed responsibility for the attacks.

## REFERENCES

Andersen, B. (1983). *Imagined communities: Reflections on the origin and spread of nationalism.* London: Verso.

Anthias, F. (2008). Thinking through the lens of translocational positionality: An intersectionality frame for understanding identity and belonging. *Translocations: Migration and Social Change, 4*(1), 5–20.

Anthias, F., & Yuval-Davis, N. (1992). *Racialised boundaries: Race, nation, gender, colour and class and the anti-racist struggle.* London: Routledge.

Archer, L. (2003). *Race, masculinity and schooling: Muslim boys and education.* Milton Keynes: Open University Press.

Bauman, Z. (1992). *Modernity and the holocaust.* Cambridge: Polity.

Beck, U. (1992). *Risk society: Towards a new modernity.* London: Sage.

Bhavnani, K., & Phoenix, A. (1994). Shifting identities, shifting racisms. *Feminism and Psychology, 4,* 5–18.

Bhopal, K. (2010). *Asian women in higher education: Shared communities.* Stoke on Trent: Trentham.

Brah, A. (1996). *Cartographies of Diaspora: Contesting identities.* London: Roultedge.

Brah, A., & Phoenix, A. (2004). Ain't I a woman? Revisiting intersectionality. *Journal of International Women's Studies, 5*(3), 75–86.

Brock, D. (1991). Talking about a revelation: feminist popular discourse on sexual abuse. *Canadian Women's Studies, 12,* 12–15.

Butler, J. (1990). *Gender trouble.* New York: Routledge.

Calderon, H., & Salvidar, H. (1991). *Criticism in the borderlands*. Durham, NC: Duke University.

Collins, P. (2005). *Black sexual politics: African Americans, gender and the new racism*. New York: Routledge.

Crenshaw, K. (1989). Demarginalising the intersection of race and sex. *University of Chicago Legal Forum, 139*, 139–167.

Crenshaw, K. (1994). Mapping the margins: Intersectionality, identity politics and violence against women of color. *Stanford Law Review, 24*–38.

Crow, G., & Allan, G. (1994). *Community life. An introduction to local social relations*. Hemel Hempstead: Harvester Wheatsheaf.

Deleuze, G., & Guattari, F. (1986). 'What is a minor literature?' in Kafka, *Towards a Minor Literature*, In D. Polan (Ed.). Minneapolis: University of Minnesota Press.

Derrida, J. (1974). White mythology: Metaphor in the text of philosophy. *New Literary History, 6*(1), 5–74.

Eghraveba, I. (2001). 'Researching an-'other' minority ethnic community: Reflections of a Black female researcher on the intersections of race, gender and other power positions in the research process'. *International Journal of Social Research Methodology, 4*(3), 225–241.

Foucault, M. (1972). *The archaeology of knowledge*. London: Tavistock.

Frazer, E. (1999). *The problem of communitarian politics. Unity and conflict*. Oxford: Oxford University Press.

Giddens, A. (1984). *The constitution of society. Outline of the theory of structuration*. Cambridge: Polity Press.

Giddens, A. (1990). *The consequences of modernity*. Blackwell: Oxford.

Giddens, A. (1993). *The transformation of intimacy*. Stanford: Stanford University Press.

Giddens, A. (1999). 'Risk and Responsibility'. *Modern Law Review, 62*(1), 1–10.

Gillborn, D. (2005). Education policy as an act of White supremacy: Whiteness, critical race theory and education reform. *Journal of Education Policy, 20*, 485–505.

Gillborn, D. (2006). Rethinking White supremacy: Who counts in 'Whiteworld'. *Ethnicities, 6*, 318–340.

Gillborn, D. (2009). 'Risk-free racism: Whiteness and so-called "free speech"', *wake forest law review, 44*(2), 535–555.

Gillborn, D., & Mirza, H. (2000). *Educational inequality: Mapping race, class and. gender*. London: Ofsted.

Goffman, E. (1959). *The presentation of self in everyday life*. University of Edinburgh Social Sciences Research Centre.

Grewal, S. et al. (1988). *Charting the journey*. London: Sheba.

hooks, b. (1990). *Yearning: Race, gender and cultural politics*. Boston, MA: Southend Press.

Hicks, E. (1991). *Border writing: The multidimensional text*. Minneapolis: University of Minnesota Press.

Leonardo, Z. (2005). The color of supremacy: Beyond the discourse of 'White privilege'. In Z. Leonardo (Ed.), *Critical pedagogy and race* (pp. 37–52). Oxford: Blackwell.

Lewis, G. (2000). *Race, gender, social welfare*. Cambridge: Polity.

McCall, L. (2005). The complexity of intersectionality. *Signs, 30,* 1771–1800.

McCracken, G. (1988). *The long interview.* London: Sage.

McMillan, D., & Chavis, D. (1996). 'Sense of community: A definition and theory'. *Journal of Community Psychology, 14*(6), 6–23.

Mirza, H. (2009). *Race, gender and educational desire.* London: Routledge.

Phoenix, A. (2001). Practising feminist research: The intersection of gender and 'race' in the research process. In K. K. Bhavnani (Ed.), *Feminism and race* (pp. 203–219). Oxford: Oxford University Press.

Reay, D. et al. (2001). 'Choices of degree or degrees of choice?' *Sociology, 35*(4), 855–874.

Redfield, R. (1971). *The little community.* New York: Harper.

Seidman, S. (1994). *Contested knowledge: Social theory in the postmodern era.* Cambridge: Blackwell.

Shain, F. (2003). *The schooling and identity of Asian girls.* Stoke on Trent: Trentham.

Shain, F. (2011). *The new folk devils: Muslim boys and education in England.* Stoke on Trent: Trentham.

Skeggs, B. (1997). *Formations of class and gender: Becoming respectable.* London: Sage.

Spivak, G. (1999). *A critique of postcolonial reason.* Harvard: Harvard University Press.

Strauss, A., & Corbin, J. (1990). *Basics of qualitative research.* London: Sage.

Weedon, C. (1996). *Feminist practice and poststructuralist theory.* Oxford: Blackwell.

# PART IV

## EDUCATIONAL POLICIES AND URBAN SPACES

CHAPTER 12

# HUMAN RIGHTS, SCHOLARSHIP, AND ACTION FOR CHANGE

**Audrey Osler**
**Buskerud University College, Norway**
**and University of Leeds, U.K.**

## INTRODUCTION

In our global age, we need tools that will support educational research and development which can be applied in a range of contexts: local, cultural, national and international. Within the human rights framework the concept of intersectionality is implicit. Here, I aim to make this implicitness explicit. The chapter considers strengths and potential limitations of the human rights framework for education research and practice, addressing, in particular, questions of universality and recognition, questions central to debates about intersectionality.

Avtar Brah and Ann Phoenix understand the concept of intersectionality as:

> signifying the complex, irreducible, varied, and variable effects which ensue when multiple axis of differentiation—economic, political, cultural, psychic, subjective and experiential—intersect *in historically specific contexts*. The concept

*Intersectionality and Urban Education*, pages 249–265
Copyright © 2014 by Information Age Publishing
All rights of reproduction in any form reserved.

emphasizes that different dimensions of social life cannot be separated out into discrete and pure strands. (Brah & Phoenix, 2004, p. 76, my emphasis)

In this chapter, I explore the possibilities offered by combining the concepts of intersectionality and human rights to provide a framework to analyse and enable social justice in and through education, focusing on concepts, language and legal frameworks. Recognising that the concepts of human rights, child rights and human rights education are infrequently discussed outside the specialist literature, I begin by focusing on human rights, identities and education, noting the over-nationalistic focus of many school curricula and problems arising from this. I then examine rights, educational scholarship and multiculturalism in the United States and Europe, exploring some similar and some divergent trends. It would appear that in both contexts the complexity of the issues involved and the wide range of identity questions require a framework of analysis which is both comprehensive and sensitive to the interplay of these various factors.

Before examining together the concepts of intersectionality and human rights and ways in which they may enhance our analysis of injustice or inform struggles for justice, I recount my own epistemological journey towards human rights. I do this not only for its own sake—so as to situate my thinking within the context of my own experiences—but because I conclude the chapter by exploring the potential of narrative to bridge the two concepts of human rights and intersectionality both in education research and practice. My own story outlines my steps towards this.

## Human Rights, Identities and Education

Since 1948 and the signing of the Universal Declaration of Human Rights, the international human rights project has accorded a central place to education as a means of enabling the full realisation of these rights to the world's people. From 2011, with the signing of the U.N. Declaration on Human Rights Education and Training (U.N., 2011), the international community has a working definition of human rights education (HRE), which we can consider a minimal entitlement for all:

> Human rights education and training comprises all educational, training, information, awareness-raising and learning activities aimed at promoting universal respect for and observance of all human rights and fundamental freedoms and thus contributing, inter alia, to the prevention of human rights violations and abuses by providing persons with knowledge, skills and understanding and developing their attitudes and behaviours, to empower them to contribute to the building and promotion of a universal culture of human rights. (U.N., 2011: Article 2:1)

Article 2.2 goes on to explain that HRE encompasses education *about* human rights, education *through* human rights, and education *for* human rights. The school is an important arena in which children and young people can learn *about* human rights, including their own rights and their role in defending the rights of others. Education about rights includes knowledge and understanding of human rights norms and principles, the values that underpin them and the mechanisms for their protection.

Human rights education is essential in supporting learners in understanding their role in shaping their communities and the wider world and in understanding that solidarity across difference is essential both in struggles for justice and for the protection of democratic thinking and democratic living. This can be characterised as education *for* human rights.

The 1989 U.N. Convention on the Rights of the Child confirms the right, not just to education, but to *human rights education* (Osler & Starkey, 1996; 2010). It has been universally signed and almost universally ratified, the two exceptions being Somalia and the United States. Significantly, as Sleeter has observed:

> human rights frameworks are rarely studied in US schools. As a result, among the general public there is little awareness of the U.N. Convention on the Rights of the Child, and even less awareness of the failure of the U.S. to endorse it. Even teachers generally do not know about the struggle for children's human rights. (Sleeter, 2013, p. viii)

Consequently, many of the struggles in the United States for equitable schooling, including struggles for multicultural curricula and 'culturally responsive' (Gay, 2010) or 'culturally relevant' teaching (Ladson Billings, 1995) have taken place on a local or national stage with little awareness of how international human rights standards might support these struggles or indeed of parallel struggles elsewhere for equal access for all to quality schooling. Thus, the concept of solidarity with other struggles for justice in education, as well as opportunities to identify allies elsewhere in the world, has sometimes been overlooked. A key defining element of quality education is one where students' rights are guaranteed. In other words, a quality education is where students are educated *through* human rights.

In the public school, learners interact with others outside their immediate family and friendship groups, encountering those whose identities, experiences and values may be different from their own. All learners have a range of identities, actual and potential. Schools are places in which students learn to live together with others, encountering others' identities and becoming aware of their own identities. Just as intersectionality provides a tool for theorising, researching, and applying research which acknowledges multiple and complex identities in education, so human rights provide a framework of analysis which is premised on intersectionality, and on the equal dignity of all human subjects, by virtue of their humanity. The human rights framework can support analysis and serve as a tool to enable social justice in education. In school, students learn to live together with others, encountering others' identities and becoming aware of their own identities. A critical approach to learning involves opening up and extending the learner's range of potential identities, rather than focusing exclusively on one identity. Regretfully, schools often promote a singular sense of national identity through their programmes of citizenship education, social studies and history (Reid et al., 2009) which may serve to mask or deny other identities. Such programmes may consequently have a negative impact on learners, particularly those from minority groups, whose histories and experiences are underplayed or misrepresented in the dominant national narrative. Likewise, those learners who are not citizens of the nation-state in which they are being educated, and who may not aspire to such citizenship, may find such programmes exclusive or irrelevant. Similarly, schools with a religious ethos or foundation which emphasise a specific religious identity and belonging, while overlooking other aspects students' identities, may fail to create an inclusive environment (Berkeley, 2008).

Education programmes which are underpinned by human rights, assume a common standing point of our shared humanity; our humanity is the status against which rights are claimed, rather than national citizenship. Such programmes have the capacity to be inclusive of all learners. Equally importantly, entitlement to rights as a human subject, rather than as a citizen of a particular nation-state, allows the educator to focus on the rights-holder as an individual with a range of identities, rather than as a citizen of a specific nation state, thereby opening up the possibilities both for a cosmopolitan worldview in which rights are not dependent on nationality[1] and an analysis premised on intersectionality in which these complex identities are acknowledged.

In our global and transnational age, schools need to draw on principles which are inclusive of all students and which promote cosmopolitan, rather than exclusive national identifications. In her book, *Flexible Citizenship* Aihwa Ong explores 'the condition of cultural interconnectedness or mobility across space' (1999, p. 4) in a global context in which there is, for many, a disjuncture between state-imposed identity (nationality) and the individual's personal identities. This disjuncture may have various causes, including political upheavals, migration and changing global markets and employment opportunities.

What degree of loyalty can the nation-state demand of its citizens? Parekh (2000, pp. 341–342) suggests that it is not essential that citizens share:

> common substantive goals, for its members might deeply disagree about these, nor a common view of history which they may read differently, nor a

particular economic or social system about which they might entertain different views.

Rather, Parekh sees this commitment or loyalty as including, minimally, commitment the state's 'continuing existence and well-being' which *'implies that one cares enough for it not to harm its interests and undermine its integrity'.* This political commitment to the nation-state (which Parekh recognises as patriotism) will be felt differently by different individuals and may range from 'quiet concern' to 'intense love'.

If we accept Parekh's understanding of political loyalty, then it is not incumbent on schools to foster uncritical patriotism, or to teach a hegemonic mainstream version of national history. As Parekh points out, political loyalty and criticism (of prevailing forms of government, institutions, policies, values, and so on) are compatible, so long as individuals do not undermine the integrity of the political entity and remain open to dialogue. Social cohesion is maintained not by shared culture or a shared version of the national story, but by a shared commitment to agreed human rights principles, which are applied and interpreted through a process of dialogue.

Human rights are necessarily cosmopolitan rather than national in their conception. Human rights appeal to and depend on human solidarity across borders, whether these be national, ethnic, religious or whatever. In struggles for justice, an individual who experiences a violation of their rights cannot always depend on the immediate community or on immediate neighbours. This was recognised by U.S. civil rights leader Malcolm X, when towards the end of his life he argued that the term human rights should replace civil rights, since then 'anybody, anywhere on this earth can become your ally' (1965, in Clark, 1992, p. 175). He wrote (1964): 'We can never get civil rights in America until our human rights are first restored. We will never be recognised as citizens there until we are first recognized as humans'. He made this claim at the climax of the civil rights struggle just a few weeks after the Civil Rights Act was passed, which enforced the constitutional right to vote, and prohibited discrimination in public facilities including education, in government, and in employment. Human rights provide a framework for research, analysis and action within which intersectionality is assumed. As Malcolm X recognised, human rights do not privilege one primary identity, other than our common humanity, implicitly acknowledging that other identities are multiple and flexible, changing according to context, as oppressed groups engage in struggles for justice and form alliances in those struggles.

Malcolm X recognized the power of human rights in enabling global solidarity for justice. The concept of human solidarity is fundamental to the human rights project. So the claim often levelled against the concept of human rights, that they are individualistic, is inaccurate. While it is generally true that individuals are rights-holders, human rights can only be exercised in community and can only be guaranteed through human solidarity.

## Rights and Educational Scholarship in Multicultural Contexts

In the United States, contemporary manifestations of multicultural education can be traced back to the civil rights movement of the 1960s and 1970s, a period in which African Americans struggled for fundamental change in U.S. society and particularly for rights and recognition. The concept of rights is often perceived, first and foremost, to be a legal one. Rights are secured through constitutional and legal frameworks and any struggle for equal rights and dignity implies structural change. Yet, legal and structural guarantees, although essential, are rarely sufficient to overcome deepseated inequalities and historical disadvantage. The struggle for rights and recognition also implies cultural change, and this, in turn, implies an educational project. Education has a key role to play in creating such a culture whereby human rights violations are not simply addressed through legal mechanisms but are prevented.

For those struggling for civil rights in the 1960s and 1970s, many demands focused on equal access to education in the nation's schools, colleges and universities. The legacy of this can be seen today in the emphasis attached within the field of scholarship of multicultural education to combatting inequalities in educational outcomes through a focus on access and achievement.

In other regions of the globe, and notably in Europe, multicultural education, or what is more commonly referred to as intercultural education, has tended to focus more on creating inclusive societies through critical examination of identities (including national identities) and strategies to support the integration of immigrant and minority youth (Gobbo, 2011). In contrast to other European nation-states, multicultural education in the United Kingdom tended, as a result of pressure from the late 1960s from minorities—initially from African Caribbean communities—to address the problem of racism and to focus on the educational outcomes of minority students (Figueroa, 2004), more so than in other European countries. Indeed Figueroa (2004) notes the impact of visits by U.S. civil rights leaders, Martin Luther King and Malcolm X on grassroots movements to promote multicultural education, develop supplementary schools and challenge racism within education services. Yet, by the first decade of the twenty-first century, there was no official multicultural policy initiative in the United Kingdom (Tomlinson, 2009).

Official education policies across Europe, both at national and international levels, during the late twentieth century and first decade of the twenty-first, continue to give higher priority to the *integration* of minorities, than to equitable educational outcomes. In practice, although mainstream society, as in the United Kingdom, may see changes in food habits, musical tastes and fashion, influenced by migrant and minority ethnic groups, integration is, in both policy and practice, understood as a one-way process, with considerably greater official emphasis placed on educational measures for the social integration of minorities, rather than extending levels of understanding and openness of mainstream learners, or explicitly combatting racism, discrimination and intolerance. Effectively, this one-way integration process, which is rarely matched by positive action for the economic or political integration of minorities, may be in many cases be one of assimilation.

While Banks (Banks & Banks, 2004; Banks, 2009) suggests a broad consensus among multicultural education theorists about the nature, aims and scope of the field internationally, he also recognises its contested nature. In the seventh edition of *Multicultural Education: issues and perspectives* (Banks & Banks, 2010) the editors acknowledge the expansion of the dimensions of multicultural education, notably with the addition of new chapters on the intersection of race and gender in the processes of marginalisation (Henry, 2010) and on sexual and gender minorities (Mayo, 2010). Grant and Zwier (2011), also presenting a north American perspective, report on efforts within the National Association for Multicultural Education (NAME) to centre intersectionality as a frame for research and practice in education, discussing the contentions and concerns this initiative has provoked.

While a number of European scholars, notably minoritised feminist scholars (for example, Bhopal, 1998; Brah & Phoenix, 2004), are embracing intersectionality in their scholarship, issues of gender, class and heterosexism are marginal or absent in the way multicultural/ intercultural education tends to be framed in Europe, with such interlocking issues rarely explored together in policy documents and only infrequently addressed in scholarship. Work on students' perspectives (Archer, 2003; Osler, 2010) and the shaping of students' multiple and flexible identities through the processes on schooling, as well as learners' contributions to a wider social justice project, is one notable exception. Another exception is Zembylas' (2010) complementary work on mainstream teachers' constructions of their own and their students' identities in the Republic of Cyprus, with some teachers reproducing racist, ethnonationalist and class-based discourses and others attempting to challenge injustices and inequalities through their everyday practices.

Discrimination related to religion has been central to debates surrounding intercultural education and citizenship education in Europe during the first two decades of the twenty-first century, not least because of the prevalence of anti-Muslim and anti-Semitic discourses (Osler, 2009). Issues of ability/disability are addressed to some degree as part of a separate educational discourse of 'inclusion'.

Educational scholarship addressing education in multicultural contexts has taken place within a broader European political context often hostile to the concept of multiculturalism. Senior European political figures, including French President Nicolas Sarkozy, German Chancellor Angela Merkel, and U.K. Prime Minister David Cameron have attacked multiculturalism (Council of Europe, 2011). Cameron claimed 'state multiculturalism' undermines community, while Merkel asserted multiculturalism has 'failed utterly' and that Germans and foreign workers cannot 'live happily side by side' (Osler, 2012). Ironically, neither Germany nor France has ever aspired to multiculturalism, nor has Britain ever developed comprehensive multicultural policies or 'multicultural citizenship' (Kymlicka, 1996).[2] What has not been tried cannot be said to have failed. Significantly, these European leaders are criticised for 'reacting in a defensive and unimaginative way' to the challenges of the twenty-first century, instead of confronting and challenging populism and extremism (Council of Europe, 2011).[3]

It can be seen that the complexity of issues impacting on national and international struggles for justice in education—legal, constitutional, social and political-, together with a complex interplay of identity questions, relating to race and ethnicity, gender, sexuality, religious, and other factors, require a framework of analysis which is both comprehensive and sensitive to the interplay of these various factors. Before discussing the concept of intersectionality and the contribution which human rights might make to intersectionality as a framework for analysis, I wish to turn briefly to a personal narrative which both contextualises and informs my thinking.

## An Epistemological Journey towards Human Rights

It was during the 1980s that I was first introduced to human rights as a framework for practice when working as an advisory teacher within a team responsible for supporting teachers in developing multicultural and anti-racist perspectives in schools in Birmingham UK, a large and diverse urban school district. At this time the national political climate was not conducive to our work, with the government of the day and then Prime Minister Margaret Thatcher expressing criticism of anti-racist initiatives in education, supported by a media campaign also hostile to such initiatives (Murray, 1986).

Interestingly, I first learned about human rights education (HRE) not in the United Kingdom but through attending a teachers' seminar in Denmark in autumn 1985, with the support of the Council of Europe. This was my first international conference and I was shocked to discover a number of Danish colleagues pitying me for living and working in a multicultural environment. They linked the riots which had taken place that autumn in Birmingham directly to the presence of visible minorities, rather than to complex problems of poverty, discrimination and inequality. Their ideal society was one of homogeneity; a multicultural society was, within this framework of analysis, one which deviated from the norm.

Nevertheless, from this conference which introduced me to HRE, I saw the possibilities in 'rebranding' much of the anti-racist work we were doing with teachers as human rights education. After all, it seemed that the U.K. government, which was overtly critical of anti-racism, would not declare itself in opposition to human rights or HRE. So my initial engagement with HRE was strategic.

At this stage I did not explore the potential of human rights as a framework for addressing a broad range of inter-locking dimensions of injustice in education practice, but through my own experiences and those of the young people with whom I had worked, I was conscious of the need for a gender dimension to our anti-racist practice.

One of the challenges facing the team of advisory teachers to which I belonged was dealing with the guilt generated among some White teachers when facing up to racism in schools and society. Another was the differential experiences of team members in working with schools and school leaders, often dependent on the identity of the advisory teacher concerned and whether s/he was from a visible minority group. The concept of solidarity, fundamental to the human rights project, helped me to recognise the ways in which all team members could contribute to the struggle for justice in education, regardless of ethnicity or identity. It was also an empowering concept for mainstream White teachers who wanted to promote greater justice through education.

These experiences informed and help shape my research when five years later I embarked on doctoral studies and an academic career. My doctoral project, examining the lives and careers of teachers from visible minority communities, produced rich data which necessarily required me to engage in an analysis which examined interlocking issues of race, ethnicity, gender and religion (Osler, 1997). At the very time my work was published Patricia Williams was giving the BBC Reith lectures: *The Genealogy of Race* (Williams, 1997). The stories that she told to highlight the complex ways in which race and racism impacted on life in the United Kingdom as well as in the United States were liberating, not simply because of her insights into U.K. society, but because these stories allowed her to discuss everyday realities which are infrequently aired in mainstream U.K. media. The lectures and stories within them confirm that the realities of race and racist oppression are not something separate from the everyday workings of society.

As Williams' scholarship makes clear, we are not only the sum of our various identities, juggling these in the face of inequality, but are shaped by and bound together and influenced by the structures, institutions and the wider society in which we study, work and live our lives. Her stories underline how the various forces of inequality combine to continuously change and re-form their outward shapes, even as we seek to make sense of these same lives. And so, I looked afresh at the life stories of the teachers in my study (Osler, 1997) and understood afresh how powerful these remain and how potent narrative can be as a tool both for exposing injustice, and perhaps more importantly, the lessons to be learned through struggles for justice.

Our analysis should not simply address the various identities we adopt, related to gender, sexuality profession and so on, but must necessarily explore how institutions and policy work to impact on those various identities. In the United Kingdom in the 1990s and beyond, the White mainstream was equated with normalcy. Similarly, the notion of demographic homogeneity was also associated with normalcy, and multicultural communities seen as exceptional, or peculiar to specific cities. In academia, visible minorities had some space to research minorities, but those studies which critiqued mainstream society, its structures, and institutions were vulnerable to criticisms of bias.

This attitude persists in academia, as I found when in 2007 I attended a symposium of renowned French sociologists meeting to debate racism in French society. It was striking that all present were White, something unimaginable in Britain in a meeting focusing on race. Remarking on this to a colleague, he expressed a degree of surprise. In his opinion, it would be difficult for non-White French academics to research race, since their research would inevitably be seen as biased. So the French principle of colour-blindness is clearly applied selectively (Osler, 2010).

Today, part of my working life is in Norway, where the concepts of equality, tolerance, democracy and respect for human rights are internalised and accepted as part of the national identity, yet where racial exclusion was part of the historical process of nation-building. The concepts of race and racism are still infrequently discussed in academe. Gullestad (2004, p. 184) suggests that conversations about racism are viewed as upsetting 'the innocent national self-image' crafted in the post-World War Two era.

## Intersectionality, Struggle and Human Rights

Drawing on the work and words of Sojourner Truth and other political campaigners struggling for justice and recognition, Brah and Phoenix (2004, p. 77) show how 'identities are 'processes constituted in and through power relations' involving complexity and multiplicity.

The modern human rights project, dating from the mid-twentieth century and the 1948 Universal Declaration of Human Rights (UDHR), is based on a concept of rights not restricted to citizens and guaranteed by national governments but a universal entitlement to all human beings, regardless of citizenship or other status. The UDHR sets out a vision. Its preamble claims that universal respect for human rights constitutes 'the foundation of freedom, justice and peace in the world'. This vision or promise is a utopia, something which is envisioned but does not yet exist. This utopian project drew its inspiration from a desire to overcome and prevent recurrences of the inhumanity and gross injustices of the Second World War.

Yet, the UDHR also recognised how a previous concept of rights tied to national citizenship and accorded by the nation-state was inadequate, not least because war, crisis, migration and displacement leave many living in nation-states where they lack citizenship rights and are thus unprotected.

Not all citizens of mid-twentieth century democracies were equally protected, with clear legal inequalities existing at the time in many contexts between the rights of women and men and according to race and ethnicity. These inequalities were reinforced by racist and patriarchal cultures as well as by legal frameworks. Thus the UDHR proclaimed and envisioned *universal* rights but the human rights project relied on subsequent use of human rights instruments as tools to realise these rights in what has proved to be an on-going struggle. The whole project depends on education and awareness-raising. In practice, a right is only a right if people know about it *and* if they are prepared to struggle for it.

## Universality

Although the concept of cosmopolitanism and understandings of the universal have been very influential in early twenty-first century discourses relating to multicultural, international and human rights education, it has been argued that, in practice, the enlightenment principles which inform the modern human rights project have sometimes functioned to standardise culture though education at the expense of cultural difference (Foucault, 1995; Popkewitz, 2007). Some feminist and post-colonialist scholars have also challenged the notion of the universal, by seeking to illustrate how discourses promoted by the powerful often serve to regulate the knowledge and values of the colonised (Mohanty, 1984; Spivak, 1999). Together, these critiques serve to remind us of asymmetrical power relations which need to be considered in any analysis and in curricula addressing human rights, cultural diversity, justice and injustice. There is the risk that human rights, designed to be liberating, can in turn become part of a hegemonic discourse, used to control, if rights and principles are applied without dialogue and without consideration of people's actual experiences. As a starting point, human rights offer a set of procedural principles in which dialogue can take place.

## Recognition

The preamble of the UDHR opens with the concept of recognition: 'recognition of the inherent dignity and of the equal and inalienable rights of all members of the human family'. The concept of recognition of equal and inherent dignity and equal and inalienable rights is fundamental to the human rights project. Article 6 states that 'Everyone has the right to recognition everywhere as a person before the law' and Article 7 affirms this equal recognition extends to equality before the law and protection under the law against discrimination.

While the UDHR and subsequent human rights instruments set a framework for policy development and legal frameworks designed to guarantee the rights of individuals and conditions for social justice, the project of social justice is itself an on-going struggle since these legal frameworks, as Habermas (1996) points out, are often in tension with shifting societal norms. So, for example, following the ratification of the CRC by the UK, and its entry into force in 1992, various legal steps have been taken to guarantee children and young people under the age of 18 the right to be consulted in decision-making processes which affect them, in keeping with Article 12. Nevertheless, education law in England has traditionally accorded rights to parents, and assumed children's interests are protected through such parental rights and this principle remains. When children's rights in education are in tension with those of their parents, children may have no legal recourse open to them.

When children enter schools they do so in specific global locations and with specific positionings in histories which privilege or repress their voices. Their identities, including ascribed identities, are related to their lived experiences. An ascribed identity is not chosen by the individual, but designated, often by powerful others. In the context of schooling, students may be ascribed an identity by teachers or education policy-makers. Today in Norway, for example, certain schools and children are labelled 'multicultural'. This identity is ascribed to children from visible minorities, generally by White mainstream teachers, and extended to many of the schools they attend. Children whose parents have both migrated to Norway from non-Nordic countries are officially counted as 'immigrant'. To the individual child the label 'multicultural' is meaningless, and that of 'immigrant' serves to position a person as 'Other'. Such ascribed identities are pernicious because they misrepresent and threaten to obscure actual identities. Needless to say, they are applied under conditions where power differentials are overlooked. An ascribed identity is one which may, in certain circumtances, effectively dehumanize the other.

According to Bhabba (2003, 2004) and Butler (2006) a postmodern ethics permits us to address the power struggles and asymmetrical power relations in which histories and identities are given recognition. The modern human rights project grew out of a periods of war and atrocities characterized by processes of dehumanization. Recognition of equal human dignity is, as we have seen, essential to that project. Butler's analysis is in keeping with this: her starting point is that violence stems from processes of dehumanization and lack of recognition. She repeatedly points to ways in which representation and misrepresentation can be a form of violence.

Bhabba (2003, pp. 180–181) emphases the importance of 'the right to narrate', offering some pointers to those wishing to decolonize school curricula and policy so as allow learners to find their own places and their own identities within an inclusive collective history:

> To protect the 'right to narrate' is to protect a range of democratic imperatives: it assumes there is an equitable access to those institutions—schools, universities, museums, libraries , theatres—that give you a sense of a collective history and the means to turn those materials into a narrative of your own.

He asserts that such 'such an assured, empowered sense of 'selfhood' depends on a public culture in which the rights-holder is confident his or her story will be heard and acted upon. This, he asserts, depends in turn on our guardianship or protection of 'the right to take part in cultural life' (Convention on Economic, Social and Political Rights, Article 5). Bhabba's 'right to narrate' is part of a global ethic which challenges and interrogates systems which create hegemonic narratives and which silence marginal voices. His understanding of culture is dynamic and he calls on us to recognise each human being and their complex identities within a historically specific context and ever-dynamic power relations. Thus the recognition which he proposes is one which humanizes, rather than dehumanizes. The form of education or curriculum which might follow from this must necessarily include opportunities to explore and reflect on various identities and cultural attributes; and create personal narratives and processes of self-learning. Effectively, it needs to allow learners to develop new collective narratives through which they can together make sense of the world (Osler, 2011).

## Linking Intersectionality and Human Rights Frameworks to Enable Justice

I have sought to argue that just as the concept of intersectionality is used by scholars to inform research analysing and addressing how multiple axes of differentiation and discrimination intersect—not privileging one axis or one identity over others in this analysis—so the human rights framework offers a way of seeing the world (and education) which does not privilege any one identity but which stresses our common humanity. Both are tools in a struggle for greater social justice. That struggle encompasses both research and action for change.

Human rights have an added dimension in this struggle since they are necessarily cosmopolitan rather than national in their conception, enabling those engaged in struggle in one context to unite in solidarity with others to support their cause. This has been recognised by oppressed groups in many different settings. This chapter highlighted the civil rights struggle in the U.S., but other struggles, including that of the African National Congress struggling against Apartheid in South Africa and those calling today for a Kurdish homeland also draw on a human rights discourse to achieve support and solidarity for their cause. It is this cosmopolitan vision which gives human rights such potency.

Human rights provide a broad perspective for multicultural learning, opportunities to promote solidarity beyond national boundaries, and one which is inclusive of a range of identities. Human rights avoid a singular exclusive focus on the nation which is a recurrent (and often exclusive) element of most citizenship curricula.

The international human rights project is relatively new—little more than 60 years—and thus is a project in progress and subject to further development. It is important to remember that the concept of universality, that human rights are due to all persons as human beings, does not necessarily imply universalising processes. Human rights are the minimal requirements on how we should treat and be treated by each other. They can acknowledge commonality as well as difference, but do not imply cultural sameness. Human rights discourses need to be open to critique, so that universalist discourses do not disguise or obscure power differentials but take into consideration asymmetrical power relations and the interpretation of human rights principles in different social and cultural settings.

Finally, although human rights incorporate the concept of recognition, specifically recognition of our equal dignity and recognition before the law, the concept of recognition in human rights discourse as it currently stands may present a potential limitation in education. The international human rights project was initiated in response to gross inhumanity and dehumanisation processes. Lack of recognition and misrepresentation are dehumanising experiences. If we see human rights as a set of minimum standards, then they can be extended to incorporate a broader concept of recognition.

Bhabba's identification of 'the right to narrate' is particularly important in the context of education, where hegemonic curricula have long served to exclude and misrepresent minoritised students. It opens up a space for students to shape their own identities within inclusive collective histories. A right to human rights education must necessarily incorporate rights in education, and this includes equitable access to quality schooling and to other education resources. By linking the concepts of human rights, intersectionality and recognition we move closer to guaranteeing social justice in education in diverse educational settings.

## NOTES

1. The European Convention on Human Rights offers protection to all those living within the 47 countries which are member-states of the Council of Europe, including those who are nationals of those member-states, those who hold national citizenship elsewhere in the world, and those who may be stateless.
2. For decades Germany denied citizenship to 'guest-workers', on the premise that German citizenship could only be acquired through bloodlines. Britain has had piecemeal multicultural polices, for example, in education, dependant on the commitment of specific local authorities (Figueroa, 2004; Tomlinson, 2009; Osler, 2011).
3. These comments are especially noteworthy since they are expressed in a publication by the Council of Europe, a respected international body, and are direct criticisms of leaders of Council of Europe member-states.

## REFERENCES

Archer, L. (2003). *Race, masculinity, and schooling: Muslim boys and education*. Maidenhead, UK: Open University Press.

Banks, J. A. (2009) *The Routledge international companion to multicultural education*. Routeldge: New York and Routledge.

Banks, J. A., & Banks, C. A. M. (2004). *Handbook of research on multicultural education* (2nd ed.). Jossey Bass: San Francisco.

Banks, J. A., & Banks, C. A. M. (2010). *Multicultural education: Issues and perspectives* (7th ed.). Wiley: Holboken, NJ.

Berkeley, R. (2008). *Right to divide? Faith schools and community cohesion*. London: Runnymede Trust.

Bhabba, H. J. (2003). On writing rights. In M. Gibney (Ed.), *Globalizing rights: The Oxford amnesty lectures* (pp. 162–183). Oxford; Oxford University Press.

Bhabba, H. J. (2004). *The location of culture*. (2nd ed.). New York: Routledge.

Bhopal, K. (1998). South Asian women in east London: Religious experience and diversity, *Journal of Gender Studies*, 7(2), 143–156.

Brah, A., & Phoenix, A. (2004). Ain't I a woman? Re-visiting intersectionality, *Journal of International Women's Studies*, 5(3), 75–86.

Butler, J. (2006). *Precarious life: The powers of mourning and violence*. New York: Verso.

Clark, S. (1992). (Ed.). *Malcolm X 1965: The final speeches*. Pathfinder: New York.

Council of Europe (2011). *Living together: Combining diversity and freedom in 21st-century Europe*. Report of the Group of Eminent Persons of the Council of Europe (Strasbourg, Council of Europe).

Figueroa, P. (2004). Multicultural education in the United Kingdom: Historical development and current status. In J. A. Banks & C. A. M. Banks (Eds.), *Handbook of research on multicultural education* (2nd ed., pp. 997–1026). Jossey Bass: San Francisco.

Foucault, M. (1995). *Discipline and punishment: The birth of the prison*. New York: Vintage Books.

Gay, G. (2010). *Culturally responsive teaching: Theory, research, and practice* (3rd ed.). New York: Teachers College Press.

Gullestad, M. (2004). Blind slaves of our prejudices: Debating 'culture' and 'race' in Norway. *Ethnos: Journal of Anthropology, 69*(2), 177–203.

Grant, C. A., & Zwier, E. (2011). Intersectionality and student outcomes: Sharpening the struggle against racism, sexism, classism, ableism, heterosexism, nationalism, and linguistic, religious, and geographical discrimination in teaching and learning, *Multicultural Perspectives, 13*(4), 181–188.

Gobbo, F. (2011). Intercultural education and intercultural learning in Europe. In J. A. Banks (Ed.), *Encyclopedia of diversity in education* (vol. 2, pp. 1217–1220). Sage: Los Angeles and London.

Habermas, J. (1996). Struggles for recognition in the democratic constitutional state. In C. Taylor & A. Gutmann (Eds.), *Multiculturalism: Examining the politics of recognition* (pp. 107–148). Princeton, NJ: Princeton University Press.

Henry A. (2010). Race and gender in classrooms: implications for teachers. In J. A. Banks & C. A. M. Banks (2010). *Multicultural education: Issues and perspectives* (7th ed., pp. 183–207). Wiley: Holboken, NJ.

Kymlicka, W. (1996). *Multicultural citizenship: A liberal theory of minority rights.* Oxford: Oxford University Press.

Ladson-Billings, G. (1995). But that's just good teaching! The case for culturally relevant pedagogy. *Theory into Practice, 34*(3), 159–165.

Malcolm X (1964). 'Racism: The cancer that is destroying America,' *Egyptian Gazette,* 25 August 1964. http://www.heroism.org/class/1960/CivilUnrest.htm Accessed 4 February 2013

Mayo, C. (2010). Queer lessons: Sexual and gender minorities in multicultural education. In J. A. Banks & C. A. M. Banks (2010). *Multicultural education: Issues and perspectives* (7th ed., pp. 209–227). Wiley: Holboken, NJ.

Mohanty, C. T. (1984). Under western eyes: Feminist scholarship and colonial discourses. *Boundary,* 12/13 3/1: 333–358.

Murray, N. (1986). Anti-racists and other demons: The press and ideology in Thatcher's Britain, *Race and Class 27*(3), 1–19.

Ong, A. (1999). *Flexible citizenship: The cultural logics of transnationality.* Duke University Press.

Osler, A. (1997). *The education and careers of Black teachers: Changing identities, changing lives.* Open University Press: Buckingham.

Osler, A. (2009). Patriotism, multiculturalism and belonging: Political discourse and the teaching of history. *Educational Review, 61*(1), 85–100.

Osler, A. (2010). École: l'égalité raciale peut-elle être inspectée? *Migrations Societé* Action public et discrimination ethnique, *22*(131) septembre–octobre, pp. 185–200.

Osler, A. (2011). Education policy, social cohesion and citizenship. In I. Newman & P. Ratcliffe (Eds.), *Promoting social cohesion: Implications for policy and frameworks for evaluation* (pp. 185–205). Bristol, UK and Portland, OR: Policy Press.

Osler, A. (2012). Higher education, human rights and inclusive citizenship. In T. Basit & S. Tomlinson (Eds), *Higher education and social inclusion.* Bristol, UK: Policy Press.

Osler, A., & Starkey, H. (1996). *Teacher education and human rights.* London: David Fulton.

Osler, A., & Starkey, H. (2010). *Teachers and human rights education.* Stoke-on-Trent, UK: Trentham.

Parekh, B. (2000). *Rethinking multiculturalism: Cultural diversity and political theory.* London: Macmillan.

Popkewitz, T. S. (2007). *Cosmopolitanism and the age of school reform: Science, education and making society by making the child.* New York: Routledge.

Reid, A., Gill, J., & Sears, A. (2009). (Eds.). *Globalisation, the nation-state and the citizen: Dilemmas and directions for civics and citizenship education.* New York and London: Routledge.

Sleeter, C. (2013). Foreword. In J. Hall (Ed.), *Children's human rights and public schooling in the United States.* Sense Publishers: Rotterdam.

Spivak, G. C. (1999). *A critique of postcolonial reasons: Towards a history of the vanishing present.* Cambridge, MA: Harvard University Press.

Tomlinson, S. (2009). Multicultural education in the United Kingdom. In J. A. Banks (Ed.), *The Routledge international companion to multicultural education* (pp. 121–133). Routledge: New York and Abingdon, UK.

United Nations (1948). *Universal declaration of human rights.* New York and Geneva: United Nations. http://www.un.org/en/documents/udhr/index.shtml

United Nations (1989). *UN convention on the right of the child.* New York and Geneva: United Nations. http://www.ohchr.org/EN/ProfessionalInterest/Pages/CRC.aspx

United Nations (2011). *UN declaration on human rights education and training.* http://www2.ohchr.org/english/issues/education/training/UNDHREducation-Training.htm

Williams, P. J. (1997). *Seeing a color-blind future: The paradox of race.* London: Virago.

Zembylas, M. (2010): Greek-Cypriot teachers' constructions of Turkish-speaking children's identities: critical race theory and education in a conflict ridden society, *Ethnic and Racial Studies, 33*(8), 1372–1391.

CHAPTER 13

# PLACE, CULTURE, AND GENDER IN INTERCULTURAL AND BILINGUAL EDUCATION PRACTICES IN A CHUJ MAYA TOWN

**Alexandra Allweiss**
*University of Wisconsin, Madison*

*"Soy maya, soy indígena; me identifico para que me respeten."/* "I am Maya, I am indigenous; I identify myself, so that they respect me," my friend and fellow educator said to me as we sat in his office discussing his thoughts on education in his community, Xantin. This conversation took place in the context of Guatemala's current Intercultural and Bilingual Education (IBE) reforms, whose stated goal is to promote greater equality throughout the country and among its diverse ethnic, linguistic, cultural, and gender groups. He continued to layout the tensions Chuj Maya students experience in formal schooling. These themes and tensions were repeated in similar ways across my conversations with Chuj educators.

*Intersectionality and Urban Education*, pages 267–291
Copyright © 2014 by Information Age Publishing
All rights of reproduction in any form reserved.

*Para mí la educación que se está dando no está ayudando a fortalecer a la persona porque el niño o la niña tiene su propia identidad, su propia cultura, su propia forma de ser, pero en la escuela esto se rompe...se rompe porque en la escuela te enseñan otra cultura... Hay maestros que [dicen], "debes aprender esto porque esta [la cultura ladina] es la buena cultura, la mejor cultura y así vas a desarrollar.".... [T]e dicen que este es el mejor, pero te das cuenta que no es así... Cuando te entras con el otro grupo se dan cuenta de que [su cultura] no es lo tuyo, no entendes también eso. Entonces al final te quedas al medio camino. Te quedas casi sin identidad... si digo "ya no soy bueno yo no soy indígena sino que ya soy ladino." Después se dan cuenta aquellos, "no sos ladino, sos indígena." Y cuando vienes en tu otro grupo, "vos ya te fuiste con aquellos." Entonces ese es el proceso que sufre el niño después por falta de identidad... si no tienes identidad no puedes desarrollarte. Y ¿al fin dónde vas a estar? Para nosotros sin identidad es como estar perdido, estar en la montaña saber dónde veniste, dónde vas o qué haces.*

For me the education that is being given is not helping strengthen the person because the boy or the girl has his/her own identity, culture, way of being, but in school that is broken... it is broken because in the school you are taught another culture... There are teachers [that say], "you should learn this because this [Ladino culture] is the good culture, the best culture and this way you will be able to develop." ... [T]hey tell you that this is the best, but you realize it that's not how it is... When you go with the other group they realize that [their culture] is not yours, you don't understand it. So in the end you are left in the middle of the road. You are left almost without identity... if I say, "I am not good, I am not indigenous anymore, rather now I am Ladino." Later they realize, "you are not Ladino, you are indigenous." And when you come back to your group, "you already went with them." So that is the process by which the child suffers later from a lack of identity... if you don't have identity you can't develop. And in the end where will you be? For those of us without identity it's like being lost in a mountain without knowing where you came from, where you are going or what you are doing.

## Xantin: The History of a Sacred Place

seeks to examine the ways student- teachers, teachers, principals and community leaders in Xantin enact and make sense of education in the community within the context national Intercultural and Bilingual Education (IBE) educational reforms. Based on ethnographic research methods, this chapter shows how educators use nuanced intersectional understandings of place, culture and gender to inform and make sense of their practice in ways that build on and push back against the educational policy frameworks and national curriculum.

This chapter focuses on Xantin (all names of places and people are pseudonyms), Guatemala. Xantin is a semi-urban Chuj Maya town situated high in the mountains of Guatemala. It is the *cabecera municipal* (municipal center) of the municipality, which is home to seventy small, remote *aldeas* (villages) and has a population of over 38,000 (FUNCEDE, 2011). This research focuses on the experiences and views of those living in the *cabecera* and the schools that they attend. The *cabecera* is home to an estimated 7,000 to 10,000 inhabitants, the majority of whom (an estimated 98 to 99%) identify as Chuj, a "minority" Maya linguistic group (the 9th largest in Guatemala). The rest identify as Ladino[2]. Some teachers and students come from nearby municipalities to study and work; the teachers from other municipalities most often identify as Ladino and the students are often Maya (Chuj or Q'anjobal).

Xantin is considered a sacred place for the Chuj who live there. It is the ancestral homeland of the Chuj who have inhabited the mountainous lands for centuries (Piedrasanta, 2009). Xantin has salt reservoirs that made Xantin a center of trade during the post-classic Mayan period. The sacred salt mines and the powerful salt spirit continue to carry deep significance for the Chuj people of Xantin.

Yet, with the violence of colonization and the continued State-led violence against the Maya of Guatemala, Xantin has been historically marginalized and suffered from much direct and indirect repression from the State. Colonization imposed formal schooling structures on Xantin, where Mayas were forced to speak Spanish and convert to Christianity. Independence brought a series of authoritarian governments that continued the violence and repression of Mayan people and forced Mayas to work on the large plantations across the country. Many Chuj men and women spent months each year on the plantations on the eastern coast. After a brief period of democracy and peace from 1944 to 1954 (known as the 10 Years of Spring), the CIA backed military coup installed a series of oppressive dictatorships that brought violence and armed conflict against the Mayas. The heightened state led repression and violence of the 1980s and 1990s had a direct affect on Xantin. The government declared Mayas enemies of the State and carried out a series of attacks on Mayan communities. Xantin was a target of army activity and forced recruitment. Schools were targets for this forced recruitment of boys, so many parents chose to protect their children by keeping them out of schools. In 1981, one of Xantin's neighborhoods was the site of a targeted massacre; in the middle of the night men, women, and children were murdered by armed soldiers as they slept. One community leader I spoke with discussed the lasting effects of the war:

*Más que todo [la guerra ha afectado] el tejido social aquí en [Xantin] tanto como el de los ancianos, y el de la gente adulta y el de la juventud. Desde el conflicto armado antes como digo había una gran comunión entre jóvenes, ancianos y mujeres.... Antes había mucha equidad... y la relación entre adulto, anciano y jóvenes era magnífico, pero lo que pasó en la guerra ... llevaron mucha gente al ejército, y gente que fue entre la guerrilla, entonces tomaron el poder así bruscamente... ya no hay nada guerra, ya todo impulsando la educación, entonces ya esto como que ya empieza a hacer sus acercamientos poco a poco.*

More than anything [the war has affected] the social fabric here in [Xantin] as much between the elders and the adults as with the youth. Before the armed conflict there was a great communion between youth, elders and women... Before there was much equity... and the relationship among adults, elders and youth was magnificent, but what happened during the war was that... they forcible recruited many people to the army and people went with the *guerrilla*, then they suddenly got power ... now there's no war, now everything goes to push education, so now it's like there's a coming together little by little. (MC11, 8/15/11)

As this educator explained, the *internal armed conflict* (as it is termed nationally) has had a lasting impact on Xantin, but following the violence there was a renewed commitment to formal education that some argue has had a positive effect on the community.

Xantin continues to be marginalized by the government. Because of its location and history, Xantin has received marginal governmental support for and access to infrastructure and social services (such as roads, schools, teachers, running water, etc.). The everyday violence of poverty continues to affect many Xantinos, since according to the 2002 census, approximately 92% of the population on the municipality lives at or below the poverty line (FUNCEDE, 2011). The few NGOs present in the community are focused on education and health services. Access to formal national schooling systems has been historically limited. National and NGO data estimate that 30% of the population in Xantin is considered literate (Lewis, 2009; FUNCEDE 2011). However, here it is important to consider the Giroux's (1987) argument that "illiteracy" is often used as a cultural and social marker to negatively label individuals and groups as deficient. Illiteracy can often be an act of resistance by "subordinate groups" and a conscious refusal to subscribe to the dominant culture's literacy (Giroux). In Mayan communities throughout Guatemala, the refusal to go to school has historically been an effort to protect Mayan children.

Currently, the community has been engaged with struggles against large transnational mining corporations and the government over rights to their land. Community members, teachers and students have all engaged in active protests and resistance to protect their sacred land.

## The New National Curriculum (CNB)

In 1997, a year after the signing of the Peace Accords following the 36-years of state sponsored violence and conflict the Guatemalan Ministry of Education began a process of educational reform. The official reforms aim to improve the quality of education in Guatemala to reflect the country's multicultural population in accordance with international standards (such as UNESCO's Education for All framework, 1990). These reforms call for IBE opportunities and have culminated in the creation of a new national curriculum (CNB) first put into effect in 2004 (after years of planning and consultation with national and international groups). At this point educators and schools across the country received the new national curriculum from government officials to implement in their schools and classrooms. However, they were also given space to use it and re/imagine it in the ways they see fit. The primary objective of the CNB is to "respect and respond to the characteristics, needs and aspirations of a multicultural, multilingual and multiethnic country..." (MINEDUC, 2005). The curriculum seeks to address social inequalities and gender and cultural discrimination through a more inclusive educational model.

The stated objectives of the new curriculum is to improve the quality of education for all involved through:

- El desarrollo de la educación multicultural y del enfoque intercultural para que todas y todos los guatemaltecos reconozcamos la riqueza étnica, lingüística y cultural del país.
- El respeto y la promoción de las distintas identidades culturales y étnicas en el marco del diálogo.
- El fortalecimiento de la participación de la niña y de la mujer en el sistema educativo en el marco de las relaciones equitativas entre los géneros.
- La promoción de una educación con excelencia y adecuada a los avances de la ciencia y la tecnología.
- El impulso a procesos educativos basados en el aprender a hacer, aprender a conocer y pensar, aprender a ser, aprender a convivir y aprender a emprender.
- La vinculación de la educación con el sistema productivo y el mercado laboral conciliado con los requerimientos de una conciencia ambiental que proponga los principios de un desarrollo personal y comunitario sostenible y viable en el presente y en el futuro."

English Translation

- The development of multicultural education and of an intercultural focus so that all Guatemalans recognize the ethnic, linguistic and cultural richness of the country.
- The respect and promotion of distinct cultural and ethnic identities within the framework of dialogue.

- The strengthening of the participation of girls and women in the educational system in the framework of equitable relations among the genders.
- The promotion of education with an excellence and relevant to the scientific and technological advances.
- The push for educational processes based in learning to do, learning to know and think, learning to be, learning to live together and learning to undertake.
- The connection of education with the production system and the labor market mediated by the requirements of an environmental consciousness that proposes the principles of personal development and a sustainable and viable community in the present and in the future."

This outline along with the content and structure of the curriculum show the governments' efforts towards a certain vision of "equality" as imagined by a neoliberal educational model that focuses human capital development as well as the promotion of better "human relations"[3] without a critique of power inequities.

However, within this framework are a number of inherent tensions that Xantin educators spoke back to and a number of scholars have also critiqued. As a top-down curriculum created in the capital, it does not fully reflect the voices of teachers or all of Guatemala's rural and indigenous communities. Additionally, within the curricular framework identities are flattened and separated in certain discrete ways as themes and topics to be addressed within the curriculum (for example gender and cultural equality as separated out as separate issues to be addressed). Similarly, within the content of the curriculum the Maya are often presented as a discrete cultural group (separate from Ladinos) with a shared set of characteristics without a full recognition of the diverse knowledges, histories and worldviews between and within Mayan linguistic and ethnic groups. Historical representations tend to look at "Guatemalan history" without a full recognition of the different histories and historical experiences of the various communities, whose histories are often taken up and silenced within this national (Ladino capital-centered) historical framework. For the Chuj this means that there is a brief mention of the Chuj in the curriculum, but much of the local history, knowledge and ways of knowing are not reflected; so it is the responsibility of educators to make these connections and create relevant curricular models within a system of formal schooling that has historically excluded and disenfranchised Chuj students and culture and has "flattened" and essentialized their culture and identities.

The government characterizes the general curriculum as "flexible" to give local communities, schools and teachers the ability to use the official curriculum as a guide, but contextualize it according to local realities and knowledges and the needs, abilities and epistemologies of the students, teachers and families. However, in practice the governmental support and funding for localized materials and curricular development has prioritized the four "majority" Mayan communities (K'iche', Kaqchikel, Q'eqchi' and Mam); there has not been much governmental support or NGO support for local curricular development in minoritized Maya communities and the Chuj Maya have yet to receive this support. This has re/created a hierarchical relationship among "majority" and "minority" Mayan communities. As López (2006) states, educational "efforts have focused on the four most-used Maya languages—Kaqchikel, Mam, Qeqchi and Quiche—to the detriment of the other 19 linguistic communities." Additionally, there has been an exclusion of Chuj voices from political and educational decisions on the national level and a framing of the Chuj people from a deficit perspective that views them as "lacking" what is deemed necessary to participate in "decision-making" (personal correspondence with official in the Ministry of Education, 2012). This is the context within which Chuj educators are positioned nationally. Within this context they are charged with contextualizing their practice without material support or direct training.

**Previous Scholarship**

Many scholars have critiqued the educational reforms in Guatemala. Most argue that it advocates "strategic essentialism" that emphasizes a certain way to "be Maya"—excluding and silencing a multiplicity of voices (Sieder, 2008); ignores the intersectionality of identities at play for individuals (Dietz & Mateos C., 2008); and solidifies the polarizing classifications of "Ladino" and "Maya" (Rodas, 2008). Hale (2002) argues that the legal recognition of many cultures does not challenge neoliberal models and structures that perpetuate inequalities; instead these policies get taken up within neoliberal frameworks. Esquit (2008) also argues that these multicultural reforms are a way for the State and those in power to continue to "discipline" the indigenous population and hinder the promotion of self-determination and political awareness. The Maya continue to be pushed to learn Spanish and Ladino culture in order to gain access to social, political and economic opportunities that are otherwise unavailable to those who only speak their native Mayan language. Through research on policy implementation, Cojtí Cuxil (2005) argues: "Ladino-centrism minimizes, hides, and disqualifies the presence, needs, and actions of indigenous nations." While some studies such as those presented above have explored the flaws inherent in the policy, few studies have focused on how these reforms are put into practice by the educators charged with enacting them.

This study seeks to add insights into and contribute to these critiques by focusing on education in a "minority" Maya community that has experienced a silencing of their needs and concerns. The experiences of "minority" Maya communities have been excluded in much of the literature and studies of education in Guatemala. This exclusion is especially problematic, because as Herdoíza-Estévez and Lenk (2010) argue, "With the state concentrating exclusively on the most widely spoken indigenous languages...lesser-spoken indigenous languages [are] threatened." In this vein, this study pushes towards a greater understanding of how Xantin educators are experiencing and envisioning education in the community by listening to and observing the educators themselves. My discussions with these educators reflected the above issues and themes, but also expanded on and pushed back against these frameworks in new and insightful ways.

**Research Focus**

Within this context I sought to understand how educators (broadly defined to include student- teachers, teachers, principals and community leaders involved in educational efforts) were understanding and making sense of education for students in Xantin within the current national framework of Intercultural and Bilingual Education (IBE) reform policies. To do so, I draw on 2.5 years of teaching experience in Xantin, Guatemala and 4-weeks of structured ethnographic data collection, including individual ethnographic interviews and classroom and participant observations. A total of 32 semi-structured interviews with Xantin educators[4] are used to inform this chapter.

Because of the apparent ways people's individual personalities, histories and intersectional identities shaped their perceptions of and responses to the IBE reforms, within my presentation of interview quotes I focus on two aspects of identity that proved to be central to IBE efforts and educational experiences across most interviews: culture and gender. While focusing on two broad categories is limiting, because of the hybrid and multiple nature of identity, the saliency and intersectional nature of gender and culture came out through interviews and readings and provide deep insights into the views and experiences of educators in Xantin. Thus, each of the interviews provides information on the individual's gender ("M" for male and "F" for female) followed by their cultural identity ("C" for Chuj and "L" for Ladino). The number that follows represents the number the interview is catalogued under and generally marks the order in which the interviews were recorded. I felt that this allowed for respondents' identity to be considered while maintaining confidentiality. I chose to use vague identifiers and numbers rather than names, so as not to suggest that interview responses came from someone else in the community.

Throughout this process I felt it was very important to consider how my positionality came into play both during the research and analysis. I am a white Jewish-American woman from the suburbs of Chicago. I am an outsider to the Chuj Maya community in a number of ways. My cultural frame of references and life experiences differ from many people in Xantin. As Linda Tuhiwai Smith (1999) states, this can cause points of tension in research with indigenous communities because "Western" research historically comes from a positivist tradition that seeks to "know" and "brings to bear, on any study of indigenous peoples, a cultural orientation, a set of values, a different conceptualization of such things as time, space and subjectivity, different and competing theories of knowledge, highly specialized forms of language, and structures of power" (p. 42). I most noticed these tensions with the nature of the questions I asked and the structure of the interviews. I visualized questions in a chronological and linear fashion that would allow those I interviewed to talk about their experiences with education in a more chronological fashion. However, Mayan conceptualizations of time and conversational styles are more cyclical. Thus, I was acutely aware of how this structure likely affected the way people felt they were able to work through the questions. At the same time, because I had spent two years living and teaching in Xantin and another 6 months doing work and conducting short-term courses, I gained somewhat of an "insider" role in the community and in the schools.

Because of this position and its inherent tensions, rather than polarizing notions of insider/outsider or native/non-native researcher I use Narayan's (1993) notion of "quality of relations" to make sense of and evaluate my positionality as a researcher. Narayan argues that the researchers' positionality is multiple and shifting. Because of my experience teaching in Xantin and close relationship within the community, I am neither an insider nor an outsider, thus, looking at the "quality of relations" I had with my participants provides more nuanced insight into my positionality and encouraged a deep reflexivity of my positionality, tensions with representation and my research goals throughout the analysis process. Considering my positionality in this way also helped ensure an honest, respectful and caring representation of my friends and colleagues, whose knowledge and insights inform this study. Thus, throughout this process I attempted to continually engage my friends and colleagues in Xantin with my research to gauge whether or not they felt comfortable with the information I was putting forth could be at all compromising and/or was reflective of their experiences.

Even with these efforts, it is important to remember that there is always an implicit "I" throughout this analysis and representation of other people's voices and experiences. My voice and positionality are woven into the way people's voices are presented. In addition there are multiple voices and interpretations that take place through the translations between and among languages. I tried to combat this by presenting interview excerpts in both Spanish and my English translations and making some of these multiple voices more explicit.

## Listening to Educators across the Intersections

My interviews with educators in Xantin, showed that while the theories and critical scholarship around the national curriculum are important and shed light on important tensions with the curricular framework, what happens in schools and the ways educators talk about their practice both builds on and pushes back against these narratives. Educators' analysis of the curriculum reflected a variety of policy analysis perspectives, but the majority argued that the CNB fails to be fully multicultural and lacks a social justice framework. Many saw the current policy within a long history of colonial educational policies and practices. Central to these arguments was the importance of place and place-based identities, histories, and experiences and understandings of gender and culture/race that intersect and play an important role in lived educational experiences.

These arguments represent a complex understanding of national policies informed by intersecting experiences that shape how teachers are responding to the curriculum and in turn carry out their practice. These experiences and intersectional understandings are flattened by the curriculum, but brought to life by the teachers who reimagine the curriculum and put it into practice.

## "You can't speak because you are Maya": Cultural Racism

I use Hale's (2002, 2008) term "cultural racism," which refers to social conflation of culture and race in Guatemala, to reflect on how Chuj students, parents and teachers complex experiences of discrimination based on racialized notions of Mayan culture. All Chuj participants talked about their experiences with "discrimination" based on racialized notions of Mayas and perceived linguistic and cultural orientations and understandings. These experiences inform how Chuj individuals interact with schools and make sense of what schools are and should be doing.

Often social discrimination and exclusion experienced by Chuj was viewed as situated in perceptions of Spanish language ability. Linguistic difference as a visible manifestation of culture is often used as justifications for social exclusion, as Ng (2007) argues linguistic exclusion "provides a stowaway for more subtle discrimination against target groups." Language is central to culture, as Anzaldúa (1987/1999) argues, "Ethnic identity is twin skin to linguistic identity—I am my language. Until I can take pride in my language, I cannot take pride in myself." In Guatemala, discrimination against Mayan language speakers perpetuates the dominance of Spanish-language and Ladino culture and leads to experiences of social marginalization both in and outside of Xantin. A student teacher explained this linguistic discrimination as follows,

> *Nosotros que hablamos nuestro idioma casi nos discriminan que no podemos hablar el español perfectamente... La discriminación es por ejemplo "tú no tienes opinión" o "tú no puedes hablar porque eres maya."*

> Those of us who speak our language are discriminated against for not being able to speak Spanish perfectly... The discrimination is, for example, "you don't have an opinion" or "you can't speak because you are Maya." (MC6, 8/13/11)

Discussions of linguistic and cultural discrimination overlapped and intersected within and across interviews in very complex ways. An educational leader spoke to the notion of cultural racism and situated it historically. He argued that situating Spanish culture as superior has impeded educational possibilities in Guatemala and has had the effect of dividing Mayan communities. He explained:

> *Entonces el sistema... es de que por ejemplo a nosotros, los chujes, la cultura castellana nos discriminaba porque "es que usted es indio es que a usted le hace falta el desarrollo mental" como que había cierto rechazo... hasta hoy me estoy dando cuenta de que este sistema no está bien; es una ideología totalmente antisocial que viene a afectar el desarrollo en la educación. Decían que la cultura Mam, ellos son aparte, la cultural Q'anjobal, aparte. Entonces como que ahí prevalecía que la cultura castellana es la mejor. Es la que tenía el poder, es la que podría desarrollarse mejor en el ámbito educativo...*

> So the system... is that for example, the Castilian culture discriminated against us, the Chuj, because "it's that you are *indio*, you lack mental development" there was a certain rejection... even today I am realizing that this system is not good; it's a completely antisocial ideology that comes to affect educational development. They said that Mam culture, they are separate, the Q'anjobal culture, separate. So it's as if there Castilian culture prevailed as the best. It had the power, it's the one that could best develop the educational environment. (MC29, 8/31/11)

This explanation also highlights the construction of the popular notion that Mayan languages and cultures are "divisive," solidifying Ladino cultural dominance through its positioning as the "unifying" national culture representative of "universal values." This discourse and positioning has created and maintained the linguistic and social hegemony of Spanish language and culture, which is also reflected in the practices occurring in classrooms and schools. Not knowing Spanish or privileged school knowledges is understood to be a driving force behind discriminatory comments about Mayas as less intelligent as Ladinos '*porque no saben.*'

This "cultural racism" has a profound affect on the school environment. One student- teacher discussed the ways he heard Ladino teachers talking to students and overtly discriminating against them as well as how this discrimination gets internalized by students and has a profound effect on their educational experiences with their teachers:

> *Sí, en la educación sí hay como mucha discriminación a nosotros. Por ejemplo los profesores hablan mal de los profesores que son mayas. "Es que no saben mucho... que no pueden." Y hasta a la vez aconsejan a sus alumnos, "hay que decir a tu papá que él no puede." Y "hay que decir ante el director que lo que está enseñando no es lo correcto." Es como que están quitando el valor a un indígena... el niño está ahí escuchando, "ah, entonces los profesores de aquí de [Xantin] no sirven..."*

> Yes, in education there is a lot of discrimination towards us. For example, teachers speak badly about the teachers that are Maya. "They don't know a lot... they aren't capable." And even at the same time they advise their students, "tell your dad that he's not capable." And "you must tell the director that what s/he is teaching is not correct." It's as if they are taking away the value from the indigenous person... the child is there listening, "ah, so the teachers from [Xantin] are worthless..." (MC6, 8/13/11)

Students receive both explicit and implicit messages about their inferiority. The deficit understandings of Chuj language and culture that many felt Ladino teachers historically had of Mayas and many argue continue to have towards Chuj students, families and teachers carries through to the overt and hidden curricula in schools. In my observations I saw a number of Chuj and Ladino teachers privileging Spanish language and ways of knowing in their lessons as I observed teachers stressing the importance of learning dominant knowledges in order to "get ahead" and be "successful". Thus, students in Xantin learn that Spanish language and Ladino culture are the most valuable.

Ladino (and some Chuj) teachers were likely to evaluate students' abilities based on their Spanish language skills, again positioning it as valuable and dominant. As one Ladina teacher explained,

> *Veo un poco de deficiencia en la forma de expresión y redacción que ellos tienen. Como sabemos ese problema viene desde primaria porque si los niños no aprenden español, ya cuando son grandes ya no van a aprender.*

> I see deficiency in the way they have of expressing and writing. We know the problem starts in primary school, because if the students don't learn Spanish then, when they're older they're not going to learn. (FL15, 8/25/11)

And many Chuj teachers also argued for the importance of Spanish based on their experiences with discrimination and formal schooling. One teacher talked about hearing other Chuj teachers say, *"no y ¿por qué tenemos que enseñar de nuestra propia cultura si es esa es un atraso?"/* "no and why do we have to teach about our own culture if it's a setback?" (FC28, 8/30/11). Because of these understandings and experiences many argued for the continued need to focus on Spanish language and dominant knowledges.

However, there were a number of educators, who felt that this continued centering of Spanish language is dangerous for Chuj language and culture. As one student-teacher explained,

> *Si vamos a hablar sólo el español sería muy malo porque estamos desapareciendo toda nuestra cultura y nos podemos quedar muy atrás.*
>
> If we are going to only talk in Spanish that would be very bad because we would be disappearing our entire culture and we could be left behind. (MC13, 8/24/11)

Thus, many Chuj educators pushed back against the dominant educational framework and argued for Chuj language and culture to be centered in schools to give it the privileged place within education. Otherwise, they argued, its continued marginalization socially and educationally would threaten their future. Some people talked about their fear that Chuj language would "disappear" and that would mean that the Chuj as a people would "disappear" as well.

This relates to the argument of a number of respondents, that it is most important for students to learn their language and culture in school to better understand who they are. Once students know who they are, many argued they can then learn other languages and knowledges and more easily navigate social power structures. As one teacher argued:

> *[S]ólo los estamos llenando de informaciones de otras cosas, pero [si] los llenamos con la cultura que ellos tienen yo creo que tendríamos a alumnos mejores... con muchos conocimientos y yo creo que lo primero es saber de lo que hay a nuestro alrededor de nuestro propio lugar, después conocer algo de esos. Por ejemplo aquí en [Xantin] nosotros no somos ladinos, somos mayas. Entonces nosotros debemos conocer primero nuestra cultura, nuestra origen y segundo conocer otros.*
>
> [W]e are just filling them with information about other things, but if we fill them with the culture they have I think that we would have better students... with lots of knowledge and I think that the first thing is to know is what there is around us in our own place and later know something of those others. For example, here in [Xantin] we are not Ladinos, we are Mayas. So we should know our culture first, our origin and second know others. (MC7, 8/14/11)

However, some people further troubled the previous arguments with a functional argument that positions schools as sites to facilitate access to the culture and language of power. This argument recognizes the opportunities that are available to those who speak Spanish and can navigate Ladino-centered social structures. This argument relates to Fanon's (1952) argument that marginalized people seek to speak the dominant or colonial language "since it is the key to open doors which only fifty years ago remained closed to [them]." Interviewees talked about how parents thought that students did not need to learn Chuj in school because they learned it at home. The idea was that students should learn in school that which their parents could not teach them at home. Thus, the schools were for students to learn the dominant language and cultural capital to better navigate dominant social structures, while Chuj language and culture were for parents to teach. As one teacher stated:

> *Pero ellos [los padres] se oponen mucho, a veces dicen, "no es que si los mandamos en la escuela es porque tienen que aprender el castellano y no el idioma chuj, porque el idioma chuj lo aprenden desde pequeños en la casa." Y tienen razón, si aprenden, pero hay cosas que ellos no saben. Por ejemplo, no saben escribir, no saben como redactar...*
>
> But they [the parents] are often very opposed, sometimes they say, "no, if we send them to school it's because they need to learn Spanish and not Chuj, because they learn Chuj language at home from the time they are young." And they are right, they do learn, but there are things that they don't know. For example, they don't know how to write, they don't know how to write it... (FC28, 8/30/11)

This quote not only highlights the ways parents see schools as spaces that provide access to different knowledge than that acquired at home, but it also shows how the push for Spanish only in schools comes into tension with the argument that education is facilitating language and culture loss and should change to privilege Chuj language, culture and knowledge. Chuj educators and community members, who argue that Spanish language should be centered in schools, may not necessarily argue that Chuj language and knowledge are not valuable, but may see school as the access point for acquiring the dominant cultural capital and the home and local community as being the sites for fostering local (non-dominant) knowledge and language. However, the way this is often carried out in schools leads to denigrative practices that marginalize the students' culture, language and knowledge.

Thus, many argued that this centering of Spanish language and knowledges comes into tension with the community and Chuj knowledges and ways of knowing. Many respondents talked about how many elders had a negative view of formal schooling, because there are particular tensions with the values that elders and adults feel are being promoted in the schools that are seen as antithetical to local values that are important for the community. Formal schooling, with its traditional focus on Ladino culture and Spanish language, was criticized for not promoting 'educated' Chuj youth, but rather for fostering rebelliousness, disrespect, and laziness because students are seen to not value traditional Chuj values (such as respect and community), cultural knowledge, and traditional work. Because of this, a number of parents were resistant to sending their children (especially their daughters) to school and some openly critiqued and opposed the schools in town.

Many talked about how it is important for schools to work to bridge these 'gaps' and become more connected to the community and the lessons parents teach at home. Thus, these parents and educators pushed for a greater centering of Chuj knowledge and cultures in schools to support students' acquisition of traditional Chuj values and skills. Yet, these perceptions are often highly gendered in what knowledges and skills are seen as valuable for girls and boys and those that are seen as detrimental for each.

Thus, the role of culture and language in formal schooling was diversely understood by different educators and community members. All responses built off individual experiences with formal schooling. These understandings and arguments became more complex as discussions moved in and out of conversations about gender and discrimination against women and girls.

## "It Hurts Me Sometimes": Gender Discrimination

Gender emerged across interviews as one of the central concerns with social and educational inequities in Xantin and in Guatemala as a whole. Discussions about gender and gendered discrimination were complex and multifaceted. For the purpose of this chapter, I will focus on certain aspects of these discussions, because I feel they show the internal tensions experienced by teachers while also recognizing that the analyses here are only partial. All participants spoke to gender as a central issue in the schools. Gender and culture are deeply intertwined and dually constructed (Anzaldúa, 1987/1999). Many respondents argued for the importance of recognizing the multiple ways gender and culture are connected and intersect. Experiences and understandings of gender came through as a central factor for all the educators I spoke with, however, the social location of the respondents emerged as central for informing how educators' made sense of gender and gender inequities. While both male and female respondents often initially argued that gender parity in schools showed reduced gender discrimination, when probed further male respondents were more likely to continue to argue this point, while female respondents often complicated this understanding with personal experiences of discrimination. While women talked about their personal experiences with gendered discrimination, men generally talked about "others" who discriminated and their own efforts to combat this discrimination. For example one male teacher talked about this issue as follows:

> *[A] mi me duele a veces ver a las mujeres discriminadas por los hombres. Estamos discriminados por otras culturas pero a veces entre nosotros nos discriminamos...*
>
> [I]t hurts me sometimes to see women discriminated against by men. We are discriminated against by other cultures, but sometimes between ourselves we discriminate against each other... (MC3, 8/8/11)

This quote also shows the ways understandings of group belonging and "othering" are shifting notions when gender is included. Here the interviewee talks about belonging to a marginalized cultural group as a potential source of solidarity, but how in reality Chuj are divided along gendered lines. This teacher offered a new way to think about the complexity of the forms discrimination takes and the multiplicity of oppressions experienced by Chuj women, from outside and within the community.

Gender comes into play in a number of different ways in the schools and classrooms. Discussions of gender inequalities in schools and classrooms centered on the ways male students, teachers and administrators acted in discriminatory and oppressive ways toward female students and teachers. This affected the ways girls and women interacted with schools and their experiences with formal schooling. Escalated instances of discrimination towards girls in the classroom occurred within a context of everyday experiences of discrimination in the community. Many of the people I spoke with discussed how timid the girls were in their classes, how they were afraid to speak up and that their male classmates made fun of them when they did. As one teacher explained:

> *Por ejemplo si una mujer habla diciendo esto, los hombres, "no, tú no sabes nada, nosotros vamos a arreglar eso... "*
>
> For example if a girl says something, the boys [say], "no, you don't know anything, we are going to take care of this...." (FC26, 8/30/11)

Similarly, all of the Chuj women I interviewed spoke of their first-hand experiences with gender discrimination in the classroom. Women talked about experiences about marginalization, ridicule, sexual coercion and violence in the classroom from male students and teachers. Across interviews, women who stood up for themselves or were more vocal were accused of *molestando* (roughly translated to disturbing or being bothersome or annoying). Framing female students as *molestando* gave male students cover to mistreat them. For example, one teacher described how when she was in middle school she would stand up for herself in class and speak up, even though the class was majority male. One day a group of the boys got angry with her and started pushing her. One even pushed her head against the wall. She told the principal what happened, but when he talked to the boys they said she was the one *molestando* and no action was taken. Because of these experiences, girls described feeling unsafe and marginalized because of the actions and attitude of male students and a lack of response by male teachers and administrators. Girls learned that schools are male-dominated spaces; they are not sites for gender equitable learning and often not safe spaces. In addition, they learned that to succeed in school they had to be "seen and not heard".

Throughout the interviews I observed how gender inequality is now recognized as an issue itself by all interviewed (both men and women). However, respondents differed in how they situated gender inequity socially and culturally—whether it is a Mayan, colonial, or Ladino construct. This was just one of the issues among many that came out of the interviews, but for this chapter I focus on this aspect of the discussions, because I feel it shows the internal tensions of teachers and the broader histories and forces connected with understandings of and experiences with gender.

Ladino educators and participants tended to situate gender discrimination within Mayan culture. Their responses were often supported by a national and international discourses that place a greater emphasis on promoting gender equality in Mayan communities, but fail to interrogate these issues historically. As one Ladino teacher stated:

> *Es por lo que la cultura ha practicado de que se le ha dado menos valor a la mujer, por eso son cuestiones de la cultura por saber cuento tiempo...*
>
> It is because of what the culture has practiced that it has given less value to women, so those are cultural issues for who knows how long... (ML16, 8/26/11)

These arguments push for cultural changes and situate the "problem" within Chuj culture and "blame" Maya cultures for gender inequalities. However, this analysis does not extend to broader social, historical and structural contexts and forces.

On the other hand a number of Chuj interviewees gave a more historicized analysis that situated gender inequalities within gendered colonial power structures and current Ladino-centered social structures. One educational coordinator countered this notion that discrimination against women is situated within Mayan culture in his assertion that the State model of education as imposed by the Spanish colonial system changed the more equal educational models the Chuj had developed.

*[C]uando entró el sistema educativo digamos del Estado entonces le daba mas prio-ridad al hombre... pero anteriormente a la educación... como decía la señora... tenían grupos... de muchachas para tejer el pop. Allí sí como que hay más equidad, porque la mamá se encargaba de enseñar a las niñas durante el trabajo y el papá se encargaba de enseñar al niño cuando se iba a trabajar con su papá. Entonces ahí sí como que hay una equidad.*

[W]hen the educational system of the State entered it gave more priority to men... but before the education... as the *señora* said... had groups... of girls to weave *pop*. There it was as if there was more equality, because the mom was in charge of teaching the girls during the work and the dad was in charge of teaching the boy when he went to work with his dad. So it's as if there was equality. (MC11, 8/15/11)

Education of boys and girls in this sense is not depicted as being identical as the content was determined by gender, but many people have argued men and women's roles were equally important and given equal priority (in reference to the complimentary energies of men and women in traditional Mayan culture). This destabilizes the notion of the Ladino State fostering greater gender equality in Mayan communities and brings into question its ability to do so given its history. Many Chuj respondents made the argument that gender discrimination has its historical roots in colonization and has been perpetuated by Ladino-centered power structures.

Another teacher talked about similar historical issues in connection to the history of the preference given to boys in access to formal schooling. He argued that gendered access was in part due to the colonial system's privileging of schooling for men (due to their perceived superiority by the Church) as well as what a number of interviewees argued was strategic decision-making on the part of the community, who felt the boys could physically handle the corporal punishments dealt out in 'colonial' and 'traditional' schools. Implicit in this argument is an understanding of women as 'carriers of culture,' who were needed to carry out their traditional roles. This led to girls being "sheltered" from formal schooling, which came to be seen "for boys". As one interviewee argued:

*Si bueno comparando a la educación maya, yo creo que anteriormente un poco ese sistema educativo digamos no daba prioridad a las mujeres. Anteriormente, "como ella es mujer, que el niño se vaya a la escuela, porque él es hombre va a aguantar allí aunque le peguen, pero la mujer no. Y es que ella se va a casar."*

Yes, well comparing to Mayan education, I think that before [the Western] educational system didn't really give priority to women. Before, "since she is a women, the boy goes to school, because he is a man and could tolerate it there even if they hit him, but the woman can't. And she is going to marry." (MC11, 8/15/11)

This, explanation shows the way culture and gender have historically inter-sected in education in such a way that formal schooling in Xantin came to be seen as male through Western education models that sought to physi-cally suppress Mayan culture, language and knowledge in the classrooms. The experiences and understandings of gender discrimination and in-equities were discussed in conflicting and divergent ways depending on participants' own positionality and experiences. Understandings of where gender discrimination is situated culturally led to very different practices and programs in schools, classrooms and community spaces for addressing these inequalities; some felt that Mayan understandings of gender differ-ences had to be suppressed or changed because they contribute to these inequities, others felt that Chuj culture and histories could be drawn on to create more equitable relations and combat oppressive colonial structures. These intersecting concepts were brought together in how teachers talked about their visions for education in Xantin.

## What is Possible: Visions and Implications of the Future

Educators in Xantin pushed back against the flattening and compart-mentalization of identities and histories through their discussions of gender and culture. They added to the scholarly critiques of the formal curriculum in new and different ways by drawing on their deep understandings of the intersections of multiple identities and histories. Yet, their understandings of the intersections of culture and gender along with place-based histories and knowledge informed their practices and educational visions. Because of their different positionalities and experiences, the curriculum looked different in each classroom and teachers visions for education in Xantin diverged. However, all of the educators I spoke with had visions for local educational models that would take into account the complex and intersec-tional experiences and knowledges of Chuj men and women that are not reflected in the national curriculum.

For many Chuj educators, a new local curriculum would make it possible to "take back" their cultural knowledge and histories by fostering a mean-ingful connection between formal education and local knowledge and tra-ditions. This would mean resituating the curriculum in the local context. One of the school principals pushing for this in his school argued:

*Todo eso pues nos puede ayudar a volver a retomar cosas importantes de repente si puede ayudar a la ciencia o el futuro que también los mayas según lo que sabemos también son, fueron, o han sido personas muy matemáticos, ingenieros, astrónomos, entonces pero ellos tenían otro tipo de educación… [H]ay muchas cosas que sí hay de aprender de acá, de eso de los sueños por ejemplo el traje, qué es significado, la historia de [Xantin]… ahora está un poco así como abandonado y nadie sabe qué ha pasado... pero lo que piensa es retomar esas historia, la cultura fuera de [Xantin] y volver a renacer, a implementar y a conocer y así vamos a... conocernos mejor y de ahí viene lo de afuera...*

All that [creating a local curriculum] could help us take back the important things that could help science or the future because according to what we know the Mayas are, were, or have been mathematicians, engineers, astronomers, but they had another type of education... [T]here are many things that it is possible to learn here, like dreams, for example, the *traje*, what is the significance, the history of [Xantin]... it is as if this has been abandoned and no one knows what has happened... but we think about re-taking those histories, culture outside of [Xantin] and come to be re-born, to implement and to know and in that way we will... know ourselves better and from there comes everything from outside... (MC2, 8/8/11)

This vision replaces the deficit notions of Chuj and Maya cultures with an understanding that situates Chuj and Mayan communities and cultural understandings as sites of knowledge and value in education. These ideas also offer the possibilities for new sources of knowledge and educational models to be incorporated into the curriculum.

A strong base in local culture, histories and knowledge is seen to provide the opportunity for students to explore and learn who they are and to have a strong sense of their own identity and history in ways that are not reflected in or fostered by the national curriculum. Chuj history is taken up within and lost in the framework of "national history" that does not reflect the diverse histories and experiences of different communities, regions and linguistic groups in Guatemala. In order to "re-take" their place-based histories, many people discussed incorporating the elders' knowledge into the schools by situating elders and leaders as teachers and promoting the use local materials with in a new curricular model.

One individual talked about how such educational models would push back against the current structures and models, since unlike neoliberal capitalist models, collectivism and collaboration are valued in traditional Mayan cultures. Current structures are antithetical to Chuj culture and ways of knowing. As one Chuj language educator explained:

*¿Cómo empezar a entender eso de la educación desde la cosmovisión maya para llegar a entender la vida en sí mismo? Porque el capitalismo es que unos tienen los pocos, y los otros que se jodan... O sea si hay que entender la propia realidad. ¿Ya? Conocer nuestra identidad dónde vinimos, dónde estamos, dónde vamos. Porque la educación como está ahorita no sé a dónde nos va a llevar. Si no nos está inculcando nuestra identidad, ¿qué nos va a pasar después?*

How to begin to understand education from Mayan cosmovision to be able to understand life itself? Because capitalism is that some have the little there is and the others are screwed... In other words it's important to understand the actual reality. Ok? To know our identity, where we came from, where we are, where we are going. Because education as it is now, I don't know where it will take us. If it's not inculcating us with our own identity, what will happen to us later? (MC21, 8/29/11)

This quote also highlights the importance of basing this new educational model within students' own culture to provide them the base from which to understand and navigate their world. Many argued that this sense of one's own identity is important for students to effectively access Spanish language and Ladino-centered social structures, especially since current structures have marginalized Chuj students and local knowledges.

These curricular visions also set out address gender inequities within Chuj culture and using Mayan educational methodologies of discussion, group work and joint reflection to bring about changes. As one teacher argued, boys and girls and women and men all need to be a part of this process with everyone working together and teaching one another how to value themselves as well as those around them.

*Formaría a todas la niñas de aquí en la escuela por ejemplo y les imparto sobre la autoestima, los derechos, las obligaciones también y que ellas también piensan, "¿Qué hacemos? Hagamos grupos entonces y llamamos a los compañeros"; un grupo de ellas hablen con ellos y otro grupo de ellas hablen con otros y así. Y si vemos el resultado de que los hombres pasen de exponer, por ejemplo, delante de las mujeres que por ejemplo un hombre y una mujer dicen, "Tú vales, yo también, hagamos conciencia de que nosotros podemos salir adelante. Aunque somos diferentes de sexo, pero somos inteligentes por naturaleza y todos lo sabemos." ... Quiero que los hombres también estén delante de las señoras por ejemplo, las señoras, ah sí, las mujeres también y que las mujeres estén delante de los hombre también. Y así podemos promover, es que hoy y mañana no, poco a poco , pero si podemos hacer.*

I would form a group with the girls here at the school for example and I teach them about self-esteem, rights, and obligations too, and so that they also think, "what should we do" Let's make groups and call the *compañeros*; a group of the girls talks to a group of the boys and another group of the girls talk with others and so on. And we can see the result when the men come up to speak, for example, in front of the women that for example a man and a woman say, "You are valuable, me too, let's raise awareness that we can move forward. Even if we are different sexes, but we are intelligent by nature and we all know it." ... I want the men to be in front of the older women, for example, the *señoras*, ah yes, women too and that the women are in front of the men too. And in this way we can promote it, not today or tomorrow, little by little, but we can do it. (FC30, 8/26&30/11)

This teacher's vision is situated within a larger discourse on human rights and women's rights in particular at the same time it builds off of local cultural practices by being collaborative involving all members of the community in promoting greater equity. She shows the possibilities of local educational models to foster gender equality in ways that also intersect with these global and national discourses and strategies.

## Discussion: Using Intersectionality to Make Sense of the Insights

Across interviews, teachers' educational visions reflected an understanding of the intersectionality of lived experiences and social issues. Their visions illuminated new possibilities for what schools can and should be doing, which both differ from and expand on the policy analysis perspectives that initially framed my research. While at times, educators talked about gender and culture separately in their analysis of the current situation and issues in Xantin schools, they also acknowledged ways they were connected and overlapped. When it came to discussions of their educational visions, issues of culture, gender and place were brought together in complex ways that deeply reflected their interconnectedness.

Listening to educators' voices adds insights into and/or disrupts popular narratives about educational policies and schools. Thus, it is important to consider how educators' insights can be used to create richer and more complex ways of honoring people's lived experiences and promoting equity in education in ways that cannot be envisioned through a top-down approach. Exploring the experiences of educators, who have on-the-ground experiences in schools in communities, illuminates the complexity of these issues and calls for the development of solutions that are locally-based and build off of community strengths, knowledges and realities. As researchers, it is our responsibility to listen to these insights. Because of the ways educators talked about their experiences, practice, and educational possibilities in complex and overlapping ways, I argue that intersectionality may be a useful framework for better understanding local educators' visions. Intersectionality examines the multiplicity of social categories that interact to produce systematic and individual inequalities (Crenshaw, 1991; Collins, 1998; McCall, 2005; Bhopal & Preston, 2012). This chapter showed how notions of culture, place and gender influence schooling experiences and practices in Xantin to highlight how these social categories are interconnected and how inequalities are perpetuated not only within the national policies, but also socially and within schools. Intersectionality illuminates how multiple oppressions, such as cultural discrimination and gender inequalities, are mutually reinforcing, as educators suggested was the case in Xantin (Roth, 2004).

Analyses of one current educational policy can be limiting as each policy is embedded in histories and ways thinking about gender and culture that are situated within intersecting histories themselves. In the case of Xantin, local Chuj histories and traditions intersect with colonial histories and policies in deep and complex ways—colonial and local histories cannot always be disentangled as was seen in discussions of gender inequalities. Similarly, educators in Xantin did not always view the current IBE policies as separate from past repressive colonial education models, showing a different way of analyzing "a current policy." This brings into questions the ways curricula and policies are often analyzed as stand-alone documents that are new and separate from previous models. Using an intersectionality model for understanding policy and educators' experiences with it can help show how these histories overlap.

By highlighting the intersectional knowledge and experience of Chuj educators that are not reflected in the national curricula, but deeply inform their practices and visions, this chapter calls for the consideration of teachers as policymakers rather than simply enactors of curriculum (Sutton & Levinson, 2001). Teachers are making decisions on a daily basis regarding what education in their classrooms, schools and communities will look like. This chapter seeks to open the discussion of education reforms and multicultural education and center the knowledge and visions of all teachers towards new models, which foster greater equity and can more fully reflect and honor the intersectional realities of people's lived experiences.

## NOTES

1. Quote from personal interview 21 (August 29, 2011).
2. Guatemala's dominant cultural group—the "mestizo" and Spanish-speaking population
3. The human relations approach to multicultural education was laid out by Grant and Sleeter (1998/2008) as an approach to multicultural education that pushes for better relations among groups without recognizing or destabilizing power inequities.
4. Student-teachers, teachers, school principals and community educators.

## REFERENCES

Anzaldúa, G. (1987/1999). *Borderlands/La Frontera: The New Mestiza.* San Francisco: Aunt Lute Books.

Bhopal, K., & Preston, J. (2012). *Intersectionality and "race" in education.* New York, NY: Routledge.

Cojtí C., D. (2005). *El racismo contra los pueblos indígenas de Guatemala.* Guatemala: CNEM.

Collins, P. H. (1998). The tie that binds: Race, gender, and US violence. *Ethnic and Racial Studies, 21*(5), 917–938.

Crenshaw, K. W. (1991). Mapping the margins: Intersectionality, identity politics, and violence against women of color. *Stanford Law Review, 43*(6), 1241–1299.

Dietz, G., & Mateos, L. S. (2008). El discurso internacional ante el paradigma de la diversidad: estructuraciones subyacentes y migraciones discursivas del multi-culturalismo contemporáneo. In S. Bastos, *Multiculturalismo y futuro en Guatemala* (pp. 23–54). Guatemala: FLACSO/OXFAM.

Esquit, E. (2008). Disciplinando al subalterno. Vínculos de violencia y de gobierno en Guatemala. In S. Bastos (Ed.), *Multiculturalismo y futuro en Guatemala* (pp. 123–148). Guatemala: FLACSO/OXFAM.

Fanon, F. (1952). *Black skin, White masks.* New York, NY: Grove Press.

FUNCEDE. (2011). *Comportamiento Electoral Municipal in Guatemala: Elecciones Generales 2007.* Serie de Estudios No. 22. Guatemala.

Giroux, H. (1987). Introduction. In P. Freire & D. Macedo, *Literacy: Reading the word and the world.* New York, NY: Bergin and Garvey.

Grant, C., & Sleeter, C. (1998/2008). *Turning on learning: Five approaches for multi-cultural teaching plans for race, class, gender and disability.* San Francisco: Wiley & Sons, Inc.

Hale, C. (2002). Does multiculturalism menace? Governance, cultural rights and the politics of identity in Guatemala. *Journal of Latin American Studies, 34*(3), 485–524.

Hale, C. (2008). *Más que un indio/More than an Indian: Racial ambivalence and neoliberal multiculturalism in Guatemala.* Santa Fe: School of American Research Press.

Herdoíza-Estévez, M., & Lenk. S. (2010, December). Intercultural dialogue: Discourse and realities of indigenous and Mestizos in Ecuador and Guatemala. *Interamerican Journal of Education for Democracy, 3*(2), 196–223.

Lewis, P. (Ed.). (2009). *Ethnologue: Languages of the world* (16th ed.). Dallas: SIL International. Retrieved from: http://www.ethnologue.com.

López, L .E. (2006). Cultural diversity, multilingualism and education in Latin America. In O. Garcia, T. Skutnabb-Kangas, & M Torres-Guzman, *Imagining Multilingual Schools: Languages in Education and Globalization* (pp. 239–261). Buffalo: Multilingual Matters.

McCall, L. (2005). The complexity of intersectionality. *Signs: Journal of Women in Culture and Society, 30*(3), 1771–1800.

MINEDUC, DICADE, DIGEBI. (2005). *Curriculum nacional base.* Guatemala.

Narayan, K. (1993). How native is a "native" anthropologist? *American Anthropologist, 95*(3), 19–32.

Ng, S. H. (2007). Language based discrimination: Blatant and subtle forms. *Journal of Language and Social Psychology, 26*(2), 106–122.

Piedrasanta, R. (2009). *Los Chuj: Unidad y rupturas en su espacio.* Guatemala: Armar Editores.

Rodas, I. (2008). El rol de las emociones en las identidades narrativas de los grupos e individuos en desplazamiento. In S. Bastos (Ed.), *Multiculturalismo y futuro en Guatemala* (pp. 157–171). Guatemala: FLACSO/OXFAM.

Roth, B. (2004). *The separate roads to feminism: Black, Chicana, and White feminist movements in America's second wave.* New York, NY: Cambridge University Press.

Sieder, R. (2008). Entre la multiculturalización y las reinvindicaciones indentitarias: construyendo ciudadanía étnica y autoridad indígena en Guatemala. In S. Bastos (Ed.), *Multiculturalismo y futuro en Guatemala* (pp. 69–96). Guatemala: FLACSO/OXFAM.

Smith, L. (1999). *Decolonizing methodologies: Research and indigenous peoples.* London: Zed Books.

Sutton, M., & Levinson, B. (2001). *Policy as practice: Toward a comparative sociocultural analysis of educational policy.* Westport: Ablex Publishing.

UNESCO. (1990, March). *World declaration on education for all.* In Jomtiem, Thailand. New York, NY: UNESCO.

CHAPTER 14

# AN INTERSECTORAL POLICY FRAMEWORK

## Technology and Obesity Intersecting on Schoolchildren

Vonzell Agosto
Anthony Rolle
*University of South Florida*

The absence of a reliable general educational production process, one that could define the specific ratio of inputs necessary to mitigate the inequalities in schooling, has sparked a history of educational policy research. Yet, it is not uncommon for actors within school systems to have very little knowledge of the public policy process – or have knowledge of the hegemonic values that typically undergird prevailing discourses, politics, and the policy process. According to Stout, Tallerico, and Scribner (1994), "[t] he politics of education ultimately resolves distributive questions in a material sense, as well as in terms of the citizenry's competing values, attitudes, and ideologies" that surface around questions such as who should go to school, what should be the purposes of schooling, what should be taught,

*Intersectionality and Urban Education*, pages 293–310
Copyright © 2014 by Information Age Publishing
All rights of reproduction in any form reserved.

who should decide issues of school direction and policy, and who should pay for schools (p. 16)? To address this knowledge gap on public policy among those working in school systems this chapter aims to codify research arguments emphasizing the application of a generalized public policy process to the pursuit of equity in education through focusing on two issues confronting education today: the role of technology in schools and obesity among schoolchildren.

This chapter begins with an introduction to a general policy framework that allows policy makers to emphasize values that are commonplace in education: efficiency, quality, choice, and equity (Stout et al., 1994). We then introduce an equity-oriented intersectoral policy framework to address the sectors of technology and healthcare. Paired with the concept of universal usability, this framework helps to center concerns about social exclusion and differential distributions of opportunities and obstacles across demographic populations. Furthermore, this approach responds to calls for policy frameworks that engage obesity and technology as complex global issues that are culturally informed and differentially experienced (i.e., Comunello, 2009; Friel, Chopra, & Satcher, 2007). How issues concerning technology and obesity are framed has implications for the well-being of schools and those who work and study in them.

## Education Policy

The intertwined democratic priorities of education and social justice practices often pursue notions of providing citizens equal access to high quality educational environments. The quality of such environments frequently is assessed through a myriad of indicators: (a) student performance; (b) teacher quality; (c) graduation rates; (d) students' sense of trust and belonging; and (d) technology utilization for learning. These multidimensional characteristics affecting quality are further linked to socio-economic outcomes measured by such concepts as educational attainment levels, income earning power, social capital, and the accumulation of wealth. Improvements along such indicators should subsequently provide a greater entrée into the middle class, more skilled career pathways, and engaged habits of democratic participation. Such current philosophical debates lead commonly to an assessment of the efficient distribution and utilization of resources. The aforementioned characteristics and values substantially complicate the capacity for researchers and practitioners to identify an objective and reliable educational production process that applies equally to the expansive variety of students and school environments. These factors vary substantially from district to district, school to school, and classroom to classroom so that establishing varying objective baselines to measure educational and social justice activities poses an equally complex challenge within each desired unit of analysis (e.g., district, school, and classroom). Further complicating matters, the landscape of politics subjectively defines the point at which the capacity to provide equal educational opportunity is trumped by competing state and local government priorities (i.e., prisons, jobs, health care, and the economy), for example, by influencing the points at which justice among the minority (e.g., 20 percent of adult citizens without a high school diploma) becomes irrelevant to a substantial majority (e.g., the remaining 80 percent) of households with higher levels of education attainment [1] (Census 2000). Ultimately, education policy-makers face the following implicit question: What types of economic and human resources and at what magnitude should they be delegated proactively to account for the disproportionate share of barriers to the well-being of those existing within low socioeconomic environments? One perspective that a plurality teachers, administrators, and policy makers support is a rapid infusion of technology into the educational landscape. Thus educators and education policy makers will continue to deliberate on how, to what extent, and to what end technological advances will be integrated into educational contexts.

## Educational Policy and Technology

Today researchers are predicting that in a few short years most students will be participating in some form of online learning (Christensen, Horn, & Johnson, 2008; Searson, Wold, & Jones, 2011). The increased attention to the integration of technology in education and leadership is evident in the standards set forth by the International Society of Technology Education (ISTE) related to digital citizenship: "Educational Administrators model and facilitate understanding of social, ethical, and legal issues and responsibilities related to an evolving digital culture" (2009, p. 1). Indicators for this standard include, among others, ensuring equitable access to digital tools and resources to meet the needs of all learners and facilitating the development of involvement in global issues through the use of communication and collaboration tools. Furthermore, researchers have focused on the role of administrators in guiding instructional technology toward universal design (Messing-Willman & Marino, 2010), supporting digital project based learning (Boss & Krauss, 2007) and modeling their usage of information and communication technologies (ICTs) to encourage faculty usage (Ashfari, Bakar, Luan, Samah, & Fooi, 2009). Fullan (2000) suggested that teachers become "pedagogical design experts" who use the power of technology (p. 582).

Despite the increasing attention to the role of technology related to educational leadership and policy studies, attention to equity and diversity is still rather incipient (e.g., Agosto & Rolle, 2012; Militello & Guajardo, 2013). For instance, Ek, Machado-Casas, Sanchez, and Alanis (2010) found that Latino/a leaders understood the need to mobilize their community through the use of technology in support of "culturally mindful social justice" (p. 842). A main challenge for educational leadership, in the face of rapidly changing technologies, is ensuring social inclusion in the building of a more equitable Network Society (Comunello, 2009). Focused on the use of technology in learning, McCombs (2000) offers a learner centered assessment approach in which the central question concerns the relationship between the benefits of technology and its service to diverse learners and values. This assessment approach reflects the perspective that the search for the impact of technology cannot be separated from the key role of humans in the process (McCombs, 2000).

The debates and critiques of the prevailing discourses on what students should and can learn via technology can inform the policy process. With the growth of distance or online education, virtual schools, and cyber charter schools (Ahn, 2011), policymakers and educators need to consider how students and educators are being shaped by technology and how they should be prepared to contend with this shaping.

## Educational Policy and Obesity

Another area of concern for K–12 education is the issue of obesity. In the United States, the increased attention to obesity rates among children over the past two decades has raised questions about the role that schooling plays in increasing or decreasing obesity for K–12 students. Central to these concerns are the discursive practices that shape common understandings of obesity (i.e., definitions of obesity, portrayals of obesity rates at crises or epidemic proportions), as well as how technology (related to food production, activity, health and media) is implicated. When constructed as an issue of weight, obesity becomes a social concern as students have been found to endure weight-based teasing or in more extreme cases of bullying (i.e., cyber) (Eisenberg, Neumark, Sztainer, & Story, 2003; Weinstock & Krehbiel, 2009). Others have brought attention to the discourse of obesity as a manifestation of fat oppression and a cultural production of fat phobia through an interdisciplinary field called Fat Studies and through anti-oppressive activist efforts (Cooper, 2010). The tyranny of a hegemonic notion of ideal body size that values slenderness, especially among women, has also been implicated in the development of the discourse of obesity (Chernin, 1986). Some argue that public opinion toward obesity and the government's role is grounded in the realm of foundational beliefs about morality and in the question of individual versus community responsibility rather than objective facts (Clemons, McBeth, & Kusko, 2012).

Policy efforts that aim to positively impact health, and health related issues from obesity to malnutrition, require a complex understanding of the global food exchange, including the consideration of how obesity results from a broad range of behavioral, social, and environmental drivers (Hardus, van Vuuren, Crawford, & Worsley, 2003). Related is the question of whether or not deliberations among policy makers on the role of schooling in addressing obesity as a nationwide problem include the perspective that obesity is a global problem that concerns health equity (Friel et al., 2007). The understanding that educators, administrators, and students have about issues related to technology and/or obesity has implications for educational policy and implementation.

## CONCEPTUAL FRAMEWORK

We draw on the concept of intersectionality as forwarded through Black feminist thought, critical race theory, and critical race feminism, to consider how identities are negotiated within power relations that transpire during the phases of policy-making informed by various sectors. Namely, we focus on the sectors of technology, health, and education to discuss issues of obesity and instructional technology. Primarily, we are concerned with how various sectors collaborate to construe (for better or worse) intersecting identities. With the intersectionality of multiple identities (Crenshaw, 1991) comes the intersectionality of privilege and subordination (Wildman & Davis, 1996) that is shaped by larger systemic structures to create interlocking systems of domination (Collins, 1990). Although society does not evenly distribute privilege, power, or subordination evenly across/within groups, patterns of disproportionality and disparities exist in the field of education. We forward an intersectoral policy framework in recognition of the convergence of intersections (identities, power, and privilege) and sectors that operate simultaneously to create complex problems. Our specific interest is in the health and well-being of schools and those who work and study in them, namely schoolchildren.

In order to provide some background on policy-making we provide a general, analytical policy framework and argue that an equity orientation is necessary to confront simplistic notions of obesity as a problem solved by physical activity or technology as a tool ensuring education that is equitable, efficient, and excellence. The phases of policy analysis below are used to generate information useful for understanding educational administration, research, and policy decisions while illuminating assumptions, evidence, and values that support them. Ultimately, it is important to remember that the goal of this analytical framework is to create a common understanding about the objectives, processes, and outcomes of public education systems. With increased levels of understanding, administrators, counselors, teachers, and policymakers can begin to address the more complex issues of producing higher levels of organizational and student learning outcomes. Education policy is a major medium through which public discourse operates on and through school environments. Some combination of the generally accepted phases of educational policy analysis (listed below) can be prevalent throughout any discussion of state, local, and federal educational policy and processes (MacPhail-Wilcox, 1984).

- *Policy Initiation:* An examination of the sources of characteristics, influences, and strategies that define the endogenous environment of policy makers such as the purpose(s) for the research request and the desired intention(s) of the analysis. This phase includes identification of a potential problem. *Sample question: How does education policy exacerbate inequity related to technology and/or obesity?*
- *Policy Context:* An examination of exogenous environmental characteristics and conditions that define the limits of policy development, content, and administration such as the value of information, timeliness of the research, and perception of results. *Sample question: What are the characteristics of the problem (conditions, discourses of obesity and/ or technology, public perception) that overlap with K–12 public education?*
- *Policy Development:* The use of the classic analytical framework that includes a statement of purpose, criteria for developing objectives, alternatives for achieving objectives, consequences of alternatives, and recommendations. *Sample question: What objectives cohere with an equity orientation to policy development concerning obesity and technology?*
- *Policy Content:* An expression of policy goals based on the projected effects of analyzed objectives which focuses on explaining relationships between new policy goals, policy processes, and policy standards. *Sample question: What are the goals of policy concerning policy and technology and what processes and standards are in place to help define the intended goals?*
- *Policy Administration:* An evaluation of the congruence between policy intentions and outcomes that focuses specifically on administrator preferences and competence in determining policy directions. *Sample question: Toward what ends should educational policy concerning technology/obesity aim and what might be some unintended outcomes and alternatives?*
- *Policy Evaluation:* An evaluation of the conditions resulting from the enactment of a policy that answers questions such as: What are

the effects of the implemented policy? Are the effects desired? How can the policy be improved? *Sample question: What are the effects of the implemented policy concerning obesity and technology? Are these effects desired? How can the policy be improved?*

An equity oriented framework engenders policy making based on understandings of obesity and technology as complex global issues that have particular causes and expressions in the United States. An equity policy framework supports leadership across the phases of policy analysis by encouraging understandings of how the larger social-political context shapes the relationships and products (i.e., physical structures, environment, education, food) that affect obesity and technology, including their (in)equitable distribution and use. Framed by the concept of social justice, this discussion of technology and obesity focuses on equity and encourages leadership development and practice attuned to the use, evaluation, and production of knowledge informing policy (Marshall Gerstl-Pepin, 2005). The discussion of the policy constructs: efficiency, adequacy, and equity is followed by current issues related to technology and obesity that suggest the need for an equity orientation to educational policy.

## BRIDGING THE DIVIDES

In the United States, where access to technology is widely available through public spaces, employment, and schools the digital divide often refers to the differences between formal access and use of technology (how, how often, and which technologies) (DiMaggio & Hargittai, 2001). Despite trends charting an increase in the use of the Internet by every demographic, Internet access in the United States remains largely stratified along lines of race, class and level of educational attainment (Lenhart et al., 2003). Various terms have been forwarded to describe inequities in the access and use of technologies across various social group differences. The terms *digital divide* and *technology gap* reflect the conditions of inequity or limitations to digital equity (Holloway, 2000; Gorski, 2009). The term *digital divide(s)* has received much attention since the mid-1990s (Gorski, 2009), informing discussions of postmodern and critical multicultural curriculum. Paul Gorski (2009) uses critical multicultural education as a theoretical framework to reframe the discourse on instructional technology by centering issues of equity and social justice in the context of K–12 schools. He contends that the inequalities that pervade schools do not disappear once technology is added to classrooms for technology can contribute to how inequity is reproduced and resisted. Although those who are growing up in the digital-age multitasking, collaboration, sharing, and publicly expressing themselves online are often referred to as *digital natives* (Prensky, 2001), there is debate over whether fluency equals literacy (Mihailidis, 2011).

## Bridging the Digital Divides

Educational systems can help reduce social exclusion by adapting their curricula to integrate new media literacy, increase people's ability to use new media in reception and production, and consider the needs of the local context (Comunello, 2009). Various frameworks, perspectives, and pedagogical approaches have been forwarded to ensure that the production and consumption of technology related to participation in the Network Society or digital culture is equitable. Comunello (2009) offers a framework for analyzing the technological and social factors of the global digital divide focused on access to technology and effective use of (ICTs) through computers and the Internet. The components of the framework are: advanced reception practices, technical skills, content production, and networking skills. Entrepreneur Mario Morino (2000) supports not-for-profit organizations through venture philanthropy. He aims to build community capacity through technology toward social development that bridges the digital divide. His vision includes the creation of an academy of technology that would help to educate leaders about the potential, applications, and risks of technology. While Johnson (2009) suggests a critical race perspective in the examination of how racism is embedded in the fabric of Internet-based learning, Voithofer and Foley (2002) advocate for a postmodern analysis of technology in relation to equity and provide an analytical framework to guide postmodern instructional technology. Their postmodern approach to instruction technology and curriculum responds to "multiple intersections of race, class, gender, and ethnicity…" (p. 7). Leadership preparation and policy studies would benefit from understandings of the relationships between schools, community development, equity, and technology.

With the expansion of the digital-age culture the notion of literacy has expanded to include new media literacies (i.e., digital literacy, global literacy, media literacy, visual literacy, cultural literacy, technological literacy) and the use of ICTs (i.e., mobile, Web 2.0). ICT's can help to improve collaboration among various stakeholders in the processes of learning and teaching (Schrum & Levin, 2009). However, they do not necessarily reduce the barriers that occur in face to face interactions among stakeholders. With the increasing amount of time that people are engaging with media and media via technology has come rising concerns expressed by cultural theorists and critical theorists who advocate for curriculum and instruction that prepares people to become critical and literate producers and consumers of media. These aims are captured by an approach to education called *new media literacy*, which promotes in students "the ability to access, analyze, evaluate, and create messages in a variety of forms" (Aufderheide & Firestone, 1993, p. 7).

In discussing new technologies and multiple and multicultural literacies, Kahn and Kellner (2007) engage the theory of critical pedagogy presented by Freire (1970) to suggest that educators constantly raise the following questions.

> Whose interests are emergent technologies and pedagogies serving? Are they helping all social groups and individuals? Who is being excluded and why? We also need to seriously question the extent to which multiplying technologies and literacies serve simply to reproduce existing inequalities in the present, as we strategize the ways in which they might also produce conditions for a more vibrant democratic society in the future. (p. 441)

Also bridging media literacy and critical theory, Morrell (2011) calls for critical (media) literacy in education. He asserts that educators should infuse critical media pedagogy into the curriculum in order to prepare people to critically "read" the multitude of texts they encounter, which "unfortunately, many educators of today's youth fail to help their students to develop critical perspectives of the media they consume" (p. 158). He further argues that critical new media literacy studies (in English curricula and pedagogy) can increase the achievement of historically under-served youth. In part, this approach helps to counter the stereotypical images of the body that corporate media and popular culture promote (Giroux, 1996; Kellner & Share, 2007). As the ideology of consumerism becomes increasingly connected to children's bodies and they become more susceptible to advertisers who target them as a profitable demographic, intervention strategies must begin teaching them how to navigate this complex political landscape of accountability and consumption (Kroner, 2009).

## A Discursive and Material Frame

Levels of obesity and activity are not uniform between countries (Gard, 2004). Even within countries, "levels of activity (and, we might add, prevalence of body fatness) are differentially distributed through the population" (Kirk, p. 124, 2006). The distribution of activity and obesity (like technology) is unevenly distributed among populations by social class, race, and gender (Gard, 2004). Furthermore, the patterns of social and environmental attributes of neighborhoods can have a determining effect on the level of physical activity and weight status. These patterns are related to the differential distribution of recreational or physical activity facilities and differential access, and are correlated with socioeconomic status (Gordon-Larsen, Nelson, Page, & Popkin, 2006).

Gard and Kirk (2007) argue that the idea of an 'obesity epidemic' is a new phase in physical education discourse enacted primarily through health and physical education (HPE) curriculum that fuses notions of bodily aesthetics, regimes of self-care and responsibility with bio-medical imperatives. Their analysis of curriculum in Ontario Canada and research on policy in other countries such as Australia and Singapore reveal a trend among responses to the 'obesity epidemic' that will likely increase the surveillance of students' bodies as schools take on a disciplinary function, monitoring and reporting conditions such as the types of snacks parents pack into lunch sacks, the weight of children, or the 'choices' that students make which affect their level of physical activity and quality of diet. Gard and Kirk (2007) argue that the focus on sport-based physical education portends a move toward corporeal regulation and the management of risk that asks students to monitor themselves and one another as a moral imperative.

Leaders in education and policy-makers would be remiss to ignore how some bodies get shaped in particular ways by schooling and discourses that pervade them (Gard & Kirk, 2007; Kirk, 1994). For instance, some have argued that the framing of childhood obesity as a crisis discourse is manufactured (Winsley & Armstrong, 2005; Kirk, 2006; Marshall, Biddle, Gorely, Cameron, & Murdy, 2004; Thorpe, 2003). Others have provided critiques of the obesity crisis discourse which include (1) the conflation of the terms obesity (a condition of excess of fat) and overweight (a condition of weight relative to a standard based on Body Mass Index (BMI) and height used to determine obesity (Evans, 2003); and (2) conflicting reports on the increase/decrease in opportunity for physical activity. As part of a larger social discourse, the related metaphor of the 'couch potato' is often used to represent the image of an obese child and reflect concerns about moral and social decay (Kirk, 2006). For example, in a study by Clemons et al., (2012), participants (college students) generally agreed that obesity is a serious problem (mean score 5.50). However, respondents believed that eating was a matter of individual responsibility rather than an appropriate realm for relevant governmental policy. More importantly they found that a policy narrative based in individual moral responsibility was more convincing to individuals than a scientific statement. This finding points to the challenge and need for articulating an intersectoral lens.

### Bridging the Obesity Divides

According to Friel et al., (2007), "Focusing only on direct action to make people eat more healthily and be more physically active misses the heart of the problem: the underlying unequal distribution of factors that support the opportunity to be a healthy weight" (p. 1241). They identify several social determinants of inequalities in obesity (sociopolitical, sociocultural, socioeconomic, socioenvironmental context) and provide examples of schools act as places where inequalities are reinforced, for instance, by providing soft drink vending machines, contracting with companies to serve lunch to reduce costs in a trade that provides food to students and faculty with little nutritional value, and reducing class participation in physical education classes through presenting barriers to student participation (i.e., allowing large class size, failing to provide equipment). Overall, they recommend policy efforts that recognize the complexity of the food system in interaction with the social and built environments to affect obesity as well make use of the capacity of multiple sectors (an intersectoral approach) to provide health equity. Rather than an individualistic approach that situates obesity in the actions of an individual. Friel et al, (2007) (1) recommend a structural approach that centers action on health equity; and (2) provide a conceptual framework in which energy expenditures are linked to global exchanges across the international market.

Similar to the *new media literacy* approaches advocated for by cultural and critical theorist, Gard and Kirk (2007) advocate for socially critical physical education as an approach based in critical pedagogy that can "assist young people to question reflectively and reflexively assumptions and received wisdom about physical education and about physical culture more broadly" (p. 34). Even in the framing of studies, critical questioning of the term obesity and its causes may be absent. For instance, in the article on ICT's and obesity among adolescents, Kautiainen, Koivusilta, Lintonen, Virtanen, and Rimpelä (2009) claim that, "In simple terms, obesity results from an imbalance between the intake and the expenditure of energy" (p. 926). Policy-makers who understand the cause of obesity in such simplistic terms may be inclined to advance the role of gaming technologies, for instance, to encourage physical activity as a single counter to obesity without considering its other causes; that some populations may not be prone to obesity, or alternative avenues to engage in physical activity. If obesity were understood and addressed more holistically, educational policies could facilitate education that responds to broader and urgent needs rather than one as narrow as increasing physical activity with the intention of countering obesity. Instead, policy that advocates for gaming technologies could focus on problem-solving to explicate how such games are tools and artifacts. Players could be asked to question what digital games teach about globalization, equitable distribution, or competing values such as cooperation and competition.

## INTERSECTORAL BRIDGING: OBESITY AND TECHNOLOGY

We turn to concepts that help to illustrate how the issues of obesity and technology can be bridged and therefore productive for thinking about leadership in educational policy: universal usability and intersectoral collaboration. The concept of "universal usability" speaks to a relationship between technology and the healthcare sector: telehealth (Shneiderman, 2003). According to Carter, Muir, and McLean (2011), telehealth is a wide range of health services delivered across distance through technology and more specifically it "is about transmitting voice, data, images, and other information across distance rather than requiring patients, health practitioners, and educators to travel for consultations, health education sessions, and health-based meetings" (p. 2). Schneiderman (2002) offers an example of telehealth through the inclusive lens of universal usability to center human needs in the discussion on computer use.

Shneiderman (2003) defines universal usability as having more than 90 percent of households successfully using information and communication technologies at least once a week. Shneiderman (2003) suggests that regardless of age, ability, or other social difference among humans computers for instance can be integrated into social life to serve the needs of people and that through the following framework this (universal usability) can be facilitated and monitored. The framework includes the following activities: *collect, relate, create, donate.* Using the context of the healthcare industry, he argues that universal usability can support human needs when computers and computer systems make medical records internationally available within seconds and screen them in the local language within seconds of arrival. Shneiderman envisions that issues of access can be overcome and barriers subverted when attention is given to social diversity (i.e., different languages or dialects) and service given (i.e., donated) to individual needs within an expansive system (i.e., health care). The framework of *collect, relate, create, and donate* can be applied to educational policy broadly or more specifically to curriculum and instructional (technology) policy. Its focus on service to human needs and donation for the public interest is congruent with equity oriented policy—as both reflect consideration of service to individuals and the public good.

Technology that offers universal usability can be used by students and educators to monitor their health, diet, and overall well-being. An example of such an application that is available through the Internet is *My Fitness Pal.* This application is one among many that helps its users to record consumption, plan a fitness program, monitor nutritional content, and communicate with pals to collaborate workout routines or other related activities. The criterion of donation is reflected in the cost of the application, which is free. Additionally, the website offers a body mass indicator (BMI) calculator that addresses some of the limitations to using BMI to create a fitness plan: "It's not accurate for pregnant women, people under 5 feet tall, and people with very muscular builds. It also does not account for age." (http: www.my-fitnesspal.com/tools/bmi-calculator). Interpreted through the framework Shneiderman (2003) offers for creating universal usability (collect, relate, create, donate), such applications allow users to collect data, relate and collaborate with others through communities and blogs, and create plans to sustain healthy lifestyles. The information offered by the application on its limitations engages the critiques of the crisis discourse of an obesity epidemic and, as encouraged by social and cultural theorists, fosters critical literacy. However, the norm upon which BMI is constructed has been critiqued as another example of White supremacy (Bonilla-Silva, 2012).

Even though the relationship between obesity and the use of technology in inconclusive, researchers have attempted to identify which engagements that children have with technology (i.e., digital gaming, television watching), if any, are correlated with an increased chance of obesity (Roberts, Foehr, & Rideout, 2005; Graves, Stratton, Ridgers, & Cable, 2008). Technology, especially video games, have been criticized for contributing to an increase in sedentary behavior and thus a culprit in the increasing rates of obesity among children and youth (Yang, Smith, & Graham, 2008). In contrast, exergaming or activity-based gaming is thought to be a solution to stem the tide of physical inactivity of students in and out of schools. Such approaches however, address obesity at the individual level and raises questions about equity in the accessibility of students to a curriculum infused with such technologies as well as the attention given in the curriculum to other contributing factors. Government and policymakers are responsible for providing the tools to help administrators, teachers, and students cultivate or develop the requisite skills and literacies that support democratic and progressive uses of technologies (Kahn & Kellner, 2007).

## POLICY IMPERATIVES

With rapid technological advances policy is sometimes reactive, responding once issues arise. Policy issues that educators face with the rapid advances in technology include: the use, ownership, and privacy of videos recorded during teacher practicums or teacher observations related to their evaluation; the evaluation of K–12 distance learning offered by brick and mortar or cyber schools (Ahn, 2011). Similar to student records, policy concerning medical records must also include attention issues of privacy. Public education and those involved in policy decisions should have and create opportunities to deliberate on the ethical use of tools, gain insight into how they can be utilized in various environments to support different outcomes whether of benefit or harm, and increase awareness of how patterns of usage can be constructed through media to promote hegemonic messages about what is in the best interest of students and educators. "Undoubtedly, technology shapes, often in unanticipated ways, how we live and work as well as how we educate our children" (Culp, Honey, & Mandinach, 2005, p. 24).

Intersectoral collaborations offer policy-makers a starting point for understanding how actors at various levels (micro-, meso-, macro-) work collaboratively from their respective sphere of influence (i.e., sector) to intervene in complex problems. Intersectoral collaboration is a response to problems that have multiple determinants, affect many people and sectors, and require action by different sectors (World Health Organization, 2006). For instance, with regard to health, its aim is to identify those policy inputs that effect health and decide what actions can be taken or avoided by those who will implement the policy framework under negotiation so as to protect, maintain or improve the health of citizens (National Institute for Health and Welfare). In the case of schools, educational leadership (at the district, state, and school level) has a central role in implementing policies that will affect the health and well-being of schools, school personnel, and schoolchildren. From an equity perspective, policy analysis "must consider whether a policy will empower and democratize, whether it will dispense goods to the have-nots as much as it considers whether a policy is efficient" (Marshall & Gerstl-Pepin, 2005, p. 91). Those crafting, implementing, or analyzing policy have a responsibility to evaluate prevailing discourses of obesity and technology and foster deliberation that takes into account less popular 'truths' about the cultures and crises students face.

## NOTE

1. Approximately 30% of the U.S. adult population over 25 have attained an Associates Degree or higher.

## REFERENCES

Ahn, J. (2011). Policy, technology, and practice in cyber charter schools: Framing the issues. *Teachers College Record, 113*(1), 1–26.

A Nation at Risk: The Imperative for Educational Reform (1983). *A Report to the Nation and the Secretary of Education United States Department of Education* by The National Commission on Excellence in Education.

Agosto, V., & Rolle, A. (2012). ). Ecology policy for educational technology. In S. Sanders & L. Witherspoon (Eds.), *Contemporary uses of technology in K–12 physical education: Policy, practice and advocacy* (pp. 57–68). Charlotte, NC: Information Age Publishing, Inc.

Ashfari, M., Bakar, K. A., Luan, W. S., Samah, B. A., & Fooi, F. S. (2009). Technology and school leadership. *Technology, Pedagogy, and Education, 18*(2), 235–248.

Aufderheide, P., & Firestone, C. M. (1993). *Media literacy: A report of the national leadership conference on media literacy*. Cambridge, UK: Polity Press.

Bonilla-Silva, E. (2012). The invisible weight of whiteness: The racial grammar of everyday life in contemporary America. *Ethnic and Racial Studies, 35*(2), 173–194.

Boss, S., & Krauss, J. (2007) Real projects in a digital world. *Principal Leadership,* (pp. 22–26).

Brown vs. Board of Education of Topeka, Kansas, 347 U.S. 483 (1954).

Carter, L. M., Muir, L., & McLean, D. (2011). Narrative as a means of understanding the multi-dimensional benefits of telehealth: An exploration of telehealth stories. *Canadian Journal of University Continuing Education, 37*(1), 1–13.

Collins, P. H. (1990). *Black feminist thought: Knowledge, consciousness, and the politics of empowerment*. London: Harper Collins.

Crenshaw, K. (1991). Mapping the margins: Intersectionality, identity politics, and violence against women of color. *Stanford Law Review, 43*(6), 1241–1299.

Chernin, K. (1986). *Womansize: The tyranny of slenderness*. London: The Women's Press.

Christensen, C. M., Horn, M. B., & Johnson, C. W. (2008). *Disrupting class* (1st ed.). New York, NY: McGraw Hill.

Clemons, R. S., McBeth, M. K., & Kusko, E. (2012). Understanding the role of policy narratives and the public policy arena: Obesity as a lesson in public policy development. *World Medical & Health Policy, 4*(2), 1–26.

Comunello, F. (2009). From the digital divide to multiple divides: Technology, society and new media skills. In E. Ferro, Y. K. Dwivedi, & J. R. Gil-Garcia. *Handbook of research on overcoming digital divides: Constructing an equitable and competitive information society* (pp. 588–605). Information Science Reference.

Cooper, C. (2010). Fat studies: Mapping the field. *Sociology Compass, 4,* 1020–1034.

Culp, K. M., Honey, M., & Mandinach, E. (2005). A retrospective on twenty years of education technology policy. *Journal of Educational Computing Research, 32*(3), 279–307.Washington, DC: U.S. Department of Education. Retrieved from http://www. nationaledtechplan. org/participate/20years.pdf

DiMaggio, P., & Hargittai, E. (2001). *From the 'digital divide' to digital inequality: Studying Internet use as penetration increases*. Working paper. Princeton, NJ: Princeton University, Center for Arts and Cultural Policy Studies.

Eisenberg, M. E., Neumark-Sztainer, D., & Story, M. (2003). Association of weight-based teasing and emotional well-being among adolescents. *Archives of Pediatrics and Adolescent Medicine, 157,* 733–738.

Ek. L. D., Machado-Casas, M., Sanchez, P., & Alanis, I. (2010). Crossing cultural borders: *La clase mágica* as a university-school partnership. *Journal of School Leadership, 20,* 820–848.

Evans, J. (2003). Physical education and health: A polemic or 'let them eat cake!' *European Physical Education Review, 9*(1), 87–101.

Friel, S., Chopra, M., & Satcher, D. (2007). Unequal weight: Equity oriented policy responses to the global obesity epidemic. *BMJ (Clinical research ed.), 335*(7632), 1241–1243. doi:10.1136/bmj.39377.622882.47

Fullan, M. (2000, February). Change forces: The sequel. 2000 CHANGE Council Keynote Address presented at the annual meeting of the Association for Educational Communications and Technology, Long Beach, CA.

Giroux, H. A. (1996). *Fugitive cultures: Race, violence, and youth.* New York: Routledge.

Gard, M. (2004). An elephant in the room and a bridge too far, or physical education and the 'obesity epidemic'. In J. Evans, B. Davies, & J. Wright (Eds.), *Body knowledge and control: studies in the sociology of physical education and health* (pp. 68–82). London: Routledge.

Gard, M., & Kirk, D. (2007). Obesity discourse and the crisis of faith in disciplinary technology. *Utbildning & Demokrati, 16*(2), 17–36.

Gordon-Larsen, P., Nelson, M. C., Page, P., & Popkin, B. M. (2006). Inequality in the built environment underlies key health disparities in physical activity and obesity. *Pediatrics, 117*(2), 417–24. doi:10.1542/peds.2005–0058

Gorski, P. (2009). Insisting on digital equity: Reframing the dominant discourse on multicultural education and technology. *Urban Education, 44*(3), 348–364.

Graves, L., Stratton, D., Ridgers, N. G., & Cable, N. T. (2008). Energy expenditure in adolescents playing new generation computer games. *British Journal of Sports Medicine, 42*(7), 592–594.

Hardus, P. M., van Vuuren, C. L., Crawford, D., & Worsley, A. (2003). Public perceptions of the causes and prevention of obesity among primary school children. *International Journal of Obesity, 27*(12), 1465–71. doi:10.1038/sj.ijo.0802463

Holloway, J. H. (2000). The digital divide. *Educational Leadership, 58*(2), 90.

International Society for Technology in Education NETS Project (2009). National educational technology standards for administrators. www.ISTE.org

Johnson, C. (2009). Meet me at the intersection of race and technology: Critical Race Theory and digital inequality in U.S. schools. *Rocky Mountain Communication Review, 6*(1), 40–46.

Kahn, R., & Kellner, D. (2007). Paulo Freire and Ivan Illich: Technology, politics, and the reconstruction of education. *Policy Futures in Education, 5*(4), 431–448.

Kautiainen, S., Koivisto, A., Koivusilta, L., Lintonen, T., Virtanen, S. M., & Rimpelä, A. (2009). Sociodemographic factors and a secular trend of adolescent overweight in Finland. *International Journal of Pediatric Obesity, 4*(4), 360–370.

Kellner, D., & Share, J. (2007). Adventures in media and cultural studies: Introducing the key works. In M. Durham & D. Kellner (Eds.), *Media and cultural studies: Key works* (pp. 1–30). Oxford, UK: Blackwell.

Kirk, D. (1994). Physical education and regimes of the body. *Australian and New Zealand Journal of Sociology, 30*(2), 165–177.

Kirk, D. (2006). The obesity 'crisis' and school physical education. *Sport, Education, and Society, 11*(2), 121–133.

Kroner, C. (2009). The body politic: Childhood obesity as a symbol of an unbalanced economy. *Policy Futures in Education, 9*(3), 381–391.

Lenhart, A., Horrigan, J., Rainie, L., Allen, K., Boyce, A., Madden, M., & O'Grady, E. (2003). The ever-shifting Internet population: A new look at Internet access and the digital divide. The Pew Internet and American Life Project. http://www.pewinternet.org/pdfs/PIP_Shifting_Net_Pop_Report.pdf

MacPhail-Wilcox, B. (1984). Tax policy analysis and education finance: A conceptual framework for issues and analyses. *Journal of Education Finance, 9*(3), 312–331.

Marshall, S. J., Biddle, S. J. H., Gorely, T., Cameron, N., & Murdy, I. (2004). Relationships between media use, body fatness, and physical activity in children and youth: A meta-analysis, *International Journal of Obesity, 28*, 1238–1246.

Marshall, C., & Gerstl-Pepin, C. (2005). *Re-framing educational politics for social justice.* Boston: Pearson.

McCombs, B. L. (2000). Assessing the role of educational technology in the teaching and learning process: A learner-centered perspective, University of Denver Research Institute. http://www2.ed.gov/rschstat/eval/tech/techconf00/mccombs_paper.html

Messenger-Willman, J., & Marino, M. T. (2010). Universal design for learning and assistive technology: Leadership considerations for promoting inclusive education in today's secondary schools. *NAASP Bulletin, 94*(1), 5–16.

Mihailidis, P. (2011). (Re)mix, (re)purpose, (re)learn: Using participatory tools for media literacy learning outcomes in the classroom. *Action in Teacher Education, 33*(2), 172–183.

Militello, M. & Guajardo, F. (2013). Virtually speaking: How digital storytelling can facilitate organizational learning. *Journal of Community Positive Practices, XIII*(2), 80–91.

Morrell, E. (2011). Critical approaches to media in urban English language arts teacher development. *Action in Teacher Education, 33*(2), 157–171.

Morino, M. (2000). Policy and philanthropy: Keys to closing the digital divide, Networks for people 2000 conference. United States Department of Commerce.

MyFitnessPal.LLC, www.Myfitnesspal.com

National Institute for Health and Welfare http://www.thl.fi/en_US/web/en/research/tools/hiap/introduction/intersectoral_collaboration

Prensky, M. (2001). Digital natives, digital immigrants. *On the Horizon, 9*(5), 1–6.

Roberts, D. F., Foehr, U. G., & Rideout, V. J. (2005). Generation M: Media in the lives of 8–18 year-olds. Menlo Park, CA: Henry J. Kaiser Family Foundation. http://www.kff.org/entmedia/loader.cfm?url=/commonspot/security/getfile.cfm&PageID=51809

Schrum, L., & Levin, B. B. (2009). *Leading 21st-century schools: Harnessing technology for engagement and achievement.* Thousand Oaks, CA: Corwin.

Searson, M., Wold, K., & Jones, W. M. (2011). Editorial: Reimaging Schools: The potential of virtual education. *British Journal of Educational Technology, 42*(3), 363–371.

Shneiderman, B. (2003). *Leonardo's laptop: Human needs and the new computing technologies.* Cambridge, Massachusetts: The MIT Press.

Stout, R. T., Tallerico, M., & Scribner, K. P. (1994). Values: The 'What?' of the politics of education. *Politics of Education Association Yearbook*, 5–20.

Thorpe, S. (2003) Crisis discourse in physical education and the laugh of Michel Foucault. *Sport, Education and Society, 8*(2), 131–151.

Voithofer, R. & Foley, A. (2002). Post-IT: Putting postmodern perspectives to use in instructional technology. A response to Solomon's "Toward a post-modern agenda in instructional technology". *Educational Technology Research and Development, 50*(1), 5–14.

Weinstock, J., & Krehbiel, M. (2009). Fat youths as common targets for bullying. In E. D. Rothblum & S. Solovay (Eds.), *The fat studies reader* (pp. 120–126). New York: New York University Press.

Wildman, S. M., & Davis, A. D. (1996). *Privilege revealed: How invisible privilege undermines America.* New York: New York University Press.

Winsley, R., & Armstrong, N. (2005). Physical activity, physical fitness, health and young people, In K. Green & K. Hardman (Eds.), *Physical education: Essential issues* (London, Sage), 65–77.

World Health Organization (2006). Focus on road traffic injuries: Why collaborate? What kind of collaboration can be developed? Definition of key concepts. http://www.who.int/violence_injury_prevention/road_traffic/activities/roadsafety_training_manual_unit_6.pdf

Yang, S., Smith, B., & Graham, G. (2008). Healthy video gaming: Oxymoron or possibility. *Journal of Online Education, 4*(4). http://www.innovateonline.info/index.php?view=article&id=186

Yau, R. (1999). Technology in K–12 public schools: What are the equity issues? *Equity Review,* 1–10.

CPSIA information can be obtained at www.ICGtesting.com
Printed in the USA
LVOW04s0202260915

455782LV00003B/23/P

9040023